Edexcel GCSE (9–1) Spanish
Higher

Rachel Hawkes, Christopher Lillington

Published by Pearson Education Limited, 80 Strand, London, WC2R 0RL.

www.pearsonschoolsandfecolleges.co.uk

Copies of official specifications for all Edexcel qualifications may be found on the website: www.edexcel.com

Text © Pearson Education Limited, 2016

Written by Rachel Hawkes and Christopher Lillington
Additional material written by Leanda Reeves

Designed and typeset by Tek-Art, West Sussex

Illustrated by: Tek-Art, West Sussex, Oxford Designers & Illustrators Ltd., KJA Artists (Mark, Andy), Beehive Illustration (Alan Rowe, Peter Lubach, Esther Pérez-Cuadrado) and John Hallett.

First published 2016

21

10 9 8

British Library Cataloguing in Publication Data
A catalogue record for this book is available from the British Library

ISBN 9781292118987

Printed in Great Britain by Bell & Bain Ltd, Glasgow

Acknowledgements

We would like to thank Christopher Lillington, Rachel Hawkes, Leanda Reeves, Teresa Martínez-Arteaga, Samantha Alzuria, Marina Barrull, Clive Bell, Gillian Eades, Nicola Lester, Ruth Manteca, Clare Dobson for their invaluable help in the development and trialling of this course. Leanda Reeves would like to thank Teresa Martínez-Arteaga for her help with the revision module. We would also like to thank María José Sierras Jimeno at the Colegio M. Mª Rosa Molas, Zaragoza, Spain.

The authors and publisher would like to thank the following individuals and organisations for permission to reproduce their photographs:

(Key: b-bottom; c-centre; l-left; r-right; t-top)

123RF.com: 6, 7 (i), 14 (c), 53l, 53c, 167, Andrey Tsidvintsev 142tl, Anna Lurye 108, Anton Gvozdikov 77l, Antonio Diaz 43, Burmakin Andrey 197b, Cathy Yeulet 36 (c), 47, 117, Daniel Ernst 34 (a), Deborah Kolbi 33l, Dmitrijs Gerciks 7 (p), Fabio Lamanna 148t, fiphoto 100 (d), 104 (c), HONGQI ZHANG 43t, Ian Allenden 153, joserpizarro 232, mitarart 213r, nito500 203t, nutthawit wiangya 176b, stillfx./123rf.com 164 (d), Tami Freed 182; **© 2016 Maraworld :** 128 (b); **Alamy Images:** agefotostock 103, 122c, Agencja Fotograficzna Caro 40tl, Alex Segre 189, 192, Alibi Productions 7 (e), Angela Hampton Picture Library 36 (d), Azk Waters 98tr, Bill Cheyrou 62cr, Cal Vornberger 22, ChaviNandez 109, Chris Mattison 14 (e), Christian Bertrand 129b, Citrus Stock 97 (h), Classic Stock 59, colau 160, dbimages 32r, Denkou Images 132, Dinodia Photos 91, Doug Houghton 96 (c), dpa picture alliance 185, epa european pressphoto agency b.v 122tl, epa european pressphoto agency b.v. 84l, Finnbar Webster 13c, Francisco Javier Fernandez Bordonarda 7 (k), Greg Balfour Evans 96 (e), Hero Images Inc. / Alamy Stock Photo 25, Iain Sharp 110, Ian Dagnall 39c, Image Source Plus 130, imageBROKER 99 (c), Images & Stories 200, Images Source 88, Izel Photography 113, Jack Sullivan 96 (b), Jean Schweitzer 31, Jeffrey Blacker 100 (e), JLImages 57r, Julie Woodhouse 98cr, Ken Walsh 104 (g), Ken Welsh 82cr, 96 (f), Marc Hill 36 (h), Maria Galan 174, Matt Fowler Photography 100 (c), Michael Dwyer 30l, 30r, Nick Lylak 40tr, Paula Solloway 63r, philipus 38 (g), Prisma Bildagentur AG 135, Radius Images 145b, Robert Harding World Imagery 122tr, Robert Kneschke 154, Rolf Richardson 16, RosalreneBetancourt 1 145c, Sergio Azenha 13tr, Simon Reddy 14 (d), Speedpix 96tr, 170tl, Steve Davey 119, ton koene 146tl, Travel Pictures 106br, Warren Faidley 172bc, WENN Ltd 171, xixia 34 (b), YAY Media AS 97 (i), Zuma Press 146cl; **Art Directors and TRIP Photo Library:** Alamy Stock Photo 97 (4), 97 (b), 97 (c); **Colegio M. Mª Rosa Molas:** 38 (b), 38 (c), 38 (d), 38 (e), 38 (h), 38 (i); **Corbis:** Imageshop 213l; **Fotolia.com:** alain wacquier 116 (h), Aleksandar Todorovic 101cr, amophoto.net 38 (f), Andres Rodriguesz 138 (3), Andriy Petrenko 69, Andy Dean 32c, 198bl, AntonioDiaz 199tl, asife 61, asikkk 7 (b), atomfotolia 7 (n), Axel Bueckert 151tr, BlueSkyImages 141cr, Brad Pict 98br, bzyxx 129t, canovass 116 (g), Christian Schwier 72b, 187, corepics 29 (d), Darren Baker 65, DragonImages 87, efired 7 (m), Eugenio Marongiu 56, fotos 593 104 (e), GalinaSt 198cl, Gelia 7 (l), gemeneacom 96 (d), GIna Sanders 98bl, goodluz 104 (d), Halfpoint 131, Hugo Felix 63l, Igor Mojzes 138 (6), Iurii Sokolov 8tl, JackF 13cl, Javier Castro 57l, JJAVA 164br, Joanna wnuk 39r, Kablonk Micro 62tr, kitzcomer 116 (e), Konstantin Kulikov 197, Leonid Andronov 96 (a), lldi 121tc, lom742 15br, M.Studio 116 (a), Maksym Gorpenyuk 107tl, Maria 20, markos86 184, Martinan 169tl, mathess 107cr, Max Topchii 8c, Maygutyak 7 (h), Mila Supynska 195, Monart Design 32l, Monkey Business 78cl, Monkey Business Images 7 (f), 35tr, 62bl, Morenovel 170tr, Morten Elm 105, mr. markin 78tl, Nebojsa Bobic 104 (b), Nina Nagovitsina 100 (b), Noam 8tr, Nobilior 39l, Olaf Speier 116 (l), papa 81t, pedrosala 202b, phanuwatnandee 36 (e), Sergey Chayko 172bl, SOMATUSCANI 104 (f), steheap 166 (c), Theirry Ryo 7 (o), uzkiland 18tl, Valeriy Velikov 121tl, ViewApart 55, Viktor 116 (d), Vladislav Gajic 7 (j), VolkerZ 34 (d), Wavebreakmedia Micro 75b, xalanx 142tr, Yuri Timofeyev 10tl, Yury Gubin 166 (d); **Getty Images:** AFP 138 (4), AFP / Stringer 167l, Alfredo Maiquez 18tr, altrendo images 44, Anadolu Agency 179, Ariel Skelley 204, Bernd Vogel 82tr, Bloomberg 126tc, Brent Winebrenner 35bl, C Flanigan 77r, CBS Photo Archive 84c, Christopher Futcher 35cr, Dave M Bennett 75t, Dennis Doyle 201, Fuse 83tl, Gaelle Beri 128 (a), Ingolf Pompe / Look Foto 13cr, JOHN GURZINSKI / Stringer 79br, JTB Photo 99 (b), Juan Naharro Gimenez / Stringer 86, Jupiter Images 161, Katarnina Wittkamp 36 (a), Michael Tran 52, Michele Falzone 106cl, MIGUEL ROJO 84r, Nigel Waldren 85, Rubberball / Mike Kemp 36 (i), Score / Aflo 40c, Sergei Supkinsky 145tr, Shane Hansen 78cr, Stockbyte 170tc, Trevor Williams 10tr; **IOC Museums Collection © IOC :** 73tr; **Ira de Reuver/Photographers Direct:** Ira de Reuver 121tr; **© Juma, 2011:** 125; **Kin Camp SA de CV:** 9; **National Geophysical Data Center:** 172tl; **Pascal Saez:** 164cl; **Pearson Education Ltd:** Gareth Boden 7 (g), 141tr, 186l, 186r, 188, Miguel Dominguez Muñoz 173 (b), John Pallister 15cr, Jules Selmes 104 (a), 217, Chris Parker 144, Rafal Trubisz 36 (inset), Sozaijiten 116 (f), Studio 8 100tl, 100tr, 101tr, 102 (a), 102 (b), 102 (c), 102 (d), 102 (e), 102 (f); **PhotoDisc:** Kevin Sanchez Cole Publishing Group 116 (k); **Reuters:** David Mercado 165, **Sergio Santana:** Sergio Santana / Lucentum Digita 38 (j); **ShelterBox:** 173tc; **Shutterstock.com:** addkm 164 (c), Alex Yeung 99 (d), Alexander Raths 33c, Anna-Mari West 209, BananaStock 36 (b), bikeriderlongon 36 (g), Blend Images 66, blvdone 104 (h), Chris Pole 7 (c), Claverinza (c), 97 (k) Dainis Derics. 166 (a), Darren Baker 82tl, David Pereiras 62cl, Denis Derics 172tr, DEPLANQUE JOEL 172 (b), Dieter H. 106, dotshock 151tl, Elzbieta Sekowska 14 (b), everydaysunshine 116 (j), Fotokostic 79tr, g-Stockstudio 100 (a), Galina Barskaya 190, Gordon Swanson 124, Greg Blok 221, holbox 138 (1), Ivan Cuzmin 99 (a), Ivan Smuk 166 (e), J Fox Photography 148b, Jason Stitt 59c, JeniFoto 7 (d), Ksenia Ragozina 98tl, Kzenon 203, Leah-Anne Thompson 176br, macro meyer 116 (b), mangostock. Shutterstock 146, marekuliasz 97 (e), Martin Good 73cl, Matej Kastelic 193, Matthew Gough 166 (b), Minerva Studio 36 (f), Monkey Business 29 (b), Monica Garza 73, 172 (f), Monkey Business Images 51, 54, 138 (2), 225, Nathalie Speliers Ufermann 123, Niv Koren 202, paol_ok 126tr, Pariny 97 (g), Poznyakov 29 (a), Pressmaster 29 (c), Quality Master 97 (1), 97 (d), Rob Bayer 62tl, Robert Wolkaniec 97 (3), 97 (f), Rose Hayes 72t, savageultralight 62br, Serg Zastavkin 19, Signature Message 166 (f), slava296 14 (a), Subotina Anna 116 (i), svry 116 (c), Tatiana Popova 98cl, Timothy Epp 106tr, Tracey Whiteside 53r, Tyler Olson 33r, u20 138 (5), vichie81 126tl, Vic Labadie 164 (a), VICTOR TORRES 73cr, wavebreakmedia 29 (e), WDG Photo 7 (a), YanLev 157; **www.imagesource.com:** Corbis / Bridge 78tr, Moosboard 83tr; **Xinhua News Agency:** Liu Dawei 140

Cover images: Front: **Alamy Images:** Kevin George

All other images © Pearson Education

Every effort has been made to contact copyright holders of material reproduced in this book. Any omissions will be rectified in subsequent printings if notice is given to the publishers. We are grateful to the following organisations for permission to reproduce copyright material:

©Kin Camp SA de CV p9; ©Grupo 20minutos SL p11; ©María Pineda & Logitravel SL p20; ©Alfaguara (Frisa, M 2013) p21; ©Just Landed p30; ©Mano a Mano Bolivia p35; ©Información Eroski Consumer p42, ©Quino, Caminito SAS p60; ©Antonia Kerrigan Agencia Literaria p64; ©Dolors Reig p65; ©Agencia EFE p72; ©INJUVE - Instituto de la Juventud p76; ©Laura Gallego p86; ©fortbravo.es p86; ©Huffington Post p108; ©AG Balcells (Allende, I 1982) p108; ©El Tiempo p109; ©Editorial Iparraguirre SA p109; ©Sandra Bruna Agencia Literaria SL (Palomas, A 2014) p125; ©Línea Directa Aseguradora SA p130; ©Organice su evento (Digital Marketing) p130; ©La Vanguardia p152; ©Jordi Galceran p153 (For play inquiries, please contact the Gurman Agency LLC (www.gurmanagency.com)); ©Ocio por Madrid p174; ©Agencia EFE p175; ©AG Balcells (Allende, I 2003) p185; ©Antonia Kerrigan Agencia Literaria (Ruiz Zafón, C 1993) p174; ©Planeta, Ignacio Martínez de Pisón p191; ©Grupo 20minutos SL p203; ©BodaMás Gestión SL p202; ©Grupo Anaya SA (Alcolea, A 2007) p204; ©Sabática Consultores SL p206.

Contenidos

Contenidos

Contenidos

1 ¡Desconéctate!
Punto de partida

- Discussing holidays and weather
- Revising the present and preterite tenses

1 leer **Completa las frases con los verbos del recuadro. Sobran <u>dos</u> verbos. Traduce las palabras en negrita al inglés.**

1 **A menudo** ———— a caballo con mi hermano.
2 **Nunca** ———— para mi familia.
3 ———— la guitarra **todos los días**.
4 **Casi nunca** ———— canciones o vídeos.
5 **De vez en cuando** ———— al polideportivo.
6 ———— al baloncesto **dos o tres veces al año**.

llevo	monto	juego
toco	cocino	voy
veo	descargo	

2 escuchar **Escucha. Escribe las <u>dos</u> letras correctas y apunta las actividades. (1–4)**

Ejemplo: 1 a – goes to park, …

¿Qué haces en verano?		
Cuando	hace	buen tiempo / mal tiempo… calor / frío / sol / viento…
	llueve / nieva…	

Pedro

3 leer **Traduce las palabras en violeta al inglés. ¿Qué significan las preguntas?**

a **¿Dónde** te gusta ir de compras?
b **¿Cuándo** te gusta hacer deporte?
c **¿Con qué frecuencia** te gusta leer?
d **¿Por qué** te gusta escuchar música?
e **¿Con quién** te gusta ir al cine?
f **¿Qué** no te gusta hacer?

4 escuchar **Escucha a Pedro y apunta los datos (1–6):**

- la expresión que usa
- la pregunta del ejercicio 3 que contesta.

Ejemplo: 1 me mola, b

Use different opinion phrases to add variety to your answers:
- Prefiero
- Me chifla
- Me encanta
- Me mola ⎫ + infinitive
- Me flipa ⎬ (e.g. *leer, escuchar*, etc.)
- No me gusta (nada)
- Odio ⎭

5 hablar **Con tu compañero/a, haz diálogos con las preguntas del ejercicio 3.**

● ¿Dónde te gusta ir de compras?
■ Me chifla ir de compras a un centro comercial.

Escucha y escribe las <u>cuatro</u> o <u>cinco</u> letras correctas. (1–5)

Ejemplo: **1** *d, g, …*

¿Adónde fuiste de vacaciones?

Fui de vacaciones a…

Francia. — Turquía. — Gales. — Italia.

¿Con quién fuiste?

Fui…

con mi insti. — con mi familia. — con mi mejor amig**o/a**. — sol**o/a**.

¿Cómo viajaste?

Viajé…

en avión. — en coche y en barco. — en tren. — en autocar.

¿Qué hiciste?

Hice turismo y saqué fotos. — Compré recuerdos. — Tomé el sol y descansé. — Comí muchos helados.

Escucha. Copia y completa la tabla en inglés. (1–7)

	day	what he/she did	what weather was like
1	*Tues*	*visited castle*	*stormy*

¿Qué tiempo hizo?	
Hizo	buen tiempo / mal tiempo calor / frío / sol / viento
Hubo	tormenta / niebla
Llovió / Nevó	

Con tu compañero/a, haz diálogos. Inventa actividades para cada día.

● *¿Qué hiciste durante tus vacaciones?*

■ *El <u>lunes</u> <u>fui</u> <u>a la playa</u> porque <u>hizo sol</u>.*

● *¿Y qué hiciste el <u>martes</u>?*

■ *…*

> **G** **Hacer *in the preterite tense*** ⟩ *Page 212*

The verb ***hacer*** is irregular in the **preterite tense**.

	hacer (to do/make)
(yo)	hice
(tú)	hiciste
(él/ella/usted)	hi**z**o
(nosotros/as)	hicimos
(vosotros/as)	hicisteis
(ellos/ellas/ustedes)	hicieron

Many activities which use 'to go' in English are translated by ***hacer*** in Spanish:

Hice *alpinismo.*   **I went** mountain climbing.

- *Saying what you do in summer*
- *Using the present tense*
- *Listening to identify the person of the verb*

1 Escucha y lee. ¿Qué significan las frases en **negrita**? Luego copia y completa la tabla en inglés.

	lives	weather	how often / activities
Maisie	Edinburgh, east...	changeable, ...	sometimes – goes...,

¿Qué haces en verano?

Vivo en Edimburgo, en el este de Escocia. En verano **el tiempo es variable**. A veces voy de paseo con mis amigos, pero casi nunca hacemos una barbacoa porque **hay chubascos** a menudo (siempre llevo un paraguas cuando salgo, ¡por si acaso!).
Maisie

el paraguas   umbrella

Vivo en Valle Nevado, en el centro de Chile. En invierno siempre hago esquí, pero en verano, no. Normalmente hace sol, pero a veces **está nublado** o **hay niebla** (¡no se puede ver nada!). Una vez a la semana trabajo como voluntario en un refugio de animales.
Jaime

Vivo en Mazatlán, en el noroeste de México. El clima **es muy soleado y caluroso** en verano, con temperaturas de más de 30 grados. ¡Qué calor! Todos los días nado en el mar. ¡Soy una fanática de la playa! De vez en cuando **hay tormenta** y por eso no salgo – chateo en la red.
Florencia

Can you work out the pronunciation of these words?

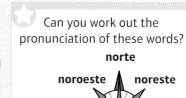
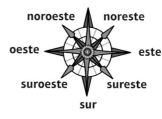

norte

noroeste   noreste

oeste   este

suroeste   sureste

sur

2 Lee los textos del ejercicio 1 otra vez. Busca <u>ocho</u> verbos diferentes. Traduce los verbos al inglés y escribe el infinitivo.

Ejemplo: salgo (I go out) – salir

> **G** **The present tense**   > *Pages 208, 210*

Remember how the present tense works:

	regular			irregular
	nad**ar** (to swim)	le**er** (to read)	viv**ir** (to live)	**ser** (to be)
(yo)	nad**o**	le**o**	viv**o**	**soy**
(tú)	nad**as**	le**es**	viv**es**	**eres**
(él/ella/usted)	nad**a**	le**e**	viv**e**	**es**
(nosotros/as)	nad**amos**	le**emos**	viv**imos**	**somos**
(vosotros/as)	nad**áis**	le**éis**	viv**ís**	**sois**
(ellos/ellas/ustedes)	nad**an**	le**en**	viv**en**	**son**

Some verbs change their stem: *ju**e**go (jugar* – to play)

Some verbs are irregular in the 'I' form only: *ha**go** (hacer* – to do/make), *sal**go** (salir* – to go out), *v**e**o (ver* – to see/watch)

3 Imagina que vives en otro país. Con tu compañero/a, haz diálogos.

- ¿Dónde vives?
- ¿Qué tiempo hace en verano?
- ¿Qué actividades haces en verano?

■ *Vivo en..., en...*
■ *Normalmente...*
■ *A menudo..., pero...*

Make use of the new weather expressions from exercise 1 to add variety.

In addition, mention lots of different activities using a range of verbs. Look back at your list of verbs from exercise 2 for ideas.

Escucha y escribe los verbos en español.
Luego traduce los verbos al inglés. (1–8)

Ejemplo: **1** *nadan – they swim*

 Escucha a David y lee las frases. Identifica las <u>tres</u> frases correctas.

a David vive en el suroeste de su país.
b Hay muchos chubascos en su región.
c David es adicto a la tele.
d David y sus amigos practican mucho deporte.
e David y sus amigos nunca hacen natación.
f David toca un instrumento.

Listen for verb endings as clues:	
Verbs ending in…	usually refer to…
–o	I
–s	you
–mos	we
–n	they

6 **Escribe un texto sobre tus vacaciones.**

- Say where you live.　　　　　　　　*Vivo en…, en el… de…*
- Say what the weather is like in summer.　*En verano normalmente…*
- Say what activities you do.　　　　*Todos los días… También… porque…*
- Say what activities your friends do.　*Mis amigos…*

7 leer **Lee el texto y completa las frases en inglés.**

Campamentos de verano con Kin Camp en México

¡El mejor verano de tu vida!

Verano Senior es la experiencia perfecta para adolescentes (de 13 a 17 años), con una combinación de diversión, juegos, deportes, aventura y amistad.

El campamento tiene actividades especiales como escalada, pista comando, tiro con arco y canoas. Además, aprendes a:
- ser un líder
- trabajar en equipo
- y lo más importante, ¡echar relajo!

Tienes la oportunidad de ir de excursión a lugares de interés increíbles. Y también ofrecemos diferentes talleres creativos de teatro, música, pintura, escultura y baile, porque ¡TODOS tenemos un artista dentro!

¡echar relajo!　　*to go wild! (Mexican slang)*

1 The summer camp is aimed at…
2 It offers a combination of fun, …
3 Special activities include climbing, …
4 You also learn to…
5 Creative workshops include theatre, …

 Zona Cultura

Cada año muchos jóvenes en España y Latinoamérica pasan quince días, o más, en un **campamento de verano**, donde disfrutan de actividades educativas, deportivas y recreativas.

- Talking about holiday preferences
- Using verbs of opinion to refer to different people
- Understanding percentages

1 leer **Lee y completa los textos con la opinión correcta. Sobra una opinión.**

a me mola leer
b le encanta hacer deportes acuáticos
c nos apasiona hacer ciclismo

d nos flipa ver películas
e odio ir de compras
f prefiero estar al aire libre

En España tenemos por lo menos once semanas de vacaciones en junio, julio y agosto. ¡Qué suerte! En verano no veo la tele en casa porque **1 ———** cuando hace sol. Todos los días mi mejor amigo y yo montamos en bici, dado que **2 ———**.

Íñigo

En Argentina tenemos las vacaciones de verano en enero y febrero. **3 ———** y por eso compro un montón de revistas en verano porque tengo más tiempo libre. A menudo voy a la pista de hielo con mi hermana y también vamos al cine, puesto que **4 ———**. Mi padre bucea en el mar, ya que **5 ———**.

Ana

2 escuchar **Escucha y comprueba tus respuestas.**

The following all mean 'since' or 'given that':
dado que
puesto que
ya que

G Verbs of opinion ⟩ Page 228

Many verbs for giving opinions need a pronoun like **me**. These verbs all take pronouns: *gustar, encantar, chiflar, molar, apasionar, flipar.*

Change the pronoun to talk about other people:

me gusta	I like	**nos** gusta	we like
te gusta	you (sing) like	**os** gusta	you (pl) like
le gusta	he/she likes	**les** gusta	they like

To give your opinion of an activity, use the infinitive after these verbs.

If you mention another person directly (for example by using their name), you need to add the word **a**.

A *mi padre* **le** chifla *cocinar*. — My dad loves cooking.
También **le** gusta *bailar*. — He also likes dancing.

3 leer **Lee los textos del ejercicio 1 otra vez. Busca las expresiones en español en el texto.**

1 loads of magazines
2 What luck!
3 at least

4 (he) goes diving
5 I go to the ice rink
6 I have more free time

4 escuchar **Escucha a Alejandra. Apunta las personas y las actividades en inglés.**

Ejemplo: Brother – loves shopping, hates…

Give reasons for <u>activities</u> you do by referring to **your wider interests**. For example:
<u>Compro muchas revistas</u> porque **me chifla leer**.

Which activities could you connect with these interests?

> *hacer deportes acuáticos*
> *hacer artes marciales*
> *estar al aire libre*
> *estar en contacto con los amigos*
> *usar el ordenador*

5 hablar **Imagina que hablas con tu compañero/a español(a). Haz diálogos.**

● ¿Cuándo tienes vacaciones?
■ *En Inglaterra tenemos…*
● ¿Qué haces durante las vacaciones?
■ *A veces hago… porque me chifla… Cuando hace calor mi hermano y yo, …*

6 leer **Lee el artículo. Apunta <u>ocho</u> detalles en inglés.**

Ejemplo: 17% prefer to go abroad

Los españoles prefieren las vacaciones... en España.

○ Según una encuesta, el 83% de los españoles prefiere veranear en España y solo un 17% en el extranjero.

○ La costa es el destino preferido de los españoles para las vacaciones (60%), comparado con el campo (17%), la montaña (14%) y la ciudad (9%).

○ Alicante, Cádiz y Málaga son los tres destinos preferidos.

En términos de alojamiento, aunque la opción preferida es ir a un hotel (33%), la segunda opción es alquilar un apartamento o una casa rural (27%). El 15% tiene una segunda residencia, y solo el 6% prefiere los campings.

| **según** | *according to* |
| **veranear** | *to spend the summer holidays* |

G **Preferir, tener *and* ir**   ❯ *Page 210*

Preferir is a stem-changing verb. **Tener** and **ir** are irregular in the present tense.

	prefer**ir** (to prefer)	**tener** (to have)	**ir** (to go)
(yo)	pref**ie**ro	ten**go**	**voy**
(tú)	pref**ie**res	t**ie**nes	**vas**
(él/ella/usted)	pref**ie**re	t**ie**ne	**va**
(nosotros/as)	preferimos	tenemos	**vamos**
(vosotros/as)	preferís	tenéis	**vais**
(ellos/ellas/ustedes)	pref**ie**ren	t**ie**nen	**van**

---

7 escuchar **Escucha la información sobre los argentinos. Copia y completa la tabla.**

a	b	c	d	e
%	%	%	%	%

⭐ Percentages are usually preceded by the word **un** or **el**. Listen out for the word **y** to help you work out numbers above 30.

| *cuarenta **y** nueve* | 49 |
| *ochenta **y** cinco* | 85 |

When listening, take extra care with the numbers *sesenta* (60) and *setenta* (70).

8 escribir **Traduce las frases al español.**

1 My best friend prefers to spend the summer holidays abroad.
2 You have at least ten weeks of holidays and you live on the coast. What luck!
3 They like to go to the ice rink in summer since they have more free time.
4 My brother and I go diving when it's hot given that we love doing watersports.

- *Saying what you did on holiday*
- *Using the preterite tense*
- *Using different structures to give opinions*

 1 escuchar

Escucha. Copia y completa la tabla en inglés. (1–4)

	when visited	best thing	worst thing
1	*two years ago*	*b*	

Hace una semana / un mes / un año...
Hace dos semanas / meses / años...

Zona Cultura

Destino: BARCELONA
Ubicación: Noreste de España, en la costa
Población: 1,6 millones de habitantes (2ª ciudad de España)
Famosa por: Los Juegos Olímpicos de 1992
La arquitectura de Antoni Gaudí
El club de fútbol FC Barcelona ('el Barça')

Lo mejor fue cuando...

a vi un partido en el Camp Nou.

b fui al acuario.

Lo peor fue cuando...

e perdí mi móvil.

f tuve un accidente en la playa.

c aprendí a hacer vela.

d visité el Park Güell.

g vomité en una montaña rusa.

h llegué tarde al aeropuerto.

 2 escuchar

Escucha otra vez. Escribe las opiniones para cada persona. (1–4)

Ejemplo: **1** *Fue flipante, ...*

G The preterite tense > Page 212

Use the **preterite tense** to talk about completed actions in the past.

visit**ar** (to visit)	beb**er** (to drink)	sal**ir** (to leave / to go out)	**irregular verbs**
			ir (to go) **ser** (to be)
visit**é**	beb**í**	sal**í**	**fui**
visit**aste**	beb**iste**	sal**iste**	**fuiste**
visit**ó**	beb**ió**	sal**ió**	**fue**
visit**amos**	beb**imos**	sal**imos**	**fuimos**
visit**asteis**	beb**isteis**	sal**isteis**	**fuisteis**
visit**aron**	beb**ieron**	sal**ieron**	**fueron**

Other irregular verbs in the preterite include:

tener (e.g. **tuve** – I had), **hacer** (e.g. **hice** – I did / made) and **ver** (e.g. **vi** – I saw / watched).

Some verbs have a spelling change in the 'I' form only:

jugar → *ju**gu**é*   *llegar* → *lle**gu**é*   *sacar* → *sa**qu**é*

⭐ Listen for ways to give opinions about the past:

- *(No) Me gustó / Me encantó*
- *Lo pasé...* bomba / fenomenal / bien mal / fatal
- *Fue...* inolvidable / increíble impresionante / flipante horroroso / un desastre

How do you pronounce these words in Spanish? Take extra care with cognates such as *desastre*.

3 hablar

Con tu compañero/a, haz diálogos sobre Barcelona. Inventa los detalles.

- ¿Cuándo visitaste Barcelona?
- ¿Cómo viajaste y con quién fuiste?
- ¿Qué fue lo mejor de tu visita?
- ¿Qué fue lo peor de tu visita?

- Visité Barcelona hace… Lo pasé…
- Viajé… y fui con… Fue…
- Lo mejor fue cuando…
- Lo peor…

4 leer

Lee el texto de la página web. Escribe <u>cinco</u> ventajas (advantages) de visitar Barcelona en Segway.

Ejemplo: It's easy

¡Explora Barcelona en Segway!
con Vamosensegway.com

- Una manera fácil, rápida y diferente de visitar la ciudad.
- Una actividad ideal para toda la familia.
- Recorridos de dos, tres o cuatro horas con guías expertos.
- Cuatro idiomas: español, catalán, inglés y francés.

La opción perfecta para conocer esta ciudad mágica donde puedes…

- disfrutar del Barrio Gótico
- subir al Monumento a Colón
- sacar fotos de la Sagrada Familia

- ver los barcos en el puerto
- descubrir el Museo Picasso
- pasear por las Ramblas

Monumento a Colón

Port Vell

Las Ramblas

5 escuchar

Escucha a Daniel. Contesta a las preguntas en inglés.

1 Look at the locations in Barcelona listed on the website. Which place did Daniel visit first?
2 What happened in the gothic quarter?
3 What was his opinion of the Sagrada Familia?
4 Where was he sick?
5 Give <u>two</u> examples of how the website information is incorrect.
6 What was his overall opinion of the experience?

 Listen again to Daniel. Can you spot examples of the following?

- Sequencers: **primero** (first), **luego** (then), **más tarde** (later), **después** (after that), **finalmente** (finally)
- Opinion phrases
- **Lo mejor /Lo peor**
- Verbs in the 'we' form
Use as many of these things as possible in exercise 6.

6 escribir

Imagina que visitaste Barcelona en Segway. Escribe un texto.

El año pasado exploré Barcelona en Segway con mi… y lo pasé bomba. Primero subí a…, donde perdí mi… Luego fuimos…

● *Describing where you stayed*
● *Using the imperfect tense*
● *Working out the meaning of new words*

1 Escucha y lee el foro. Escribe la letra correcta para cada persona. Sobra una foto.

Me quedé en un albergue juvenil y me gustó mucho. **Estaba** cerca de la playa y **tenía** una cafetería y un aparcamiento. Además, **era** bastante moderno – ¡y muy barato! **Hassan**

Me alojé en una pensión pequeña. **Estaba** en el centro de la ciudad, y por eso **era** un poco ruidosa. No **tenía** ni restaurante ni bar. Tampoco **había** piscina, pero **era** acogedora. **Alejandro**

Nos alojamos en un camping en las afueras de la ciudad. **Era** muy tranquilo y **había** mucho espacio para mi tienda. También **tenía** una lavandería. **Asun**

Fui de crucero por el Mediterráneo. **Era** caro, pero me encantó. En el barco **había** una piscina cubierta y un gimnasio. **Era** como un hotel de cinco estrellas – ¡pero más lujoso! **Yoli**

2 ¿Qué significan las palabras en violeta en los textos del ejercicio 1?

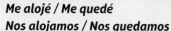

Me alojé / Me quedé	*I stayed*
Nos alojamos / Nos quedamos	*We stayed*

3 Lee los textos del ejercicio 1 otra vez y escribe el nombre correcto.

Who stayed somewhere…

1 with good sports facilities?
2 on the outskirts of the city?
3 with facilities for washing clothes?
4 with a car park?
5 noisy?
6 cheap?
7 expensive?

4 Escribe un texto para el foro con una descripción del hotel.

☆ ☆ ☆ hotel
Outskirts of city
Comfortable + cheap
✓ swimming pool, car park
✗ gym, restaurant
Loved it

Pay attention:

*El hotel **tenía** un bar.* — The hotel **had** a bar.
but: *En el hotel **había** un bar.* — In the hotel **there was** a bar.

*No tenía **ni** un bar **ni** una sauna.* — It **didn't** have a bar **or** a sauna.
Tampoco tenía un gimnasio. — **Nor** did it have a gym.

G **The imperfect tense** ❯ Page **214**

The **imperfect tense** is used for describing things in the past.

*El hotel **estaba** en la costa.* — The hotel **was** on the coast.
***Tenía** una piscina antigua.* — It **had** an old swimming pool.

	est**ar** (to be)	ten**er** (to have)
(yo)	est**aba**	ten**ía**
(tú)	est**abas**	ten**ías**
(él/ella/usted)	est**aba**	ten**ía**
(nosotros/as)	est**ábamos**	ten**íamos**
(vosotros/as)	est**abais**	ten**íais**
(ellos/ellas/ustedes)	est**aban**	ten**ían**

–er and *–ir* **verbs** have the same endings.
Only three verbs are irregular in the imperfect, including *ser* (to be) ⟶ ***era*** (it was).
The verb ***había*** is the imperfect tense of *hay* and means 'there was / there were'.

5 leer Lee el texto y elige los verbos correctos. Luego traduce el texto al inglés.

Nos alojamos en un hotel pequeño. **1 Era / Tenía** muy acogedor y **2 era / estaba** en el centro de la ciudad, cerca de la bolera. Lo bueno de la ciudad era que **3 había / era** animada y **4 había / estaba** muchos lugares de interés. Sin embargo, lo malo era que no **5 estaba / tenía** ni tiendas ni cine. Tampoco **6 estaba / había** espacios verdes. Además, **7 había / era** muchos turistas, y por eso **8 era / tenía** demasiado ruidosa.
Blanca

Use **era** (*ser*) for describing what something was like.
*La ciudad **era** ruidosa.*
The city **was** noisy.

Use **estaba** (*estar*) for talking about a location or a temporary state.
*El hotel **estaba** en las afueras.*
The hotel **was** on the outskirts.

6 escuchar Escucha. Para cada persona apunta los detalles en inglés. (1–4)

- Accommodation:
- Location:
- Good points:
- Bad points:

el parador state-run luxury hotel, usually in a historic building

Lo bueno / Lo malo (del pueblo / de la ciudad) era que…			
era	demasiado muy bastante	animad**o/a** bonit**o/a** pintoresc**o/a** tranquil**o/a**	antigu**o/a** históric**o/a** turístic**o/a** ruidos**o/a**
tenía / había… También tenía / había…		much**o**	ambiente / tráfico que hacer
		much**a**	contaminación gente
no tenía / había… Tampoco tenía / había…		much**os**	espacios verdes lugares de interés monumentos turistas
		much**as**	discotecas tiendas
no tenía ni cine ni bolera			

7 hablar Con tu compañero/a, completa las preguntas.

- *¿Adónde*
- *¿Cómo*
- *¿Qué*
- *¿Dónde*
- *¿Cómo era*
- *¿Lo pasaste*

- *hiciste?*
- *viajaste?*
- *(el hotel) / (la ciudad)?*
- *bien?*
- *fuiste de vacaciones?*
- *te alojaste?*

8 hablar Mira las fotos y habla de tus vacaciones. Utiliza las preguntas del ejercicio 7.

- Use your imagination – don't just say what you can see in the photo!
- Extend your sentences by giving extra details (e.g. when, who with, etc.).
- Try to add an opinion phrase to <u>every</u> answer.
- Include negative phrases (e.g. *No… ni… ni…, Tampoco…*).
- Use the **preterite** for saying what you did (e.g. *Descansé en…, Jugué al…*).
- Use the **imperfect** for descriptions in the past (e.g. *Era…, Había…, Estaba…*).

5 Quisiera reservar…

- Booking accommodation and dealing with problems
- Using verbs with usted
- Using questions to form answers

1 **Lee la página web. Escribe el precio correcto.**

Ejemplo: 1 95 + 14 = 109 euros

1 Single room + full board
2 Double room + breakfast
3 Double room + sea view + half board

4 Wifi access
5 Single room + sea view + half board

Hotel Dos Palomas, Alicante

En pleno centro de Alicante, el hotel Dos Palomas cuenta con piscina climatizada, tienda de recuerdos, restaurante y terraza. Todas las habitaciones disponen de:

- Aire acondicionado
- Wifi gratis
- Televisor de pantalla plana
- Baño con bañera o ducha
- Servicio de limpieza todos los días

Restaurante abierto hasta medianoche.
Recepción abierta 24 horas.
Desayuno entre las 7.00 y las 10.00.
No se admiten mascotas.

Tipo de habitación	con…	Precio por noche
Habitación individual* Opciones • con / sin balcón	desayuno incluido	79 €
	media pensión**	95 €
Habitación doble* Opciones • con dos camas • con cama de matrimonio	desayuno incluido	116 €
	media pensión**	~~145 €~~ **Oferta especial 122 €**

* Vistas al mar – suplemento de 18 €
** Pensión completa – suplemento de 14 €

2 **Lee el texto del ejercicio 1 otra vez y escucha la conversación.**
Escribe en inglés las <u>ocho</u> diferencias entre el texto y la conversación.

Ejemplo: It <u>does</u> have a pool.

3 **Con tu compañero/a, haz un diálogo sobre la información del ejercicio 1.**

- *¿Hay… en el hotel?*
- *¿Hay… en las habitaciones?*
- *¿Cuánto cuesta una habitación… con…?*
- *¿A qué hora se sirve…?*
- *¿Cuándo está abierto/a el/la…?*
- *¿Cuánto es el suplemento por…?*
- *¿Se admiten…?*

Take care with question words.

¿Cuánto(s)…?	How much / How many…?
¿Cuándo…?	When…?
¿A qué hora…?	At what time…?

When answering questions in the 'he/she/it' or 'they' form you can usually re-use the same verb in your answer.

*¿Cuánto **cuesta** una habitación doble?*
How much does a double room cost?

*Una habitación doble **cuesta** 122 €.*
A double room costs 122 euros.

4 escuchar **Escucha los dos diálogos. Escribe las palabras que faltan en español. (1–2)**

Ejemplo: **a** *individual*

- Hotel Dos Palomas, ¿dígame?
- Quisiera reservar una habitación **a** ——— con **b** ———.
- ¿Quiere una habitación **c** ——— o **d** ———?
- Pues, **e** ———, por favor.
- ¿Para cuántas noches?
- Para **f** ——— noches, del **g** ——— al **h** ——— de **i** ———.
- ¿Cómo se llama usted?
- Me llamo **j** ———. Se escribe…
- ¿Puede repetir, por favor?
- …
- Muy bien. Son **k** ——— € por noche.
- De acuerdo. ¿Hay **l** ———?
- Por supuesto, señor(a).

> **G** *Using usted*
>
> Use **usted** (polite form of 'you') in formal situations, such as when booking a room. It uses the same verb endings as the 'he/she/it' form of the verb.
>
> The plural form is **ustedes**, which uses the 'they' form of the verb.
>
> | | |
> |---|---|
> | *¿Cómo se llam**a** usted?* | What are you (polite singular) called? |
> | *¿De dónde **son** ustedes?* | Where are you (polite plural) from? |
>
> Often the word **usted/ustedes** is omitted.
>
> | | |
> |---|---|
> | *¿Puede repetir, por favor?* | Can you repeat, please? |
> | *¿Puede hablar más despacio?* | Can you speak more slowly? |

5 hablar **Con tu compañero/a, haz <u>dos</u> diálogos. Utiliza el ejercicio 4 como modelo.**

a Double, inc half board
Sea view
3–6 Feb
140 €
Air con?

b Single, inc breakfast
Balcony
14–19 Sep
79 €
Pool?

6 escribir **Escribe <u>tres</u> frases para cada dibujo.**

¿Cuál es el problema?

Quiero	quejarme hablar con el director cambiar de habitación
El ascensor El aire acondicionado La ducha / La luz	no funciona está estropead**o/a**
La habitación	está suci**o/a**
Hay	ratas en la cama
No hay Necesito	papel higiénico (un) secador / toallas champú / jabón
¡Socorro!	Es inaceptable.
Perdone / Lo siento…	El hotel está completo. Voy a llamar el servicio de limpieza. Tenemos otra habitación libre.

7 escuchar **Escucha. Copia y completa la tabla en inglés. (1–4)**

	room	problems	guest satisfied in the end? (✓/✗)
1	226	no toilet paper, …	

8 hablar **Con tu compañero/a, inventa <u>dos</u> diálogos cómicos.**

- ● ¡Socorro! Hay ratas en la ducha y… Estoy en la habitación… Quiero…
- ■ Lo siento,…
- ● ¡Es inaceptable! Quiero…

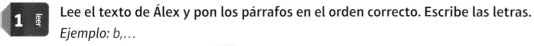

- *Giving an account of a holiday in the past*
- *Using three tenses together*
- *Identifying positive and negative opinions*

1 leer **Lee el texto de Álex y pon los párrafos en el orden correcto. Escribe las letras.**
Ejemplo: b,…

los Picos de Europa

el teleférico a Fuente Dé

a Sin embargo, este año decidimos **acampar** en Cantabria, en el norte de España. Por un lado lo pasamos muy bien, pero por otro lado tuvimos varios problemas. Primero, en Dover el barco tuvo **un retraso** de tres horas porque hubo tormenta. ¡Qué aburrido!

b Normalmente veraneamos en Grecia todos los años ya que a mis padres les chifla **el paisaje**. Además, hace mucho calor. Siempre nos alojamos en un apartamento en una de las islas donde tomo el sol, leo ¡y como demasiado! No hay mucho que hacer, pero es muy relajante.

c El último día salimos del camping muy temprano y fuimos a Santander para **volver** a Inglaterra en barco. Esta vez no tuvimos ningún problema con el viaje. ¡Menos mal! Estaba muy cansado y dormí durante todo el viaje.

d El primer día mi hermano y yo alquilamos unas bicicletas y visitamos el pueblo medieval de Santillana del Mar. Fue impresionante. **Por desgracia**, mi hermano chocó con un coche aparcado y tuvo que ir al hospital. ¡Qué miedo!

e Continuamos el viaje a Cantabria en coche, pero luego tuvimos **una avería** en **la autopista** y tuvimos que llamar a un mecánico. Cuando llegamos al camping, la recepción ya estaba cerrada, dado que era muy tarde.

f Al día siguiente fuimos de excursión a los Picos de Europa. No hicimos **alpinismo**, pero decidimos coger el teleférico a Fuente Dé. ¡Me encantó! No había mucha gente, así que no tuvimos que **esperar** mucho tiempo. Hizo buen tiempo y las vistas eran preciosas.

¡Menos mal! *Just as well!*

2 escuchar **Escucha y comprueba tus respuestas. Luego traduce las palabras en negrita al inglés.**

3 leer **Lee el texto del ejercicio 1 otra vez. Busca las expresiones en español en el texto. ¿Es presente, pretérito o imperfecto?**

Ejemplo: 1 chocó con – preterite

1 (he) crashed into
2 I was very tired
3 (it) was closed
4 we always stay
5 we decided to
6 (they) love
7 we hired
8 the views were
9 There isn't much to do
10 I slept

G **Using three tenses together**　　　　> *Pages 208, 212, 214*

Use the **present tense** to describe what things <u>are</u> like or to say what usually happens.

Es *relajante.*　　　　**It's** relaxing.
Como *demasiado.*　　　**I eat** too much.

Use the **imperfect tense** to describe what something <u>was</u> like.

Las vistas **eran** *preciosas.*　　The views **were** beautiful.

Use the **preterite tense** to say what you did / what happened.

Llegamos *tarde.*　　　　**We arrived** late.

Remember that irregular verbs do not follow the usual patterns. For example:

	ser (to be)	tener (to have)	haber
present	es	tiene	hay
imperfect	era	tenía	había
preterite	fue	tuvo	hubo

4 escuchar **Escucha y escribe P (positivo), N (negativo) o P+N (positivo y negativo). (1–6)**

Tuve	un accidente
Tuvimos	un pinchazo
	un retraso
	una avería
Tuve que ir	a la comisaría
Perdí	el equipaje
Perdimos	la cartera
	la maleta
	las llaves

When listening for positive and negative opinions, don't jump to conclusions! Listen to the end of the sentence, and listen for clues:

Lo bueno / Lo malo — The good thing / The bad thing
Lo mejor / Lo peor — The best thing / The worst thing
Lo que más / menos me gustó — What I liked most / least

Remember that *tampoco* introduces a negative sentence.

For mixed opinions you may hear phrases like *pero* (but), *sin embargo* (however) or *por un lado… por otro lado* (on one hand… on the other hand).

5 hablar **Con tu compañero/a, describe las <u>dos</u> vacaciones e inventa más detalles. Luego describe tus propias vacaciones.**

Say:

- where you normally go and why
- what you do there
- where you went last year
- what you did and what went wrong
- what the town was like
- what the weather was like.

Usually
Wales
beautiful + hot weather
tennis + relax

2 years ago
Ireland – campsite
sightseeing + photos
puncture
lost suitcase
windy

Usually
Turkey
quiet + sunny
sunbathe + swim

3 months ago
France – apartment
shopping + walks
breakdown
lost keys
stormy

6 escribir **Traduce el texto al español. ¡Cuidado con los verbos! (¿Presente, pretérito o imperfecto?)**

Look back at Unit 2.

Which negative expression do you need?

Which tense do you need here? And which verb?

Do you need *tener* or *tener que* here?

Every year we spend the summer holidays abroad. My Mum likes to rent a house in the south of France, but my Dad prefers to go camping.

However, last year we decided to go to Scotland, where we had a great time. On one hand, the town didn't have a cinema or a swimming pool, but on the other hand, the landscape was beautiful and it was sunny every day.

The best thing was when we went sightseeing. My sister bought a camera and took lots of photos. However, unfortunately I lost my wallet, and we had to go to the police station.

1 leer Lee la información sobre actividades para el verano.

Ideas para ocupar las vacaciones

❶
Club de prensa

¿Te interesa participar en la creación de una revista para adolescentes? ¿Quieres escribir artículos sobre las últimas películas? ¿O prefieres la fotografía? Actividad gratis.

❷
Actividades creativas para niños

¡No tienes que pasar el verano jugando a los videojuegos! Ofrecemos una variedad de actividades artísticas (dibujo, pintura, manualidades, baile, teatro), así como talleres de cocina.

❸
Cursos de verano

Inscríbete en nuestras clases de windsurf y vela para toda la familia. Clases de natación y buceo para principiantes también. Instructores expertos.

❹
Talleres deportivos

Actividades deportivas en pleno campo. Disfruta de unas vistas preciosas mientras practicas una variedad de deportes: baloncesto, tenis, voleibol, ciclismo… Menores de dieciséis años.

¿Cuál es la actividad ideal? Escribe el número correcto.

a No tienes mucho dinero.
b Te encanta montar en bici.
c Quieres hacer una actividad con tu madre.
d Quieres aprender a preparar tu comida favorita.
e Eres un fanático del cine.
f Te gusta mucho el paisaje bonito.

> ⭐ Remember that the texts and questions will usually use different words to express the same thing. Look at the questions and try to predict what clues you might find in the text. For example, the first question says that you haven't got much money. What information might you look for in the texts?

2 leer Read the article about Havana. Answer the questions at the top of page 21.

Descubre La Habana

los coco-taxi

Hace más de tres años que decidí visitar la capital cubana y todavía recuerdo perfectamente el viaje del aeropuerto al hotel en uno de esos curiosos taxis, popularmente conocidos como 'coco-taxi'.

Durante el trayecto, vi parte de lo que ofrece esta ciudad: pintorescas calles con los viejos coches clásicos, una elegante arquitectura colonial y casas pintadas con colores vivos, donde la actividad, la creatividad y la música están siempre presentes.

Decidí conocer el país con unos amigos, combinando la comodidad de un hotel con régimen 'todo incluido' con la libertad que tienes cuando alquilas un coche. Aunque para conocer La Habana Vieja, lo mejor es recorrerla a pie. Así puedes disfrutar de uno de los entornos coloniales mejor conservados de América Latina, con su Catedral, los palacios señoriales… y descubrir lo mejor de este país: los cubanos.

(a) What does the article tell us?
Choose the <u>three</u> correct statements.

A The writer travelled to Havana by plane.
B She saw lots of brightly coloured cars.
C She was impressed by the buildings.
D She was surprised by how quiet the city was.
E The hotel only served breakfast.
F She hired a car during her visit.
G The old buildings are now in a poor state.

Answer the following questions **in English**.
You do not need to write full sentences.

(b) According to the article, what is the best way to visit Old Havana?
(c) What does the writer like best about Cuba?

3 leer

Read the extract. Sara is staying at a summer camp called Happy English.

> *75 consejos para sobrevivir en el campamento* by María Frisa (abridged)

Normalmente los campamentos están alejados de la civilización. Nuestro fantástico 'Happy English' está en medio del monte, a casi dos horas del pueblo más cercano. Por eso nos sorprende cuando una tarde, Nicole nos dice que podemos bajar al pueblo para comprar regalos y recuerdos.

—Es una actividad voluntaria. Los que quieran venir deben estar aquí a las cinco —nos informa Nicole.

A las tres y media ya estamos TODOS aquí. Esperando. El sol pega tan fuerte que llevamos gorras y sombreros.

Answer the following questions **in English**. You do not need to write full sentences.

a Where **exactly** is the Happy English summer camp located?
b What is the purpose of their trip down to the village?
c What time were the children told to meet?
d What are the children wearing when they meet up? Name <u>one</u> item.

> ⭐ When reading extracts from novels, plays or poems there will be lots of language that you don't know. Don't panic – you are not expected to understand every word! Use the questions to give you clues about the information you are looking for. Also, use your common sense.

1 escuchar

You hear a travel bulletin on the radio. Listen and answer the following questions **in English**.

a What is causing congestion on Madrid's roads?
b Why is there so much traffic in the Nuevos Ministerios area?
c Why are there delays on the M-40 motorway?
d How exactly is the weather affecting public transport?

2 escuchar

Escuchas un anuncio para un centro de vacaciones.
Rellena el espacio de cada frase con una palabra del recuadro. Hay más palabras que espacios.

los coches	acuáticas	niños	deportivas
la montaña	dos semanas	doble	los perros
cinco días	~~familias~~	la ciudad	individual

> ⭐ There are usually two possible options for each gap. Before you listen, try to spot the pairs. Remember that you may hear different words used to mean the same thing as one of the options. Watch out for distractors, too!

Ejemplo: El Centro de Vacaciones Mirasol Sierra es ideal para <u>familias</u>.

a Está situado en ————.
b Ofrece una gran variedad de actividades ————.
c Hay una oferta especial si reservas una habitación ————.
d No hay suplemento para ————.
e Es más barato si te quedas ————.

A – Role play

1 *leer* Look at the role play card and prepare what you are going to say.

Topic: Travel and tourist transactions

Instructions to candidates:

You are talking to the receptionist at a hotel in Spain and wish to book a room. The teacher will play the role of the receptionist and will speak first.

You must address the receptionist as *usted*.

You will talk to the teacher using the five prompts below.
- where you see – ? – you must ask a question.
- where you see – ! – you must respond to something you have not prepared.

Task

Usted está en un hotel en España. Quiere reservar una habitación y habla con el/la recepcionista.

1 Habitación - tipo

2 hotel - razón

3 !

4 ? Desayuno – precio

5 ? Piscina – horaric

The third bullet point always asks you to give an unprepared answer in the **past tense**. What could the receptionist ask you here?

In the role play task you don't need to expand your answers. Focus on the **accuracy** of what you say.

What reason could you give for choosing this hotel? Keep it simple!

Start your question with '¿Cuánto …?'.

If you don't know the meaning of 'horario', can you work it out from the word 'hora'?

2 *escuchar* Practise what you have prepared. Then, using your notes, listen and respond to the teacher.

3 *escuchar* Now listen to Ryan doing the role play task. **In English,** note down what he says for the first three points on the card.

Role play tasks always require you to ask two questions. Look at the text in the bullet point to see if you can use it to help form the question and decide whether you need to start with a question word. Can you remember what these question words mean?

¿Qué?   ¿Cuándo?   ¿Cuánto?   ¿Dónde?

¿Quién?   ¿Cómo?   ¿Por qué?   ¿A qué hora?

B – Picture-based task

Topic: Holidays

Mira la foto y prepara las respuestas a los siguientes puntos:
- la descripción de la foto
- tu opinión sobre las vacaciones en el extranjero
- dónde pasaste tus últimas vacaciones
- tus planes para el próximo verano
- !

1 escuchar **Look at the photo and read the task. Then listen to Lucy's response to the first bullet point.**

1 Why does she think this is a photo of New York?
2 What do you think *edificios muy grandes* are?
3 Which <u>three</u> Spanish weather phrases does she use?
4 What does she say about the people in the photo?

2 escuchar **Listen to and read Lucy's response to the second bullet point.**

1 Write down the missing word for each gap.
2 Look at the Answer Booster on page 24. Note down <u>six</u> examples of language which Lucy uses to give a strong answer.

A mí me encanta ir al extranjero porque soy una **1** ━━━━ de la playa. Me encanta tomar el sol, **2** ━━━━ y escuchar música con mi hermana. Además, nos chifla hacer deportes acuáticos, pero en Inglaterra es difícil, puesto que **3** ━━━━ demasiado. Cuando voy de vacaciones siempre hago vela y a veces **4** ━━━━ en el mar también. Normalmente veraneamos en Egipto o Grecia, donde el clima es muy **5** ━━━━. ¡Qué suerte! Sin embargo, lo malo es que es muy **6** ━━━━.

3 escuchar **Listen to Lucy's response to the third bullet point.**

1 Which negative expressions does she use?
2 **In English**, note down <u>six</u> details that she gives.

4 escuchar **Listen to Lucy's response to the fourth bullet point. In Spanish, note down <u>six</u> near future tense verbs that she uses.**

> ⭐ To talk about what you **are going to do** use the **near future tense**. Use the present tense of the verb **ir** + **a** + **infinitive**.
>
> **Voy a ir** *a Francia con mi familia.*
> I'm going to go to France with my family.
>
> **No vamos a viajar** *en coche.*
> We aren't going to travel by car.

5 escuchar **Prepare your own answers to the first <u>four</u> bullet points. Try to predict which unexpected question you might be asked. Then listen and take part in the full picture-based task with the teacher.**

C – General conversation

1 escuchar **Listen to Stephen introducing his chosen topic. Read the statements and correct the mistakes.**

1 Stephen lives in south Wales.
2 Tourists like it because it's historic.
3 Stephen plays football on the beach.
4 His brother goes sailing.

2 escuchar **The teacher asks Stephen *'¿Dónde prefieres pasar las vacaciones?'*. Listen and note down <u>three</u> examples of how Stephen also includes other people's opinions.**

3 escuchar **Listen to Stephen's response to the second question *'¿Adónde fuiste de vacaciones el año pasado?'*. Look at the Answer Booster on page 24. Note down <u>six</u> examples of language which Stephen uses to give a strong answer.**

4 hablar **Prepare your own answers to Module 1 questions 1–6 on page 198. Then practise with your partner.**

Answer booster	Aiming for a solid answer	Aiming higher	Aiming for the top
Verbs	**Different time frames**: past, present, future	**Different persons** of the verb **Verbs with an infinitive**: *tener que, decidir*	**Preterite and imperfect to talk about the past**: *Cuando llegamos, era…* **Phrases with more than one tense**: *creo que voy a visitar…*
Opinions and reasons	**Verbs of opinion**: *Me chifla(n), me encanta(n), me apasiona(n)…* **Reasons**: *porque…*	**Exclamations**: *¡Qué suerte!* **Verbs of opinion for other people**: *A mi padre le mola…*	**Reasons**: *ya que, dado que, puesto que, por eso, así que* **Verbs of opinion in the past**: *me gustó*
Connectives	*y, pero, también*	*además, sin embargo, desafortunadamente, por desgracia*	**Balancing an argument:** *aunque… por un lado… por otro lado…*
Other features	**Qualifiers**: *muy, un poco, bastante* **Sequencers**: *primero, luego, después* **Other time phrases**: *a menudo, siempre*	**Sentences with *cuando, donde***: *Cuando llegamos…* **Negatives**: *no… ni… ni…, tampoco…*	**Positive/negative phrases**: *lo bueno/malo, lo mejor/peor, lo que más/menos me gustó, una desventaja es…* **Interesting vocabulary**: *veranear, un pinchazo*

A – Short writing task

 1 **Look at the task and answer the questions.**

- What type of text are you asked to write?
- What is each bullet point asking you to do?
- Which tense(s) will you need to use to answer each one?

* saber = to know

 2 **Read Mohammed's answer on page 25. What do the phrases in bold mean?**

 3 **Look at the Answer Booster. Note down <u>eight</u> examples of language which Mohammed uses to write a strong answer.**

4 **Look at the plan of Mohammed's answer. Write down the missing word for each gap.**

5 **Prepare your own answer to the task.**

- Look at the Answer Booster and Mohammed's plan for ideas.
- Think about how you can develop your answer for each bullet point.
- Write a detailed plan. Organise your answer in paragraphs.
- Write your answer and carefully check what you have written.

Mis vacaciones

Tu amigo español, Ricardo, quiere saber cómo pasas las vacaciones.

Escribe un correo electrónico a Ricardo.

Debes incluir los siguientes puntos:
- adónde fuiste de vacaciones el año pasado
- por qué (no) te gustó el pueblo / la ciudad
- las ventajas de diferentes tipos de alojamiento
- qué planes tienes para este verano.

Escribe aproximadamente 80–90 palabras **en español**.

Paragraph 1
- Where I **1** ━━━━━
- The **2** ━━━━━ thing about it
- The **3** ━━━━━ thing about it

Paragraph 2
- Where the **4** ━━━━━ was located
- What the **5** ━━━━━ was like

Paragraph 3
- Opinion of staying in a **6** ━━━━━
- Opinion of staying in a **7** ━━━━━

Paragraph 4
- **8** ━━━━━ I'm going to go this year
- Opinion of the **9** ━━━━━
- What I'm going to **10** ━━━━━

Hola Ricardo

En febrero fui de vacaciones a **una estación de esquí** en Austria con mi insti. Nos alojamos en un albergue juvenil y viajamos en autocar. **¡Qué incómodo!** Lo mejor fue que aprendí a esquiar, pero lo peor fue cuando **me caí en la pista** y tuve que ir al hospital.

El albergue estaba en un pueblo pequeño que tenía vistas bonitas. Era pintoresco, pero **desafortunadamente**, no tenía ni tiendas ni cafeterías. Tampoco había mucho que hacer.

En mi opinión, es mejor alojarse en un hotel dado que hay aire acondicionado. Lo bueno de un camping es que se admiten perros, pero **una desventaja es que es ruidoso**.

Este año creo que vamos a ir a Pakistán ya que mis abuelos viven allí. Me chifla viajar en avión, aunque **el vuelo es agotador**. Voy a **ir de pesca** con mi abuelo porque le encanta.

¡Hasta luego!

Mohammed

Mohammed

⭐ Remember, to talk about what you **are going to do** you need to use the **near future tense**. Use the present tense of the verb *ir* + *a* + **infinitive**.

B – Translation

1 escribir

Read the English text and Laura's translation of it. Write down the missing word for each gap.

In summer I go out every day because I love being outdoors. When it's nice weather I go sailing, but when it rains I prefer to chat online with my friends. Yesterday we went to the beach, but we didn't swim in the sea since it was cold. Next week it's my birthday and therefore I'm going to go to the bowling alley.

En **1** ———— salgo todos los **2** ———— porque me encanta estar al **3** ———— libre. Cuando hace buen tiempo **4** ———— vela, pero cuando **5** ———— prefiero **6** ———— en la red con mis **7** ————. Ayer **8** ———— a la playa, pero no **9** ———— en el mar dado que hizo **10** ————. La semana que viene es mi cumpleaños y por eso **11** ———— a ir a la **12** ————.

2 escribir

Translate the following passage into Spanish.

In the holidays I often go to the cinema given that I love watching films. Last summer I went to Fréjus in the south of France, where my best friend has a caravan. It was sunny every day and so we went sightseeing, took photos and ate lots of ice creams. Next year my parents are going to rent a house in the country.

⭐ Look out for phrases which don't translate word for word. For example, which verb do you need to use for 'we <u>went</u> sightseeing'?

¿Dónde vives?
Vivo en el…
   norte/noreste/noroeste…
   sur/sureste/suroeste…

Where do you live?
I live in the…
   north/northeast/northwest…
   south/southeast/southwest…

   este/oeste/centro…
     de Inglaterra/Escocia
     de Gales/Irlanda (del Norte)

   east/west/centre…
     of England/Scotland
     of Wales/(Northern) Ireland

¿Qué haces en verano?
En verano/invierno…
   chateo en la red
   cocino para mi familia
   descargo canciones
   escribo correos
   hago natación/esquí/windsurf
   hago una barbacoa
   juego al baloncesto/fútbol

What do you do in summer?
In summer/winter…
   I chat online
   I cook for my family
   I download songs
   I write emails
   I go swimming/skiing/windsurfing
   I have a barbecue
   I play basketball/football

   monto a caballo/en bici
   nado en el mar
   salgo con mis amigos/as
   toco la guitarra
   trabajo como voluntario/a
   veo la tele
   voy al polideportivo/al parque/
     a un centro comercial
   voy de paseo

   I go horseriding/cycling
   I swim in the sea
   I go out with my friends
   I play the guitar
   I work as a volunteer
   I watch TV
   I go to the sports centre/to the park/
     to a shopping centre
   I go for a walk

¿Con qué frecuencia?
siempre
a menudo
todos los días
a veces

How often?
always
often
every day
sometimes

de vez en cuando
una vez a la semana
dos o tres veces al año
(casi) nunca

from time to time
once a week
two or three times a year
(almost) never

¿Qué tiempo hace?
Hace buen/mal tiempo.
Hace calor/frío/sol/viento.
Llueve/Nieva.
El tiempo es variable.

What's the weather like?
It's good/bad weather.
It's hot/cold/sunny/windy.
It's raining/snowing.
The weather is changeable.

El clima es caluroso/soleado.
Hay niebla/tormenta.
Hay chubascos.
Está nublado.

The climate is hot/sunny.
It's foggy/stormy.
There are showers.
It's cloudy.

¿Qué te gusta hacer?
Soy adicto/a a…
Soy un(a) fanático/a de…
ya que/dado que/puesto que
Prefiero…
Me gusta…
Me encanta/Me mola/Me chifla/
Me flipa/Me apasiona…
No me gusta (nada).
Odio…
A (mi padre) le gusta…
Nos encanta…
   bucear
   estar al aire libre

What do you like doing?
I'm addicted to…
I'm a … fan/fanatic.
given that/since
I prefer…
I like…

I love…
I don't like… (at all)
I hate…
(My dad) likes…
We love…
   diving
   being outdoors

   estar en contacto con los amigos
   hacer artes marciales
   hacer deportes acuáticos
   ir al cine/a la pista de hielo
   ir de compras
   leer (un montón de revistas)
   usar el ordenador
   ver películas
Prefiero veranear…
   en el extranjero/en España
   en la costa/en el campo
   en la montaña/en la ciudad

   being in touch with friends
   doing martial arts
   doing water sports
   going to the cinema/ice rink
   going shopping
   reading (loads of magazines)
   using the computer
   watching films
I prefer to spend the summer…
   abroad/in Spain
   on the coast/in the country
   in the mountains/in the city

¿Adónde fuiste de vacaciones?
hace una semana/un mes/un año
hace dos semanas/meses/años
fui de vacaciones a…
   Francia/Italia/Turquía
¿Con quién fuiste?
Fui…
   con mi familia/insti

Where did you go on holiday?
a week/month/year ago
two weeks/months/years ago
I went on holiday to…
   France/Italy/Turkey
Who did you go with?
I went…
   with my family/school

   con mi mejor amigo/a
   solo/a
¿Cómo viajaste?
Viajé…
   en autocar/avión
   en barco/coche/tren

   with my best friend
   alone
How did you travel?
I travelled…
   by coach/plane
   by boat/car/train

¿Qué hiciste?
primero
luego
más tarde
después
finalmente
Lo mejor fue cuando…
Lo peor fue cuando…
   aprendí a hacer vela
   comí muchos helados
   compré recuerdos
   descansé
   fui al acuario
   hice turismo

What did you do?
first
then
later
after
finally
The best thing was when…
The worst thing was when…
   I learned to sail
   I ate lots of ice creams
   I bought souvenirs
   I rested
   I went to the aquarium
   I went sightseeing

   llegué tarde al aeropuerto
   perdí mi móvil
   saqué fotos
   tomé el sol
   tuve un accidente en la playa
   vi un partido
   visité el Park Güell
   vomité en una montaña rusa
Puedes…
   descubrir el Museo Picasso
   disfrutar del Barrio Gótico
   pasear por las Ramblas
   subir al Monumento a Colón
   ver los barcos en el puerto

   I arrived at the airport late
   I lost my mobile
   I took photos
   I sunbathed
   I had an accident on the beach
   I saw/watched a match
   I visited Park Güell
   I was sick on a roller coaster
You can…
   discover the Picasso Museum
   enjoy the gothic quarter
   walk along Las Ramblas
   go up the Columbus Monument
   see the boats in the port

¿Qué tal lo pasaste?
Me gustó/Me encantó.
Lo pasé bomba/fenomenal.
Lo pasé bien/mal/fatal.
Fue…
   inolvidable/increíble
   impresionante/flipante
   horroroso

How was it?
I liked it/I loved it.
I had a great time.
I had a good/bad/awful time.
It was…
   unforgettable/incredible
   impressive/awesome
   awful

   un desastre
¿Qué tiempo hizo?
Hizo buen/mal tiempo.
Hizo calor/frío/sol/viento.
Hubo niebla/tormenta.
Llovió/Nevó.

   a disaster
What was the weather like?
It was good/bad weather.
It was hot/cold/sunny/windy.
It was foggy/stormy.
It rained/snowed.

¿Cómo era el hotel?

Me alojé/Me quedé…	*I stayed…*
Nos alojamos/Nos quedamos…	*We stayed…*
en un albergue juvenil	*in a youth hostel*
en un apartamento	*in an apartment*
en un camping	*on a campsite*
en un hotel de cinco estrellas	*in a five-star hotel*
en un parador	*in a state-run luxury hotel*
en una casa rural	*in a house in the country*
en una pensión	*in a guest house*
Fui de crucero.	*I went on a cruise.*
Estaba…	*It was…*
cerca de la playa	*near the beach*
en el centro de la ciudad	*in the city centre*
en las afueras	*on the outskirts*
Era…	*It was…*
acogedor(a)	*welcoming*
antiguo/a	*old*
barato/a	*cheap*
caro/a	*expensive*
grande	*big*
lujoso/a	*luxurious*
moderno/a	*modern*
pequeño/a	*small*
ruidoso/a	*noisy*
tranquilo/a	*quiet*
Tenía/Había…	*It had/There was/were…*
No tenía ni… ni…	*It had neither… nor…*
No había ni… ni…	*There was neither… nor…*
Tampoco tenía…	*Nor did it have…*
(un) aparcamiento	*a car park*
(un) bar	*a bar*
(un) gimnasio	*a gym*
(un) restaurante	*a restaurant*
(una) cafetería	*a café*
(una) lavandería	*a launderette*
(una) piscina cubierta	*an indoor pool*
mucho espacio para mi tienda	*lots of space for my tent*

¿Cómo era el pueblo?

Lo bueno/Lo malo…	*The good thing/The bad thing…*
del pueblo…	*about the town/village…*
de la ciudad…	*about the city…*
era que era…	*was that it was…*
demasiado/muy/bastante…	*too/very/quite…*
animado/a	*lively*
bonito/a	*pretty*
histórico/a	*historic*
pintoresco/a	*picturesque*
turístico/a	*touristic*
Tenía…	*It had…*
mucho ambiente/tráfico	*lots of atmosphere/traffic*
mucho que hacer	*lots to do*
mucha contaminación/gente	*lots of pollution/people*
muchos espacios verdes	*lots of green spaces*
muchos lugares de interés	*lots of places of interest*
muchas discotecas	*lots of discos*

Quisiera reservar…

¿Hay…	*Is/Are there…*
wifi gratis…	*free wifi…*
aire acondicionado…	*air conditioning…*
en el hotel/las habitaciones?	*in the hotel/the rooms?*
¿Cuánto cuesta una habitación…?	*How much does a… room cost?*
¿A qué hora se sirve el desayuno?	*What time is breakfast served?*
¿Cuándo está abierto/a el/la…?	*When is the… open?*
¿Cuánto es el suplemento por…?	*How much is the supplement for…?*
¿Se admiten perros?	*Are dogs allowed?*
Quisiera reservar…	*I would like to book…*
una habitación individual/doble	*a single/double room*
con/sin balcón	*with/without balcony*
con bañera/ducha	*with a bath/shower*
con cama de matrimonio	*with double bed*
con desayuno incluido	*with breakfast included*
con media pensión	*with half board*
con pensión completa	*with full board*
con vistas al mar	*with sea view*
¿Para cuántas noches?	*For how many nights?*
Para… noches	*For… nights*
del… al… de…	*from the… to the… of…*
¿Puede repetir, por favor?	*Can you repeat, please?*
¿Puede hablar más despacio?	*Can you speak more slowly?*

Quiero quejarme

Quiero hablar con el director.	*I want to speak to the manager.*
Quiero cambiar de habitación.	*I want to change rooms.*
El aire acondicionado…	*The air conditioning…*
El ascensor…	*The lift…*
La ducha…	*The shower…*
La habitación…	*The room…*
está sucio/a	*is dirty*
La luz…	*The light…*
no funciona	*doesn't work*
Hay ratas en la cama.	*There are rats in the bed.*
No hay…	*There is no…*
Necesito…	*I need…*
papel higiénico	*toilet paper*
jabón/champú	*soap/shampoo*
toallas/(un) secador	*towels/a hairdryer*
¡Socorro!	*Help!*
Es inaceptable.	*It's unacceptable.*
Lo siento/Perdone.	*I'm sorry.*
El hotel está completo.	*The hotel is full.*

Mis vacaciones desastrosas

Por desgracia	*Unfortunately*
Por un lado… por otro lado…	*On the one hand… on the other hand…*
El primer/último día	*(On) the first/last day*
Al día siguiente	*On the following day*
Tuve/Tuvimos…	*I had/We had…*
un accidente/un pinchazo	*an accident/a puncture*
un retraso/una avería	*a delay/a breakdown*
Tuve/Tuvimos que…	*I had to/We had to…*
esperar mucho tiempo	*wait a long time*
ir al hospital/a la comisaría	*go to the hospital/to the police station*
llamar a un mecánico	*call a mechanic*
Perdí/Perdimos…	*I lost/We lost…*
el equipaje/la cartera	*the luggage/the wallet*
la maleta/las llaves	*the suitcase/the keys*
Cuando llegamos…	*When we arrived…*
era muy tarde	*it was very late*
estaba cansado/a	*I was tired*
la recepción ya estaba cerrada	*the reception was already closed*
acampar	*to camp*
decidir	*to decide (to)*
alquilar bicicletas	*to hire bicycles*
coger el teleférico	*to catch/take the cable car*
chocar con	*to crash into*
hacer alpinismo	*to go mountain climbing*
volver	*to return*
el paisaje	*the landscape*
la autopista	*the motorway*
precioso/a	*beautiful*

2 Mi vida en el insti
Punto de partida 1

● *Giving opinions about school subjects*
● *Describing school facilities*

Escucha y escribe las asignaturas que faltan. (1–5)

Mi horario

hora	lunes	martes	miércoles	jueves	viernes
08.15	biología	**c**	inglés	inglés	informática
09.00	**a**	religión	**e**	**g**	**i**
09.45	R E C R E O				
10.15	lengua	empresariales	lengua	historia	educación física
11.00	**b**	biología	**f**	lengua	**j**
11.45	R E C R E O				
12.15	química	**d**	física	arte dramático	matemáticas
13.00	física	inglés	matemáticas	**h**	tecnología

lengua	Spanish class

Lee las opiniones y mira el horario del ejercicio 1.
¿Cuál es su día preferido?

1 Me encantan los idiomas porque son interesantes e importantes.
2 ¡No me gusta escribir! Prefiero las asignaturas prácticas.
3 No me gustan las ciencias porque son aburridas y difíciles. Mi día preferido es el día que no tengo ciencias.
4 Me chifla el arte dramático porque es creativo y me interesa mucho la historia porque es útil.
5 ¿Mi día favorito? Es el día que tengo las materias fáciles: geografía, religión, música y empresariales.
6 No me gusta nada el insti, pero mi día preferido es el día que no tengo inglés. ¡Odio el inglés!

> **G** Opinion verbs 　　　　　　　 ⟩ Page 222

Interesar works like *gustar* and *encantar*. It uses a pronoun like *me* or *te*.

Me interes**a** el dibujo.　Art interests **me**.
¿*Te* interes**an**　　　　　Do languages
　los idiomas?　　　　　　interest **you**?

Odiar and *preferir* don't need a pronoun.

Remember to use the definite article (*el/la/los/las*) when giving opinions about nouns.

Con tu compañero/a, haz diálogos.

● *¿Qué día tienes inglés?*
■ *Tengo inglés los martes. Me interesa el inglés porque es útil, pero no me gustan las ciencias porque son difíciles.*
● *¿Cuál es tu día preferido?*
■ *Mi día preferido es el jueves porque tengo educación física. Me chifla porque es práctica y divertida.*

(no) me gust**a** (no) me encant**a** (no) me interes**a**	**el** francés **la** geografía	porque es	práctic**o/a**, creativ**o/a**, aburrid**o/a** útil, fácil, difícil importante, interesante
(no) me gust**an** (no) me encant**an** (no) me interes**an**	**los** idiomas **las** empresariales	porque son	práctic**os/as**, creativ**os/as**, aburrid**os/as** útil**es**, fácil**es**, difícil**es** importante**s**, interesante**s**

4 leer **Mira el horario del ejercicio 1. Completa las frases.**

1 Los lunes a las doce y cuarto tengo _____.

2 Los martes a las diez y cuarto tengo _____.

3 Los miércoles a la una tenemos _____.

4 Los jueves a las _____ tenemos una clase de lengua.

5 Los viernes a las _____ tenemos informática.

6 Todos los días a las _____ y las _____ hay un recreo.

5 escuchar **Escucha y mira el horario del ejercicio 1. Corrige las frases. (1–5)**

6 leer **Lee las frases. ¿Verdadero o Falso? Escribe V o F.**

Educación infantil
0–6 años

Educación primaria
6–12 años

Educación Secundaria
Obligatoria (ESO)
12–16 años

Bachillerato o
formación profesional
16–18+ años

1 Los niños españoles empiezan la educación primaria a los seis años.

2 En los institutos normalmente los alumnos tienen que llevar uniforme.

3 Los alumnos empiezan la educación secundaria más tarde en España que en Inglaterra.

4 La Educación Secundaria Obligatoria generalmente dura seis años en España.

5 A los 16 años los alumnos tienen dos opciones.

6 El bachillerato es obligatorio para todos.

7 escuchar **Escucha e identifica las <u>tres</u> letras correctas. Sobra una letra. (1–3)**

a muchas aulas

b una biblioteca

c un comedor

d un gimnasio

e una piscina

f un laboratorio

g un campo de fútbol

h un salón de actos

i una pista de tenis

j un patio

8 escuchar **Escucha otra vez. ¿Las opiniones son positivas o negativas? Escribe P (positivo), N (negativo) o P+N (positivo y negativo). (1–3)**

Lo bueno / malo es que…
Lo mejor / peor es que…
Lo que más me gusta es / son…
Lo que menos me gusta es / son…

Unidad 2

Punto de partida 2

- *Describing school uniform and the school day*
- *Using adjectives*

1 escribir

Mira los uniformes. Escribe los artículos de ropa y los colores en español.

Ejemplo: **a** *una camisa blanca*

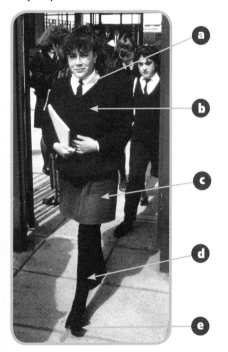

a
b
c
d
e

el uniforme escolar en Chile

f
g
h
i

Zona Cultura

En Chile es muy normal llevar uniforme en las escuelas, públicas y privadas. Normalmente es una chaqueta azul oscuro, pantalones grises y camisa blanca para los chicos, y una falda gris, camisa blanca y medias azules para las chicas. Por eso los alumnos chilenos tienen el apodo 'pingüinos'.

(No...)	un jersey (de punto)
Llevo...	un vestido
Llevamos...	una camisa
Tengo que llevar...	una camiseta
Tenemos que llevar...	una chaqueta (a rayas)
	una corbata
	una falda (a cuadros)
	unos pantalones
	unos calcetines
	unos zapatos
	unos vaqueros
	unas medias

G *Adjectival endings for colours*

Remember to make colour adjectives agree with the noun.

ending	singular		plural	
	masculine	feminine	masculine	feminine
–o	blanc**o**	blanc**a**	blanc**os**	blanc**as**
–e	verd**e**	verd**e**	verd**es**	verd**es**
consonant	azul	azul	azul**es**	azul**es**

Naranja, *rosa* and *violeta* often do not change, but some people add an –s with plural nouns.

A colour followed by **claro** (light) and **oscuro** (dark) always takes the masculine form:

*un**os** calcetines **azul claro**, un**as** medias **azul oscuro***

2 escuchar

Escucha. Copia y completa la tabla en inglés. (1–4)

	uniform details (2)	opinions (2)
1		

gris **morado / violeta** blanco **negro**

amarillo **naranja** **azul**

marrón **rosa** **verde** **rojo**

cómodo anticuado bonito

fácil feo incómodo

práctico elegante

3 leer **Lee los textos. Busca las expresiones en español en el texto.**

¿El uniforme te mola?

En mi insti todos llevamos uniforme y es superfeo. ¡Qué horror! Tengo que llevar una falda verde oscuro a cuadros y una chaqueta de punto del mismo color. Pienso que es aburrido y formal, pero mi madre dice que el uniforme mejora la disciplina y da una imagen positiva de nuestro insti. **Alicia**

Tenemos que llevar uniforme. Llevamos unos pantalones grises, una corbata azul y roja, y una chaqueta negra. Mi amiga dice que limita la individualidad, pero me gusta porque me ahorra tiempo por la mañana. Además, es importante porque así las diferencias económicas no son tan obvias. **Fran**

1 we all wear	**5** gives a positive image of our school
2 checked	**6** we have to wear
3 a cardigan of the same colour	**7** it saves me time
4 improves discipline	**8** economic differences are not as apparent

4 hablar **Con tu compañero/a, haz un diálogo sobre el uniforme.**

● *¿Qué llevas en el insti?*
● *¿Qué opinas?*

■ *Tengo que llevar uniforme. Llevo…*
■ *(No) me gusta porque es… y…*

5 escuchar **Escucha y lee. Traduce las expresiones en negrita al inglés.**

- Mayra, ¿cómo vas al insti **por la mañana**?
- Voy en taxi. **Salgo de casa** a las siete. **¡Es demasiado temprano**!
- ¿A qué hora empiezan las clases?
- **Las clases empiezan** a las siete y media y **terminan** a las dos de la tarde.
- ¿Cuántas clases tienes al día?
- Tenemos siete clases al día y **cada clase dura** cincuenta minutos.
- ¿A qué hora es el recreo?
- Hay dos recreos de veinte minutos, pero no hay **hora de comer**.
- ¿Qué días tienes ciencias?
- Tengo ciencias los lunes y los miércoles. **Me fascinan** las ciencias porque me interesa mucho el mundo natural.

Mayra vive en Arequipa en Perú

¿Cómo vas al insti?

a pie / andando	en metro
en bici	en taxi
en autobús	en tren
en coche	

6 hablar **Habla sobre tu día escolar. Utiliza el diálogo del ejercicio 5 como modelo.**

7 escribir **Escribe un párrafo sobre tu uniforme y tu día escolar. Incluye opiniones y razones.**

⭐ To say you do things on certain days use **los** + the day of the week.

Los viernes tengo matemáticas.

To say 'in the morning / afternoon' use **por**:

Por la mañana tenemos dibujo.
Por la tarde hay tres clases.

→ Unidad 4

1 ¿Qué tal los estudios?

- *Talking about subjects and teachers*
- *Using comparatives and superlatives*
- *Justifying opinions using a range of language*

1 leer **Lee y empareja las opiniones con las razones.**

¿Qué asignaturas te gustan?

Sergio

Cristina

Julián

1 Una asignatura que me gusta un montón es el inglés porque…

2 Lo que más me gusta es el dibujo porque…

3 Me interesa mucho la biología porque…

4 La física me gusta menos porque…

5 La historia me fascina, pero…

6 Una asignatura muy buena es la educación física porque…

7 Me chiflan las matemáticas porque…

a **es más práctica y relevante que** las demás ciencias. Vemos temas de la naturaleza, como las células, y hacemos experimentos.

b **no es tan difícil como** el inglés. Para mí, **es la mejor asignatura**. El profe me deja trabajar a mi manera, ¡incluso con música! Me dice que pinto y dibujo muy bien.

c me gusta resolver problemas. **Es mejor que** las otras asignaturas porque **es la asignatura más exacta y lógica**.

d no puedo memorizar las fechas. Soy **la peor** de la clase y no saco buenas notas en las pruebas.

e **es menos complicado que** los otros idiomas que estudio. Además, ya sabemos mucha gramática y mucho vocabulario.

f **es más difícil que** la biología.

g **es la asignatura más divertida y activa**

2 escuchar **Escucha y comprueba tus respuestas.**

3 leer **Traduce las expresiones en negrita del ejercicio 1 al inglés.**

4 hablar **Con tu compañero/a, haz un diálogo. Utiliza el texto del ejercicio 1 como modelo. Da opiniones y razones.**

- ● *¿Qué asignaturas te gustan?*
- ■ *A mí me chifla(n)… porque… Es la asignatura más importante. Otra asignatura que me gusta un montón es… porque…*
- ● *¿Qué asignaturas no te gustan?*
- ■ *No me gusta mucho la tecnología porque es menos interesante que la informática.*

G Comparatives and superlatives

Comparatives

más… que	more… than
menos… que	less… than
mejor que…	better than…
peor que…	worse than…
tan… como…	as… as…

*El español es **más fácil que** el mandarín.*
*La informática es **tan creativa como** la tecnología.*

Superlatives

el/la más…	the most…
el/la menos…	the least…
el/la mejor…	the best…
el/la peor…	the worst…

*Mi profesora de inglés es **la más divertida**.*
*El español es la asignatura **más interesante**.*

Giving reasons adds length and interest to what you say. Check that your answers have 12 or more words. Repeat the task with your book closed.

5 Lee y busca las expresiones en el texto.

¿Qué tal tus profes?

Me llamo Laura y estoy en 3º de ESO. Mi nuevo profesor de matemáticas me cae bien porque es muy listo y divertido. Tiene buen sentido del humor, así que crea un buen ambiente de trabajo. También es muy trabajador. Nos pone muchos deberes y tiene expectativas altas, pero aprendo mucho con él porque me hace pensar. Antes tenía problemas con el cálculo. Lo peor era que mi profesora de 2º de ESO era muy impaciente y no era nada tolerante.

1 creates a good working atmosphere
2 makes me think
3 has a good sense of humour
4 I like my new maths teacher

5 I learn a lot
6 was not at all tolerant
7 has high expectations
8 gives us lots of homework

6 Lee el texto otra vez. Busca el antónimo de los siguientes adjetivos.

aburrido   paciente   tonto

severo   perezoso

Zona Cultura

La **E**ducación **S**ecundaria **O**bligatoria (ESO) tiene cuatro cursos académicos, que se llaman 1º de ESO, 2º de ESO, etc. Generalmente, la ESO se inicia a los 12 años y se acaba con 16 años. Si los alumnos suspenden tres o más asignaturas, tienen que repetir el curso.

el curso académico   academic year
suspender   to fail

7 Escucha a Andrés. Completa el resumen con las opciones correctas. Luego traduce el texto al inglés.

La nueva profe de **ciencias / inglés** es mucho más **estricta / simpática** que su profe de antes. La señora Martínez **enseña / explica** muy bien y por eso le resulta **menos / más** difícil comprender. También da **consejos / estrategias** para estudiar mejor. Cree que no va a **aprobar / suspender** sus evaluaciones este año.

evaluaciones   assessments

8 Escribe <u>dos</u> párrafos sobre tus asignaturas y tus profes.

¿Qué tal tus asignaturas y tus profes?
- *A mí me chifla(n)… porque es la asignatura más…*
- *Otra asignatura que me gusta…*
- *Me gusta menos… porque no es tan… como…*
- *Me gusta mi profe de… porque…*
- *Siempre… así que…*
- *También…*
- *Nunca…*

Mi profesor(a) / profe…
    enseña bien
    explica bien
    tiene buen sentido del humor
    tiene expectativas muy altas
    me hace pensar
    crea un buen ambiente de trabajo
    nos da consejos / estrategias
    nos pone muchos deberes
    nunca se enfada

- *Describing your school*
- *Using negatives*
- *Comparing then and now*

1 **Escucha y lee el podcast de Josué. Contesta a las preguntas en inglés.**

Josué es de Ecuador, pero ahora vive en España.

¡Hola a todos! ¿Qué hay?

Hoy fue mi primer día de clase en mi nuevo instituto, que se llama IES Martín Galeano. Como ya sabéis, mi mamá tiene un nuevo empleo y ahora vivimos en Gijón.

¿Cómo es mi insti? Pues, es mixto y público. Hay unos quinientos alumnos y setenta profes. El edificio es bastante pequeño y moderno, muy diferente a mi insti de antes en Quito, que era mucho más grande y antiguo.

Tiene muchas aulas, pero no son parecidas a las aulas de Quito. ¡Todos los muebles (las mesas y la sillas) son verdes! Incluso las pizarras son verdes, y no hay ninguna pizarra interactiva. Sin embargo, hay un salón de actos y una biblioteca bien equipada.

Como estamos en el centro de la ciudad, no hay ningún espacio verde para practicar deporte, ni campo de fútbol, ni pista de atletismo. Lo bueno es que estamos a ciento cincuenta metros de la playa, donde tenemos las clases de educación física. ¡Qué guay!

Tampoco hay comedor, pero no es un problema porque las clases terminan a las dos y ¡vamos a casa para comer!

Todavía no conozco a nadie y no tengo nada que hacer esta tarde porque todavía no tengo deberes, por lo tanto voy a ir a la playa. ¡Hasta luego!

Gijón, España

1 Why has Josué moved to Spain?
2 What is different about the classrooms? (<u>two</u> details)
3 What does he say about the library?
4 Explain one advantage and one disadvantage of the sports facilities.
5 Why is the lack of canteen not a problem?
6 Why is Josué going to the beach this afternoon? (<u>two</u> details)

IES	*Instituto de Educación Secundaria*
todavía	*still*

2 **Escucha y apunta las preguntas en español. Luego contéstalas como Josué. (1–6)**

Ejemplo: **1** *¿Cómo se llama tu instituto? Se llama IES Martín Galeano.*

Ⓖ Negatives ❯ *Page 227*

These negatives are often used after the verb as a 'sandwich' with **no** before the verb.

3 **Traduce los párrafos 4 y 5 del podcast al inglés.**

No hago *nada.*	I **don't** do **anything**.
No conozco a *nadie.*	I **don't** know **anyone**.
No tenemos *ni* tabletas *ni* ordenadores.	We **don't** have **either** tablets **or** computers.
No tiene *ningún* laboratorio.	It **doesn't** have a **single** laboratory.
No tiene *ninguna* pista de tenis.	It **doesn't** have a **single** tennis court.

4 **Escribe un párrafo sobre tu instituto. Contesta a las preguntas del ejercicio 2. Utiliza diferentes expresiones negativas.**

Nunca can go **before** or **after** the verb. When after, use *no* in front of the verb as well.

Nunca estudia.	He/She **never** studies.
No estudia *nunca.*	He/She **never** studies.

Tampoco (not either) usually goes in front of the verb.

Tampoco hay piscina.	There **isn't** a swimming pool **either**.

mi insti

mi escuela primaria

5 escuchar

Escucha. Copia y completa la tabla en inglés.

	my primary school	my secondary school
Camilo		
Noa		

> ⭐ *antes* + **imperfect tense**, *ahora* + **present tense**
> *Antes no **había** donde jugar.*   Before there wasn't anywhere to play.
> *Ahora **hay** un patio cubierto.*   Now there is a covered playground.

6 hablar

Con tu compañero/a, compara tu escuela primaria con tu instituto.

● *¿Cómo era tu escuela primaria?*
■ *Mi escuela primaria era <u>bastante antigua</u> y…*
  No había <u>pizarras interactivas</u> ni…
  pero había…
  Tampoco había…
  Antes <u>los recreos</u> eran <u>más largos</u> y <u>los profes</u> eran… pero…

● *¿Cómo es tu insti de ahora?*
■ *Mi insti de ahora es <u>muy grande</u> y…*
  Tiene <u>buenas instalaciones</u> y…
  Las clases son <u>más duras</u>, pero hay <u>más oportunidades</u> para hacer…

En mi escuela primaria En mi insti	(no) había (no) hay	(una) piscina (un) polideportivo (unas) pizarras (interactivas) (unas) aulas de informática
Mi escuela primaria Mi insti	(no) tenía (no) tiene	exámenes / deberes (un) uniforme espacios verdes más tiempo libre más alumnos / profesores más oportunidades para hacer…
El edificio Las instalaciones El día escolar Las asignaturas Las clases	(no) era(n) (no) es (no) son	(in)adecuado / colorido moderno / antiguo más corto / largo más fácil / duro mejor / peor

> ⭐ Use the correct endings!

7 leer

Lee el texto. Elige las respuestas correctas.

Jatun Kasa – antes y ahora

Jatun Kasa es una comunidad remota de unas 40 familias en los Andes de Bolivia. Hoy hay un nuevo colegio allí, con seis aulas modernas, servicios y un patio cubierto para el recreo.

Sara, una alumna de 15 años, describe cómo era el colegio antes:

'Bueno, la verdad es que las instalaciones no eran apropiadas para aprender. El aula era estrecha y fría. No había ninguna ventana y el techo estaba roto. Tampoco había mesas ni sillas suficientes – ¡estábamos como sardinas en lata!'

Ramón Darío, profesor, vive ahora en una de las nuevas casas para los profesores:

'Antes era muy difícil vivir allí porque yo tenía una sola habitación. Igual que en el colegio, no había electricidad ni agua corriente. Estaba sucia y había ratas, arañas y serpientes. Ahora mi casa es una de las mejores. Tiene dos habitaciones, una cocina y un baño. Mi mujer y yo estamos supercontentos y trabajamos con ganas.'

1 Jatun Kasa es…
  a una ciudad.
  b un colegio.
  c un pueblo.
  d una persona.

2 Antes el colegio tenía…
  a instalaciones inadecuadas.
  b muchos muebles.
  c ventanas sucias.
  d aulas grandes.

3 Antes el profesor tenía…
  a electricidad y agua corriente.
  b dos habitaciones.
  c muy poco espacio.
  d una mascota.

4 Ahora Ramón está…
  a muy feliz.
  b triste.
  c en otro colegio.
  d cansado.

- *Talking about school rules and problems*
- *Using phrases followed by the infinitive*
- *Tackling harder listening exercises*

1 leer

Lee y empareja las fotos con las expresiones. Luego haz una frase para cada foto. Utiliza diferentes expresiones.

Ejemplo: **a** *No se debe usar el móvil en clase.*

¿Cuáles son las normas de tu insti?

mantener limpio el patio · comer chicle · respetar el turno de palabra · correr en los pasillos · ser puntual

usar el móvil en clase · dañar las instalaciones · ser agresivo o grosero · llevar piercings en el insti

💬 When reading from a text, apply the pronunciation patterns you know. E.g. the **ll** in **ll**evar and pasi**ll**o as in came**ll**o, and the **u** in **u**sar, p**u**ntual and t**u**rno as in b**ú**falo.

G *Verbs with an infinitive*

To describe rules, use these structures followed by the infinitive:

está prohibido	it is forbidden to
no se permite	you are not allowed to
no se debe	you/one must not
hay que	it is necessary to
tenemos que	we have to

No se permite ser agresivo o grosero.

2 escuchar

Escucha y escribe las letras del ejercicio 1. ¿La opinión es positiva (P), negativa (N) o positiva y negativa (P+N)? (1–3)

3 hablar

Con tus compañeros, haz un debate sobre las normas de tu instituto.

- ● *Está prohibido llevar piercings en el colegio. Creo que es justo. ¿Qué opinas?*
- ■ *Sí, estoy de acuerdo.*
- ▲ *¡Qué va!*
- ◆ *Yo tampoco estoy de acuerdo. En mi opinión, es injusto. No me gusta esta norma.*

⭐ Speak more expressively by using exclamations.

¡Qué va!	No way!
¡Qué horror!	How awful!
¡Qué bien!	How great!

4 escuchar · Escucha a Alejandra y a Román. Apunta sus respuestas.

¿Necesitamos normas?

1 ¿Qué opinas del uniforme escolar en general?
a es una buena idea
b es feo
c es caro

2 ¿Cuáles son las normas más importantes de tu instituto?
a cuidar el material y las instalaciones
b respetar a los demás
c llevar el uniforme correcto

3 ¿Qué piensas de las normas de tu instituto?
a son necesarias
b son demasiado severas
c unas son positivas

4 ¿Por qué tenemos reglas?
a para fomentar la buena disciplina
b para limitar la libertad de expresión
c para fastidiar a los alumnos

5 ¿Hay problemas en tu insti?
a no hay ningún problema
b sí, a veces
c muchos

6 ¿Qué es lo mejor de tu insti?
a las oportunidades después del colegio
b los amigos
c las calificaciones

para	in order to
cuentan	they count
restringir	to restrict

Listening questions often include <u>distractors</u>. More than one option is mentioned, so listen to the end before jumping to conclusions.

They also require you to listen out for things expressed <u>in different words</u> from the ones you read on the page.

---

5 leer · Lee los textos y escribe la letra correcta. Sobra una opción.
Luego traduce las expresiones en **negrita** al inglés.

exigir	to demand
hacer novillos	to skive
la pandilla	gang

1 Este año es duro porque en el insti nos exigen más que en otros años. Los profes nos dan mucho trabajo. Nos dicen que **debemos aprobar los exámenes**, pero **estoy superestresado** y **tengo miedo de suspender mis pruebas**. *Adrián*

2 Hay alumnos que sufren intimidación en el insti porque hay otros alumnos que siempre **se burlan de ellos** y no los dejan en paz. ¡No es justo! Se refugian en la biblioteca durante los recreos y a la hora de comer, pero la verdad es que tienen mucho miedo. *Mateo*

3 Hay algunos alumnos que son una mala influencia. Hacen novillos y otros compañeros quieren ser amigos de ellos porque quieren ser parte de su pandilla. **Todos tenemos que sacar buenas notas**, pero **los amigos cuentan más**. *Ivanna*

a el acoso escolar   **b** las normas estrictas   **c** la presión del grupo   **d** el estrés de los exámenes

---

6 hablar · Entrevista a tu compañero/a.

- Use the questions from exercise 4.
- Use additional ideas from the texts in exercise 5.
- Answer the questions with whole sentences.

---

7 escribir · Escribe un texto sobre las normas de tu insti.

Include:
- if uniform is compulsory and what you have to wear
- a positive and negative opinion and justification
- any other rules and what you think of them
- one problem that exists in your school
- the best thing about your school

- *Talking about plans for a school exchange*
- *Using the near future tense*
- *Asking and answering questions*

1 escuchar **Escucha y lee el vídeo mensaje de Víctor.**
Escribe las letras en el orden correcto.

Víctor

Colegio M. Mª
Rosa Molas

¡Hola! Te quiero dar la bienvenida al Colegio M. Mª Rosa Molas. Ahora **voy a contestar** a tus preguntas sobre la visita de intercambio.

Vas a llegar el martes a las tres al aeropuerto de Zaragoza. Allí **vamos a estar** todos, y nuestras familias también.

El miércoles nos toca ir al colegio. Algunos compañeros **van a ir** en coche, pero nosotros **vamos a ir andando** porque vivimos muy cerca, como la mayoría de los alumnos.

Las clases empiezan a las ocho y para 3º y 4º de ESO terminan a las dos. Por la mañana tenemos tres clases y un recreo a las once menos cinco. Luego hay otras tres clases.

Es obligatorio llevar uniforme (excepto los de bachillerato, que 'van de calle'). Llevamos pantalón o falda gris, polo blanco y jersey azul marino. Pero vosotros **vais a llevar** ropa de calle.

El primer día **vamos a comer** juntos en el comedor, donde comen normalmente los de 1º y 2º de ESO.

Después de la hora de comer, tenemos dos horas de lengua castellana, y luego una hora de inglés, lo que **va a ser** superfácil para vosotros.

El resto de la semana tenemos una programación variada. ¡Seguro que **te va a gustar**!

Zona Cultura

Destino:	ZARAGOZA
Ubicación:	Noreste de España, en el interior
Población:	666 mil habitantes (4ª ciudad de España)
Famosa por:	Su fiesta en honor a la Virgen del Pilar

nos toca ir	*we have to go*
ropa de calle	*casual clothes / non-uniform*

2 leer **Lee el texto del ejercicio 1 otra vez.**
Traduce las expresiones en negrita al inglés.

3 leer **Escribe la programación para el miércoles en inglés.**
Ejemplo: Walk to school. Classes start at…

G *The near future* ⟩ *Page 216*

Use the **near future tense** to say what you are going to do. Use the present tense of **ir** + *a* + infinitive.

voy		
vas		
va		visitar
vamos	a	comer
vais		salir
van		

4 leer

Lee el mensaje del ejercicio 1 otra vez. ¿A qué preguntas contesta Víctor? Empareja las mitades de las preguntas.

1	¿Cuándo vamos	vamos a hacer el miércoles?
2	¿Qué	empiezan y terminan las clases?
3	¿Cómo	a llegar a Zaragoza?
4	¿A qué hora	que llevar?
5	¿Qué ropa tenemos	vamos a comer?
6	¿Dónde	vamos a ir al instituto?

G *Asking questions*

To form questions, follow the question word with the verb.

Vamos a llegar a las dos.　We are going to arrive at two.

¿*Cuándo* **vamos a llegar**?　When are we going to arrive?

Simply start 'Yes/No' questions with the verb.

¿**Llevas** uniforme?　Do you wear a uniform?

Remember to use an inverted question mark at the start, and a 'tilde' on each question word.

5 escuchar

Escucha. Copia y completa la tabla en español. (1–3)

Castillo de Loarre

Zaragoza

chocolate con churros

	por la mañana	por la tarde
1 miércoles		
2 jueves		
3 viernes		

los/las demás　the others

voy a	llegar…　　　　salir…
vas a	practicar…　　　ir a…
vamos a	ir (juntos/as) a…　comer…
vais a	pasar todo el día en…
	hacer una visita guiada de…
	ver los edificios…
	ir de excursión el día entero
	pasarlo bien
va a	ser guay

6 hablar

Con tu compañero/a, improvisa un diálogo. Pregunta y contesta.

You and your Spanish exchange partner are talking about a day in your school. Your partner wants to know:

- when lessons start and finish
- what times break and lunch are
- where he/she is going to have lunch
- what he/she is going to wear in school
- how he/she is going to get to school
- what lessons he/she is going to have
- what he/she is going to see and do during his/her stay

7 escribir

Escribe un correo a tu estudiante de intercambio. Describe los planes para su próxima visita.

Programación: Intercambio

Primer día: Día en Londres

Mañana
Excursión en barco a Westminster

Tarde
Visita al Palacio de Buckingham

Segundo día: Día en el colegio

Mañana
Asistir a clases

Tarde
Trabajos en grupo
Actividades deportivas

Vary your writing by including general details about your school routine as well as specific plans for the exchange. Use sequencers and time expressions to give structure:

Primero…, después…, por la mañana…, por la tarde…, después del cole…, a las once…

- *Talking about activities and achievements*
- *Using object pronouns*
- *Saying how long you have been doing something*

1 **Lee los textos. Completa las frases en inglés.**

Amelia

Asisto a mi instituto desde hace tres años y me encanta porque hay muchísimos clubs extraescolares. Voy al club de ajedrez todas las semanas. Juego desde hace cuatro años y se me da muy bien. Me encanta porque te ayuda a pensar estratégicamente. Participamos en torneos nacionales y el año pasado gané un trofeo en mi categoría.

Tomás

Toco la trompeta en el club de jazz de mi insti. Me mola la música Big Band porque te enseña a improvisar y es superdivertida. El verano pasado dimos un concierto para los padres y yo toqué un solo de trompeta. ¡Fue un éxito! Ahora voy a aprender a tocar el saxofón también.

Gael

Me chiflan las artes marciales y soy miembro del club de judo de mi instituto. Practico el judo desde hace nueve años. El trimestre pasado gané el cinturón marrón. ¡Qué guay! Tengo clases particulares para mejorar mi técnica porque quiero conseguir el cinturón negro.

solemos ganar	*we usually win*

1 In the summer jazz concert, Tomás ▬▬▬.
2 Now he is going to ▬▬▬.
3 Gael has been ▬▬▬ for nine years.
4 He is having lessons to ▬▬▬.
5 Amelia is very good at ▬▬▬.
6 Last year, she ▬▬▬.

> **G** **Desde hace**
>
> To say how long you've been doing something use **desde hace** and the <u>present tense</u> of the verb.
>
> **¿Desde hace** cuánto tiempo <u>tocas</u> el piano?
> How long have you been playing the piano?
>
> <u>Toco</u> el piano **desde hace** seis años.
> I have been playing the piano for six years.

2 **Escucha y apunta los detalles en inglés. (1–3)**

a Activity?
b How long?
c Opinion of the activity?
d Achievements?
e Opinion of clubs more generally?

3 **Con tu compañero/a, pregunta y contesta.**

- *¿Desde hace cuánto tiempo asistes a este instituto?*
- *¿Qué actividades extraescolares haces?*
- *¿Desde hace cuánto tiempo (tocas / juegas al / haces)…?*
- *¿Participaste en algún (concierto / concurso / torneo)?*
- *¿Qué opinas de las actividades extraescolares?*

Para mí / En mi opinión / Creo que… las actividades extraescolares…	
son	algo diferente / muy divertidas
te ayudan a	olvidar las presiones del colegio desarrollar tus talentos hacer nuevos amigos
te dan	una sensación de logro más confianza la oportunidad de ser creativo/a la oportunidad de expresarte

4 escuchar **Escucha y lee. Copia y completa la tabla en inglés.**

	past events	present	future plans
José		*drama club*	
Kiara			

Kiara: ¿Qué actividades extraescolares haces este año, José?

José: Este trimestre voy al club de teatro. **Lo hago** todos los lunes. En marzo fuimos a ver una obra de teatro y en dos meses **la vamos a montar**. Y tú, ¿qué haces?

Kiara: Pues soy miembro del club de periodismo y canto en el coro del colegio. En julio cantamos en un concurso nacional y **lo ganamos**.

José: ¡Qué guay! ¿Vas a seguir con los mismos clubs el próximo trimestre?

Kiara: Sí, por supuesto. **No los voy a dejar** porque me molan. ¿Y tú?

José: Sí, voy a continuar con el club de lectores. El trimestre pasado tuvimos una charla de un escritor que nos leyó una parte de su última novela. ¡Me inspiró mucho!

Kiara: A mí me mola leer novelas. En casa **las leo** todo el tiempo. Voy a ir al club contigo.

José: ¡Genial! También voy a apuntarme al club de Ecoescuela.

Kiara: ¡Qué bien! **Lo hice** el trimestre pasado cuando conseguimos la clasificación como escuela ecológica. ¡Tenemos muchos planes para mejorar el insti!

⭐ Time expressions can help you decide if people are talking about the past, present or future:

Past: *el año pasado, el trimestre pasado*
Present: *ahora, este trimestre*
Future: *el próximo trimestre, el año que viene*

The preterite tense is used to refer to past achievements and successes.

Gané…	I won…
Participé…	I took part…
Toqué…	I played…
Di…	I gave…

 5 leer **Lee el diálogo otra vez. Traduce las expresiones en negrita al inglés.**

6 escribir **Traduce el texto al español.**

Where do you put the direct object pronoun? Which one do you need?

Use *desde hace* here.

In my school there are lots of extracurricular activities. I love photography and I've been a member of the photography club for two years. I do it on Tuesdays at lunchtime. Sometimes we take part in exhibitions. Last term I won a prize with my best photo. Last year I did swimming too, but I am going to stop it because it is a bit dull.

Use a dictionary to look up any words you don't know.

Will you use *lo* or *la* here?

Use the preterite here.

 G *Direct object pronouns* ❯ *Page 228*

Direct object pronouns replace the **noun** which has just been mentioned and avoid repetition.

The pronoun agrees with the noun it replaces:

	masculine	feminine
singular	lo	la
plural	los	las

It usually goes before the verb:

*Toco **el saxofón**. **Lo** toco.*
I play **the saxophone**. I play **it**.

*Participé en **una competición**. **La** gané.*
I took part in **a competition**. I won **it**.

With the near future tense, the direct object pronoun can go either at the end of the infinitive or before the present tense of *ir*:

*Voy a hacer**los**.* — I am going to do **them**.
***Los** voy a hacer.* — I am going to do **them**.

The pattern is the same for other verb + infinitive structures:

*Puedo hacer**lo**.* — I can do **it**.
***Lo** puedo hacer.* — I can do **it**.

7 escribir **Escribe un artículo sobre tus actividades extraescolares.**

- *¿Qué actividades extraescolares haces? ¿Desde hace cuánto tiempo?*
- *¿Qué opinas de las actividades extraescolares?*
- *¿Participaste en algún evento especial como un concurso, torneo o concierto el trimestre pasado?*
- *¿Qué actividades quieres hacer el trimestre / año que viene?*
- *¿Vas a participar en algún evento en el futuro?*

1 leer **Lee el artículo sobre los internados en España.**

Clases de refuerzo

Estos centros ofrecen cursos intensivos de refuerzo escolar a aquellos alumnos que lo necesitan.

Clases y estudio dirigido en lugar de playa y piscina sin límite. Cada año durante los meses de verano, un millar de jóvenes españoles se enfrenta a la disciplina de estos internados de verano. El objetivo principal de estos programas intensivos es ayudar a superar en septiembre las asignaturas suspensas.

Siete de la mañana: levantarse y desayuno. Ocho de la mañana: clases. Una del mediodía: almuerzo y descanso. Tres de la tarde: estudio. Seis y media de la tarde: deportes. Ocho y media de la tarde: cena... Éste es un ejemplo del estricto horario que tienen los estudiantes. ¿Y los resultados? En la mayoría de los casos, los resultados finales de sus alumnos son positivos.

> You don't need to understand every word of the text. Start by working out the meaning of the question and the four options. Then scan the text for synonyms or parallel phrases that match one of the options.

Elige la opción correcta para cada frase.

(a) Los cursos en estos centros se ofrecen…
  A en invierno.
  B los fines de semana.
  C durante las vacaciones.
  D todo el año.

(b) Los alumnos pasan el día…
  A en la playa.
  B estudiando.
  C descansando.
  D en la piscina.

(c) Su rutina diaria…
  A es flexible.
  B es muy variada.
  C tiene horas fijas.
  D es imposible.

(d) Al final de los cursos, la mayoría de los alumnos tiene…
  A sueño.
  B hambre.
  C éxito.
  D suerte.

2 leer **Read the extract. Apolodoro has recently started school.**

Amor y pedagogía by Miguel de Unamuno (abridged and adapted)

Y vuelve Apolodoro de la escuela, y hoy le dice a su padre:
—Papá, ya sé quién es el más inteligente de la escuela...
—¿Y quién es?
—Joaquín es el más inteligente de la escuela, el que sabe* más...
—¿Y crees tú, Apolodoro, que la persona que sabe más es la persona más inteligente?
—Claro que es la persona más inteligente...
—Pero uno puede saber menos y ser más inteligente.
—Entonces, ¿en qué se le conoce?
Y el pobre padre, confundido por todo esto, dice: "¡Parece imposible que sea hijo mío! ¡Qué niño tan extraño!"
—Vamos, Apolodoro escribe a tu tía.

*** saber = to know**

Answer the following questions in English. You do not need to write full sentences.

(a) When exactly does the conversation between Apolodoro and his father take place?
(b) According to Apolodoro, who is Joaquín?
(c) Apolodoro's father disagrees with Apolodoro. What does he say?
(d) What does Apolodoro's father tell him to do?

3 leer **Translate the following passage into English.**

Hoy fue mi primer día de clase en el nuevo instituto, y estaba un poco nerviosa. Primero conocimos a nuestra tutora, que era muy simpática. Tenemos más profesores que en la escuela primaria, y no recuerdo todos los nombres. Las clases acaban a las dos y los miércoles por la tarde hay actividades extraescolares opcionales. Mañana creo que voy a estar mucho más tranquila.

When there are unfamiliar words, consider the overall context and look at the surrounding words in the sentence. For example, in a new school with lots of new teachers, what could *no recuerdo todos los nombres* mean?

1 escuchar **You are listening to a radio debate. What are the arguments put forward in favour of school uniforms in Spanish schools?**
Listen and choose the three correct options.

A improves achievement in exams
B reduces bullying
C contributes to the school identity
D makes pupils take their learning more seriously
E saves time
F saves money
G improves concentration

With this type of task you may not hear the same words as in the question. Instead you often hear a longer description which is summarised in the short statements you are given. Also, beware of the occasional distractor in these questions!

2 escuchar **You are listening to a radio news item about changes to the primary curriculum in Spain. What does the journalist say?**
Listen and write the correct letter for each phrase.

The new subject being introduced is… *Example: B*
A computing.
B chess.
C drama.
D physical education.

(a) Until now it has been…
A taught only in secondary schools.
B compulsory in private schools.
C an extra-curricular activity.
D used to improve concentration.

(b) A recent study showed that pupils got better at…
A reading.
B maths.
C social skills.
D homework.

(c) Those experts in favour say that it improves…
A friendships.
B academic performance.
C the ability to cope with setbacks.
D creativity.

(d) Opponents of the new subject argue that…
A it is not as important as other academic subjects.
B creative subjects also bring benefits.
C learning English should be the priority.
D there are not enough specialist teachers.

A – Role play

1 leer Look at the role play card and prepare what you are going to say.

Topic: What school is like

Instructions to candidates:

You are at home talking to your Spanish friend about school life. The teacher will play the role of your Spanish friend and will speak first.

You must address your Spanish friend as *tú*.

You will talk to the teacher using the five prompts below.
- where you see – **?** – you must ask a question
- where you see – **!** – you must respond to something you have not prepared

Task

Estás en tu casa con tu amigo/a español/a. Habláis sobre la vida escolar.

1 Ir al instituto - cómo

2 Clubs - participación

3 !

4 ? Asignatura preferida

5 ? Instituto - opinión

> Think about the form of the verb you need here. Start your answer 'I go...'

> Don't be tempted to use the prompt to form your answer. Think through what you know how to say. 'I am...' and 'I go to ...'

> Use the tú form of the verb. What do you think...?

> Take a few seconds to understand the question. Pay attention to the tense of the verb as this question asks about past actions.

> Which question word do you need here?

2 escuchar Practise what you have prepared. Then, using your notes, listen and respond to the teacher.

3 escuchar Now listen to Zoah doing the role play task. **In English**, note down what she says for the first three points on the card.

B – Picture-based task

Topic: School activities

Mira la foto y prepara las respuestas a los siguientes puntos.
- la descripción de la foto
- tu opinión sobre tocar instrumentos en el colegio
- tu participación en un viaje o en una excursión extraescolar
- un viaje escolar que vas a hacer en el futuro
- (!)

1 **Look at the photo and read the task. Then listen to Cameron's response to the first bullet point.**

1 Why does he think they are in school?
2 What is his impression of the drummer?
3 What does he say about the mood of the pupils in the photo?
4 Which <u>four</u> expressions does he use to introduce his impressions?

2 **Listen to and read Cameron's response to the second bullet point.**

1 Write down the missing word for each gap.
2 Look at the Answer Booster on page 46. Note down <u>six</u> examples of language which Cameron uses to give a strong answer.

> ★ This question gives you the ideal opportuniy to use the object pronoun **te** (you). Remember that it usually goes in front of the verb:
> **Te** *da la oportunidad de expresarte.*
> It gives **you** the opportunity to express yourself.

Me encanta la música porque para mí, es la actividad más **1** ―――― y más divertida. No toco **2** ―――― instrumento, pero canto en el coro desde hace cinco años. Antes en mi escuela primaria **3** ―――― un coro muy pequeño, pero **4** ―――― en mi insti hay un coro muy grande y muy bueno. El año pasado **5** ―――― en un concurso nacional y ganamos. ¡Fue guay! Lo que más me gusta es que te da la oportunidad de **6** ―――― tus talentos y de hacer nuevos amigos.

3 **Listen to Cameron's response to the third bullet point.**

1 **In Spanish**, note down <u>six</u> verbs that he uses. How many different persons of the verb does he use?
2 Which tense does each of them use?

3 How does Cameron say 'you learn a lot on a school trip because it makes the subject more real and relevant'? Transcribe the phrase he uses.

4 **Listen to Cameron's response to the fourth bullet point. In English**, note down the <u>three</u> benefits that he mentions.

5 **Prepare your own answers to the first <u>four</u> bullet points. Try to predict which unexpected question you might be asked. Then listen and take part in the full picture-based task with the teacher.**

C – General conversation

1 **Listen to Joe introducing his chosen topic. Complete the sentences in English.**

a Joe has been going to this school…
b He likes it because…
c His primary school was… and had neither…
d His dad gives him a lift in the car when…

e The good thing about finishing at quarter to three is that…
f Today Joe is going to…

2 The teacher asks Joe, *'¿Qué asignaturas te gustan y no te gustan?'* Look at the Answer Booster on page 46. Note down <u>six</u> examples of language which Joe uses to give a strong answer.

> ★ Try to include different tenses in your answer, even if the question doesn't explicitly require it.

3 Listen to Joe's response to the second question, *'¿Qué opinas del uniforme escolar?'* Note down in English the <u>three</u> negative and <u>three</u> positive aspects of school uniform that Joe mentions.

> ★ You can produce a more developed answer if you describe both positive and negative points of view. Use *por un lado… por otro lado…* to introduce opposing opinions.

4 Prepare your own answers to Module 2 questions 1–6 on page 198. Then practise with your partner.

Answer booster	Aiming for a solid answer	Aiming higher	Aiming for the top
Verbs	**Different time frames**: past (preterite or imperfect), present, near future	**Different persons** of the verb: *improvisamos, vamos a escribir* **Verbs with an infinitive**: *hay que, está prohibido*	**More than one tense to talk about the past** (preterite and imperfect) **Unusual verbs**: *parecer, desarrollar, enseñar, suspender*
Opinions and reasons	**Verbs of opinion**: *me interesa(n), me encanta(n), me fastidia(n), pienso que, creo que…* **Reasons**: *porque…*	**Exclamations**: *¡Qué va! ¡Qué horror!* **Comparatives**: *es más relevante que…*	**Opinions**: *lo que más me gusta es…, lo peor es…, para mí…* **Reasons**: *así que, ya que…* **Comparatives/Superlatives**: *tan…como…, es la asignatura más exigente*
Connectives	*y, pero, también*	*además, sin embargo, no obstante*	**Linking past and present**: *antes…, pero ahora…* **Balancing an argument**: *por un lado… por otro lado…, aunque…*
Other features	**Qualifiers**: *muy, un poco, bastante* **Time phrases**: *el año que viene, el trimestre pasado*	**Desde hace**: *desde hace tres años* **Negatives**: *no… ni… ni…, tampoco, nunca, ningún / ninguna*	**Object pronouns**: *me/te/lo/la/los/las* **Interesting phrases**: *me permite expresarme, te da la oportunidad de…, recién renovado*

A – Short writing task

1 leer Look at the task and answer the questions.

- What **type** of text are you asked to write?
- What is each bullet point asking you to do?
- Which tense(s) will you need to use to answer each one?

2 leer Read Rebekah's answer on page 47. What do the phrases in **bold** mean?

3 leer Look at the Answer Booster. Note down <u>eight</u> examples of language which Rebekah uses to write a strong answer.

4 leer Look at the plan of Rebekah's answer. Write down the missing word for each gap.

5 escribir Prepare your own answer to the task.

- Look at the Answer Booster and Rebekah's plan for ideas.
- Think about how you can develop your answer for each bullet point.
- Write a detailed plan. Organise your answer in paragraphs.
- Write your answer and carefully check what you have written.

Mi instituto

Tu corresponsal española Maya va a visitar tu instituto.

Escribe un correo electrónico a Maya.

Debes incluir los puntos siguientes:

- describe tu instituto
- compara tu instituto con tu escuela primaria
- lo que piensas de las normas y por qué
- lo que vas a hacer con Maya en tu colegio durante su visita.

Escribe aproximadamente 80–90 palabras **en español**.

Paragraph 1
- What the **1** ———— are like
- The **2** ———— thing about it

Paragraph 2
- What the **3** ———— were like
- What the **4** ———— were like
- Why I **5** ———— my secondary school

Paragraph 3
- Opinion of some **6** ————
- Opinion of the rule on **7** ————
- What I'm going to **8** ———— next year

Paragraph 4
- The plan for the **9** ———— of Maya's visit
- The reason why my science teacher is the **10** ————
- What we will do in the **11** ————

Hola Maya

Mi instituto es grande, mixto y público. Hay edificios modernos, pero también edificios antiguos y **recién renovados**, aunque no hay ni piscina ni pista de atletismo. Lo peor es que hay bastante **estrés por los exámenes**.

Antes, en mi escuela primaria, las clases eran más fáciles, los profesores eran menos estrictos y **el día escolar era más corto**. No obstante, ahora mi insti **nos ofrece más oportunidades** y lo prefiero.

En mi opinión, algunas normas son justas y necesarias. Sin embargo, está prohibido llevar piercings y creo que esta norma **limita mi libertad de expresión**. El año que viene voy a hacer el bachillerato y voy a llevar **ropa de calle** y muchos piercings. ¡Qué guay!

El miércoles durante tu visita vamos a ir **juntas a clase**. Lo que más me gusta de los miércoles es la clase de ciencias porque mi profe es el mejor. Enseña muy bien porque **relaciona los temas** de la clase **con noticias actuales**. Por la tarde vamos a ir al club de fotografía, donde vamos a sacar y a editar fotos.

¡Hasta pronto!
Rebekah

Rebekah y Maya

> ⭐ Remember, even when a bullet does not require it, you can improve your answer by including more than one tense. Can you spot an example of this in the third paragraph?

B – Translation

1 escribir
Read the English text and Grace's translation of it. Write down the missing word(s) for each gap.

My school is in the centre of the city and **1** ――――― walk. It is important to pass the exams and get **2** ――――― but the best thing about my school is the **3** ―――――. I've been learning Spanish for three years so last year I took part in the **4** ―――――. I had an amazing time! **5** ――――― I want **6** ――――― with Spanish.

Mi insti **7** ――――― en el centro de la ciudad y puedo ir a pie. Es importante **8** ――――― los exámenes y sacar buenas notas, pero **9** ――――― de mi insti son las excursiones. **10** ――――― español desde hace tres años, así que el año pasado **11** ――――― en el intercambio. ¡Lo pasé bomba! El año que viene **12** ――――― continuar con el español.

> ⭐ Look out for phrases which don't translate word for word. For example, which tense do you need for 'I've been learning'?

2 escribir
Translate the following passage into Spanish.

Normally I cycle, given that I live quite near to my school. Lessons start at quarter to nine so I leave home early. I like my school because the facilities are good, but the worst thing is the rules, which are too strict. I've been a member of the orchestra for two years and last summer we did a concert in the school hall. It was great!

¿Te interesa(n)...? — Are you interested in...?

el arte dramático	drama
el dibujo	art / drawing
el español	Spanish
el inglés	English
la biología	biology
la educación física	PE
la física	physics
la geografía	geography
la historia	history
la informática	ICT
la lengua	language
la química	chemistry
la religión	RE
la tecnología	technology
los idiomas	languages
las empresariales	business studies
las matemáticas	maths
las ciencias	science
la materia / la asignatura	subject
me encanta(n) / me chifla(n)	I love
me interesa(n) / me fascina(n)	I'm interested in / fascinated by
me gusta(n) / no me gusta(n)	I like / I don't like
odio	I hate
prefiero	I prefer
porque es / son	because it is / they are
Mi día preferido es (el viernes).	My favourite day is (Friday).
mi horario	my timetable
¿Qué día tienes...?	What day do you have...?
Tengo inglés los martes.	I have English on Tuesdays.
¿A qué hora tienes...?	What time do you have...?
a la una / a las dos	at one o'clock / at two o'clock
y / menos cuarto	quarter past / to
y / menos cinco	five past / to
y media	half past
la educación infantil / primaria	pre-school / primary education
la educación secundaria	secondary education
el bachillerato	A levels
la formación profesional	vocational training
el instituto	secondary school

¿Qué tal los estudios? — How are your studies?

La física es más / menos ... que...	Physics is more / less ... than...
Es mejor / peor que...	It's better / worse than...
tan ... como	as ... as
fácil / difícil	easy / difficult
divertido/a / aburrido/a	fun / boring
útil / relevante / práctico/a	useful / relevant / practical
creativo/a / relajante	creative / relaxing
exacto/a / lógico/a / exigente	precise / logical / demanding
Mi profesor(a) (de ciencias) es...	My (science) teacher is...
paciente / impaciente	patient / impatient
tolerante / severo/a	tolerant / harsh
listo/a / tonto/a	clever / stupid
trabajador(a) / perezoso/a	hard-working / lazy
simpático/a / estricto/a	nice / strict
Mi profe...	My teacher...
enseña / explica bien	teaches / explains well
tiene buen sentido del humor	has a good sense of humour
tiene expectativas altas	has high expectations
crea un buen ambiente de trabajo	creates a good working atmosphere
nunca se enfada	never gets angry
me hace pensar	makes me think
nos da consejos / estrategias	gives us advice / strategies
nos pone muchos deberes	gives us lots of homework
el curso académico	academic year
las pruebas / las evaluaciones	tests / assessments
suspender / aprobar	to fail / to pass

¿Cómo es tu insti? — What is your school like?

En mi instituto hay... /	In my school there is... /
Mi instituto tiene...	My school has...
un salón de actos	a hall
un comedor	a canteen
un campo de fútbol	a football pitch
un patio	a playground
un gimnasio	a gym
una piscina	a pool
una biblioteca	a library
una pista de tenis / atletismo	a tennis court / an athletics track
unos laboratorios	some laboratories
muchas aulas	lots of classrooms
Lo bueno / malo es que...	The good / bad thing is that...
Lo mejor / peor es que...	The best / worst thing is that...
Lo que más me gusta es / son ...	What I like most is / are...
Lo que menos me gusta es / son ...	What I like least is / are...
no...ningún / ninguna	not a single...
ni...ni...	(n)either...(n)or
nada	nothing / anything
nadie	no-one / anyone
tampoco	not either
Mi insti es...	My school is...
mixto / femenino / masculino	mixed / all girls / all boys
público / privado	state / private
pequeño / grande	small / large
moderno / antiguo	modern / old
En mi escuela primaria había...	In my primary school there was/were...
Mi escuela primaria tenía...	My primary school had...
más / menos...	more / fewer, less
exámenes / deberes / alumnos	exams / homework / pupils
muebles / espacios verdes	furniture / green spaces
tiempo libre	free time
oportunidades / instalaciones	opportunities / facilities
pizarras interactivas / clases	interactive whiteboards / lessons
aulas de informática	ICT rooms
donde jugar	somewhere to play
poco espacio	little space
antes / ahora	before / now
El edificio / El colegio /	The building / The school /
El día escolar	The school day
es / era...	is / was...
(in)adecuado/a / corto/a / largo/a	(in)adequate / short / long
Las clases son / eran...	The lessons are / were...
Instituto de Educación Secundaria (IES)	secondary school

Las normas del insti — School rules

Tengo que llevar ...	I have to wear ...
Tenemos que llevar ...	We have to wear ...
(No) Llevo ...	I (don't) wear ...
(No) Llevamos ...	We (don't) wear ...
Es obligatorio llevar	It's compulsory to wear
un jersey (de punto)	a (knitted) sweater
un vestido	a dress
una camisa	a shirt
una camiseta	a T-shirt
una chaqueta (a rayas)	a (striped) jacket
una chaqueta de punto	a cardigan
una corbata	a tie
una falda (a cuadros)	a (checked) skirt
unos pantalones	trousers
unos calcetines	socks
unos zapatos	shoes
unos vaqueros	jeans
unas medias	tights
amarillo/a	yellow

blanco/a	white	llevar piercings	to have piercings
negro/a	black	Hay que…	It is necessary…
rojo/a	red	ser puntual	to be on time
morado/a / violeta	purple	respetar el turno de palabra	to wait for your turn to speak
naranja	orange	mantener limpio el patio	to keep the playground clean
rosa	pink	La norma más importante es…	The most important rule is…
azul	blue	respetar a los demás	to respect others
verde	green	Las normas son…	The rules are…
gris	grey	necesarias / demasiado severas	necessary / too strict
marrón	brown	para fomentar la buena disciplina	for promoting good discipline
oscuro / claro	dark / light	para limitar la libertad de expresión	for limiting freedom of expression
a rayas / a cuadros	striped / checked	para fastidiar a los alumnos	for annoying the pupils
bonito / feo	pretty / ugly	sacar buenas / malas notas	to get good / bad grades
cómodo / incómodo	comfortable / uncomfortable	Estoy de acuerdo.	I agree
anticuado / elegante / formal	old-fashioned / smart / formal	¡Qué va!	No way!
El uniforme…	Uniform…	¡Qué horror!	How awful!
mejora la disciplina	improves discipline	¡Qué bien!	How great!
limita la individualidad	limits individuality	Un problema de mi insti es…	One problem in my school is…
da una imagen positiva del insti	gives a positive image of the school	el estrés de los exámenes	exam stress
ahorra tiempo por la mañana	saves time in the morning	el acoso escolar	bullying
Está prohibido…	It is forbidden…	la presión del grupo	peer pressure
No se permite…	You are not allowed…	Hay (unos) alumnos que…	There are (some) pupils who…
No se debe…	You / one must not…	se burlan de otros	make fun of others
comer chicle	to chew chewing gum	sufren intimidación	are victims of intimidation
usar el móvil en clase	to use your phone in lessons	tienen miedo de…	are afraid of…
dañar las instalaciones	to damage the facilities	hacen novillos	skive
ser agresivo o grosero	to be agressive or rude	quieren ser parte de la pandilla	want to be part of the friendship group
correr en los pasillos	to run in the corridors	son una mala influencia	are a bad influence

¿Cómo es tu día escolar? — What is your school day like?

normalmente	usually	Las clases empiezan / terminan a las…	Lessons start / finish at …
Salgo de casa a las…	I leave home at…	Tenemos … clases al día.	We have … lessons per day.
Voy…	I go…	Cada clase dura … minutos.	Each lessons lasts … minutes.
a pie / andando	on foot / walking	El recreo / La hora de comer…	Break / Lunch is at…
en bici / en autobús / en coche	by bike / by bus / by car	es a la(s)…	
en metro / en taxi / en tren	by underground / by taxi / by train		

¿Qué vas a hacer? — What are you going to do?

Voy / Vas / Vamos a…	I'm going / You're going / We're going to…	pasar todo el día en…	spend the whole day in…
		asistir a clases	attend lessons
llegar / salir / estar	arrive / go out / be	practicar el español	practise Spanish
ir en coche / andando	go by car / walk	ir de excursión	go on a trip
llevar ropa de calle	wear casual clothes / non-uniform	tener una programación variada	have a varied programme
ir / comer juntos	go / eat together	Va a…	It's going to…
hacer una visita guiada	do a guided tour	ser fácil / guay	be easy / cool
ver los edificios	see the buildings		

Las actividades extraescolares — Extra-curricular activities

Toco la trompeta…	I play / I've been playing the trumpet…	El año / trimestre / verano pasado…	Last year / term / summer…
Canto en el coro…	I sing / I've been singing in the choir…	participé en un evento especial/ un concierto / un concurso / un torneo	I took part in a special event/ a concert / a competition / a tournament
Voy al club de…	I go / I've been going to the … club	gané un trofeo	I won a trophy
Soy miembro del club de…	I am / I've been a member of the … club	toqué un solo	I played a solo
ajedrez / judo / teatro / periodismo	chess / judo / drama / reporters	conseguimos la clasificación como…	we achieved the award / designation as…
lectores / Ecoescuela / fotografía	reading / eco-schools / photography	tuvimos una charla	we had a talk / presentation
desde hace … años / meses	for … years / months	ganamos una competición nacional	we won a national competition
Para mí…	For me…	dimos un concierto	we gave a concert
Pienso que / Creo que…	I think that…	¡Fue un éxito!	It was a success!
las actividades extraescolares son…	extra-curricular activities are	Este trimestre / El próximo trimestre…	This term / Next term
muy divertidas	a lot of fun	voy a	I'm going to…
algo diferente / un éxito	something different / an achievement	aprender a …	learn to …
te ayudan a…	they help you to…	continuar con…	continue with…
olvidar las presiones del colegio	forget the pressures of school	dejarlo	stop doing it
desarrollar tus talentos	develop your talents	apuntarme al club de…	sign up for the … club
hacer nuevos amigos	make new friends	vamos a…	we are going to…
te dan…	they give you…	montar una obra de teatro	put on a play
una sensación de logro	a sense of achievement	conseguir…	achieve…
más confianza	more confidence		
la oportunidad de ser creativo/a	the opportunity to be creative		
la oportunidad de expresarte	the opportunity to express yourself		

3 Mi gente
Punto de partida 1

- *Talking about socialising and family*
- *Using verbs in the present tense*

1 escuchar

Escucha. Identifica las <u>dos</u> actividades y la persona del verbo. (1–6)

Ejemplo: **1** <u>I</u> play on phone, <u>I</u> read texts.

hablar por Skype
sacar fotos
mandar mensajes
chatear con mis amigos
descargar canciones y aplicaciones
jugar con mi móvil
ver vídeos o películas
leer mis SMS
compartir mis vídeos favoritos

2 escribir

Traduce las frases al español.

1. I talk via Skype with my friends.
2. Do you (singular) take photos with your phone?
3. They chat with their friends.
4. We download songs and apps.
5. He watches his favourite videos.
6. She plays on her phone.
7. We read our texts.
8. Do you (plural) share your photos?

G Possessive adjectives

Most possessive adjectives have two forms, singular and plural.

	singular	plural
my	mi	mi**s**
your (singular)	tu	tu**s**
his/her/its	su	su**s**
our	nuestr**o**/nuestr**a**	nuestr**os**/nuestr**as**
your (plural)	vuestr**o**/vuestr**a**	vuestr**os**/vuestr**as**
their	su	su**s**

Nuestro (our) and *vuestro* (your – plural) also have masculine and feminine forms:

| nuestr**os** hermanos | our brothers |
| nuestr**as** hermanas | our sisters |

For *usted* (you – polite, singular) and *ustedes* (you – polite, plural) use *su/sus* to mean 'your'.

3 hablar

¿Qué significan los adjetivos? ¿Cómo se pronuncian?

animado   popular   útil

práctico   necesario   rápido

peligroso   fácil   cómodo

Words ending in –*n*, –*s* or a vowel are stressed on the penultimate syllable, whereas words ending in any other consonant are stressed on the final syllable. Any exceptions have a tilde (or accent) to indicate the stress. E.g. *difícil, canción*.

4 escuchar

Escucha y comprueba.

5 escuchar

Escucha y escribe la forma correcta de querer o poder. Luego tradúcelas al inglés. (1–7)

Ejemplo: **1** *podemos = we can*

> ⭐ When identifying the person of the verb, remember that the last letter(s) usually give(s) you a clue.

6 escribir

Completa las frases con la forma correcta del presente de poder o querer. Traduce las frases al inglés.

1 ¿(**querer**) ir de compras con nosotros? (you singular)
2 No (**poder**) ir a la bolera porque tengo que estudiar. (I)
3 ¿Miguel no viene? No, no (**poder**) venir al partido hoy. (he)
4 ¿(**querer**) ir al centro con nosotros? (you plural)
5 ¡Sí, (**poder**) ir! ¡Qué guay! (we)
6 Señor Gómez, ¿(**querer**) usted tomar algo en la cafetería? (you, polite singular)

> **G** **Poder *and* querer** 〉*Page 208*
>
> **Poder** (to be able to / 'can') and **querer** (to want) are stem-changing verbs usually followed by the infinitive.
>
> | | | | |
> |---|---|---|---|
> | *pue*do | I can | *qui*ero | I want |
> | *pue*des | you can | *qui*eres | you want |
> | *pue*de | he/she can | *qui*ere | he/she wants |
> | *po*demos | we can | *que*remos | we want |
> | *po*déis | you can | *que*réis | you want |
> | *pue*den | they can | *qui*eren | they want |

7 leer

Completa las frases en español con las palabras del recuadro. Usa un diccionario si es necesario. Sobran <u>cuatro</u> opciones. ¿Qué significan?

1 El marido de tu abuela es tu ⸺.
2 El hermano de tu padre es tu ⸺.
3 La mujer de tu padre es tu ⸺.
4 La hija de tus tíos es tu ⸺.
5 El hijo de tus padres es tu ⸺.
6 La abuela de tu padre es tu ⸺.
7 La hermana de tu padre es tu ⸺.
8 El hijo de tu hermano es tu ⸺.

hermanastra · hermano · abuelo · bisabuela · marido · tío · hija · madre · sobrino · prima · padrastro · tía

8 escribir

Escribe las palabras en español.

1 niece
2 stepbrother / half-brother
3 wife
4 male cousin
5 great-grandfather
6 son

> ⭐ Adapt the family members from exercise 7 to do exercise 8.
>
> E.g. If *sobrino* = nephew, what is niece?
>
> If *padrastro* = stepfather, what is stepbrother / half-brother?

Punto de partida 2

- *Describing people*
- *Using adjectival agreement*

1 escuchar

Escucha y escribe la letra correcta. (1–6)

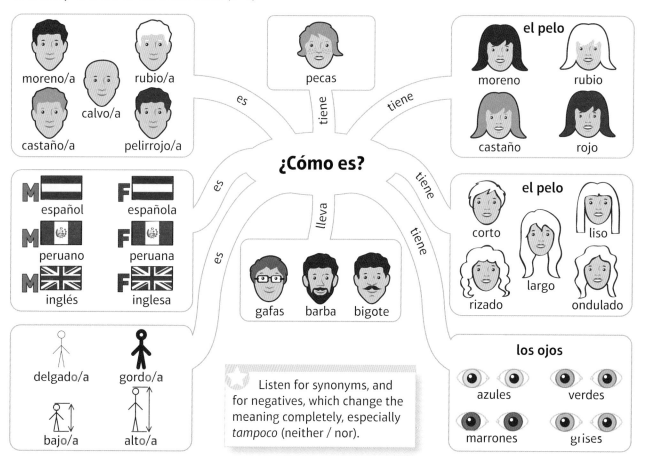

Listen for synonyms, and for negatives, which change the meaning completely, especially *tampoco* (neither / nor).

1 La madre de Lola…
a) es colombiana.
b) tiene el pelo castaño.
c) no es gorda.

2 Su padre…
a) es bajo.
b) es delgado.
c) no tiene pelo.

3 Su hermano menor…
a) tiene 15 años.
b) lleva barba.
c) es más bajo que Lola.

4 Su hermana mayor…
a) tiene una hija.
b) tiene el pelo rubio.
c) tiene los ojos azules.

5 Su abuela…
a) es peruana.
b) lleva ropa verde.
c) tiene 97 años.

6 Lola…
a) tiene pecas.
b) tiene el pelo largo.
c) lleva gafas.

2 leer

Traduce el texto al inglés.

Jesse & Joy es un dúo mexicano de pop latino. Son hermanos. Su padre es mexicano y su madre es estadounidense. Joy es bastante baja y delgada. Tiene el pelo castaño, largo y ondulado, y los ojos marrones. No lleva gafas. En el grupo toca la guitarra y canta. Jesse es más alto que su hermana y tiene los ojos marrones y bigote. Tiene menos pelo que Joy y a veces lleva un sombrero.

3 hablar

Describe a un(a) cantante de pop.
Tu compañero/a adivina la identidad.
Usa el texto del ejercicio 2 como modelo.

> ★ Use comparatives to give more
> precision to your description.
> *más… que…* more… than…
> *menos… que…* less… than…
> *tan… como…* as… as…

 4 leer

Completa las frases con los adjetivos antónimos.
Sobran <u>cuatro</u> adjetivos.

1 Soy bastante pesimista, pero mi hermano es siempre <u>optimista</u>.
2 Mi profesora de español es ━━━━, pero mi profe de historia es muy serio.
3 Un buen amigo es ━━━━; nunca es infiel.
4 Mi perro es muy travieso, pero a veces también puede ser ━━━━.
5 Normalmente mi padre es ━━━━, pero los fines de semana es un poco perezoso.

simpático
~~optimista~~
bueno
trabajador
generoso
hablador
divertido
inteligente
fiel

G *Adjectival endings* ❯ *Page 224*

Adjectives in Spanish usually come after the noun and 'agree' with the noun they describe.

You have seen the *–o/a, e* and consonant endings already. Adjectives ending in *–or/ora* and *–ista* follow a slightly different pattern.

adjective ending	masculine singular	feminine singular	masculine plural	feminine plural
–o/a	seri**o**	seri**a**	seri**os**	seri**as**
–e	inteligent**e**	inteligent**e**	inteligent**es**	inteligent**es**
consonant	fiel	fiel	fiel**es**	fiel**es**
–or/ora	hablad**or**	hablad**ora**	hablad**ores**	hablad**oras**
–ista	optim**ista**	optim**ista**	optim**istas**	optim**istas**

 5 hablar

Describe tu carácter y el carácter de un(a) amigo/a.
¿Tu compañero/a está de acuerdo?

● ¿Cómo eres? Y tu amigo (David), ¿cómo es?
■ *Pienso que soy <u>bastante alto</u>, y tengo… (David) es…*
● ¿Cómo eres de carácter?
■ *Creo que soy <u>muy hablador</u>. (David) es…*

Sí, es verdad.
Sí, estoy de acuerdo.
No, no estoy de acuerdo.
¡Qué va!

6 leer Lee los textos y contesta a las preguntas.

Who has…
1 an Argentinian aunt?
2 Spanish parents?
3 nephews?

Who is…
4 smaller than one of her parents?
5 taller than her sister?
6 more impatient than her sibling?

Mi madre tiene siete hermanos. ¡Todos tienen niños! Mi hermana y su marido viven en Berlín con sus tres hijos. Lola, mi hermana, es más pequeña que yo, y mucho más paciente y tranquila. **Luna**

De momento vivo con mi tía porque estudio en Buenos Aires. Ella es argentina y trabaja como médica. No es nunca perezosa. Mis padres son de Valencia y viven allí con mi hermano menor. **Isaac**

Mi padrastro es de Argentina y es ambicioso y trabajador. Es más alto que yo. No tenemos mucho en común, pero es más simpático y comprensivo que mi madre. **Alba**

- *Talking about social networks*
- *Using **para** with infinitives*
- *Extending responses by referring to others*

1 Escucha y escribe la letra correcta. ¡Ojo! Sobran <u>tres</u> frases. (1–6)

Ejemplo: **1** *d*

¿Qué aplicaciones usas?

a buscar y descargar música

b controlar mi actividad física

c pasar el tiempo

d compartir fotos

e contactar con mi familia

f conocer a gente nueva

g subir y ver vídeos

h organizar las salidas con mis amigos

i chatear y mandar mensajes

1 Uso Instagram para…

2 Uso WhatsApp para…

3 Uso Skype para…

4 Uso Spotify para…

5 Uso YouTube para …

6 Uso Facebook para…

2 **Escucha otra vez.**
Escribe <u>dos</u> **razones para cada aplicación. (1–6)**

Es / No es…		
barat**o**/**a**	popular	necesari**o**/**a**
divertid**o**/**a**	útil	rápid**o**/**a**
práctic**o**/**a**	gratis	cómod**o**/**a**
fácil de usar	peligros**o**/**a**	ampli**o**/**a**

G *Para + infinitive*

Use ***para*** to mean 'in order to…' or 'for –ing'. It is followed by the infinitive.

*Uso Moves **para controlar** mi actividad física.*
I use Moves **in order to record** my physical activity.

*Es una aplicación muy buena **para descargar** música.*
It is a very good app **for downloading** music.

3 **Con tu compañero/a, haz diálogos.**

- *¿Qué aplicación usas para <u>compartir fotos</u>?*
- *Uso <u>Instagram</u>.*
- *¿Por qué te gusta?*
- *Me gusta porque es <u>fácil de usar</u>.*

Extend your responses by referring to others, using different parts of the verb.

E.g. *Mis amigos y yo **usamos** WhatsApp para chatear, pero mi madre **usa** Twitter.*

Remember to change the pronoun to say what others like:
E.g. *A mi madre **le** gusta Twitter porque es práctica y rápida.*

escuchar

4 Escucha y lee. Contesta a las preguntas en inglés.

Las redes sociales – lo bueno y lo malo

La red social que más me gusta es WhatsApp. Lo bueno es que todos mis amigos la usan, así que es el canal de comunicación más importante en mi vida. Además, uso Netflix para ver mis series favoritas desde mi móvil. La tengo desde hace seis meses y es muy práctica para pasar el rato en el autobús o en casa. Lo único malo es que te engancha.

Mi hermana Jessica está completamante enganchada. Es un problema porque no puede estar sin su móvil – ¡lo utiliza para todo! Le chiflan las fotos y usa varias apps para editar. Personaliza las fotos con efectos y filtros y luego las sube a Instagram.

Mi padre tiene que viajar a menudo a otros países y por eso mis padres usan Skype para estar en contacto. En cada país mi padre usa Duolingo. Dice que es la mejor app para mejorar sus idiomas. Antes mi madre no tenía un Smartphone, pero ahora lo usa para todo. Usa una app para controlar las calorías. ¡Yo pienso que es una pérdida de tiempo!

Alejandro

pasar el rato	to pass the time	**no puede estar sin**	(she) can't be without
te engancha	it gets you hooked	**una pérdida de tiempo**	a waste of time

1 Why is WhatsApp Alejandro's most important means of communication?

2 Why does he think Netflix is so handy?

3 What does Alejandro say about Jessica's relationship with her phone? Give <u>two</u> details.

4 What does Jessica do with her photos? Give <u>two</u> details.

5 What does Alejandro's dad use Duolingo for?

6 What does Alejandro's mum use her phone for, in particular?

5 Lee el texto del ejercicio 4 otra vez. Copia y completa la tabla con frases del texto.

frases positivas	frases negativas
es el canal de comunicación más importante en mi vida	*lo único malo es que te engancha*

6 Traduce las frases al español. Usa el texto del ejercicio 4 como modelo.

1 I am hooked on my mobile. I use it for everything.

2 Twitter is my favourite social network. I have been using it for six months.

3 My friends use Duolingo to improve their Spanish.

4 Before I didn't have Instagram, but now I use it every day.

5 My parents use Facebook to keep in touch with their friends.

6 My friend Gabriela uses lots of apps to personalise her phone.

7 *Nuestras aplicaciones favoritas de la A a la Z.* En grupos de 4 a 6 personas, prepara un post. Incluye la información siguiente:

- *¿Para qué usas la aplicación?*
- *¿Desde hace cuánto tiempo la tienes?*
- *¿Por qué te gusta?*
- *¿Tiene algún inconveniente?*

> Improve the flow of your writing. Use direct object pronouns (it/them) to refer to things you have already mentioned. Look back at exercise 4. What do the pronouns refer to?

- *Making arrangements*
- *Using the present continuous tense*
- *Improvising dialogues*

 1 **leer** **Lee y busca las expresiones en los mensajes.**

Ejemplo: **1** *estoy esperando*

Sara Moya Cortés
¡Holaaaaaaaaaaaa a todooooosss! ¿Qué estáis haciendo ahora mismo?

Carlos Santos Bedoya
Estoy escuchando música, estoy tomando el sol en el balcón y estoy esperando a David, que está en la ducha.

Elena Fernández
Rebecca y yo estamos viendo una peli en casa. Mi madre está preparando algo para merendar.

James Baker
¡Hola Sara! Estoy leyendo porque Mateo está repasando para un examen de matemáticas. Y sé que Bea y Tom están haciendo footing. ¿Y los demás? ¿Qué estáis haciendo?

Alfonso Peresín Rojas
Nada especial. Estoy haciendo el vago porque Phil está durmiendo ¡desde hace dos horas ya! ☺ ☺

Gabriela Reyes Telmo
Yo estoy escribiendo aquí en Facebook para responderte. ¡Ja ja ja! Y tú, Sara, ¿qué estás haciendo?

Sara Moya Cortés
¿Yo? Estoy pensando en salir para dar una vuelta por la Plaza Mayor. ¿Queréis venir conmigo?

la Plaza Mayor, Salamanca

hacer el vago   *to laze around*

1 I am waiting
2 He is revising
3 They are jogging
4 We are watching a film
5 She is preparing something for tea
6 What are you doing?

 2 **escuchar** **Escucha. Apunta los detalles en inglés. (1–4)**

- Where are they in Salamanca?
- What are they doing?

charlar   *to chat / talk*

> When listening or reading you may encounter different forms of familiar verbs. E.g. You know *comer* (to eat) but hear *comiendo*. What does this mean?

3 **hablar** **Improvisa una conversación con tu compañero/a.**

- ● *¿Qué está haciendo Carlos?*
- ■ *Pues, está…*

Rebecca y Elena   James

Mateo   Bea y Tom

Phil   Gabriela

G *The present continuous tense*   > *Page 218*

Use the **present continuous tense** to say what you are doing at the moment. Take the present tense of the verb *estar* and the **present participle** ('–ing' form) of the action verb.

	estar (to be)	**present participle**
(yo)	estoy	
(tú)	estás	mir**ando**
(él/ella/usted)	está	beb**iendo**
(nosotros/as)	estamos	escrib**iendo**
(vosotros/as)	estáis	
(ellos/ellas/ustedes)	están	

To form the present participle, take the infinitive, remove the *–ar*, *–er* or *–ir* and add the endings *–ando*, *–iendo*, *–iendo*.

Estoy buscando *canciones.*   **I am looking** for songs.
No **estamos haciendo** *nada.*   **We are not doing** anything.

Irregular present participles include: **leer** → **leyendo**, **dormir** → **durmiendo**

¿Quieres salir conmigo?

4 **Escucha. Copia y completa la tabla en inglés. (1–4)**

	activity	excuses
1		

No puedo porque…		
tengo que quiero	salir… terminar… subir… visitar a…	cuidar a… hacer… quedarme en casa… hacer el vago
está lloviendo		
estoy estamos	actualizando… viendo…	editando… descansando

5 **Lee la conversación. Rellena los espacios en blanco con el verbo correcto.**

Lucas: Hola, Ana. ¿Qué estás **1**⸺?
Ana: No mucho. Estoy **2**⸺ una serie.
Lucas: ¿**3**⸺ salir conmigo? Podemos **4**⸺ una vuelta por la ciudad.
Ana: Ahora no **5**⸺ porque **6**⸺ que visitar a mi tía.
Lucas: ¡Qué rollo! Pues, ¿más tarde, entonces?
Ana: ¡Claro que sí! ¿A qué hora quedamos?
Lucas: A las seis.
Ana: Vale. ¿Dónde **7**⸺?
Lucas: En la Plaza Mayor, debajo del reloj. ¡Qué bien! Hasta las seis.

el reloj   clock

quedamos

puedo

viendo

tengo

quieres

haciendo

dar

6 **Escucha y comprueba tus respuestas.**

el Puente Nuevo, Salamanca

Zona Cultura

Salamanca está en la parte central de España, a 212 kilómetros al oeste de Madrid. Su Plaza Mayor es el punto de encuentro más popular. La gente pasa mucho tiempo allí charlando, paseando, tomando el sol o disfrutando de un helado en una de las cafeterías. Es ideal por la tarde, pero es aún más bonita por la noche, cuando la iluminación es impresionante.

7 **Organiza un encuentro en la Plaza Mayor de Salamanca con tu estudiante de intercambio. Utiliza el ejercicio 5 como modelo.**

● *Hola Víctor. ¿Qué estás haciendo?*
■ *No mucho. Estoy escuchando música. ¿Por qué?*
● *¿Quieres salir? Podemos…*

detrás de	behind
delante de	in front of
debajo de	underneath
enfrente de	opposite
al lado de	next to
en (el/la)	in (the)

- *Talking about reading preferences*
- *Using a range of connectives*
- *Recognising similar ideas expressed differently*

1 escuchar **Escucha. Apunta las <u>dos</u> letras correctas para cada persona. (1–5)**

Ejemplo: **1** *a, c*

¿Qué te gusta leer?

a los blogs

b los tebeos / los cómics

c los periódicos

d las revistas

e las poesías

f las novelas de ciencia ficción

g las novelas de amor

h las historias de vampiros

i las biografías

2 escuchar **Escucha otra vez. Apunta la expresión de frecuencia que se menciona. (1–5)**

Ejemplo: **1** *una vez a la semana*

¿Con qué frecuencia lees?
  cada día / todos los días
  a menudo
  generalmente
  de vez en cuando
  una vez a la semana
  dos veces al mes
  una vez al año
  nunca

3 hablar **Habla con tu compañero/a.**

- ¿Qué te gusta leer?
- *Me gusta leer <u>revistas</u> y <u>biografías</u>.*
- ¿Con qué frecuencia lees?
- *Leo revistas <u>muy a menudo</u> y biografías <u>de vez en cuando</u>.*
  En este momento (no) estoy leyendo…
- ¿Qué no te gusta leer? ¿Por qué no?
- *No me gusta leer <u>novelas</u> porque son <u>aburridas</u>.*

4 leer **Lee los textos y apunta la información en inglés.**

- Who:
- What he/she likes reading:
- How often:
- Preferred format:
- Reason:

Mi tía Salomé es el mayor ratón de biblioteca de mi familia. Lee cada noche y le interesan mucho las biografías y las novelas históricas. Prefiere leer libros en papel porque le gusta pasar las páginas a mano y escribir anotaciones.

A mi primo Rafael le encantan los cómics y es un fan del manga. Lee a través de una aplicación en su móvil, lo cual prefiere porque es más práctico. Lee a veces por la mañana cuando está esperando el autobús.

5 leer Lee las opiniones sobre leer en formato digital. Busca <u>tres</u> ventajas y <u>tres</u> desventajas.

Ejemplo: Ventajas: 1, …, …,
Desventajas: …, …, …

Leer en formato digital…

1 protege el planeta, ya que no malgasta papel.

2 cansa la vista más que leer libros en papel.

3 depende de la energía eléctrica.

4 te permite llevar contigo miles de libros.

5 cuesta mucho menos que leer en formato tradicional.

6 fastidia porque no hay numeración de páginas.

fastidiar to annoy / be annoying

6 escuchar Escucha y comprueba tus respuestas.

7 leer Lee el blog. Busca las opiniones en **negrita** que significan lo mismo que las frases del ejercicio 5.

*Ejemplo: **1** los libros digitales son más ecológicos*

E-book o libro en papel, ¿cuál es mejor?

¡Hola, ratones de biblioteca! El tema de hoy es: e-book o libro en papel, ¿cuál es mejor?

Primero, yo personalmente prefiero leer en papel, porque me gusta tocar las páginas. Además, **no leo más que una página en formato digital y ya tengo los ojos cansados**, mientras que con un libro de verdad puedo leer horas y horas.

Sin embargo, sé que leer libros electrónicos tiene muchas ventajas. Una ventaja es que **son mucho más fáciles de transportar**, ya que no ocupan espacio. También **los libros digitales son más ecológicos**. Mis amigos fanáticos de lo digital dicen que **son mucho más baratos que los libros tradicionales**.

Por otro lado, **una desventaja de los ebooks es el uso de batería**. Si se te acaba la batería, tienes que recargarla. Otra desventaja es que así **no se pueden numerar las páginas,** y por lo tanto no es muy práctico.

En resumen, pienso que leer es algo muy personal. Si puedo escoger, prefiero en papel, pero también puedo leer perfectamente en e-book. Y vosotros, ¿qué pensáis?

recargar to recharge

8 escribir Escribe un blog sobre las ventajas y desventajas de **los libros en papel**.

 Adapt language from exercise 7 and use a range of connectives to structure your arguments clearly:

- Introduction: *primero*
- Addition: *además, también*
- Opposition: *sin embargo, por otro lado, mientras que*
- Justification: *porque, ya que*
- Consequence: *por lo tanto, así que*
- Conclusion: *en resumen*

Zona Cultura

'El que lee mucho y anda mucho, ve mucho y sabe mucho.' Miguel de Cervantes
Miguel de Cervantes Saavedra (1547–1616) fue un soldado y autor español. Es el autor de la novela más famosa de la literatura española, ***Don Quijote de la Mancha***. Es el libro más editado y traducido de la historia, solo superado por la Biblia.

4 Retratos

- *Describing people*
- *Using **ser** and **estar***
- *Understanding more detailed descriptions*

1 ler **Lee el texto. Apunta los detalles en inglés.**

- Name:
- Age:
- From:
- Physical description:
- Character:

- Position:
- Place:
- Activity:
- Emotion:

Ésta es Mafalda. Es una niña de ocho años de Buenos Aires, Argentina. Es morena y baja, con el pelo negro y los ojos marrones. Como persona, es simpática, pensativa y pesimista. En la imagen está sentada en el jardín, con los ojos cerrados. Está escuchando música y sonriendo. Está feliz.

Zona Cultura

Mafalda es un personaje de una tira argentina que se publicó de 1964 a 1973. Su creador fue el humorista gráfico Quino. Mafalda es una niña que está preocupada por la humanidad y la paz mundial, y a menudo está desilusionada por la realidad. Es un cómic muy popular en Latinoamérica, así como en muchos países europeos. Ha sido traducido a más de 30 idiomas.

la tira comic strip

G Ser *and* estar ❯ *Page 210*

Ser is used for:
Description: **Soy** *alto y bastante delgado.*
Origin: *¿****Eres**** de Colombia?*
Character: **Es** *muy honesto.*
Time: **Son** *las cinco de la tarde.*
Occupation: **Somos** *mecánicos.*
Relation: *¿****Sois**** mis primos, no?*

Estar is used for:
Position: **Estoy** *de pie.*
Location: *¿****Estás**** en Madrid?*
Action: **Está** *estudiando.*
Condition: **Estamos** *cansados. ¿****Estáis**** bien?*
Emotion: **Están** *contentos.*

2 escuchar **Escucha y escribe la letra correcta. (1–3) Sobran <u>dos</u> personajes (y Mafalda).**

 a Miguelito

 b Manolito

c Felipe

 d Susanita

 e Guille

el racimo de plátanos bunch of bananas

3 escuchar **Escucha otra vez. ¿Cómo son de carácter? Apunta <u>tres</u> detalles en inglés para cada personaje.**

*Ejemplo: **1** ambitious, …, …*

4 hablar **Mira la imagen del ejercicio 2. Describe a los <u>dos</u> personajes que quedan. Usa también los adjetivos de carácter.**

● *Se llama… Es… En la imagen está…*

⭐ For exercises 2 and 3, you will hear adjectives you have seen already as well as some new, more descriptive, language for character and appearance:

Es *alegre / ambicioso / cómico / dinámico / egoísta / explosivo / histérico / idealista / modesto / molesto / pensativo / romántico / sincero / tímido / travieso*

Tiene *los ojos grandes / pequeños / brillantes*
el pelo de punta / ondulado
la cara redonda / alargada
los dientes prominentes / la piel blanca
En la imagen…
Está *de pie / sentado / al lado izquierdo / derecho de…*
sonriendo / hablando / mirando
feliz / contento / triste

5 leer Lee el texto. Busca las expresiones en español.

Mi hermana y yo, ¡qué diferentes somos!

Sandra y Lorena

Mientras que yo soy baja y mido 1,60, mi hermana es bastante alta, ya que mide 1,80. No nos parecemos físicamente, pues yo tengo el pelo negro como el carbón y ella es rubia como el sol. Ella tiene los ojos grandes y redondos, mientras que mis ojos son tan pequeños como dos botones.

Por otra parte, yo soy una persona muy enérgica porque no puedo estar sentada y siempre estoy haciendo algo. No obstante, mi hermana es tan tranquila como el agua de un pozo, y no se impacienta nunca con nadie.

Por último, ella es una persona muy ordenada, así que siempre sabe dónde está todo. En cambio, yo paso horas y horas buscando mis cosas porque soy una persona muy caótica.

el pozo   well

1   I am 1.60 m tall
2   we are not physically alike
3   I can't be sitting / sit still

4   she never gets impatient with anyone
5   she always knows where everything is
6   I spend hours and hours looking for my things

6 leer Busca ejemplos con **ser** y **estar** en el ejercicio 5. Explica la razón de su uso.

Ejemplo: yo <u>soy</u> baja – ser – description

7 leer Lee el texto del ejercicio 5 otra vez. Completa los símiles en inglés.

1   My hair is as black as ▬▬▬.
2   She is as blonde as ▬▬▬.

3   My eyes are as small as ▬▬▬.
4   She is as calm as ▬▬▬.

8 escuchar Escucha. Completa la tabla en español. (1–2)

	persona	descripción física	carácter	comparaciones / símiles
1	abuela	pelo – fino, blanco, …	alegre, …	piel blanca como el papel, …

la piel   skin

Listen out for negatives. They often change the meaning completely. Sometimes the negative is in two parts, sometimes not.

No se pelea nunca. He/She doesn't **ever** argue.
Nunca se pelea. He/She **never** argues.
No es ni gordo ni delgado. He is **neither** fat **nor** thin.
Tampoco tiene pecas. **Nor** does he/she have freckles.

9 escribir Escribe una descripción de una persona, real o imaginaria. Incluye:

• adjetivos físicos
• adjetivos de carácter
• comparaciones
• símiles

No es ni alto ni bajo. Es moreno con los ojos…
Como persona, es optimista y alegre.
No es tan inteligente como Einstein, pero…
Es tan enérgico como una pila Duracell.

Including similes adds a literary dimension to description.
Use a photo or drawing if you have one. Add specific details about the person's location, position and mood, and what he/she is doing.

- *Talking about friends and family*
- *Using a range of relationship verbs*
- *Referring to the present and past*

1 **Escucha y lee los textos. ¿Qué significan las expresiones en violeta en inglés?**

¿Te llevas bien con tu familia y tus amigos?

1 **Me llevo muy bien con** mi madre porque es paciente y simpática. **Me apoya** en todos los momentos difíciles.

2 **Me peleo con** mi hermana a menudo porque es tonta y egoísta.

3 **No me llevo bien con** mis padres porque son muy estrictos. ¡Me dan demasiados consejos!

4 **Me divierto con** mi padre porque tenemos mucho en común. Siempre es optimista y **nunca me critica**.

5 Mi amigo y yo **nos llevamos superbién** porque es muy divertido y **me hace reír**.

6 Mi amiga y yo **nos divertimos** siempre porque es muy graciosa. Además, **es fiel** y **me acepta como soy**.

2 **leer** **Lee los textos del ejercicio 1 otra vez. Busca las frases en español.**

1 She supports me in hard times.
2 They give me too much advice!
3 We have a lot in common.
4 He never criticises me.
5 He makes me laugh.
6 She is loyal.
7 She accepts me as I am.

3 **hablar** **Con tu compañero/a, haz diálogos.**

- ● *¿Te llevas bien con* <u>tu madre</u>*?*
- ■ *Sí, me llevo bien con* <u>mi madre</u> *porque es* <u>generosa</u> *y* <u>siempre me apoya</u>*. Y tú, ¿te llevas bien con* <u>tus padres</u>*?*

Increase the interest of your speaking by using a wide variety of adjectives. Can you find all ten in exercise 1?

Remember to use adverbs to add detail: *siempre, a veces, de vez en cuando, nunca…*

G **Reflexive verbs for relationships** 〉 *Page 211*

Some verbs for describing relationships are reflexive in Spanish.

	llevarse (to get on)	
(yo)	me llevo	
(tú)	te llevas	
(él/ella/usted)	se lleva	bien con…
(nosotros/as)	nos llevamos	mal con…
(vosotros/as)	os lleváis	
(ellos/ellas/ustedes)	se llevan	

Me llevo bastante **bien** con mis padres.
I get on quite **well** with my parents.

Verbs like this include: *pelearse* (to argue) and *divertirse* (to have fun).

Other verbs use reflexive pronouns to mean 'each other'.

conocerse →
Nos conocemos desde hace cinco años.
We have known each other for five years.

apoyarse →
Se apoyan en todo.
They support each other in everything.

● **Zona Cultura**

'Deben buscarse los amigos como los buenos libros: pocos, buenos y bien conocidos.'

Mateo Alemán (1547–1615), novelista español

4 Escucha y completa la tabla en inglés. (1–4)

	where they met	what a good friend is like (2 details)
1	at badminton club	

¿Cómo es un buen amigo / una buena amiga?
Un buen amigo / Una buena amiga es alguien que…

te apoya / te ayuda	te escucha
te conoce bien	te hace reír
te acepta como eres	no te critica
te da consejos	nunca te juzga

 5 Lee los textos. Contesta a las preguntas para cada texto en español.

¿Cómo conociste a tu mejor amigo/a?

Santi y John

Tom y Kiara

Pues, yo conocí a mi amigo John hace cuatro años en Málaga, cuando él estaba de vacaciones. Nos conocimos en la playa, jugando al fútbol. Como tenemos el deporte en común, nos llevamos muy bien. Es muy alto y bastante delgado. Es moreno con los ojos marrones y el pelo corto y rizado. Es una gran persona, siempre animado y optimista. Aunque vive en Inglaterra, estamos en contacto por MSN. Para mí, un buen amigo es alguien que te conoce bien y nunca te juzga.

Mi mejor amiga es Kiara, mi mujer. La conocí en el colegio, cuando tenía 10 años. Nos hicimos amigos un día en clase. A los 15 años nos hicimos novios. Convivimos después de la universidad y luego nos casamos. Kiara es baja y rubia, con los ojos verdes. Como persona, es creativa, tolerante y enérgica. Nos llevamos superbién. Bueno, a veces nos llevamos como el perro y el gato porque tenemos opiniones distintas, pero ella es el amor de mi vida. Nos encantan las películas, y por lo tanto vamos cada semana juntos al cine. Para mí, un buen amigo es alguien que te quiere mucho y te ayuda en todo.

convivir	*to live together*
casarse	*to get married*

1 ¿Cuándo conoció a su mejor amigo/ su mejor amiga?
2 ¿Dónde lo/la conoció?
3 ¿Qué tienen en común?
4 ¿Cómo se llevan?
5 ¿Cómo es su carácter?
6 En su opinión, ¿cómo es un buen amigo/una buena amiga?

G *The personal 'a'*

When the object of the verb is a specific, known person, use the personal '*a*'.
*Conocí **a** mi mejor amigo Félix.*   I met my best friend Félix.

Do not use it when the person is not someone you can picture.
*Busco **a** mi amigo.*   I'm looking for **my** friend.
Busco un amigo.   I'm looking for **a** friend.

 6 Escribe un texto de 80–90 palabras. Incluye:

- what a good friend does
- how you met a good / your best friend
- what he/she looks like
- what he/she is like as a person
- why you get on well
- what you have in common / do together

Para mí, un buen amigo es alguien que…
Conocí a mi (mejor) amigo/a…
Es bastante alto/a. Tiene el pelo…
Como persona, es divertido/a y fiel.
Nos llevamos bien porque…
Nos gusta… / Tenemos… en común y por eso…

Remember to use the **preterite tense** for completed actions in the past.

Use the **imperfect tense** for describing in the past.

1 leer **Lee la información sobre los cumpleaños.**

> Aquí en Ecuador no organizamos tanto la fiesta... Los niños están felices haciendo algunos concursos o juegos, o corriendo por todos lados – nada más. **Pilar, Ecuador**

> Cuando son pequeños, normalmente lo celebran a la hora del té y hoy vamos a un sitio donde hay personas que organizan las actividades. **Ángel, Argentina**

> Para los niños en nuestra familia siempre hay dos celebraciones: una cena con la familia y una fiesta para los amiguitos. Además del 'Cumpleaños feliz', también cantamos 'Las mañanitas', una canción muy popular. **Sergio, México**

> Si es el cumpleaños de un niño, hacemos una celebración en casa. Los invitados traen regalos y hay una tarta de cumpleaños con velas. Hacemos lo mismo que cuando yo era joven. **Yoli, España**

¿Cómo es el cumpleaños ideal? Escribe el nombre correcto.

Ejemplo: Te gusta celebrar tu cumpleaños con la familia. *Sergio.*

(a) No quieres organizar una fiesta en casa.
(b) Para ti, la música es muy importante.
(c) Te gustan las fiestas sin mucha organización.

(d) No quieres tener la responsabilidad de las actividades.
(e) Prefieres comer algo dulce*.   * *dulce = sweet*

2 leer **Read the dialogue between Max and Roland.**

El príncipe de la niebla by Carlos Ruiz Zafón (abridged)

> —Hola. ¿Tú eres de la familia que se ha instalado en la casa al final de la playa?
> Max asintió. —Soy Max.
> El chico, con los ojos verdes penetrantes, le tendió su mano. —Roland. Bienvenido a *ciudad aburrimiento*.
> Max sonrió y aceptó la mano de Roland.
> —¿Qué tal la casa? ¿Os gusta?— preguntó Roland.
> —Hay opiniones divididas. A mi padre le encanta. El resto de la familia lo ve diferente— explicó Max.
> —Conocí a tu padre hace unos meses, cuando vino al pueblo— dijo Roland—. Me pareció un tipo divertido.
> Max asintió.
> —Es un tipo divertido— corroboró Max—, a veces.
> —¿Por qué habéis venido al pueblo?— preguntó Roland.
> —La guerra— contestó Max—. Mi padre piensa que no es un buen momento para vivir en la ciudad. Supongo que tiene razón.

Choose the correct letter for each phrase.

(a) Roland finds his village...
  A busy.
  B peaceful.
  C boring.
  D touristy.

> Written dialogues often include words like 'she nodded' or 'he said'. Some of these verbs are cognates in Spanish (e.g. *explicar, corroborar*). Other verbs include **asentir** (to nod), **preguntar** (to ask), **contestar** (to answer) and **decir** (to say).
>
> Don't get distracted by these words! Instead focus on the dialogue itself to work out what they are saying.

(b) Max...
  A loves the new house.
  B doesn't love the new house.
  C and his father love the new house.
  D and his family love the new house.

(c) Roland has already...
  A met Max before.
  B been to Max's house.
  C met Max's parents.
  D met Max's father.

(d) Max and his family have moved out of the city because of the...
  A pollution.
  B war.
  C sea air.
  D job opportunities.

3 leer   Read the article about multitasking.

¡La multitarea no existe!

Parece que los adolescentes pueden hacer multitarea, y dicen que las mujeres estamos orgullosas a veces de hacerlo: hablamos por el móvil, enviamos un correo y leemos una carta, todo al mismo tiempo…, pero existe un problema: la multitarea es un mito.

La multitarea implica participar en dos tareas al mismo tiempo, y eso solo es posible si se cumplen dos condiciones:

1) al menos una de las tareas es automática, es decir, no requiere atención o pensamiento para hacerla (por ejemplo, caminar o comer) y,

2) las dos tareas necesitan diferentes tipos de procesamiento cerebral*. Por ejemplo, podemos leer mientras escuchamos música clásica, porque el cerebro* procesa la música y el texto en dos partes diferentes.

Sin embargo, no ocurre lo mismo cuando leemos y escuchamos música *con letra* porque las dos tareas requieren la activación de la misma parte del cerebro.

> * **el procesamiento cerebral = mental processing**
> * **el cerebro = brain**

**Answer the following questions in English.
You do not need to write full sentences.**

(a) According to the article, which <u>two</u> groups of people seem to multitask?

(b) Give <u>two</u> examples of activities that don't require conscious attention.

(c) According to the article, why is it possible to read and listen to classical music at the same time?

(d) Why is listening to music with lyrics considered to be different?

1 escuchar   **Escuchas un anuncio de un nuevo lector digital*. ¿Qué dice el anuncio?
Escoge entre: grande, rápido, fácil, barato. Puedes usar las palabras más de una vez.**

Ejemplo: El nuevo lector digital es más grande

(a) Comprar una batería nueva no es ⎯⎯⎯ .

(b) Recargar la batería es ⎯⎯⎯ .

(c) Hacer la letra más grande es ⎯⎯⎯ .

(d) Comprar libros digitales es ⎯⎯⎯ .

(e) El tamaño de la memoria es ⎯⎯⎯ .

* **el lector digital = e-book reader**

2 escuchar   **You are listening to an interview about the importance of social media.
Listen and choose the <u>two</u> correct statements for each question.**

(a) One advantage of social media is that…
  A you can chat to friends and family very cheaply.
  B social media enable family members who live far apart to keep in touch.
  C your world goes with you wherever you go.
  D young people are better informed about events in their local area.
  E world news is shared quickly and easily via your mobile.

(b) A potential danger is that…
  A people become addicted to social media.
  B people only share good news.
  C people become less physically active when using social media.
  D people don't do anything useful on social media.
  E virtual friendship is not real friendship.

A – Role play

 1 leer Look at the role play card and prepare what you are going to say.

Topic: Cultural life

Instructions to candidates:

Your Spanish friend is staying at your house. The teacher will play the role of your Spanish friend and will speak first.

You must address your Spanish friend as *tú*. You will talk to the teacher using the five prompts below.

- where you see – **?** – you must ask a question
- where you see – **!** – you must respond to something you have not prepared

Task

Tu amigo/a español/a está en tu casa. Hacéis planes para esta tarde

1 Esta tarde - adónde

2 Salir - hora

3 !

4 ? comer - dónde

5 ? después - actividad

> Be sure to read all the information given on the task card. What is '*Hacéis planes para esta tarde*' telling you?

> You can keep your answer short here – just give an appropriate time.

> Take time to consider how to answer. You usually have to refer to 'I' or 'we' in your response.

> Always keep the situation in mind. You are arranging to go out. What do you want to know here?

> Keep it simple. How would you ask 'What are we doing...?.

 2 escuchar Practise what you have prepared. Then, using your notes, listen and respond to the teacher.

 3 escuchar Now listen to Zach doing the role play task. **In English**, note down what he says for the first three points on the card.

B – Picture-based task

Topic: Who am I?

Mira la foto y prepara las respuestas a los siguientes puntos:

- la descripción de la foto
- quiénes son más importantes, tus amigos o tus padres
- lo que hiciste la última vez que celebraste algo con tu familia
- tus planes con tus amigos para la semana que viene
- (!)

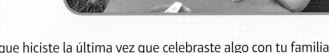

 1 escuchar Look at the photo and read the task. Then listen to Anya's response to the first bullet point.

1 Why does she think this is a family occasion?

2 Which person does she describe in detail, and why?

3 What makes her think the people in the photo are happy?

4 Can you write down the Spanish for the following phrases: 'of different ages', 'birthday cake', 'presents'?

2 **escuchar**

Listen to Anya's response to the second bullet point. Note down the Spanish for the following expressions as you hear them.

it depends   one advantage of… is   whereas

however   although   as / given that

> Questions like this give you the opportunity to justify and qualify your opinions. Give more sophisticated answers by using **aunque** and **mientras que** to include opposing viewpoints within the same sentence.

3 **escuchar**

Listen to and read Anya's response to the third bullet point.

1 Write down the missing word(s) for each gap.
2 Look at the Answer Booster on page 68. Note down <u>six</u> examples of language which Anya uses to give a strong answer.

La última vez que **1** ———— algo con mi familia fue el Día del Padre. Mis padres, mi hermano y yo fuimos en tren a Londres **2** ———— ir a un concierto. Es el tipo de actividad que más **3** ———— gusta a mi padre porque le chifla la música clásica, pero a mí no me interesa nada, así que **4** ———— un poco monótono. Sin embargo, después fuimos a cenar a un restaurante mexicano, donde **5** ———— fajitas y tacos. ¡Qué rico!

 4 **escuchar**

Listen to Anya's response to the fourth bullet point. She uses <u>three</u> time frames. Note down <u>two</u> details for each.

- How things are for her at the moment.
- How she spent last weekend.
- Her plans for this weekend.

> In Anya's answer, she uses the following phrases:
> - *para divertirme un poco*
> - *vamos a poner una tienda de campaña*
>
> What do they mean? How can you work out their meaning?

 5 **escuchar**

Prepare your own answers to the first <u>four</u> bullet points. Try to predict which unexpected question you might be asked. Then listen and take part in the full picture-based task with the teacher.

C – General conversation

 1 **escuchar**

Listen to Jennifer introducing her chosen topic. Read the statements and correct the mistakes.

a Ana y Jennifer se conocen desde hace siete años.
b Se llevan superbién, pero no tienen mucho en común.
c Ana y Jennifer se parecen físicamente.
d A Ana y a Jennifer les gusta llevar ropa de diferentes estilos.
e Ana es una buena amiga, pero a veces no le dice la verdad a Jennifer.

2 **escuchar**

The teacher asks Jennifer, *'¿Qué aplicaciones usas para estar en contacto con tus amigos y con tu familia?'* Look at the Answer Booster on page 68. Note down <u>six</u> examples of language which Jennifer uses to give a strong answer.

3 **escuchar**

Listen to Jennifer's response to the second question, *'¿Estás enganchada a tu móvil?'* Note down <u>three</u> examples of how Jennifer uses different persons of the verb.

> Take every opportunity to refer to others, even when the question asks about you. This is an excellent way to develop your answer.

 4 **hablar**

Prepare answers to Module 3 questions 1–6 on page 198. Then practise with your partner.

Answer booster	Aiming for a solid answer	Aiming higher	Aiming for the top
Verbs	**Different time frames**: past, present, near future	**Different persons** of the verb **Verbs with an infinitive**: *poder, querer, tener que*	**Unusual verbs**: *apoyar, escoger, conocerse, llevarse, divertirse* **Mixed tenses**: present tense and present continuous
Opinions and reasons	**Verbs of opinion**: *me interesa(n), me chifla(n), me fastidia(n), pienso que…* **Reasons**: *porque…* **Adjectives**: *simpático, monótono*	**Comparatives**: *es más paciente que, es más barato que…* **Exclamations**: *¡Qué pesado! ¡Qué rico!*	**Opinions**: *creo que, lo que más/ menos me gusta…* **Reasons**: *por lo tanto, así que* **Comparatives/Superlatives**: *no es tan… como…, la persona más importante…*
Connectives	*y, pero, también*	*además, sin embargo, aparte de eso*	**Balancing an argument**: *depende, una ventaja…, otra ventaja…, una desventaja…, aunque, mientras que…*
Other features	**Qualifiers**: *muy, un poco, bastante* **Sequencers**: *primero, después* **Other time phrases**: *la última vez que…, a menudo, siempre*	**Sentences with *cuando, donde, si***: *fuimos a…, donde…* ***Desde hace*** **Negatives**: *nunca, no… ni… ni…* ***Para* + infinitive**: *para ir a un concierto*	**Object pronouns**: *me/te/lo/la/los/las* **Interesting phrases**: *una pérdida de tiempo, una relación amor-odio*

A – Extended writing task

1 Look at the task and answer the questions.
- What **type** of text are you asked to write?
- What is the **purpose** of the text?
- Who is the intended **audience**?

2 Read Martyn's answer on page 69. What do the phrases in **bold** mean?

3 Look at the Answer Booster. Note down <u>eight</u> examples of language which Martyn uses to write a strong answer.

4 Look at the plan of Martyn's answer. Correct the <u>nine</u> mistakes.

5 Prepare your own answer to the task.
- Look at the Answer Booster and Martyn's plan for ideas.
- Write a detailed plan. Organise your answer in paragraphs.
- Write your answer and carefully check what you have written.

La tecnología

Usted es un(a) fanático/a de la tecnología.

Escriba usted un artículo para informar a los lectores de una revista española sobre la importancia de la tecnología.

Debe incluir los puntos siguientes:
- cómo usa su móvil todos los días
- cómo usó las redes sociales la semana pasada
- un pequeño inconveniente de la tecnología
- cómo va a usar la tecnología en el instituto la semana que viene.

Justifique sus ideas y sus opiniones.

Escriba aproximadamente 130–150 palabras **en español**.

Paragraph 1
- For searching for and downloading music
- Useful when waiting in school

Paragraph 2
- Not really for passing time/communication
- Last week used for sharing photos for a school project

Paragraph 3
- Major problem – depends on electricity
- Power cut causes waste of money
- Reading online tires your brain

Paragraph 4
- Brings the world into the home
- Allows you to personalise learning
- Next week going to make a film

Me mola la tecnología y soy un fanático de mi móvil, sobre todo porque **me ayuda a organizar** y a descargar música. Lo uso todos los días para escuchar música, y es muy práctico cuando **estoy haciendo el vago en casa** o esperando el autobús por la mañana. **Nunca me aburro** si tengo música. Además, lo uso para mandar mensajes a mis amigos y a mi familia.

Sin embargo, las redes sociales no son solo útiles **para pasar los ratos libres**, ni para contactar con la familia y los amigos. La semana pasada usé Facebook para buscar y compartir información con mis amigos para un proyecto de historia, así que también **sirven para** ayudarte con los deberes.

Martyn

Un pequeño inconveniente de la tecnología es que depende de la energía eléctrica. Un corte de energía puede resultar en **una pérdida de tiempo**. Además, mi profesor de historia, que **tiene una relación amor-odio con la tecnología**, dice que leer en pantalla* es malo porque cansa la vista.

En mi opinión, **no es posible imaginarse la vida** en el insti sin Internet. La tecnología **lleva el mundo al aula** y permite **personalizar el aprendizaje**. La semana que viene vamos a crear nuestra propia página web. ¡Viva la tecnología!

* la pantalla = screen

B – Translation

1 leer **Read the English text and Emily's translation of it. Correct the <u>five</u> mistakes in the Spanish translation.**

My mum works in Germany, so we talk via Skype during the week. We get on really well because she is fun and she always supports me. My best friend is from Spain. I met her when we did an exchange. I want to visit her in the holidays, but I can't go now because I have to study for my exams.

Mi madre trabaja en Austria, así que hablamos por Skype durante el fin de semana. Nos llevamos bastante bien porque es divertida y siempre me ayuda. Mi mejor amiga es de España. La conocí cuando hicimos un examen. Quiero visitarla en las vacaciones, pero no puedo ir ahora porque tengo que estudiar para mis exámenes.

> ⭐ Translations will always include high-frequency language that is not specific to any one topic. For example, time expressions such as 'during the week', 'in the holidays' and 'now'. Make sure you keep a list of this language and revisit it often.

2 escribir **Translate the following passage into Spanish.**

My sister, Tia, and I are quite different. She is talkative and can be annoying, but I get on well with her because we love technology. We are always looking for new apps for editing photos or sending messages. Last year I made an app and won a competition, and this year Tia is going to take part in the competition too.

> ⭐ Always check your Spanish adjectives carefully, as they change their form to match gender and number. Think about how you will spell the Spanish words for 'different', 'talkative' and 'new'.

¿Qué aplicaciones usas?

Uso … para…
  ver mis series favoritas
  organizar las salidas con mis amigos
  controlar mi actividad física /
  las calorías
  contactar con mi familia
  chatear con mis amigos
La tengo desde hace … meses.
Es una aplicación buena para…
  buscar y descargar música
  pasar el tiempo / el rato
  sacar / editar / personalizar fotos
  compartir / subir fotos
  estar en contacto
  conocer a nueva gente
  subir y ver vídeos
  chatear y mandar mensajes
Es / No es…

What apps do you use?

I use … (in order) to…
  watch my favourite series
  organise to go out with my friends
  monitor my physical activity / my
    calorie intake
  get in touch with my family
  chat with my friends
I've had it for … months
It's a good app for…
  looking for and downloading music
  passing the time
  taking / editing / personalising photos
  sharing / uploading photos
  keeping in touch
  meeting new people
  uploading and watching videos
  chatting and sending messages
It is / It isn't…

una red social — a social network
amplio/a — extensive
cómodo/a — convenient
divertido/a — fun
necesario/a — necessary
peligroso/a — dangerous
práctico/a — practical
rápido/a — quick
fácil de usar — easy to use
popular — popular
útil — useful
gratis — free
un canal de comunicación — a channel / means of communication
una pérdida de tiempo — a waste of time
Soy / Es adicto/a a… — I am / He/She is addicted to…
Estoy / Está enganchado/a a… — I am / He/She is hooked on…
Lo único malo es que… — The only bad thing is that …
  te engancha — it gets you hooked

¿Qué estás haciendo?

Estoy…
  actualizando mi página de Facebook
  editando mis fotos
Estás / Está / Están…
  escuchando música
  esperando a (David)
  descansando
  pensando en salir
  preparando algo para merendar
  repasando para un examen
  tomando el sol
  haciendo footing
  haciendo el vago
  leyendo
  viendo una peli
  escribiendo
¿Quieres salir conmigo?
No puedo porque…

What are you doing?

I am…
  updating my Facebook page
  editing my photos
You are / He/She is / They are…
  listening to music
  waiting for (David)
  relaxing
  thinking about going out
  preparing something for tea
  revising for an exam
  sunbathing
  jogging
  lazing about
  reading
  watching a film
  writing
Do you want to go out with me?
I can't because…

está lloviendo — it's raining
tengo que… — I have to…
  salir — go out
  visitar a (mi abuela) — visit (my grandmother)
  cuidar a (mi hermano) — look after (my brother)
  hacer los deberes — do homework
quiero… — I want to…
  subir mis fotos a… — upload my photos to…
  quedarme en casa — stay at home
¡Qué rollo! — What a pain!
¿A qué hora quedamos? — What time shall we meet?
¿Dónde quedamos? — Where shall we meet?
en la Plaza Mayor — in the main square
debajo de — underneath
detrás de — behind
delante de — in front of
enfrente de — opposite
al lado de — next to

¿Qué te gusta leer?

los blogs
los tebeos / los cómics
los periódicos
las revistas
las poesías

What do you like reading?

blogs
comics
newspapers
magazines
poems

las novelas de ciencia ficción — science fiction novels
las novelas de amor — romantic novels
las historias de vampiros — vampire stories
las biografías — biographies

¿Con qué frecuencia lees?

cada día / todos los días
a menudo
generalmente
de vez en cuando

How often do you read?

every day
often
generally
from time to time

una vez a la semana — once a week
dos veces al mes — twice a month
una vez al año — once a year
nunca — never

¿Qué es mejor, leer en papel o en la red?

Leer en formato digital…
  protege el planeta
  no malgasta papel
  cansa la vista
  depende de la energía eléctrica
  te permite llevar contigo miles
    de libros
  cuesta mucho menos
  fastidia porque no hay
    numeración de páginas
Los libros electrónicos / Los e-books…
  son fáciles de transportar
  son más ecológicos / baratos

What is better, reading paper books or online?

Reading in digital format…
  protects the planet
  doesn't waste paper
  tires your eyes
  relies on electricity
  allows you to take thousands of books
    with you
  costs a lot less
  is annoying because there is no
    page numbering
Electronic books / E-books…
  are easy to transport
  are more environmentally-friendly /
    cheaper

no ocupan espacio — don't take up space
Una desventaja es… — One disadvantage is…
  el uso de batería — the battery use
Me gusta / prefiero… — I like / I prefer…
  tocar las páginas — to touch the pages
  pasar las páginas a mano — to turn the pages by hand
  escribir anotaciones — to write notes
  leer horas y horas — to read for hours and hours
un ratón de biblioteca — a bookworm
un fan del manga — a manga fan
un libro tradicional — a traditional book
un libro de verdad — a real book

La familia / Family

el padre / la madre	father / mother	el primo / la prima	male cousin / female cousin
el padrastro / la madrastra	step-father / step-mother	el sobrino / la sobrina	nephew / niece
el hermano / la hermana	brother / sister	el marido / la mujer	husband / wife
el hermanastro / la hermanastra	step-brother / step-sister	el hijo / la hija	son / daughter
el abuelo / la abuela	grandfather / grandmother	el nieto / la nieta	grandson / granddaughter
el bisabuelo / la bisabuela	great grandfather / great grandmother	mayor / menor	older / younger
el tío / la tía	uncle / aunt		

¿Cómo es? / What is he/she like?

Tiene los ojos… — He/She has … eyes
  azules / verdes / marrones / grises — blue / green / brown / grey
  grandes / pequeños / brillantes — big / small / bright
Tiene el pelo… — He/She has… hair
  moreno / rubio / castaño / rojo — dark brown / blond / mid-brown / red
  corto / largo — short / long
  rizado / liso / ondulado — curly / straight / wavy
  fino / de punta — fine / spiky
Tiene… — He/She has…
  la piel blanca / morena — fair / dark skin
  la cara redonda / alargada — a round / oval face
  los dientes prominentes — big teeth
  pecas — freckles
Lleva… — He/She wears / has…
  gafas — glasses
  barba — a beard

bigote — a moustache
Es… — He/She is…
  alto/a / bajo/a — tall / short
  delgado/a / gordito/a / gordo/a — slim / chubby / fat
  calvo/a — bald
  moreno/a — dark-haired
  rubio/a — fair-haired
  castaño/a — brown-haired
  pelirrojo/a — a redhead
  español / española — Spanish
  inglés / inglesa — English
  peruano / peruana — Peruvian
Mide 1,60. — He/She is 1m60 tall.
No es ni alto ni bajo. — He/She is neither tall nor short.
(No) Nos parecemos físicamente. — We (don't) look like each other.

¿Cómo es de carácter? / What is he/she like as a person?

Como persona, es… — As a person, he/she is…
  optimista / pesimista — optimistic / pessimistic
  simpático/a / antipático/a — nice / nasty
  trabajador(a) / perezoso/a — hard-working / lazy
  generoso/a / tacaño/a — generous / mean
  hablador(a) / callado/a — chatty / quiet
  divertido/a / gracioso/a / serio/a — fun / funny / serious
  fiel / infiel — loyal / disloyal
  feliz / triste — happy / sad
  ordenado/a / caótico/a — tidy / chaotic

enérgico/a / animado/a / tranquilo/a — energetic / lively / calm
pensativo/a — thoughtful
comprensivo/a — understanding
honesto/a — honest
alegre — cheerful
molesto/a — annoying
ambicioso/a — ambitious
egoísta — selfish
Está feliz / triste. — He/She is happy / sad.

¿Te llevas bien con tu familia? / Do you get on well with your family?

(No) Me llevo bien con…porque… — I (don't) get on well with… because…
  me apoya — he/she supports me
  me acepta como soy — he/she accepts me as I am
  nunca me critica — he/she never criticises me
  tenemos mucho en común — we have a lot in common

Me divierto con… — I have a good time with…
Me peleo con… — I argue with…
Nos llevamos superbién. — We get on really well.
Nos llevamos como el perro y el gato. — We fight like cat and dog.
Nos divertimos siempre. — We always have a good time.

¿Cómo es un buen amigo / una buena amiga? / What is a good friend like?

Un buen amigo es alguien que… — A good friend is someone who…
  te apoya — supports you
  te escucha — listens to you
  te conoce bien — knows you well
  te acepta como eres — accepts you as you are
  te quiere mucho — likes / loves you a lot
  te da consejos — gives you advice
  te hace reír — makes you laugh
  no te critica — doesn't criticise you
  nunca te juzga — never judges you

Conocí a mi mejor amigo/a… — I met my best friend…
Nos conocimos — We met / got to know each other
Nos hicimos amigos — We became friends
Nos hicimos novios — We started going out
convivimos — we lived together
nos casamos — we got married
Es el amor de mi vida. — He/She is the love of my life.
Tenemos … en común. — We have … in common.
  nos gustan (las mismas cosas) — we like (the same things)
  nos encantan (las películas) — we love (films)

4 Intereses e influencias
Punto de partida 1

- *Talking about free-time activities*
- *Using stem-changing verbs*

1 escuchar **Escucha y lee. Rellena los espacios en blanco.**

Alex, 16

¿Qué haces en tus ratos libres?

Tengo **1** ———— pasatiempos. Después del insti toco la **2** ———— y también juego al futbolín y a los **3** ————. Los fines de semana normalmente **4** ———— con mis amigos. A veces vamos al polideportivo, donde **5** ———— al squash y montamos en **6** ————.

El problema es que no tengo **7** ———— dinero. Mis padres me dan **8** ———— euros a la semana, pero gasto mi paga en saldo para el **9** ————. De vez en cuando compro **10** ———— también.

quedar con	*to meet up with*
gastar	*to spend (money)*

2 hablar **Con tu compañero/a, haz un diálogo.**

- *¿Qué haces después del insti?*
- *¿Adónde vas los fines de semana?*
- *¿Tus padres te dan dinero? ¿Cuánto?*
- *¿Qué haces con la paga?*

Después del insti Los fines de semana Cuando tengo tiempo,	voy de compras toco la flauta / trompeta monto en bici / monopatín juego al billar / futbolín
Mis padres me dan… Mi madre/padre me da…	a la semana al mes
Gasto mi paga en También compro	saldo para el móvil ropa, joyas y maquillaje zapatillas de marca videojuegos y revistas

3 escribir **Escribe un texto. Usa el texto del ejercicio 1 como modelo.**

Say:
- what you do in your free time, and when
- how much pocket money you receive
- what you spend it on

Use:
- verbs in the 'I' form and the 'we' form
- connectives and adverbs of frequency

G The verb jugar　　　　　　　　　〉 *Page 208*

Jugar is a stem-changing verb.

	jug**ar** (to play)
(yo)	j**ue**go
(tú)	j**ue**gas
(él/ella/usted)	j**ue**ga
(nosotros/as)	jugamos
(vosotros/as)	jugáis
(ellos/ellas/ustedes)	j**ue**gan

4 leer **Lee el texto. Escribe un resumen en inglés.**

Los padres españoles, entre los más generosos

Según los resultados de una encuesta, los padres españoles son de los más generosos de Europa.
- Los españoles son los terceros de Europa en dar más cantidad de paga a sus hijos, después de los italianos y franceses.
- El 41% de los niños españoles de entre 5 y 15 años reciben de cinco a diez euros por semana.
- Un 13,8% de niños mayores de 15 años reciben más de cincuenta euros a la semana.

5 leer · **Empareja el deporte con el dibujo correcto.**

Ejemplo: **1** *e*

Juego / Jugué al…
1 baloncesto
2 fútbol
3 rugby
4 bádminton
5 ping-pong
6 hockey

Hago / Hice…
7 gimnasia
8 atletismo
9 equitación
10 natación
11 ciclismo
12 remo

6 escuchar · **Escucha y escribe la letra del deporte que mencionan <u>en el pasado</u>. ¡Ojo! Cada persona menciona <u>dos</u> o <u>tres</u> deportes. (1–6)**

Ejemplo: **1** *g*

7 leer · **Lee y apunta <u>ocho</u> detalles en inglés.**

Ejemplo: She's addicted to sport.

Para mí, el deporte es como una droga – ¡estoy enganchada! Me chifla hacer judo y también juego al pádel desde hace dos años. Tenemos un partido todas las semanas. Sin embargo, nunca juego al golf, puesto que es un poco aburrido.

En septiembre participé en un triatlón Ironman en Mallorca. Primero nadé casi dos kilómetros en el mar. ¡Qué frío! Luego recorrí 90 kilómetros en bici y finalmente corrí más de 21 kilómetros por la playa de Alcúdia. ¡Fue alucinante! No gané, pero lo importante es participar, ¿no?

Sara, 32

recorrer	*to cover (distance)*
correr	*to run*

Zona Cultura

El pádel es muy popular en España y Latinoamérica. Este deporte de raqueta, que fue inventado en México, se juega con una pala especial y una pelota.

Cognates and near-cognates look like English words, but usually follow Spanish pronunciation rules. Practise saying these words:

críquet   tenis   rugby
fútbol   gimnasia   voleibol

However, the words for some sports break these rules.
hockey   judo

8 hablar · **Con tu compañero/a, habla del deporte.**

Say:

- Which sports you do / play
- Which sports you never do
- Which activity you did recently
- How it went

Hago / Juego… ya que es sano / emocionante / fácil… También…
Sin embargo, … porque es…
(En febrero) participé / hice / jugué…
(No)…

1 escuchar

Escucha. Copia y completa la tabla in inglés. (1–5)

¿Eres teleadicto/a?

Sí, soy teleadicto/a.

No, no soy teleadicto/a.

	telly addict?	likes	dislikes
1	✓	h – informative	…

a un concurso

b un programa de deportes

c un reality

d un documental

e un culebrón / una telenovela

f una comedia

g una serie policíaca

h el telediario / las noticias

2 hablar

Con tu compañero/a, haz diálogos.

- ¿Eres teleadicto/a?
- ¿Qué tipo de programas te gustan? ¿Por qué?
- ¿Cuál es tu programa favorito?
- ¿Qué tipo de programas no te gustan? ¿Por qué?

Es Son…	muy bastante más… que… menos… que…	aburrido/**a**/**os**/**as** adictivo/**a**/**os**/**as** divertido/**a**/**os**/**as** entretenido/**a**/**os**/**as** tonto/**a**/**os**/**as** informativo/**a**/**os**/**as** malo/**a**/**os**/**as** emocionant**e**(**s**) interesant**e**(**s**)

3 escribir

Escribe una entrada para el foro.

¿Eres teleadicto/a?

- En mi opinión, (no) soy…
- Veo la tele…
- Me gusta(n)… porque…
- Creo que los/las… son más/menos… que…
- Mi programa favorito es…
- No me gusta(n)… porque…

When giving your opinion about a type of programme, remember to use the definite article and the plural form of the noun:

un concurso ⟶ Me chiflan **los** concursos.
una telenovela ⟶ No me gusta ver **las** telenovelas.

El telediario is always singular in Spanish.

4 escuchar

Escucha y apunta la nacionalidad correcta en español. (1–8)

Ejemplo: **1** *italiana*

Premios Festival de Izarra

1 Mejor película de amor.

2 Mejor película de terror.

3 Mejor película de acción / aventuras.

4 Mejor película de animación.

5 Mejor película de ciencia ficción.

6 Mejor película de fantasía.

7 Mejor actor.

8 Mejor director.

los **goya**

Zona Cultura

Cada año los Premios Goya celebran lo mejor del cine español. Los ganadores de los Goya incluyen al actor Javier Bardem y la actriz Penélope Cruz, que se casaron en 2010, y a los directores Guillermo del Toro y Pedro Almodóvar.

G *Adjectives of nationality* ❯ *Page* **224**

Adjectives of nationality do not start with a capital letter in Spanish.

Like all adjectives, they have to agree with the noun.

Those ending in a **vowel** usually follow the regular pattern:

| italian**o** | italian**a** | italian**os** | Italian**as** |

Adjectives of nationality ending in a **consonant** follow an irregular pattern (the same pattern as adjectives ending in **–or**, like *hablador*).

ending in **–l**	español	español**a**	español**es**	español**as**
ending in **–n**	alemán	aleman**a**	aleman**es**	aleman**as**
ending in **–s**	inglés	ingles**a**	ingles**es**	ingles**as**

americano	alemán
argentino	danés
británico	español
chino	francés
griego	holandés
italiano	inglés
mexicano	irlandés
sueco	japonés

5 leer

Lee el texto y completa las frases.

Soy una fanática de las películas extranjeras y mi actor favorito es el mexicano Gael García Bernal. ¡Qué guapo es! También es muy dinámico e idealista. Me chiflan las pelis de Escandinavia, sobre todo los misterios daneses y suecos. Sin embargo, no me gustan las películas de dibujos animados japoneses porque son un poco infantiles.

Voy al cine todos los sábados por la noche, y la semana pasada vi una película de Bollywood con mi novio, que es chino. Me gustó, pero era un poco larga. Después fuimos a un restaurante italiano. ¡Fue una noche muy cosmopolita!

Paula

extranjero/a   *foreign*

1 Paula is a fan of ▬▬.

2 She thinks that Gael García Bernal is ▬▬.

3 Her favourite Scandinavian films are ▬▬.

4 She doesn't like ▬▬ because ▬▬.

5 Last week she ▬▬.

6 She mentions ▬▬ different nationalities.

6 escribir

Escribe un texto sobre el cine. Usa el texto del ejercicio 5 como modelo.

Give details about:

- types of films you like/don't like, and why.
- how often you go to the cinema
- a recent trip to the cinema
- your opinion of the film you saw.

- Talking about what you usually do
- Using soler + infinitive
- Identifying correct statements about a text

1 **escuchar**

Lee el artículo. Luego escucha y apunta los detalles para cada persona en español. (1–6)

- su nombre
- el número de la actividad
- ¿con qué frecuencia?
- ¿cuándo?

> los (lunes)
> por la mañana / tarde / noche
> después del insti
> a la hora de comer
> mientras desayuno / como

Los pasatiempos de los jóvenes españoles

Según una encuesta del Instituto de la Juventud, en España los jóvenes suelen tener una media de 32,6 horas de tiempo libre a la semana.

Las diez actividades de ocio más populares son:

1 **usar el ordenador**
2 **salir con amigos**
3 **escuchar música**
4 **ver la tele**
5 **descansar**
6 **leer periódicos o revistas**
7 **escuchar la radio**
8 **leer libros**
9 **hacer deporte**
10 **ir al cine**

el ocio   leisure

G **soler + infinitive**   > *Page 208*

To say what you usually do or tend to do, you can use **soler** + infinitive.

> **Suelo** *salir con amigos.*
> I usually / I tend to go out with friends.

Soler is a stem-changing verb.

(yo)	**sue**lo
(tú)	**sue**les
(él/ella/usted)	**sue**le
(nosotros/as)	solemos
(vosotros/as)	soléis
(ellos/ellas/ustedes)	**sue**len

2 **hablar**

Con tu compañero/a, haz diálogos.

- ● *¿Cuándo sueles escuchar música?*
- ■ *Suelo escucharla por la noche.*
- ● *¿Con qué frecuencia haces deporte?*
- ■ *Lo hago…*

⭐ Remember to avoid repetition by using direct object pronouns: **lo/la/los/las**.
These usually come before the verb, but can be added to the end of an infinitive.

> *¿Cuando ves la tele?*
> **La** *veo por la noche.*
> but *Suelo ver**la** por la noche.*

3 **escuchar**

Escucha y apunta en inglés: (a) ¿qué actividades hacen? (b) ¿por qué? (1–5)

Ejemplo: **1** (a) *Plays the saxophone…*
            (b) *needs…, ….*

Es	divertido	informativo
	relajante	sano
Soy	creativo/a	sociable
	perezoso/a	activo/a
	adicto/a a…	
Me ayuda a	relajarme	
	olvidarme de todo	
Me hace	reír	
Me encanta	estar al aire libre	
Necesito	practicar…	
	salir / comunicarme (con otra gente)	
Mi pasión es	la lectura	el deporte
	la música	

4 **escribir**

Escribe un texto sobre tus pasatiempos.

- Mention four activities you do.
- Say how frequently / when you do them.
- Give reasons.

5 leer Lee el texto. Identifica las <u>cuatro</u> frases correctas.

Silvano, 15
Puerto Plata

En la República Dominicana hay una gran variedad de pasatiempos. Mi padre juega al dominó desde hace muchos años (es muy popular aquí) y recientemente participó en un torneo. ¡Ahora es el campeón de nuestra región! Mucha gente suele practicar deporte también, sobre todo el béisbol.

Sin embargo, a mí me interesa más la música. Mi madre adora a Juan Luis Guerra, un cantante muy conocido por la bachata y el merengue (dos estilos de música y baile tradicionales), pero yo suelo escuchar el R 'n' B. Mis hermanos y yo tenemos nuestra propia banda – yo toco la batería, José toca el teclado y Félix canta.

Soy fan de Bruno Mars. Su música es una mezcla de muchos estilos distintos y tiene una voz hermosa. Asistí a un concierto suyo cuando visitó Santo Domingo, nuestra capital, durante su gira mundial. El espectáculo fue increíble y cuando entró en el escenario, el público empezó a gritar y a aplaudir. Cantó todas mis canciones favoritas y fue una noche inolvidable.

MAR CARIBE

el merengue

Bruno Mars

1 Su padre es un buen jugador de dominó.
2 El béisbol no es muy popular.
3 Juan Luis Guerra toca un instrumento.
4 Silvano y su madre prefieren diferentes estilos de música.
5 Silvano tiene tres hermanos.
6 La música de Bruno Mars es muy variada.
7 Bruno Mars empezó su gira en la República Dominicana.
8 Los espectadores disfrutaron del concierto.
9 Silvano cantó mucho en el concierto.

> To identify the correct statements, look at each one and decide whether:
>
> 1 it gives information that doesn't quite match the text (not correct!)
>
> 2 it is talking about something which is simply not mentioned (not correct!)
>
> 3 it is true, though it may use different words from those in the text (correct!)

6 leer Lee el texto otra vez y busca el equivalente de las expresiones.

1 he took part in a tournament
2 a singer very well known for
3 our own band
4 I play the drums
5 he has a beautiful voice

6 I went to a concert of his
7 during his world tour
8 the show
9 when he came on stage

7 escribir Escribe un texto sobre los pasatiempos y la música en tu país.

Use both the present and the preterite tenses, and include language from exercise 5 to write about:

- Which hobbies are popular in your country
- What people in your family do in their free time
- What type of music you like
- A concert you have been to.

> Most types of music in Spanish are cognates or near-cognates. For example:
> *el soul, el rap, el funk, el dance, el hip-hop, el pop, el rock, el jazz, la música clásica, la música electrónica.*
> When talking about a concert you have been to, use a variety of preterite tense verbs to:
>
> - say what you did   *Saqué muchas fotos.* (I took lots of photos.)
> - talk about other people *El público cantó.* (The audience sang.)
> - give your opinion   *Fue inolvidable.* (It was unforgettable.)

- *Talking about sports*
- *Using the imperfect tense to say what you used to do*
- *Listening for different tenses*

1 Escucha y lee. Escribe el nombre correcto.

¿Qué dicen los alumnos de 4º de ESO de sus pasiones deportivas?

Cuando tenía diez años jugaba al balonmano, pero ya no juego. Ahora soy miembro de un club de natación y entrenamos todos los días. ¡Me flipa! También hago tiro con arco de vez en cuando.
Rocío

Cuando era más joven hacía gimnasia e iba a clases de equitación. Ya no hago equitación porque es caro, pero todavía hago gimnasia y soy miembro de un equipo. A veces voy de pesca con mi padre. ¡Es guay!
Diego

Soy muy deportista. Voy al gimnasio todos los días, juego al baloncesto, hago kárate... ¡Soy un fanático del deporte! Antes jugaba al fútbol y era aficionado del Athletic de Bilbao, pero ya no me interesa.
Joaquín

Cuando era más pequeña, iba a clases de judo, pero ahora prefiero deportes como la escalada y el parkour. ¡Soy adicta a la adrenalina! También soy miembro de un club de piragüismo, y en verano hago submarinismo.
Gloria

1 Hago dos deportes acuáticos.
2 Voy a la piscina a menudo.
3 Ya no practico artes marciales.
4 Me molan los deportes de riesgo.
5 ¡El deporte es mi vida!
6 Antes montaba a caballo.

> Use **ya no** to say that you **no longer** do something.
>
> **Ya no** juego al fútbol.
> I **no longer** play football.
>
> Use **todavía** to say that you **still** do something.
>
> **Todavía** hago judo. I **still** do judo.

2 Lee los textos otra vez. Apunta los deportes mencionados. ¿Presente o imperfecto?

Ejemplo: handball (imperfect), ...

3 Con tu compañero/a, haz diálogos.

- ¿Eres muy deportista?
- ¿Qué deportes hacías cuando eras más joven?
- ¿Qué deportes haces ahora?
- ¿Eres miembro de un club / un equipo?
- ¿Cuándo entrenas?
- ¿Eres aficionado/a de un equipo?

Cuando era más joven tenía (ocho) años	Ahora (no) Ya no Todavía	
(no) era	soy	deportista miembro de... aficionado/a de... un(a) fanático/a de...
jugaba	juego	al balonmano
hacía	hago	piragüismo
iba	voy	a clases de...

Ⓖ The imperfect tense ❯ *Page 214*

You have seen the **imperfect tense** for describing things in the past. It is also used for saying what you <u>used to</u> do.

***Jugaba** al baloncesto.* **He/She used to play** basketball.

	jug**ar** (to play)	hac**er** (to do/make)	viv**ir** (to live)
(yo)	jug**aba**	hac**ía**	viv**ía**
(tú)	jug**abas**	hac**ías**	viv**ías**
(él/ella/usted)	jug**aba**	hac**ía**	viv**ía**
(nosotros/as)	jug**ábamos**	hac**íamos**	viv**íamos**
(vosotros/as)	jug**abais**	hac**íais**	viv**íais**
(ellos/ellas/ustedes)	jug**aban**	hac**ían**	viv**ían**

Only three verbs are irregular in the imperfect. These are:

ser (to be) → ***era**, **eras**, etc.*

ir (to go) → ***iba**, **ibas**, etc.*

ver (to see / watch) → ***veía**, **veías**, etc.*

4 escuchar

Escucha. Copia y completa la tabla en inglés. (1–5)

	sport in past	details	sport now	details
1	basketball	3 times…		

> ⭐ Listen carefully to work out whether the sports are mentioned in the present or the imperfect.
>
> Remember that 'I' form regular verbs end in –aba or –ía in the imperfect.
>
> Also, listen out for time markers such as *antes*, *todavía*, *ahora*, etc.

5 escuchar

Lee el texto y escribe los verbos correctos. Luego escucha y comprueba tus respuestas.

Ejemplo: **1** *era*

Cuando **1** (**ser**) más joven, **2** (**hacer**) gimnasia dos veces a la semana. También **3** (**ir**) a clases de patinaje sobre hielo con mi hermana.

Me chifla la gimnasia y todavía la **4** (**hacer**) cuando tengo tiempo, pero ya no **5** (**patinar**). Ahora mi pasión es el fútbol y **6** (**jugar**) en un equipo de fútbol femenino. **7** (**Ser**) delantera y **8** (**soler**) entrenar cada domingo. Hace dos semanas **9** (**marcar**) mi primer gol de la temporada en un partido contra otro equipo de mi ciudad. ¡Qué ilusión!

Mi hermano y yo **10** (**ser**) hinchas del Barça y nuestro jugador preferido es el argentino Lionel Messi, el mayor goleador de la Liga de Campeones. ¡Es un crack! Messi **11** (**ganar**) el Balón de Oro por primera vez en 2009, aunque para mí, su punto culminante fue cuando **12** (**batir**) el récord de mayor cantidad de goles en un mismo año.

un(a) hincha   *a fan*

Begoña, 15

> ⭐ Take care to choose the correct **tense** and **person** of the verb.
>
> Use the **imperfect** tense for what you used to do.
>
> Use the **preterite** tense for completed actions in the past.
>
> Remember that some verbs have a spelling change in the 'I' form of the preterite (e.g. *marcar, jugar*).

6 escribir

Escribe un texto sobre el deporte. Usa el texto del ejercicio 5 como modelo.

Write about:
- Sports you used to do.
- Sports you do / don't do now.
- Whether you are a member of a club / team.
- Your favourite player / team.
- A highlight of their career.

Cuando era…
Todavía…, pero ya no… Ahora…
(No) soy…
Mi… preferido/a es…
Su punto culminante fue cuando (ganó / batió)…

7 leer

Lee el texto y tradúcelo al inglés.

Estrella del boxeo con orígenes humildes

Ganador de docenas de títulos mundiales, hoy es uno de los boxeadores más ricos del mundo. Pero la vida no era siempre así para Manny Pacquiao, que nació en Filipinas en 1978. Con seis hijos, sus padres eran muy pobres, y a la edad de 14 años Pacquiao decidió escaparse de casa. Fue a Manila, donde vivía en las calles y dormía en una caja de cartón. Vendía pan y donuts en la calle, y de esta manera ganaba bastante dinero para sobrevivir.

así / de esta manera   *like this / in this way*
la caja   *box*

- *Talking about what's trending*
- *Using the perfect tense*
- *Using words which have more than one meaning*

1 leer **Lee los tuits. Busca las expresiones en español.**

Juana @JMtopbajista
#temasdelmomento ¿**Has leído** la última novela de Ruiz Zafón? Ya **ha vendido** más de un millón de ejemplares y es fenomenal.

Aitor @AitorP-Getxo
#temasdelmomento En mi página de Facebook **he compartido** las fotos del cumpleaños de Joseba. También **he subido** un vídeo. ¡Fiesta brutal!

Daniela @DaniJsevilla
No he visto todavía la nueva peli de Jennifer Lawrence, pero mis padres me **han comprado** el CD de la banda sonora. ¡Me flipa! #temasdelmomento

Marina López @mariluzL
¿Ya **has oído** la nueva canción de Paloma Faith? **La he descargado** y creo que es preciosa. #temasdelmomento

Ignacio Torres @NachoTgamer
¿**Has jugado** al videojuego *Gladiador Valiente 3*? #temasdelmomento Yo **no lo he probado** todavía porque ¡mi hermano me **ha roto** la consola!

temas del momento	*trending topics*
la banda sonora	*sound track*

1 I have uploaded
2 I haven't tried it
3 (they) have bought
4 Have you read…?
5 I have downloaded it
6 (he) has broken
7 I haven't seen
8 Have you heard…?
9 I have shared
10 it has sold
11 Have you played…?

2 escuchar **Escucha. Copia y completa la tabla en inglés. (1–6)**

	have you…?	✓/✗	extra details
1	bought new edition of…	✗	has spent…

Listen out for five examples of the perfect tense with verbs that you didn't see in exercise 1. Can you spot them?

3 hablar **Con tu compañero/a, haz diálogos sobre:**

- los últimos videojuegos / libros / diseños de moda / programas
- las últimas películas / canciones / revistas / aplicaciones / noticias

● ¿Ya has (descargado / visto)…?
■ Sí, **ya** (lo/la) he (descargado / visto) y creo que es…
■ No, no (lo/la) he… **todavía** porque…

 When used with the perfect tense, **ya** and **todavía** have different meanings.

*¿**Ya** has visto la nueva peli?*	Have you **already** seen the new film?
*Sí, **ya** la he visto.*	Yes, I've **already** seen it.
*No, no la he visto **todavía**.*	No, I haven't seen it **yet**.

G **The perfect tense** > *Page 219*

This is used to talk about what you <u>have done</u>.

Use the present tense of the verb **haber** + **past participle**.

(yo)	**he**	
(tú)	**has**	escuch**ado**
(él/ella/usted)	**ha**	vend**ido**
(nosotros/as)	**hemos**	compart**ido**
(vosotros/as)	**habéis**	
(ellos/ellas/ustedes)	**han**	

To form the past participle, remove the **–ar**, **–er** or **–ir** from the infinitive and add:

–ado (–ar verbs)
–ido (–er/–ir verbs)

Some past participles are irregular:

escribir (to write) → **escrito**
poner (to put) → **puesto**
hacer (to do / make) → **hecho**
romper (to break) → **roto**
morir (to die) → **muerto**
ver (to see / watch) → **visto**

4 leer Lee la página web y las frases 1–6. Escribe C (cine), V (videojuegos) o T (televisión).

Estrenos de la semana

Cine

Esta semana se ha estrenado la nueva película de aventuras *Dina*, que ya ha ganado varios premios. **Cuenta la historia de** una chica rusa con poderes mágicos. **La mezcla de** comedia y misterio y la banda sonora muy original son aspectos positivos, pero el argumento es **débil** y los efectos especiales son **decepcionantes**.

Videojuegos

El nuevo título multijugador *Gladiador Valiente 3* acaba de **salir al mercado**. **Disponible** para diferentes plataformas, este juego de acción tiene gráficos **de alta calidad**, aunque también tiene una melodía irritante y los personajes principales son poco plausibles. Sin embargo, tiene un buen argumento, y las animaciones parecen muy naturales.

Televisión

Acaba de estrenarse **la nueva temporada** de la comedia *Big Bang Theory*, la serie americana que ha tenido mucho éxito en todo el mundo. **Sigue las vidas de** los siete **protagonistas**, con situaciones hilarantes, como siempre. Recomendamos que la veas **en versión original**.

estrenarse	to be released
el argumento	plot
tener éxito	to be successful

1 Buen aspecto visual.
2 Es muy popular en diferentes países.
3 No me gustan los personajes.
4 Combina el suspense con el humor.
5 Es mejor verla en inglés.
6 Banda sonora malísima.

> ⭐ Use the perfect tense to say what you <u>have done</u>. However, to say what you <u>have just done</u> use the present tense of **acabar de** + **infinitive**.
>
> | | | |
> |---|---|---|
> | | ***He visto*** un buen documental. | **I have seen** a good documentary. |
> | but | ***Acabo de ver*** un buen documental. | **I have just seen** a good documentary. |
>
> ***Acabar de*** is an example of a phrase which cannot be translated word for word.

5 leer Lee la página web otra vez. Escribe las palabras en **negrita** en inglés.

6 escuchar Escucha y apunta los detalles en inglés. (1–5)

Ejemplo: **1** *watched new soap – good plot, …*

- What have they just done?
- What is their opinion of it?

7 hablar Con tu compañero/a, habla de un videojuego, un programa o una película.

- *¿Qué acabas de hacer?*
- *¿Qué tipo de videojuego / programa / película es?*
- *¿De qué trata?*
- *¿Te gustó? ¿Por qué (no)?*

Acabo de ver / jugar a…	
Es un/una…	
Cuenta la historia de…	
Trata de …	
Combina el misterio / la comedia / la acción con…	

El argumento	es
La banda sonora	buen**o/a**, fuerte, débil, guapo
El protagonista	

Los personajes	son
Los gráficos	buen**os/as**, estupend**os/as**
Los efectos especiales	guap**os/as**, guay
Los actores	impresionantes
Las animaciones	interesantes
Las canciones	mal**os/as**, originales naturales, repetitiv**os/as**

- Discussing different types of entertainment
- Using **algunos / ciertos / otros / muchos / demasiados / todos**
- Adapting a model dialogue to fit different situations

1 leer Lee los anuncios y contesta a las preguntas en español.

Nuevo espectáculo de baile

La compañía de danza flamenca *Flamencomás* pone en escena su nuevo espectaculo *Alma Ajena* en el teatro Lope de Vega. Una experiencia auténtica de cante, toque y baile flamenco.

Horario: 19.45 y 22.15
(todos los días excepto los lunes)

Duración: 1 hora y media

Entradas: 40 € (bebida incluida)

1 ¿De qué tipo de baile es el espectáculo?
2 ¿Cuántas sesiones hay al día?
3 ¿Dónde tiene lugar el circo?
4 ¿Cuánto cuesta una entrada para niños?
5 ¿Cuándo termina el festival de cine de verano?
6 ¿Cuántas películas distintas ponen?

¡El Circo Mil Sueños ha vuelto!

El Circo Mil Sueños presenta *Viaje a Venús* en la plaza de toros de Santa María. En un espectáculo de dos horas, cincuenta acróbatas, ilusionistas, contorsionistas y bailarines nos llevan a otro planeta. Funciones a las 15.00 y 19.30.

Tarifas: 32 € (20 € menores de 18 años)

Cine de verano

Con la llegada del calor vuelve el festival de cine al aire libre. Disfruta de más de 140 películas de todos los géneros en una pantalla gigante. Algunos de los mejores estrenos del año, incluso *Star Wars Episodio VIII*. A diario a las 20.15 / 22.45 hasta el 12 de septiembre.

Entrada general – **7 €**
Carné de estudiante – **5 €**
Abono 10 sesiones – **60 €**

2 escuchar Escucha. Rellena los espacios en blanco. (1–2)

- ¿Qué vamos a hacer **a** ▬▬▬▬ ?
- ¿Tienes ganas de ir **b** ▬▬▬▬ ?
- Depende. ¿Qué ponen?
- **c** ▬▬▬▬ . Es **d** ▬▬▬▬ .
- ¿Cuánto cuesta?
- Son **e** ▬▬▬▬ euros.
- Vale. ¿A qué hora empieza?
- Empieza a las **f** ▬▬▬▬ y termina a las **g** ▬▬▬▬ .
- De acuerdo.

- Dos entradas para **h** ▬▬▬▬ , por favor.
- ▲ ¿Para qué sesión?
- Para la sesión de las **i** ▬▬▬▬ .
- ▲ Lo siento, no quedan entradas.
- Pues, para la sesión de las **j** ▬▬▬▬ .
- ▲ Muy bien.
- ¿Hay un descuento para estudiantes?
- ▲ Sí. ¿Tiene su carné de estudiante?
- Aquí tiene.

To say what you <u>are going to do</u>, remember to use **ir + infinitive** (the near future):

*¿Qué **vamos a hacer**?* — What **are we going to do**?
***Voy a ir** al cine.* — I'm going to go to the cinema.

To say what you <u>fancy / feel like doing</u>, use **tener ganas de + infinitive**:

***Tengo ganas de ver** la tele.* — I **fancy / feel like watching** TV.

esta tarde / noche mañana el (viernes)		
ir al	cine / teatro / circo	
ir a	un concierto / un festival / un espectáculo	
es	un musical una película / obra de…	

3 *hablar* Con tu compañero/a, inventa diálogos. Usa el ejercicio 2 como modelo. Habla de los anuncios del ejercicio 1 o inventa los detalles.

⭐ **¿Qué ponen?** means 'What's on?' when talking about cinema, etc.

To talk about a concert use **¿Quién canta / toca?** (Who's singing / playing?)

How would you change the dialogue to talk about a football match?

4 *leer* Lee las opiniones. ¿Quién habla? Escribe B (Berto) o Y (Yolanda).

Prefiero ver las pelis en casa.
Berto

Prefiero ir al cine.
Yolanda

a Las palomitas que venden están ricas.

b El ambiente es mejor con muchas personas.

c Es mejor porque no tienes que hacer cola.

d Hay demasiadas personas y los otros espectadores me molestan.

e Me encanta porque ponen tráilers para todas las nuevas pelis.

f No me gusta, dado que los asientos no son cómodos.

g La imagen es mejor en la gran pantalla.

h Las entradas son muy caras.

i Si vas al baño te pierdes una parte.

hacer cola *to queue*

5 *escuchar* Escucha. Copia y completa la tabla. (1–4)

en directo *live*
la corrida de toros *bull fight*

	prefers…	opinions from exercise 4	other points
1	*watching a band live*	b, …	*can buy…*

6 *escuchar* Escucha otra vez y mira la gramática. ¿Qué palabras menciona cada persona?

Ejemplo: **1** *muchos, …*

G **Useful adjectives** ❯ *Page 224*

These adjectives are useful in lots of different topics:
algunos/**as** (some)   **ciert**os/**as** (certain)
otros/**as** (other)   **much**os/**as** (many/lots of)
demasiados/**as** (too many)   **tod**os/**as** (all/every)

Todos/**as** is followed by **los/las**:
*Me gustan **todas las** películas.*   I like **all** films.

7 *escribir* Traduce el texto al español.

Look back at Unit 3.

I have just seen a new animated film and it was incredible. I tend to go to the cinema every week because I love the big screen. However, some cinemas show too many trailers. I like certain science fiction films because the special effects are brilliant, but others are stupid and the plot is boring.

Look back at Unit 1.

- *Talking about who inspires you*
- *Using a range of past tenses*
- *Talking about dates*

1 escuchar **Escucha y elige la respuesta correcta.(1–4)**

¿Crees que los famosos son buenos modelos a seguir?

1 La cantante Taylor Swift es un buen modelo a seguir porque…
  a tiene mucho talento.
  b tiene mucho éxito.
  c usa su fama para ayudar a otros.

2 El actor Ryan Gosling es un buen modelo a seguir porque…
  a apoya varias organizaciones benéficas.
  b trabaja en defensa de los animales.
  c recauda fondos para Amnistía Internacional.

3 La actriz Angelina Jolie es un buen modelo a seguir porque…
  a lucha contra la pobreza.
  b lucha contra la homofobia.
  c lucha por los derechos de los refugiados.

4 Muchos futbolistas son malos modelos a seguir porque…
  a se emborrachan.
  b se comportan mal en el campo de fútbol.
  c se meten en problemas con la policía.

2 leer **Has oído estas expresiones en el ejercicio 1. ¿Qué significan?**

a organizaciones que ayudan a las víctimas de desastres naturales
b apoya muchos proyectos de educación
c apoya varias campañas para mejorar las condiciones de vida

d hace mucho para combatir la injusticia en el mundo
e un buen modelo a seguir es alguien que ayuda a los demás
f los jóvenes imitan su comportamiento

3 escuchar **Empareja las fotos con los textos. ¿A quién se refiere el texto que sobra? Escucha y comprueba tus respuestas.**

1 Rigoberta Menchú

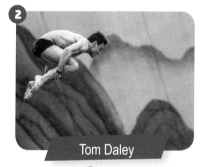

2 Tom Daley

3 Emma Watson

a Es un joven nadador que ha ganado varias medallas de oro. Además, ha hablado abiertamente de su sexualidad e inspira a muchos jóvenes.

b Tiene mucho talento como cantante. Ha creado la *Fundación Pies Descalzos* para ayudar a los niños pobres de Colombia.

c Lucha por la justicia social en Guatemala. Ha ganado el Premio Nobel de la Paz por su trabajo como activista.

d Lucha por los derechos de la mujer y es embajadora de buena voluntad de la ONU. Ha tenido mucho éxito como actriz.

un(a) embajador(a) de buena voluntad *a goodwill ambassador*

4 hablar **Con tu compañero/a, habla de los modelos a seguir.**

- *¿En qué consiste un buen modelo a seguir?*
- *Da un ejemplo de un buen modelo a seguir.*
- *¿Y un mal modelo a seguir?*

■ *Un buen modelo a seguir es alguien que…*
■ *En mi opinión… es un buen modelo a seguir porque…*
■ *Creo que… es un mal modelo a seguir…*

5 escuchar **Escucha. Apunta los detalles en inglés.**

¿A quién admiras?
Malala Yousafzai

- Qualities: <u>brave, ...</u>
- Fights for: _____
- Childhood: _____
- 2009: _____
- 2012: _____
- 2013: _____
- 2014: _____

> ⭐ When referring to a year in Spanish, say it as if it is a number. For example, 1995 is said as 'one thousand nine hundred and ninety-five'.
>
> To make it easier, break it down into its separate elements.
>
> **1995** mil   novecientos   noventa y cinco
> **2017** dos mil   diecisiete

valiente	*brave*

6 leer **Lee los textos. ¿Qué significan las palabras en negrita? Luego contesta a las preguntas en español para las <u>dos</u> personas.**

Mi inspiración es el tenista Rafa Nadal, dado que tiene todas las **cualidades** importantes de un buen deportista: talento, dedicación, perseverancia y resistencia física y mental. Nació en Mallorca en 1986 y de niño practicaba varios deportes. Sin embargo, su pasión era el tenis, y a los 15 años **empezó** su carrera profesional.

A pesar de todas las **lesiones** físicas que ha sufrido, Nadal ha batido varios récords, y fue el primer jugador en ganar nueve veces el mismo torneo de Grand Slam. También ha ganado más títulos que **cualquier** otro español, y en 2008 ganó una medalla de oro en los Juegos Olímpicos de Pekín.

Más que nada, admiro a Nadal porque es buena persona, y porque en 2007 estableció la *Fundación Rafa Nadal* para ayudar a los **niños desfavorecidos** en España y en la India.

Bea

Mi ídolo no es ni rico ni famoso, pero es una persona cariñosa, amable y muy fuerte. Y como todos los héroes anónimos, no ha ganado **ningún** premio. Es mi abuela, Conchita Jiménez.

De pequeña vivía en Canarias, donde conoció a mi abuelo cuando tenía diez años. Se casaron ocho años más tarde, pero con solo 25 años se quedó **viuda** con cuatro hijos pequeños cuando mi abuelo murió en un accidente marítimo.

Su vida no ha sido fácil, y ha sufrido varias **enfermedades** graves. Sin embargo, siempre ha superado sus problemas para ayudar a otras personas, y en los últimos 25 años **ha acogido temporalmente** a más de cien niños en casa.

Sobre todo, admiro a mi abuela porque siempre **sonríe** y nunca es egoísta. Solo piensa en los demás.

Enrique

a pesar de	*despite*
el héroe anónimo	*unsung hero*

1 ¿Qué cualidades tiene?
2 ¿Cómo era su infancia?
3 ¿Qué problemas ha tenido?

4 ¿Qué ha hecho a pesar de sus problemas?
5 ¿Qué premios o títulos ha ganado?
6 ¿Por qué es un buen modelo a seguir, sobre todo?

> **G Using past tenses** 〉 Pages **212, 214, 219**
>
> Use the **imperfect tense** for saying what someone <u>used to do</u>, or for describing things in the past.
> *Vivía* en Pakistán.   **He/She used to live** in Pakistan.
> No **era** justo.   **It wasn't** fair.
>
> Use the **preterite tense** for saying what they <u>did</u>.
> ***Ganó*** un premio.   **He/She won** a prize.
>
> Use the **perfect tense** for saying what they <u>have done</u>.
> ***Ha superado*** muchos problemas.   **He/She has overcome** lots of problems.

7 leer **Lee los textos otra vez. Busca <u>cuatro</u> ejemplos de cada tiempo verbal.**

- Imperfect
- Preterite
- Perfect

8 escribir **Escribe un texto sobre una persona que admiras. Contesta a las preguntas del ejercicio 6.**

1 leer **Lee la página web de unos decorados de cine* en España que están abiertos al público.**

Visita Fort Bravo, ¡más que un parque temático!

Fort Bravo / Texas Hollywood son los decorados de cine estilo western más grandes de Europa, que se encuentran situados en pleno desierto de Tabernas, Almería. Se construyeron a principios de los años sesenta para la filmación de las numerosas películas de Sergio Leone, los famosos *spaguetti-western*, y todavía filmamos películas, spots publicitarios y videoclips.

Abrimos desde las 9.00 hasta las 20.00. En su visita va a descubrir un auténtico poblado de madera del Viejo Oeste americano, un típico pueblo mexicano y un poblado indio. Puede disfrutar de un día inolvidable paseando por sus calles y viendo el espectáculo de cowboys con peleas de salón, asalto al banco y baile de cancán con trajes típicos. También hay alquiler de caballos y estudio fotográfico. Disponemos de Saloon-Bar, restaurante y tienda de recuerdos, y puede dormir en el Oeste en nuestras cabañas de madera rurales totalmente equipadas.

* los decorados de cine = film sets

Contesta a las preguntas en español. No tienes que escribir frases completas.

(a) ¿Dónde está Fort Bravo?
(b) ¿Cuándo empezó la producción de películas allí?
(c) ¿Qué tipo de películas produjo Sergio Leone?
(d) ¿Cuál es el horario para los visitantes?
(e) ¿Qué ropa llevan las bailarinas de cancán?
(f) ¿Qué tipo de alojamiento ofrece Fort Bravo?

> Start by working out what information you are asked to give. In your answers you should be able to 'lift' words from the text.

2 leer **Read the dialogue between Sara and her team mates.**

Sara y las Goleadoras: El último gol by Laura Gallego (abridged and adapted)

Me gusta el fútbol, pero creo que los estudios son más importantes —dijo Dasha.
—Yo prefiero el fútbol —suspiró Eva— pero mi padre no me deja salir de casa por las tardes porque dice que tengo que estudiar.
—Tienes que ser razonable, Eva —intervino Mónica. —A todas nos encantaría poder entrenar todos los días y jugar fenomenal en los *play-off*, pero hay que aceptar que no podemos hacerlo todo.
—Además —añadió Vicky— las jugadoras de los otros equipos también tienen exámenes, así que están en la misma situación que nosotras.
—No exactamente —murmuró Sara— porque las chicas de los otros equipos ya juegan mejor que nosotras, así que debemos entrenar más que ellas.
—Bueno, considerando que es nuestro primer año, lo hemos hecho muy bien —razonó Dasha.

Answer the following questions in English. You do not need to write full sentences.

(a) Why is Eva unhappy?
(b) Mónica gives a balanced view. What are the two sides to her argument?
(c) What is Vicky's opinion?
(d) According to Sara, why should they train more than the other teams?
(e) Why does Dasha think their team has done well?

> Written dialogues often include words like 'she said' or 'he added'. These may include *añadir* (to add), *gritar* (to shout), *suspirar* (to sigh), *decir* (to say), *intervenir* (to intervene), *murmurar* (to murmur) and *razonar* (to reason).

3 leer Translate the following passage into English.

Ver la tele es el pasatiempo favorito de mucha gente. A pesar de la reciente popularidad de los realitys, los españoles todavía prefieren los programas deportivos. Sin embargo, una excepción notable tiene que ser *La Voz*. Este concurso musical ha tenido un éxito enorme en todo el mundo y ha ganado muchos premios en otros países.

 1 escuchar You are listening to an interview with a Mexican singer.

Listen and answer the following questions **in English.**

(a) What has the singer recently organised?

(b) Who did she want to help? Give <u>two</u> details.

(c) What does performing live enable her to do? Give <u>one</u> detail.

(d) What is different about her new tour? Give <u>two</u> details.

2 escuchar You are listening to a programme in which Spanish teenagers are talking about who they admire. **What does Omar say?**

Listen and choose the correct word(s) for each phrase.

(a) Sam Simon died in 2015…
  A   during a fight.
  B   in a car crash.
  C   whilst appearing on TV.
  D   from an illness.

(b) In the United States, *The Simpsons* is…
  A   the funniest TV programme.
  B   the longest-running animated series.
  C   the oldest TV programme.
  D   the most popular comedy show.

(c) Omar admires Sam Simon most because of his…
  A   success.
  B   creativity.
  C   generosity.
  D   talent.

(d) Sam Simon set up a foundation to…
  A   give shelter to homeless dogs.
  B   cure sick dogs.
  C   train dogs to help deaf people.
  D   raise awareness of cruelty to dogs.

 3 escuchar You are listening to a news report about the popularity of cinema in Spain.

Listen and choose the <u>two</u> correct statements for each question.

(a) What comments are made about the cost of cinema tickets?
  A   Cinemas charge less in larger cities.
  B   Tickets are now cheaper in the middle of the week.
  C   The *Fiesta del Cine* offers tickets from as little as 3,00 €.
  D   The *Fiesta del Cine* takes place twice per year.
  E   Tickets are cheaper if you buy them online.

(b) What comments are made about cinema-going habits?
  A   Cinema is less popular in Spain than in most European countries.
  B   Spanish films always break box office records.
  C   Spain has more than 3900 cinema screens.
  D   Each year Spaniards spend eight billion euros on tickets.
  E   Spaniards buy more than 80 million tickets a year.

When listening to statistics, pay attention to words like *medio/a* (half), *más de* (more than), *menos de* (less than), *casi* (almost) and *unos* (about / some).

A – Role play

1 leer Look at the role play card and prepare what you are going to say.

Topic: Who am I?

Instructions to candidates:

You are at your house with your Spanish friend. You are planning to go to a concert. The teacher will play the role of your Spanish friend and will speak first.

You must address your Spanish friend as *tú*.

You will talk to the teacher using the five prompts below.
- where you see – **?** – you must ask a question.
- where you see – **!** – you must respond to something you have not prepared.

Task
Estás en tu casa con un/a amigo/a español/a. Estáis hablando de los planes para ir a un concierto.

1 Concierto – dónde

2 Cantante preferido/a – razón

3 !

4 ? Concierto – hora

5 ? Después del concierto – planes

> Don't be fooled if you see a question word. For this bullet point you have to answer a question, not ask one!

> Make sure you give both details.

> Start with an appropriate question word or phrase.

> Remember that this question will require you to answer in the **past tense**. What could you be asked in this particular context?

> You could ask 'What plans …?' or 'What are we …?'

2 escuchar Practise what you have prepared. Then, using your notes, listen and respond to the teacher.

3 escuchar Now listen to Megan doing the role play task. **In English**, note down what she says for the first three points on the card.

> ⭐ Listen carefully to the unknown question (!). If you don't understand, ask the teacher (in Spanish!) to repeat the question – *¿Puede(s) repetir, por favor?*
>
> For the other bullet points, don't get distracted by what the teacher says – stick to what you have prepared!

B – Picture-based task

Topic: Cultural life

Mira la foto y prepara las respuestas a los siguientes puntos:

- la descripción de la foto
- tu opinión de los deportistas como modelos a seguir
- la última vez que practicaste un deporte
- tus planes para probar otros deportes en el futuro
- (!)

1 escuchar **Look at the photo and read the task. Then listen to Ben's response to the first bullet point.**

  1 Which athlete is he describing?
  2 Note down the two present continuous verbs that he uses.
  3 What do you think the word *carrera* means in this context?

2 escuchar **Listen to and read Ben's response to the second bullet point.**

  1 Write down the missing word for each gap.
  2 Look at the Answer Booster on page 90. Note down six examples of language which Ben uses to give a strong answer.

En mi opinión, **1** ——— deportistas son buenos modelos a seguir, pero otros no. Por ejemplo, creo que el futbolista **2** ——— Cristiano Ronaldo es el mejor modelo a seguir porque es dinámico y muy trabajador. Es un **3** ——— rápido que no es ni egoísta ni agresivo. **4** ——— es arrogante. Ha jugado en equipos como el Sporting, el Manchester United y el Real Madrid, y ha batido muchos récords. Por ejemplo, en **5** ——— marcó sesenta y nueve goles. Sobre todo, admiro a Ronaldo **6** ——— que es muy generoso y siempre usa su fama para ayudar a otras personas. Por eso es mi inspiración.

3 escuchar **Listen to Ben's response to the third bullet point.**

  1 In English, note down six details that he gives.
  2 Can you work out the meaning of *estilo libre* and *mariposa* from the context?

> ⭐ Try to develop your answers as much as possible to ensure that the conversation lasts for between three and three and a half minutes.

4 escuchar **Listen to Ben's response to the fourth bullet point. In Spanish**, note down examples of how he justifies what he says.

5 escuchar **Prepare your own answers to the first four bullet points. Try to predict which unexpected question you might be asked. Then listen and take part in the full picture-based task with the teacher.**

C – General conversation

1 escuchar **Listen to Aisha introducing her chosen topic. In which order does she mention the following?**

  a what instrument she plays
  b what instrument she used to play
  c who her favourite singer is
  d what type of person she is
  e where she is going to go
  f what she has just done

2 escuchar **The teacher asks Aisha, *'¿Eres teleadicta?'* Listen to how Aisha develops her answer. What 'hidden questions' does she also answer?**

  Example: How often do you watch TV?

> ⭐ A good way of developing your answer is to think about what 'hidden questions' you could also respond to in order to give a full, well-developed answer.

3 escuchar **Listen to Aisha's response to the second question, *'¿Prefieres ver películas en casa o en el cine?'* Look at the Answer Booster on page 90. Note down six examples of language which Aisha uses to give a strong answer.**

4 hablar **Prepare your own answers to Module 4 questions 1–6 on page 198. Then practise with your partner.**

Answer booster	Aiming for a solid answer	Aiming higher	Aiming for the top
Verbs	**Different time frames**: past (preterite or imperfect), present, near future	**Different persons** of the verb **Verbs with an infinitive**: *tener ganas de, soler, acabar de*	**More than one tense to talk about the past** (preterite, imperfect and perfect)
Opinions and reasons	**Verbs of opinion**: *me chifla(n), me interesa(n)…* **Reasons**: *porque…*	**Exclamations**: *¡Qué guay!* **Comparatives**: *más… que…, menos… que…*	**Opinions**: *creo que, a mi modo de ver, en mi opinión* **Reasons**: *dado que, por eso, por lo tanto, así que, como* **Comparatives**: *tan… como…*
Connectives	*y, pero, también*	*sin embargo, por desgracia, por ejemplo, sobre todo*	*ya no, todavía* **Balancing an argument**: *aunque, por un lado… por otro lado…*
Other features	**Negatives**: *no, nunca* **Qualifiers**: *muy, un poco, bastante* **Adjectives**: *emocionante, original* **Time phrases**: *hace dos semanas*	**Sentences with *cuando, donde***: *Cuando tenía…* **Negatives**: *ni… ni…, tampoco…* ***para* + infinitive**: *para ayudar*	**Object pronouns**: *lo/la/los/las* **Specialist vocabulary**: *el / la guardameta, la campeona* **Interesting phrases**: *me ayuda a desconectar, la gran pantalla*

A – Extended writing task

1 leer **Look at the task and answer the questions.**

- What **type** of text are you asked to write?
- What is the **purpose** of the text?
- Who is the intended **audience**?

2 leer **Read Rahma's answer on page 91. What do the phrases in bold mean?**

3 leer **Look at the Answer Booster. Note down <u>eight</u> examples of language which Rahma uses to write a strong answer.**

4 leer **Look at the plan of Rahma's answer. Write down the missing word(s) for each gap.**

5 escribir **Prepare your own answer to the task.**

- Look at the Answer Booster and Rahma's plan for ideas.
- Write a detailed plan. Organise your answer in paragraphs.
- Write your answer and carefully check what you have written.

El deporte

Usted es un(a) fanático/a del deporte. Escriba un informe para una revista española para convencer a los lectores de la importancia del deporte.

Debe incluir los puntos siguientes:

- por qué el deporte es importante para usted
- qué deportes practicaba en el pasado
- por qué los deportistas son buenos modelos a seguir
- un evento deportivo al que va a asistir en el futuro.

Justifique sus ideas y sus opiniones.

Escriba aproximadamente 130–150 palabras **en español**.

Paragraph 1
- Why I **1** ⎯⎯⎯
- How long I've been **2** ⎯⎯⎯
- Which other **3** ⎯⎯⎯

Paragraph 2
- Sports I **4** ⎯⎯⎯
- Which position I **5** ⎯⎯⎯

Paragraph 3
- My opinion of **6** ⎯⎯⎯
- Why I admire **7** ⎯⎯⎯
- Her greatest **8** ⎯⎯⎯

Paragraph 4
- Which event **9** ⎯⎯⎯
- What I'm going to **10** ⎯⎯⎯

Soy muy deportista, dado que **soy una persona competitiva y enérgica**. El **deporte me ayuda a desconectar** y a olvidarme de todo, y además es muy sano. Soy miembro de un club de natación desde hace cinco años y acabamos de ganar el torneo regional. También me flipan los deportes de equipo, ya que **me permiten hacer nuevos amigos** y **mantenerme en forma**.

Cuando tenía doce años jugaba en el equipo de netball de mi instituto – un deporte popular en Inglaterra que es **parecido al baloncesto**. Jugaba **en posición de guardameta**. También hacía gimnasia, pero ya no la hago. En mi opinión, es menos interesante que la natación.

A mi modo de ver, los deportistas son buenos modelos a seguir porque tienen mucha disciplina y perseverancia. **Admiro a la campeona olímpica** Jessica Ennis-Hill puesto que tiene mucho talento y es ambiciosa. Ha ganado muchos títulos por eventos como **el salto de altura**, pero su punto culminante fue cuando ganó la medalla de oro en heptatlón en los Juegos Olímpicos de Londres.

Rahma

Me mola ver los partidos de fútbol **en directo** porque es muy emocionante cuando ves a todos los otros **hinchas**, y el sábado voy a ir a Old Trafford con mi padre. ¡Qué guay! Vamos a llevar nuestras **bufandas** y el ambiente va a ser fenomenal, ya que nuestro equipo va a jugar contra el Liverpool.

> ⭐ What extra information could you give for each bullet point to make your answer fuller and more interesting? For example, mention which sports you do now / have never done / would like to try. Remember that you must **convince** the readers of the importance of sport, so make sure you **justify** your answers.

B – Translation

1 escribir

Read the English text and Lauren's translation of it. Write down the missing word(s) for each gap.

I'm a music fanatic and I used to play the drums. I tend to listen to the radio while I do my homework, since it helps me to relax. Last week I went to a concert with my cousin, where we sang lots of our favourite songs. The atmosphere was incredible and I'm going to buy the DVD.

1 ———— un fanático de la música y **2** ———— la batería. **3** ———— escuchar la radio mientras **4** ———— mis deberes, dado que me **5** ———— a relajarme. La semana pasada **6** ———— a un concierto con mi primo, donde **7** ———— muchas de nuestras canciones favoritas. El ambiente **8** ———— increíble y **9** ———— el DVD.

2 escribir

Translate the following passage into Spanish.

I used to be a telly addict, but I no longer watch television because I don't have time. I tend to spend my pocket money on computer games and tomorrow I'm going to buy a new game. Yesterday I played with my brother, but I lost. He is addicted to the computer and uses it every day.

> ⭐ Examiners test your ability to use different types of verbs in different tenses and to talk about different people (for example, I, he/she, …). Think about which person and tense you need and take extra care with irregular verbs and those with a spelling change.

La paga / Pocket money

Mis padres me dan…	My parents give me…
Mi madre / padre me da…	My mum / dad gives me…
…euros a la semana / al mes	…euros a week / a month
Gasto mi paga en…	I spend my pocket money on…
También compro…	I also buy…
saldo para el móvil	credit for my phone
ropa / joyas / maquillaje	clothes / jewellery / make-up
zapatillas de marca	designer trainers
videojuegos / revistas	computer games / magazines

Mis ratos libres / My free time

las actividades de ocio	leisure activities
Tengo muchos pasatiempos.	I have lots of hobbies.
A la hora de comer…	At lunchtime…
Cuando tengo tiempo…	When I have time…
Después del insti…	After school…
Los fines de semana…	At weekends…
Mientras desayuno / como…	Whilst I have breakfast / lunch…
juego al billar / futbolín	I play billiards / table football
monto en bici / monopatín	I ride my bike / I skateboard
quedo con mis amigos	I meet up with friends
voy de compras	I go shopping
mi pasión es la música / la lectura	my passion is music / reading
Suelo…	I tend to / I usually …
descansar	rest
escuchar música / la radio	listen to music / the radio
hacer deporte	do sport
ir al cine	go to the cinema
leer libros / revistas / periódicos	read books / magazines / newspapers
salir con amigos	go out with friends
usar el ordenador	use the computer
ver la tele	watch TV
Es divertido / relajante / sano	It's fun / relaxing / healthy
Soy creativo/a / perezoso/a / sociable	I'm creative / lazy / sociable
Soy adicto/a a…	I'm addicted to…
me ayuda a relajarme	it helps me to relax
me ayuda a olvidarme de todo	it helps me to forget everything
me hace reír	it makes me laugh
necesito comunicarme / relacionarme con otra gente	I need to have contact with other people

La música / Music

Me gusta el soul / el rap / el dance / el hip-hop / el pop / el rock / el jazz / la música clásica / electrónica	I like soul / rap / dance / hip-hop / pop / rock / jazz / classical / electronic music
asistir a un concierto	to attend a concert
cantar (una canción)	to sing (a song)
tocar el teclado / el piano /	to play the keyboard / the piano /
la batería / la flauta / la guitarra / la trompeta	the drums / the flute / the guitar / the trumpet
mi cantante preferido/a es…	my favourite singer is…
un espectáculo	a show
una gira (mundial)	a (world) tour

El deporte / Sport

Soy / Era…	I am / I used to be…
(bastante / muy) deportista	(quite / very) sporty
miembro de un club / un equipo	a member of a club / a team
aficionado/a / hincha de…	a fan of…
un(a) fanático/a de…	a … fanatic
juego al…	I play…
jugué al…	I played…
jugaba al…	I used to play…
bádminton / baloncesto	badminton / basketball
béisbol / balonmano	baseball / handball
críquet / fútbol	cricket / football
hockey / ping-pong	hockey / table tennis
rugby / tenis / voleibol	rugby / tennis / volleyball
hago…	I do…
hice…	I did…
hacía…	I used to do…
baile / boxeo / ciclismo	dancing / boxing / cycling
deportes acuáticos	water sports
equitación / escalada	horseriding / climbing
gimnasia / judo	gymnastics / judo
kárate / natación	karate / swimming
patinaje sobre hielo	ice skating
piragüismo / remo	canoeing / rowing
submarinismo	diving
tiro con arco	archery
voy…	I go…
fui…	I went…
iba…	I used to go…
a clases de…	to … classes
de pesca	fishing
ya no (juego)…	(I) no longer (play)…
todavía (hago)…	(I) still (do)…
batir un récord	to break a record
correr	to run
entrenar	to train
jugar un partido contra…	to play a match against…
marcar un gol	to score a goal
montar a caballo	to go horseriding
participar en un torneo	to participate in a tournament
patinar	to skate
mi jugador(a) preferido/a es…	my favourite player is…
su punto culminante fue cuando…	the highlight (of his/her career) was when…
el campeón / la campeona	the champion
la temporada	the season

La tele / TV

(No) Soy teleadicto/a.	I'm (not) a TV addict.
Mi programa favorito es…	My favourite programme is…
un concurso	a game / quiz show
un programa de deportes	a sports programme
un reality	a reality TV show
un documental	a documentary
un culebrón / una telenovela	a soap
una comedia	a comedy
una serie policíaca	a crime series
el telediario / las noticias	the news
Me gustan las comedias.	I like comedies.
Es / Son…	It is / They are…
aburrido/a/os/as	boring
adictivo/a/os/as	addictive
divertido/a/os/as	fun
entretenido/a/os/as	entertaining
tonto/a/os/as	silly
informativo/a/os/as	informative
malo/a/os/as	bad
emocionante(s)	exciting
interesante(s)	interesting

Las películas — Films

un misterio	a mystery
una película de amor	a love film
una película de terror	a horror film
una película de acción	an action film
una película de aventuras	an adventure film
una película de animación	an animated film
una película de ciencia ficción	a sci-fi film
una película de fantasía	a fantasy film
una película extranjera	a foreign film

Nacionalidades — Nationalities

americano/a	American	alemán/alemana	German
argentino/a	Argentinian	danés/danesa	Danish
británico/a	British	español(a)	Spanish
chino/a	Chinese	francés/francesa	French
griego/a	Greek	holandés/holandesa	Dutch
italiano/a	Italian	inglés/inglesa	English
mexicano/a	Mexican	irlandés/irlandesa	Irish
sueco/a	Swedish	japonés/japonesa	Japanese

Temas del momento — Trending topics

he compartido…	I have shared…	cuenta la historia de…	it tells the story of…
he comprado…	I have bought…	trata de…	it's about…
he jugado…	I have played…	combina el misterio con la acción	it combines mystery with action
he leído…	I have read…	el argumento es fuerte / débil	the plot is strong / weak
he oído…	I have heard…	la banda sonora es buena / mala	the soundtrack is good / bad
he roto…	I have broken…	los actores…	the actors…
he subido…	I have uploaded…	los efectos especiales…	the special effects…
¿Has probado…?	Have you tried…?	los gráficos…	the graphics…
mi hermano ha descargado…	my brother has downloaded…	los personajes…	the characters…
se ha estrenado…	…has been released.	las animaciones…	the animations…
la nueva canción	the new song	las canciones…	the songs…
el último libro	the latest book	son guapos/as / guay	are good looking / cool
Ya lo/la/los/las he visto.	I have already seen it/them.	son estupendos/as / impresionantes	are great / impressive
No lo/la/los/las he visto todavía.	I haven't seen it/them yet.	son originales / repetitivos/as	are original / repetitive
acabo de ver / jugar a…	I have just seen / played…		

Ir al cine, al teatro, etc. — Going to the cinema, theatre, etc.

¿Qué vamos a hacer…	What are we going to do…	Es una película / obra de…	It's a … film / play
esta tarde?	this afternoon / evening?	¿A qué hora empieza / termina?	What time does it start / finish?
esta noche?	tonight?	Empieza / Termina a las…	It starts / finishes at…
mañana / el viernes?	tomorrow / on Friday?	Dos entradas para…, por favor.	Two tickets for …, please.
¿Tienes ganas de ir…	Do you fancy going…	para la sesión de las…	for the … showing / performance
a un concierto / un festival?	to a concert / a festival?	No quedan entradas.	There are no tickets left.
a un espectáculo de baile?	to a dance show?	¿Hay un descuento para estudiantes?	Is there a discount for students?
al cine / al teatro / al circo?	to the cinema / theatre / circus?	Aquí tiene mi carné de estudiante.	Here is my student card.
¿Qué ponen?	What's on?		

¿En el cine o en casa? — At the cinema or at home?

(No) Me gusta ir al cine porque…	I (don't) like going to the cinema because…	las palomitas están ricas	the popcorn is tasty
		los asientos no son cómodos	the seats aren't comfortable
Prefiero ver las pelis en casa porque…	I prefer watching films at home because…	los otros espectadores me molestan	the other spectators annoy me
el ambiente es mejor	the atmosphere is better	ponen tráilers para las nuevas pelis	they show trailers for new films
hay demasiadas personas	there are too many people	si vas al baño te pierdes una parte	if you go to the toilet you miss part of it
la imagen es mejor en la gran pantalla	the picture is better on the big screen	tienes que hacer cola	you have to queue
las entradas son muy caras	the tickets are very expensive	una corrida de toros	a bull fight
		en directo	live

Los modelos a seguir — Role models

Admiro a…	I admire…	la pobreza / la homofobia	poverty / homophobia
Mi inspiración / ídolo es…	My inspiration / idol is…	los derechos de la mujer	women's rights
…es un buen / mal modelo a seguir	…is a good / bad role model	los derechos de los refugiados	the rights of refugees
Un buen modelo a seguir es alguien que…	A good role model is someone who…	los niños desfavorecidos	underprivileged children
		la justicia social	social justice
apoya a organizaciones benéficas	supports charities	a pesar de sus problemas…	despite his/her problems…
recauda fondos para…	raises money for…	ha batido varios récords	he/she has broken several records
tiene mucho talento / éxito	is very talented / successful	ha creado…	he/she has created…
trabaja en defensa de los animales	works in defence of animals	ha ganado … medallas / premios	he/she has won … medals / awards
usa su fama para ayudar a los demás	uses his / her fame to help others	ha sufrido varias enfermedades	he/she has suffered several illnesses
se emborrachan	they get drunk	ha superado sus problemas	he/she has overcome his/her problems
se comportan mal	they behave badly	ha tenido mucho éxito como…	he/she has had lots of success as…
se meten en problemas con la policía	they get into trouble with the police	siempre sonríe	he/she always smiles
es amable / cariñoso/a / fuerte	he/she is nice / affectionate / strong	solo piensa en los demás	he/she only thinks of other people
lucha por / contra…	he/she fights for / against…		

5 Ciudades
Punto de partida 1

- *Talking about places in a town*
- *Asking for and understanding directions*

1 leer **Lee los textos. Pon los dibujos en el orden correcto. (NB Not all places mentioned are shown in the pictures!)**

1 En mi ciudad hay un cine y una piscina. También hay muchas tiendas y unos museos, pero no hay ni mercado ni biblioteca. Tampoco hay pista de hielo.

2 Vivo en un pueblo tranquilo donde solo hay una iglesia, un parque y Correos. También hay un castillo en ruinas, pero no hay ni bolera ni ayuntamiento.

3 Mi ciudad tiene un centro comercial con muchos restaurantes y bares. Está en la costa, así que hay playas y un puerto también. Desafortunadamente, no hay polideportivo.

2 escribir **Escribe una lista en español e inglés de los lugares del ejercicio 1.**

3 escuchar **Escucha y mira los dibujos. ¿Hay uno, unos o muchos? (1–3)**
Ejemplo: **1** e ✓✓, …, …

Hay	un / una ✓
	unos / unas ✓ ✓
	muchos / muchas ✓ ✓ ✓
No hay	--- ✗

4 leer **Lee y empareja las preguntas y respuestas.**

1 ¿Dónde vives?
2 ¿Dónde está?
3 ¿Cómo es tu ciudad?
4 ¿Qué hay en tu ciudad?
5 ¿Te gusta vivir allí?

a Está bien porque siempre hay algo que hacer.
b Hay muchos lugares de interés.
c Está situada en el sur del país.
d Vivo en Córdoba.
e Es una ciudad bastante grande, turística y muy bonita.

5 hablar **Con tu compañero/a, pregunta y contesta a las preguntas del ejercicio 4.**

> **No** hay **ni** un̶ polideportivo **ni** una̶ plaza mayor. | There **isn't** a sports centre **or** town square.
> **Tampoco** hay un̶ teatro. | **Nor** is there a theatre.

Vivo en	Manchester, Cardiff,	una ciudad un pueblo	grande pequeño/a		y/e pero	histórico/a moderno/a tranquilo/a ruidoso/a turístico/a industrial bonito/a feo/a
Está situado/a en	el norte / el sur / el este / el oeste		de Inglaterra / Gales / Escocia / Irlanda (del Norte)		cerca de…	
En… hay Mi ciudad tiene	un ayuntamiento una bolera / unos bares unas pistas de tenis		pero no hay		teatro muchos espacios verdes	
(No) me gusta porque	(no) hay mucho que hacer / siempre hay algo que hacer / no hay nada que hacer					

6 escribir **Escribe un párrafo sobre tu ciudad o pueblo.**

Use **e** to mean 'and' when the next word begins with *i*- or *hi*-.
*Vivo en una ciudad pequeña **e** histórica.*

7 leer **Pon la conversación en el orden correcto.**
Luego tradúcela al inglés.

a De nada.

b ¿Dónde está?

c Perdón. ¿La Plaza Mayor está lejos de aquí?

d Muchas gracias.

e No, está muy cerca.

f Toma la primera calle a la izquierda. Luego sigue todo recto y está a la derecha.

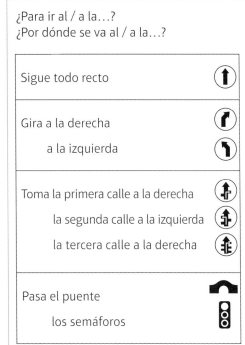

¿Para ir al / a la…?
¿Por dónde se va al / a la…?

¿Dónde está el / la…?
¿El / La … está cerca / lejos?

Sigue todo recto

Gira a la derecha
a la izquierda

Toma la primera calle a la derecha
la segunda calle a la izquierda
la tercera calle a la derecha

Pasa el puente
los semáforos

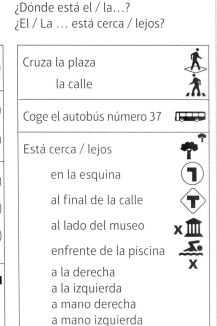

Cruza la plaza
la calle

Coge el autobús número 37

Está cerca / lejos
en la esquina
al final de la calle
al lado del museo
enfrente de la piscina
a la derecha
a la izquierda
a mano derecha
a mano izquierda

8 escuchar **Escucha y mira el mapa. Escribe la letra correcta (a–f). (1–6)**

Remember:
a + el = al
de + el = del

Estas aquí

9 hablar **Con tu compañero/a, pregunta y contesta. Utiliza el mapa.**
● *¿Dónde está la iglesia / el mercado / la biblioteca / el cine / la bolera?*

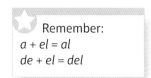

1 leer ¿Qué se compra en estas tiendas? Copia y completa la tabla en español.

tienda	cosa
la panadería	*pan*
la zapatería	
la frutería	
la papelería	
la cafetería	
la joyería	
la carnicería	
la pastelería	
la pescadería	
la librería	

Many shop names contain the word for what they sell. Try to work out what these shops are without a dictionary.

FRUTERIA BRENES

2 escuchar Escucha. ¿Adónde van? Escribe la letra correcta. (1–6)

a la estación de trenes

b el banco

c la tienda de ropa

d la peluquería

e la farmacia

f el estanco

The place name is not mentioned, so listen carefully for clues to help you identify where each person is going.

3 escribir Lee la lista de Carolina, ¿adónde va? Escribe los lugares en español.

4 escribir Escribe frases para cada lugar.

Ejemplo: **1** *De lunes a viernes la panadería* **abre** *a las ocho y* **cierra** *a la una.*
Por la tarde **abre** *de las dos hasta las siete…*

– buscar un regalo para mi madre (¿unos pendientes?)
– comprar carne para la barbacoa
– recoger la tarta de cumpleaños para la fiesta
– devolver la camiseta nueva que compré la semana pasada
– comprar sellos para mandar unas cartas

1
Panadería El Faro
Horario comercial:
lunes–viernes
08.00–13.00
14.00–19.00
sábados
09.00–13.00

2
Heladería San Isidro

bar   bar
helados   helados
bebidas   bebidas
lunes–viernes 11.00–21.00
sábados y domingos 13.00–23.00
no cierra a mediodía

3
Centro comercial
Horario
lunes–sábado 10.00–22.00
cerrado domingos y festivos

4
Pescadería Cangrejo
Horas de apertura:
abierto todos los días 8.15–14.00
fines de semana 07.30–12.30

5 hablar ¿Cuánto cuesta? Pregunta y contesta.

● Creo que el llavero cues**ta** tres euros noventa y cinco (céntimos). ¿Y tú?
■ Sí, yo también. En mi opinión, los pendientes cuest**an** cincuenta y seis euros.

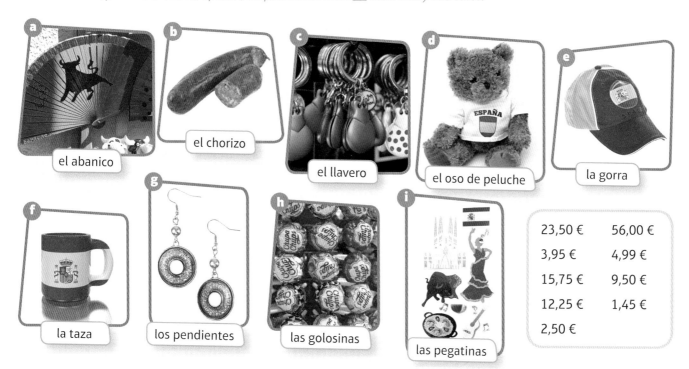

a el abanico

b el chorizo

c el llavero

d el oso de peluche

e la gorra

f la taza

g los pendientes

h las golosinas

i las pegatinas

23,50 €	56,00 €
3,95 €	4,99 €
15,75 €	9,50 €
12,25 €	1,45 €
2,50 €	

6 escuchar Escucha y comprueba tus respuestas. Escribe la letra correcta y el precio. (1–9)

7 escuchar Escucha y lee. Escribe las palabras que faltan en español. (1–2)

● Buenos días. ¿Me puede ayudar? Quiero comprar **a** ————.
■ Muy bien. ¿Para quién es?
● Es para **b** ————.
■ Vale. ¿De qué color?
● **c** ————, por favor.
■ De acuerdo. Aquí tiene.
● ¿Tiene uno/una/unos/unas **d** ————, por favor?
■ Sí, por supuesto.
● Gracias. ¿Cuánto es / son?
■ **e** ————.
● Solo tengo un billete de cincuenta / cien euros.
■ No pasa nada, tengo cambio.

> ⭐ Prices can be said in different ways:
> * ocho euros **y** cincuenta y cinco
> * ocho **con** cincuenta y cinco
> * ocho euros cincuenta y cinco

G Polite form of address

Use the **usted** (polite) form of the verb with an adult you don't know well.

¿Me **puede** ayudar?	**Can you** help me?
Aquí **tiene**.	Here **you are**.

8 hablar Con tu compañero/a, haz diálogos. Utiliza los siguientes detalles.

brother
red
smaller
13,25 €

dad
purple
cheaper
9,75 €

girlfriend
blue
longer
35,95 €

sister
white
larger
18,40 €

> ⭐ *Largo* means 'long', not 'large'!
> 'Big' or 'large' = *grande*.

1 ¿Cómo es tu zona?

- Describing the features of a region
- Using se puede and se pueden
- Asking and responding to questions

1 escuchar **Escucha y lee. Escribe la ciudad correcta para cada frase.**

¿Cómo es tu zona?

Arequipa, Perú

Arequipa está rodeada de tres volcanes y tiene unos impresionantes paisajes naturales. Es un oasis verde entre el desierto y la sierra. Me encanta el clima soleado. Solo llueve un poco en verano, así que se puede pasar mucho tiempo al aire libre. **Lidia**

Vivo en Coroico, un pueblo situado en un valle de la cordillera de los Andes. Es una región muy húmeda con muchas nieblas, pero es un paraíso de selva subtropical, ríos y bosques, perfecto para los que quieren caminar o ir en bici. **Alberto**

Coroico, Bolivia

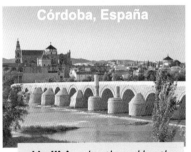

Córdoba, España

Córdoba es mi ciudad natal y me gusta mucho. Las varias influencias culturales (árabe, romana y judía) la hacen acogedora y atractiva, y se pueden visitar edificios de estilos muy diferentes. **Vicente**

La verdad es que en Valencia tenemos de todo: el bullicio de una ciudad, pero al lado del mar Mediterráneo. Mi lugar favorito es la Ciudad de las Ciencias, donde se pueden alquilar bolas de agua para pasear por los lagos artificiales. **Mariana**

Valencia, España

el bullicio   hustle and bustle

1   Aquí se puede apreciar la arquitectura variada.
2   Aquí se pueden practicar senderismo y ciclismo.
3   Aquí se puede disfrutar del ambiente urbano y de la costa al mismo tiempo.
4   El clima es seco en invierno, otoño y primavera.
5   Es una zona muy montañosa y pintoresca, donde llueve a menudo.
6   Aquí se puede aprovechar el buen tiempo.

G se puede / se pueden + *infinitive*

Use these to say 'you can...'.
(Singular noun) *Se puede visitar **la galería** de arte.*
(Plural noun) *Se pueden probar **platos** típicos.*

2 leer **Lee los textos de nuevo. Haz dos listas en español y luego traduce las palabras al inglés:**

- diez palabras relacionadas con la geografía física
- cuatro palabras relacionadas con el clima

3 escuchar **Escucha. Copia y completa la tabla en inglés. (1–4)**

city	geography	climate	two things you can do there
Rosario			

4 escribir **Busca información y escribe un texto sobre una de estas ciudades.**

Está	situado/a en un valle / al lado del río rodeado/a de sierra lleno/a de bosques a... metros sobre el nivel del mar
El clima es	soleado, caluroso, seco, frío, templado
Hay	riesgo de tormentas mucha marcha
Es	famoso/a por (la Alhambra) conocido/a por (sus playas)
Aquí se puede	subir a la torre esquiar en invierno hacer un recorrido en autobús disfrutar de las vistas viajar en el AVE
Aquí se pueden	probar platos típicos practicar deportes acuáticos

Sevilla   Palma de Mallorca   La Habana   Santiago de Compostela

5 escribir · Estás en la oficina de turismo. Empareja las mitades de las preguntas. Escribe frases completas.

1 ¿Me puede dar más información…
2 ¿Cuándo abre…
3 ¿Cuánto cuesta una…
4 ¿Dónde se pueden…
5 ¿A qué hora…
6 ¿Hay visitas guiadas…
7 ¿Me puede dar…
8 ¿Me puede recomendar…

un plano de la ciudad?
la cueva?
sale el autobús?
entrada?
sacar las entradas?
un restaurante típico?
a caballo o en Segway?
sobre la excursión a la Cueva de los Murciélagos?

6 escuchar · Escucha el diálogo y comprueba tus respuestas.

7 hablar · Estás en la oficina de turismo en Córdoba. Con tu compañero/a, haz diálogos.

- Say which excursion you would like more information about.
▪ Sí, por supuesto.
- Ask about times. (¿ Cuándo abre / empieza(n)?)
▪ Abre a las / Empieza(n) a las…
- Ask the price.
▪ Cuesta…
- Ask where you can buy tickets.
▪ Aquí en la oficina de turismo.
- Ask what time the bus leaves.
▪ Sale…
- Ask for another item (brochure, map of the city).
▪ Aquí tiene (un folleto) / (un plano de la ciudad).

Excursión		Día / Horario	Tarifa
Cueva de los Murciélagos		ma.–vi. 12.30–17.00	6 €
Castillo de Almodóvar		lu.–do. 10.00–15.00	7 €
Visitas guiadas (a caballo, en bici, en Segway)		todos los días, cada dos horas, a las 10, 12…	40 €
Costa del Sol (Málaga)		cada hora diariamente 9–18	27 €

8 leer · Lee el texto. Contesta a las preguntas utilizando frases completas.

calleja de las Flores

24 horas en Córdoba. ¡Todo es posible!

Por la mañana: ¡Merece la pena madrugar! A primera hora hace menos calor y se puede aprovechar para visitar la Mezquita, que hasta las 9.30 es gratis. Luego puedes bajar al río Guadalquivir y contemplar la ciudad desde el puente romano. Para desayunar, podemos comer unos *jeringos* (o churros) en la churrería de la plaza del Campo Santo de los Mártires. Después es hora de descansar en los baños árabes Hammam Al Ándalus.

Al mediodía: Tenemos el bar Casa Santos y sus tortillas, hechas con cinco kilos de patatas y treinta huevos, quizá las más grandes y las mejores del mundo.

Por la tarde: Conocer el barrio más popular de Córdoba: la Judería, un laberinto de calles estrechas. La más pintoresca es la calleja de las Flores. Está llena de geranios y es un imán para los aficionados a la fotografía.

la Mezquita

Por la noche: El espectáculo ecuestre que se ofrece en las Caballerizas Reales es algo que no te puedes perder.

1 ¿Cuándo se puede visitar la Mezquita sin pagar?
2 ¿Dónde se puede desayunar?
3 ¿Qué se puede hacer en los baños árabes?
4 ¿Qué se puede comer en el bar Casa Santos?
5 ¿Qué se puede hacer en la calleja de las Flores?
6 ¿Qué animales se pueden ver por la noche?

2 ¿Qué haremos mañana?

- Planning what to do
- Using the future tense
- Understanding the geography of Spain

1 leer   Lee el texto y elige las <u>tres</u> frases correctas. Luego traduce las expresiones en **negrita**.

San Cristóbal de la Laguna, 7 de junio

¡Hola mamá!

Ya estoy muy a gusto en casa de Elena. ¡Su familia es guay! La zona donde viven es muy bonita, pero también es bastante lluviosa. ¡No ha dejado de llover en dos días! Por lo tanto, todavía no he visto mucho de Tenerife, pero mañana **el papá de Elena nos llevará** al Pico del Teide, donde **subiremos en teleférico**. Elena me dice que **pasaremos entre las nubes** para llegar a la cumbre. Aunque es verano, **habrá nieve** en la sierra. **¡Será genial!** Luego **bajaremos a pie** para disfrutar del paisaje. **Sacaré muchas fotos** y **las subiré** a mi Facebook. **Te enviaré** un comentario mañana por la noche. Hoy, si sale el sol, **iremos a la playa**. ¿Qué tiempo hace allí en Cartagena?

Un beso, Juliana

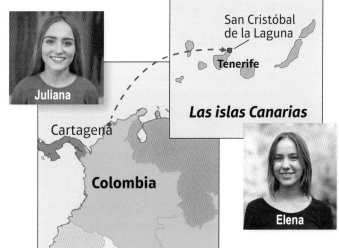

Juliana

San Cristóbal de la Laguna

Tenerife

Cartagena

Las islas Canarias

Colombia

Elena

1 Juliana está muy feliz en casa de Elena.
2 Siempre hace buen tiempo en San Cristóbal de la Laguna.
3 Juliana y Elena irán de excursión en barco.
4 Mañana Juliana y Elena irán a la montaña.
5 Juliana escribirá otro mensaje a su madre.
6 Hoy hará sol.

G The future tense > Page 216

Add these endings to the infinitive stem of regular –ar, –er and –ir verbs.

visitar**é**	I will visit
visitar**ás**	you will visit
visitar**á**	he/she/you (polite) will visit
visitar**emos**	we will visit
visitar**éis**	you (plural) will visit
visitar**án**	they/you (plural, polite) will visit

A few verbs have an **irregular stem** in the future tense:
haré (I will do)   **podr**ás (you will be able to)
tendré (I will have)   **saldr**ás (you will leave, go out)
dirá (he/she/you will say)   **habr**á (there will be)

2 escuchar   Escucha. Escribe los detalles en inglés. (1–4)
Ejemplo: **1** *if good weather – go on boat trip, …*

está despejado   *it's fine / cloudless*

Use 'if' clauses to discuss plans:
Si + **present**, + **future**
   Si **hace** *calor,* **nadaremos** *en el mar.*
   If **it's** hot, **we'll swim** in the sea.

3 hablar   Con tu compañero/a, habla de los planes posibles.

- ¿Qué haremos el lunes?
- *Si hace sol, jugaremos al tenis.*
- ¡Qué bien! ¿Y si llueve?
- *Iremos al cine.*

lunes	☀	jueves	🌡☀
martes	🌡❄	viernes	🌧
miércoles	👎☁		

4 escuchar **Escucha y lee. Contesta a las preguntas en inglés.**

E: Bueno, ¿qué haremos el resto de la semana? Ya has visto el Pico del Teide y el parque nacional…

J: Sí, ¡fue genial! También hemos pasado un día en la playa.

E: Pues, mira. Hoy es martes. Según el pronóstico del tiempo, hará viento en la costa, así que será mejor ir al zoo que a la playa. ¿Qué te parece?

J: ¡Qué bien! Quiero ver los monos. Mañana parece que lloverá bastante.

E: ¿Por qué no vamos a la Cueva del Viento? El tiempo no nos importará allí.

J: Buena idea. ¿Y el jueves?

E: Será muy variable, según el pronóstico. Habrá nubes y claros, con chubascos. Bueno, iremos a Santa Cruz. Si no hace viento, podremos hacer paddle surf, y si hace demasiado viento, haremos piragüismo.

J: ¡Qué guay! Me encantan los dos.

E: El viernes será tu último día.

J: ¡Qué triste!

E: Sí, pero iremos al centro comercial y podrás comprar regalos para tu familia.

J: De acuerdo.

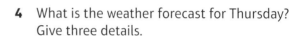

Santa Cruz de Tenerife

1 Name <u>three</u> things that Juliana has already done.
2 Why does Elena suggest going to the zoo on Tuesday?
3 Where does Elena think they should go tomorrow and why?

4 What is the weather forecast for Thursday? Give <u>three</u> details.
5 What are the <u>two</u> options for Thursday?
6 Give <u>two</u> details about the plan for Juliana's last day.

5 escribir **Estás en España. Escribe un post para el blog de tu clase.**

Mention:
- something you have already visited   *Ya he visitado…*
- something you have not yet seen   *Todavía no he visto…*
- an activity you will do if the weather is good   *Si hace buen tiempo, …*
- an activity you will do if the weather is bad   *Si llueve, …*
- what you will do on the last day   *El último día…*

6 escuchar **Escucha el pronóstico meteorológico. Escribe las letras correctas.**

¿Qué tiempo hará en…?
1 el sur
2 la costa cantábrica
3 el norte
4 el este
5 las Baleares

Habrá…
a una ola de calor *(heatwave)*
b truenos y relámpagos *(thunder and lightning)*
c temperaturas más altas *(higher temperatures)*
d temperaturas más bajas *(lower temperatures)*
e granizo *(hail)*
f brisas fuertes *(strong breezes)*
g periodos soleados *(sunny spells)*

Las temperaturas…
h subirán *(will rise)*
i bajarán *(will fall)*

El tiempo…
j se despejará *(will clear up)*
k cambiará *(will change)*
l lloverá *(It will rain)*

Océano Atlántico
Picos de Europa
Galicia Asturias **Santander**
Cantabria
Pirineos
Cataluña
Madrid **Barcelona**
Valencia
Valencia
Sevilla Islas
Andalucía Murcia Baleares
Mar Mediterráneo

Islas Canarias

Spain has 17 *comunidades autónomas.*

● *Shopping for clothes and presents*
● *Using demonstrative adjectives*
● *Explaining preferences*

1 escuchar **Escucha y lee. Busca las frases en español.**

Aquí tienen de todo. ¿Por dónde quieres empezar?

Primero quiero devolver algo.

Perdone, señora. Ayer compré **esta camiseta**, pero tiene un agujero. ¿Puede reembolsarme el dinero, por favor?

Aquí tiene el recibo. N• quiero otra camiseta. ¿Qué me recomienda?

No, lo siento. Pero podemos hacer un cambio.

¿Qué tal **este cinturón** de cuero?

No, gracias ¿Me puedo probar **esta falda amarilla**?

Elena, ¿qué te parece?

Bueno, **esta falda** me la llevo. ¡Y estas sandalias también! Ahora necesito regalos para mi familia…

¡Qué bonitos!

Por supuesto. ¿Qué talla tiene? ¿La 36? ¿Y qué tal con **aquellos zapatos negros**?

La falda te queda muy bien, pero **esos zapatos** te quedan demasiado grandes. Prefiero **estas sandalias**.

1 I want to return something.	**4** We can exchange it.	**7** What size are you?
2 It has a hole.	**5** Here is the receipt.	**8** The skirt looks very good on you.
3 Can you refund me?	**6** Can I try on this yellow skirt?	**9** I'll take it.

2 leer **Lee la historia del ejercicio 1 otra vez. Traduce las palabras en negrita al inglés.**

G *Demonstrative adjectives*

	singular		plural	
	masculine	**feminine**	**masculine**	**feminine**
this, these	est**e** bolso	est**a** corbata	est**os** bolsos	est**as** corbatas
that, those	es**e** bolso	es**a** corbata	es**os** bolsos	es**as** corbatas
that, those… over there	aqu**el** bolso	aqu**ella** corbata	aqu**ellos** bolsos	aqu**ellas** corbatas

3 escuchar **Escucha. Copia y completa la tabla en inglés. (1–4)**

en rebajas   on sale
una talla más grande   a bigger size

	item bought	problem	solution
1			

4 hablar **Con tu compañero/a, haz diálogos.**

1
– Say what you bought, what the problem is, and ask for a refund
– Say yes, of course, ask for the receipt
– Say here you are
– Say here's the money
– Say thank you and goodbye

2
– Say what you bought, what the problem is, and ask for a refund
– Say no, sorry, but you can change it
– Say OK, ask what he/she recommends
– Say what about this (T-shirt)?
– Say you like it and you'll take it

está	roto/a
es demasiado	estrecho/a, largo/a
tiene	una mancha un agujero
le falta	un botón

5 leer ¿Quién dice las siguientes frases? Escribe el nombre correcto.

¿Te gustan los centros comerciales?

Bruno
A mí me mola ir de tiendas con mis amigos. Solemos ir al nuevo centro comercial. Tiene prácticamente todas las tiendas que necesitas y grandes almacenes donde se puede comprar de todo, incluso artículos de marca en las tiendas de diseño. Prefiero ir allí que al centro porque es un buen sitio para pasar la tarde con mis amigos.

Iker
Odio los centros comerciales porque siempre hay demasiada gente. La última vez que fui de compras en la ciudad hacía mucho calor y tuve que hacer cola en todas las tiendas. Fue una absoluta pérdida de tiempo. Desde entonces compro todo por Internet porque es mucho más cómodo. Hago mis compras sin salir de casa. ¡Es genial!

Fabiana
Me encanta la ropa alternativa y por eso nunca me ha gustado comprar en las cadenas. Tengo un estilo muy diferente, y por eso busco lo que necesito en tiendas de segunda mano. Allí siempre puedes encontrar gangas y ropa con mucha originalidad.

Clara
Prefiero comprar cosas por Internet porque creo que hay más variedad que en las tiendas. Además, los precios son más bajos y hay más ofertas. No obstante, como no se pueden probar las cosas antes de comprar, hay que devolverlas a menudo. ¡Qué rollo!

grandes almacenes	*department stores*
las cadenas	*chain stores*
las gangas	*bargains*

1 Es más económico comprar en la red.
2 Ir de compras con tus amigos es muy divertido.
3 No compro ropa de moda.
4 Me gusta comprar por Internet, pero hay inconvenientes también.
5 Me gustan los centros comerciales.
6 Es mucho más práctico comprar por Internet.

6 leer Traduce el post de Clara al inglés.

7 escuchar Escucha. Apunta en inglés (a) dónde prefiere comprar y (b) por qué. (1–4)

8 hablar Con tu compañero/a, pregunta y contesta.

- ¿Adónde vas de compras normalmente?
- ¿Dónde prefieres comprar? ¿Por qué?
- ¿Te gusta comprar por Internet? ¿Por qué?
- ¿Adónde fuiste de compras la última vez y qué compraste?
- ¿Vas a ir de compras el próximo fin de semana?

 Adapt the opinions and reasons from exercise 5 to explain your preferences.

Normalmente voy Suelo ir	a los centros comerciales al centro de la ciudad		
Prefiero comprar Me gusta comprar Odio comprar	en	(las) cadenas (los) grandes almacenes (las) tiendas de diseño (las) tiendas de segunda mano	porque...
	por	Internet	
La última vez que fui de compras	compré... y...		
El próximo fin de semana	voy a... para comprar...		

4 **Los pros y los contras de la ciudad**

● *Talking about problems in a town*
● *Using the conditional*
● *Using synonyms and antonyms*

1 escuchar **Escucha. Escribe las <u>dos</u> letras correctas. (1–4)**

Lo mejor de vivir en la ciudad es que... ## Lo peor es que...

a
es tan fácil desplazarse.

b
hay tantas diversiones.

e
el centro es tan ruidoso.

f
se lleva una vida tan frenética.

c
las tiendas están tan cerca.

d
hay muchas posibilidades de trabajo.

g
hay tanto tráfico.

h
la gente no se conoce.

2 leer **¿Qué <u>dos</u> cosas cambiaría cada persona? Apunta los datos en inglés.**

La vida aquí en la ciudad es bulliciosa, pero a mí me gusta. Tienes todas las tiendas a poca distancia y es imposible aburrirse. También es fácil encontrar empleo. Lo único que cambiaría sería el centro. Introduciría más zonas peatonales y renovaría algunos edificios antiguos. **Julio**

Se dice que en la ciudad no hay un gran sentido de comunidad, pero yo conozco a todos mis vecinos. Por otro lado, opino que la gente siempre tiene prisa. Por mi parte, pondría más áreas de ocio, donde la gente podría descansar. También plantaría más árboles. **Valentina**

Se lleva una vida muy relajada en el campo. ¡Es tan tranquila! No hay tanto que hacer, pero diría que tienes todo lo necesario para vivir bien. Sin embargo, el transporte público no es fiable y por eso hay tantos coches. Mejoraría el sistema de transporte público y sería gratis para todos. **Ariana**

Aunque vivo en el campo, ahora hay una red de transporte público muy buena y no hay tantos atascos como antes. Sin embargo, las tiendas están demasiado lejos y por eso construiría un nuevo centro comercial. Otro problema es que hay bastante desempleo. Invertiría en el turismo rural porque crearía una mejor oferta de empleo. **Hugo**

G **The conditional** > *Page* **220**

Most verbs in the conditional translate as 'would'. You already know *me gustaría* (I would like). To form the conditional, add the imperfect endings of *–er/–ir* verbs to the infinitive:

mejorar**ía**	I would improve
mejorar**ías**	you would improve
mejorar**ía**	he/she/you (polite) would improve
mejorar**íamos**	we would improve
mejorar**íais**	you (plural) would improve
mejorar**ían**	they/you (plural, polite) would improve

G **Irregular verbs in the conditional** > *Page* **220**

Verbs which are irregular in the future tense are also irregular in the conditional. Here are the most common:

decir → *diría* (I would say)
haber → *habría* (there would be)
hacer → *haría* (I would do)
poder → *podría* (I would be able to)
poner → *pondría* (I would put)
tener → *tendría* (I would have)

3 leer — Busca en el texto del ejercicio 2 frases sinónimas a las frases del ejercicio 1.

Ejemplo: **a** *Es tan fácil desplazarse.*
→ *Hay una red de transporte público muy buena.*

so…, so much…, so many…		
tan + adjective	*tan* tranquilo	**so** quiet
tanto/a + singular noun	*tanta* contaminación	**so much** pollution
tantos/as + plural noun	*tantos* problemas	**so many** problems

4 leer — Busca en el texto del ejercicio 2 frases antónimas a las frases del ejercicio 1. Tradúcelas al inglés.

Ejemplo: **a** *El transporte público no es fiable.*
→ *Public transport is not reliable.*

5 escuchar — Escucha y apunta en inglés (a) <u>tres</u> problemas y (b) <u>seis</u> soluciones.

Ciudad de Panamá

6 hablar — Con tu compañero/a, habla de donde vives.

● *¿Qué es lo mejor del lugar donde vives?*
■ *Lo mejor es que <u>las tiendas están tan cerca</u> y…*
● *¿Qué es lo peor?*
■ *Lo peor es que <u>hay tanto tráfico</u> y…*
● *¿Cómo cambiarías tu zona?*
■ *<u>Mejoraría el sistema de transporte público</u> y…*

7 escuchar — Escucha. Copia y completa la tabla en inglés. (1–4)

	past problem	improvement made	improvement needed
1			

 You may hear expressions you have met before but in a different tense. Listen out for both past problems in the **imperfect tense** and the improvements that have already been made in the **perfect tense**.

han mejorado	*they have improved*
han introducido	*they have introduced*
han renovado	*they have renovated*
han construido	*they have built*
han creado	*they have created*
han plantado	*they have planted*
han abierto	*they have opened*

8 leer — Lee el artículo. Contesta a las preguntas en inglés.

Mi ciudad se llama Bilbao. Antes era muy industrial, pero ahora es un lugar muy atractivo para vivir. Lo mejor es que hay mucho que ver en la ciudad, como por ejemplo el famoso Museo Guggenheim. Todavía es ruidosa, pero han creado muchas áreas de ocio que son muy tranquilas. Han mejorado la red de transporte e incluso han introducido un sistema de alquiler de bicis. Es tan fácil desplazarse que se puede coger el metro o el tranvía para pasar un día en un pueblo en la costa.

1 How did Bilbao use to be and how is it now?
2 What is the best thing about the city?
3 Name one disadvantage.
4 List three improvements that have been made.
5 What evidence is there that it is easy to get around nowadays?

9 escribir — Escribe un artículo sobre el lugar donde vives.

 Use:
• the **present tense** for describing your town/village and saying what the best/worst thing is
• the **imperfect tense** for saying what problems there used to be (*Antes (no) había… / era… / estaba…*)
• the **perfect tense** for saying what improvements have been made (*Han renovado / creado…*)
• the **conditional** for saying what else you would do to improve it (*Mejoraría… / Construiría…*)

5 ¡Destino Arequipa!

- Describing a visit in the past
- Using different tenses together
- Recognising and using idioms

1 Escucha y lee. Busca las expresiones en español.

Aventura sudamericana

El estudiante Lucas Walker nos cuenta cómo va su año sabático, y su visita a Arequipa en el sur del país.

¿Qué tal tu visita a Arequipa, Lucas?
¡Fue fenomenal! Me quedé impresionado con la ciudad. Vimos lugares interesantes como el monasterio de Santa Catalina. Tuvimos un guía que nos hizo un recorrido y nos ayudó a entender toda la historia.

Lucas Walker

¿Visitaste la ciudad a pie?
Sí, recorrí a pie el centro histórico, donde vi la plaza de Armas y la Catedral Blanca. Y en el Mundo Alpaca compré tantas cosas que ¡casi me quedé sin dinero!

Otro día alquilé una bici de montaña. Subimos en grupo al pie del volcán Misti, donde había unas vistas maravillosas. Luego bajamos en bici de la montaña a la ciudad. ¡Fue una experiencia única, pero al final de cada día estaba muy cansado!

la alpaca

¿Cómo era la ciudad?
Era muy acogedora porque la gente era muy abierta y comunicativa. Aprendí mucho sobre la cultura peruana.

¿Qué tal la comida?
La comida estaba muy buena. Comí de todo: pollo, patatas (o papas, como se llaman en Perú) y rocoto relleno.

¿Qué es lo que más te gustó?
Lo que más me gustó fue el clima porque hizo mucho sol. Lo que menos me gustó fueron los taxis. Eran baratos, pero iban demasiado rápido. ¡Qué miedo!

¿Vas a volver algún día?
Por supuesto que volveré algún día. Primero voy a visitar otras ciudades. Creo que voy a ir a Trujillo, en el norte de Perú, donde aprenderé a hacer surf. Luego quiero viajar a Colombia y a Ecuador. Allí trabajaré unas semanas como voluntario en un orfanato.

la gente peruana

el volcán Misti

rocoto relleno stuffed rocoto peppe.

Completed actions
1 We saw...
2 He/She did a tour for us...
3 I went on foot round the historic centre.
4 We went up...
5 What I liked most...

Description in the past
6 There were amazing views.
7 The people were very open.
8 I was very tired.
9 The food was very good.

Future plans
10 I will return...
11 I'm going to visit...
12 I think I'm going to...
13 I will work...

> **G** *Using the preterite and the imperfect* > *Pages 212, 214*

Remember, you use the **preterite** for completed actions in the past.
Comí de todo.   **I ate** everything.
Use the **imperfect** to describe what something was like, and for repeated actions in the past.
La ciudad era acogedora.   The city **was** welcoming.

Zona Cultura

Arequipa, 'la Ciudad Blanca'

Destino:	AREQUIPA
Ubicación:	Sur de Perú, en el interior
Población:	1,3 millones (2ª ciudad de Perú)
Famosa por:	el volcán Misti
	la arquitectura blanca
	los textiles de alpaca

2 Lee la entrevista otra vez. Luego identifica las cuatro frases correctas.

1 Lucas visitó el monasterio de Santa Catalina con un guía.
2 A Lucas le gustó mucho la ciudad de Arequipa.
3 Cogió un autobús turístico para visitar la ciudad.
4 No comió rocoto relleno porque es vegetariano.
5 No le gustó el clima porque hizo mucho calor.
6 Lucas tiene la intención de regresar a Perú en el futuro.
7 Primero Lucas visitará otra ciudad en Perú.

3 escuchar **Escucha y escribe las letras correctas. Sobran <u>tres</u> opciones. (1–3)**
Escucha otra vez. ¿La opinión es positiva (P) o negativa (N)?

a museums   **d** atmosphere   **g** language
b food   **e** people   **h** architecture
c music and culture   **f** transport   **i** shopping

la plaza de Armas, Arequipa

⭐ ***Quedarse*** literally means 'to stay' or 'to remain'.

Me quedé en un hotel.   **I stayed** in a hotel.

It is also used idiomatically to mean 'to end up', but we sometimes translate it into English using other verbs.

Me quedé sin dinero.   **I ended up** without money / I ran out of money.

Can you work out what these expressions mean?

Me quedé sin palabras.
Me quedé dormido.
Me quedé jugando al fútbol todo el día.
Me quedé enamorado de la ciudad.

4 hablar **Con tu compañero/a, habla de una visita a una ciudad.**

● *¿Adónde fuiste?*   ■ *Fui a <u>Londres</u>.*
● *¿Cuánto tiempo pasaste allí?*   ■ *Pasé…*
● *¿Qué tal tu visita a <u>Londres</u>?*   ■ *¡Fue genial! Vi… Fui a…*
● *¿Visitaste la ciudad a pie?*   ■ *Visité… a pie / Cogí… / Alquilé…*
● *¿Qué tiempo hizo?*   ■ *Hizo…*
● *¿Qué tal la comida?*   ■ *La comida estaba…*
● *¿Qué es lo que más te gustó?*   ■ *Lo que más me gustó fue / fueron… pero lo que menos me gustó…*
● *¿Vas a volver?*   ■ *Sí, volveré… Creo que… Quiero….*

5 escribir **Traduce este texto al español.**

mucho, mucha, muchos or *muchas*?

Say 'did a guided tour for us'. Use the preterite of *hacer*, with *nos* (us) in front of it.

Do you need the preterite or the imperfect here?

Last year I visited Santander, a city in the north of Spain, with my school. We saw **a lot of** interesting places. The teacher **took** us on a guided tour and I learned a lot. **The food was** very good, but what I liked most was the windsurfing. It was amazing! I wIll go back one day, but next year I think I am going to go to Italy.

cuy chactado

🔵 **Zona Cultura**

Aunque se habla español en Perú, hay unas palabras diferentes.

Por ejemplo:

España		Perú		
coche		carro		
patata		papa		
cobaya		cuy		
zumo de naranja		jugo de naranja		
ordenador		computadora		
móvil		celular		
plaza Mayor		plaza de Armas		

¿Qué significan en inglés?

1 leer **Read the article about cities of the world.**

La mejor ciudad del mundo para vivir está en España: es Palma de Mallorca, según el diario británico *The Times*.

'La capital de las islas Baleares tiene playas a las que se puede llegar andando y un clima excepcional', concluye *The Times*. Palma supera a rivales como Toronto en Canadá (el mejor destino para los urbanitas), Auckland en Nueva Zelanda (la mejor ciudad marítima), Hoi An en Vietnam (el número uno de la gastronomía) y Berlín.

El equipo de periodistas especializados en viajes de *The Times* ha utilizado diversas estadísticas sobre la calidad de vida, las infraestructuras, la gastronomía, el clima, el entorno y la facilidad de 'asimilación' de los británicos. El diario describe Palma como 'una de las ciudades más pintorescas de España', y también la recomienda para unas vacaciones o para vivir.

Los primeros países de la lista son Estados Unidos (con diez ciudades entre las cincuenta elegidas), Francia (con cinco), España, Italia y Australia (con cuatro cada una).

Palma de Mallorca

(a) What does the article tell us? Choose the <u>three</u> correct statements.

A One reason for Palma de Mallorca being the best city is the proximity of its beaches.
B The report lists three reasons why Palma tops the list.
C Toronto is listed as the best coastal city.
D The list was compiled by *The Times*' team of travel correspondents.
E The quality of the food was one of the criteria.
F Palma is described as one of the most popular cities in Spain.
G Overall, Spain has five cities in the list of top 50 cities.

Answer the following questions in English. You do not need to write full sentences.

(b) For what purposes does the newspaper recommend Palma to its readers? Give <u>two</u> details.
(c) What does the article say about the United States? Give <u>two</u> details.

2 leer **Read the extract. Esteban is talking to his sister, Férula, about a house he owns called *Las Tres Marías*.**

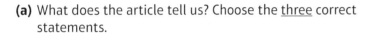

La casa de los espíritus by Isabel Allende (abridged)

—Creo que me iré al campo, a Las Tres Marías.
—Eso es una ruina, Esteban. Siempre te he dicho que es mejor vender esa tierra, pero tú eres testarudo como una mula.
—Nunca hay que vender la tierra. Es lo único que queda cuando todo lo demás se acaba*.
—No estoy de acuerdo. La tierra es una idea romántica, lo que enriquece** a los hombres es el buen ojo para los negocios*** —alegó Férula. —Pero tú siempre decías que algún día te ibas a ir a vivir al campo.
—Ahora ha llegado ese día. Odio esta ciudad.
—¿Por qué no dices mejor que odias esta casa?
—También —respondió él brutalmente. […]
Terminaron de comer en silencio.

* acabarse = to finish
** lo que enriquece = what enriches
*** los negocios = business

Answer the following questions in English. You do not need to write full sentences.

(a) What does Esteban say he is planning to do?
(b) What does Férula want him to do with the land?
(c) In response, how does Esteban explain his point of view?
(d) What does Férula feel is better for men than owning land?
(e) How did Férula and Esteban finish their meal?

With texts that include dialogue, it's important to be clear who is speaking. In the exam you can write F (Férula) and E (Esteban) next to each line of speech to help you pinpoint the correct information to answer each question.

3 leer **Lee el artículo.**

Un ejecutivo con traje y corbata pedalea, camino de su trabajo. Al otro lado de la marcha, una joven con mochila se dirige en bici a su primera clase de la mañana en la universidad. ¿Ámsterdam? No, Bilbao.

¿Cómo sabemos que el uso de la bici está en alza? Las cifras de alquiler de las bicicletas públicas dan una pista: el pasado octubre se alquilaron en Bilbao 27.000 bicis frente a las 17.000 del mismo mes de 2011.

Pero, ¿por qué las bicicletas han tomado este año la ciudad? En Bilbao dicen que es una forma de ahorrar el billete del autobús o el metro.

De los datos de alquiler de bicis se puede obtener un perfil del ciclista urbano: joven y hombre, en la mayoría de los casos. Otro factor es la climatología. En mayo se alquilaron 27.012 bicis, por las 11.666 de febrero. También creen algunos que el boom del uso de la bici responde a la ecología, es decir, al respeto al medio ambiente.

Contesta a las preguntas en español. No tienes que escribir frases completas.

(a) ¿De qué ciudad trata el artículo?

(b) ¿Adónde van en bici los ciudadanos? Escribe <u>dos</u> detalles.

(c) Según el artículo, ¿por qué prefieren ir en bici?

(d) ¿Cómo es el típico ciclista urbano?

(e) ¿Qué otros factores afectan al alquiler de bicis? (<u>dos</u> factores)

1 escuchar **You are in a shopping centre in Santander and overhear a conversation between a mother and her son.**

Listen and answer the following questions in English.

(a) Why is the mother cross with her son? Give <u>one</u> reason.

(b) Why is he unhappy? Give <u>two</u> reasons.

(c) What does the mother say about their last shopping trip?

(d) What does the son say about online shopping? Give <u>two</u> details.

2 escuchar **You are listening to the news. The reporter is talking about the city of Medellín, in Colombia.**

Listen and choose the correct word(s) for each phrase.

(a) The award was announced…
  A yesterday morning.
  B today.
  C this week.
  D this month.

(b) Medellín has improved…
  A water quality.
  B innovation in the city.
  C the quality of life.
  D tourism.

(c) The judges were most impressed by the…
  A reduction in crime.
  B focus on education.
  C unemployment figures.
  D focus on public transport.

(d) There were… other finalists.
  A 25
  B 2
  C 70
  D 200

A – Role play

1 leer   Look at the role play card and prepare what you are going to say.

Topic: Travel and tourist transactions

Instructions to candidates:

You are talking to a travel agent in a tourist office in Spain. The teacher will play the role of the agent and will speak first.

You must address the agent as *usted*.

You will talk to the teacher using the five prompts below.

- where you see – **?** – you must ask a question
- where you see – **!** – you must respond to something you have not prepared

Task

Usted está en una oficina de turismo en España. Habla con el/la agente sobre una excursión

1 Excursión – reservar

2 Día preferido

3 !

4 ? Autocar – hora (salir)

5 ? Otra excursión

> Be specific. Name a city or specific attraction that you want to visit…

> You can keep your answer short here.

> Anticipate the question. What might you be asked by a friendly travel agent?

> Start your question with 'At what time…'. Which form of the verb do you need?

> What verb can you use here to ask 'Is there / are there…?'

2 escuchar   Practise what you have prepared. Then, using your notes, listen and respond to the teacher.

3 escuchar   Now listen to Mark doing the role play task.

1   Which excursion does he want to book?
2   How does he answer the unexpected question?

B – Picture-based task

Topic: Daily life

Mira la foto y prepara las respuestas a los siguientes puntos:

- la descripción de la foto
- tu opinión sobre comprar en los mercados
- un problema que tuviste cuando fuiste de compras
- qué te gustaría comprar si tuvieras* mucho dinero
- (!)

* si tuvieras = if you had / were to have

1 *escuchar* **Look at the photo and read the task card. Then listen to Karolina's response to the first bullet point.**

1. What do you think the words for 'pedestrian zone' and 'market stall' are?
2. Note down <u>two</u> things she says about the street.
3. What season does she think it is, and why?

> ⭐ You hear Karolina use the following positional phrases. What do they mean?
>
> *en primer plano*   *detrás de*
> *al otro lado*   *en el fondo*
> *a la derecha*

2 *escuchar* **Listen to and read Karolina's response to the second bullet point.**

1. Write down the missing verb for each gap.
2. Look at the Answer Booster on page 112. Note down <u>six</u> examples of language which Karolina uses to give a strong answer.

> Me gusta mucho **1** ———— a los mercados. Lo bueno es que siempre puedes **2** ———— gangas. Los precios suelen ser más bajos que en las tiendas, y a menudo **3** ———— negociar el precio. Además, a mi modo de ver, **4** ———— ropa más variada e interesante en los mercados. No obstante, un inconveniente es que no es tan fácil **5** ———— las cosas y tampoco hay donde **6** ———— la ropa. Sin embargo, me chifla el bullicio de los mercados, sobre todo en Navidad, cuando siempre hay mucho ambiente.

3 *escuchar* **Listen to Karolina's response to the third bullet point. Note down answers to the following questions in English.**

- When?
- Where?
- Why?
- What did she buy?
- What was the problem? (<u>two</u> details)
- How was it resolved?

> ⭐ The question on the third bullet is in the perfect tense. However, Karolina's answer is in the preterite. This is because she's talking about a specific shopping trip in the past.

4 *escuchar* **Listen to Karolina's response to the fourth bullet point. Which of these conditional verbs does she use? What do they mean?**

compraría	saldría	tendría	gastaría	me gustaría
pondría	iría	ahorraría	haría	habría

5 *escuchar* **Prepare your own answers to the first <u>four</u> bullet points. Try to predict which unexpected question you might be asked. Then listen and take part in the full picture-based task with the teacher.**

C – General conversation

1 *escuchar* **Listen to Leigh introducing her chosen topic. Identify the <u>five</u> aspects that she mentions.**

- **a** weather
- **b** geography
- **c** buildings
- **d** why it is special
- **e** a previous visit
- **f** food
- **g** an annual event
- **h** disadvantages

> ⭐ To develop your answer as fully as possible, use one or more of the following strategies:
> - include the views of others
> - present a balanced view by including opposing opinions
> - narrate a specific event to exemplify your opinion
> - say what something is **not**, as well as what it is.

2 *escuchar* **The teacher asks Leigh *'¿Cómo es la ciudad o el pueblo donde vives?'* Listen and note down which <u>four</u> additional hidden questions she answers.**

3 *escuchar* **Listen to Leigh's response to the second question, *'¿Qué es mejor, vivir en la ciudad o en el campo?'* Look at the Answer Booster on page 112. Note down <u>six</u> examples of language which Leigh uses to give a strong answer.**

4 *hablar* **Prepare your own answers to Module 5 questions 1–6 on page 199. Then practise with your partner.**

Answer booster	Aiming for a solid answer	Aiming higher	Aiming for the top
Verbs	**Different time frames**: past, present, near future **Different types of verbs**: regular, irregular, reflexive, stem-changing	**Different persons** of the verb **Verbs with an infinitive**: *se puede(n), querer, soler, acabar de*	**A wide range of tenses**: present, preterite, imperfect, perfect, future, conditional **Less common verbs**: *disfrutar de, desplazarse*
Opinions and reasons	**Verbs of opinion**: *me chifla(n), me encanta(n), pienso que…, creo que…* **Reasons**: *porque…*	**Exclamations**: *¡Qué pena!, ¡Qué rollo!* **Comparatives**: *más bajo que…*	**Opinions**: *desde mi punto de vista, a mi modo de ver, para mí* **Reasons**: *ya que, dado que, puesto que, así que, por lo tanto*
Connectives	*y, pero, también*	*además, sin embargo, por desgracia, sobre todo, incluso*	*todavía* **Balancing an argument**: *por un lado… por otro lado, lo bueno es, un inconveniente es… aunque, a pesar de…*
Other features	**Qualifiers**: *muy, un poco, poco, bastante, demasiado* **Adjectives**: *pintoresco/a, lluvioso/a, conocido/a*	**Sentences with *cuando, donde, si***: *Si hace buen tiempo,…* **Tan, tanto/a/os/as**: *es tan tranquilo/a, no hay tantos coches*	**Positive/Negative phrases**: *lo bueno/malo/mejor/peor…* **Specialist vocabulary**: *gangas, la mayoría, zona peatonal* **Idioms**: *me quedé enamorado/a de la ciudad*

A – Extended writing task

1 leer **Look at the task and answer the questions.**

- What is the **purpose** of the text that you are asked to write?
- What is each bullet point asking you to do?
- Which tense(s) will you need to use to answer each one?

2 leer **Read George's answer on page 113. What do the phrases in bold mean?**

3 leer **Look at the Answer Booster. Note down <u>eight</u> examples of language which George uses to write a strong answer.**

4 leer **Complete the essay plan based on George's answer.**

5 escribir **Prepare your own answer to the task.**

- Look at the Answer Booster and George's plan for ideas.
- Write a detailed plan. Organise your answer in paragraphs.
- Write your answer and carefully check what you have written.

Mi área local

Le gusta mucho la región donde vive.

Escriba un artículo para convencer a los lectores de la importancia de mejorar su zona.

Debe incluir los puntos siguientes:

- qué tiempo hace normalmente en verano y en invierno
- lo que hay en su zona para los turistas
- cómo han mejorado la zona recientemente
- sus ideas para mejorar su ciudad / pueblo en el futuro.

Justifique sus ideas y sus opiniones.

Escriba aproximadamente 130–150 palabras **en español**.

Paragraph 1
- My home town size / location
- Climate
- Number of visitors and why

Paragraph 2
- Lots for…

As you complete the essay plan, try to write a couple of words or a short phrase for each sentence of George's answer. In the exam, you will not want to spend too long writing your plan.

Mi ciudad natal es Newcastle, la ciudad más grande del noreste de Inglaterra. Es una ciudad genial, **aunque tiene un clima bastante frío y variable**. A pesar del tiempo, **la ciudad acoge a** más de dos millones de visitantes todos los años, quizás porque la gente es tan alegre y abierta.

Newcastle **ofrece muchas posibilidades para los turistas**. **Se puede salir a la montaña** con solo un corto viaje en coche o en autobús. Además, las familias con niños **pueden disfrutar de un día interesante** en el Centro de Ciencias de la Vida, mi lugar favorito, que está situado en el centro.

En los últimos años han mejorado el sistema de transporte público, así que ahora es una ciudad bien conectada por tren con otras ciudades importantes. Además, han renovado varios edificios antiguos, incluso el centro comercial, donde **acaban de abrir nuevas tiendas de marca**.

Desde mi punto de vista, ahora **se debería construir más casas** y crear más oportunidades de empleo en Newcastle para los jóvenes. También introduciría más zonas peatonales y pondría más áreas verdes en el centro **para hacerlo todavía más pintoresco y acogedor**.

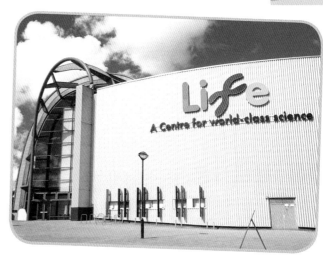

⭐ Focus on making links to join your phrases and sentences. How many different links can you spot in George's answer? What do *a pesar de* and *incluso* mean?

B – Translation

1 escribir   **Translate the passage into Spanish.**

Which tense do you need to use to describe things in the past?

My town used to be horrible because there was so much pollution, but they have introduced a new system to control traffic and now there are not as many cars. I like living here because there is a lot to do, and all the shops are nearby. However, in the future I will live in another city as there is a lot of unemployment here.

Don't translate this idiomatic phrase word for word. How do you translate 'to'?

Do you need *ser* or *estar* here? In which person of the verb?

Translate these using the same word in Spanish, but don't forget to use the correct ending.

You have lots of possibilities here. The meaning is 'because' or 'given that'.

2 escribir   **Now translate the following passage into Spanish. Use your answer to exercise 1 to help you.**

My life in the country used to be too quiet but now I think it is fun because I have so many friends who live nearby. They have introduced more buses so therefore public transport is more reliable. In the future, I will live here if there are more job opportunities.

En mi ciudad | In my town

Hay… / Mi ciudad tiene…	There is/are… / My town has…
un ayuntamiento	a town hall
un bar / muchos bares	a bar / lots of bars
un castillo (en ruinas)	a (ruined) castle
un cine	a cinema
un mercado	a market
un museo / unos museos	a museum / a few museums
un parque	a park
un polideportivo	a sports centre
un puerto	a port
muchos restaurantes	lots of restaurants
un teatro	a theatre
una biblioteca	a library
una bolera	a bowling alley
una iglesia	a church
una piscina	a swimming pool
una playa / unas playas	a beach / a few beaches
una Plaza Mayor	a town square
una pista de hielo	an ice rink
una oficina de Correos	a post office
una tienda / muchas tiendas	a shop / lots of shops
muchos lugares de interés	lots of sights
algo / mucho que hacer	something / a lot to do
no hay nada que hacer	there is nothing to do
Vivo en un pueblo…	I live in a … village
histórico / moderno	historic / modern
tranquilo / ruidoso	quiet / noisy
turístico / industrial	touristy / industrial
bonito / feo	pretty / ugly
Está situado/a en … del país.	It is situated in … of the country.
el norte / el sur / el este / el oeste	the north / the south / the east / the west

¿Por dónde se va al / a la…? | How do you get to the…?

¿Dónde está el / la…?	Where is the…?
¿El / La …. está cerca / lejos?	Is the …nearby / far away?
sigue todo recto	go straight on
gira a la derecha / izquierda	turn right / left
toma la primera / segunda / tercera calle a la derecha / a la izquierda	take the first / second / third road on the right / left
pasa el puente / los semáforos	go over the bridge / the traffic lights
cruza la plaza / la calle	cross the square / the street
coge el autobús número 37	take the number 37 bus
está…	it is…
en la esquina / al final de la calle	on the corner / at the end of the street
al lado del museo / enfrente de…	next to the museum / opposite…

¿Cómo es tu zona? | What is your area like?

está situado/a en un valle	it is situated in a valley
entre el desierto y la sierra	between the desert and the mountains
al lado del río / mar Mediterráneo	by the river / Mediterranean sea
Está…	It is…
rodeado/a de volcanes / sierra	surrounded by volcanoes / mountains
lleno/a de bosques / selvas	full of woods / forests
a … metros sobre el nivel de mar	at … metres above sea level
Tiene…	It has…
unos impresionantes paisajes naturales	some amazing natural landscapes
varias influencias culturales	various cultural influences
el bullicio del una ciudad	the hustle and bustle of a city
El clima es…	The climate is…
soleado / caluroso / seco / templado / frío	sunny / hot / dry / mild / cold
llueve (muy) poco / a menudo	it rains (very) little / often
en primavera / verano / otoño / invierno	in spring / summer / autumn / winter
hay mucha marcha	there is lots going on
Es…	It is…
mi ciudad natal / mi lugar favorito	My home town / my favourite place
acogedor/a / atractivo/a	welcoming / attractive
famoso/a / conocido/a por	famous for / well-known for
una región muy húmeda	a very humid region
una zona muy montañosa / pintoresca	a mountainous / picturesque area
tan fácil desplazarse	so easy to get around
Se puede…	You / One can…
estar mucho tiempo al aire libre	spend lots of time in the open air
subir a la torre	go up the tower
hacer un recorrido en autobús	do a bus tour
disfrutar de las vistas / del ambiente	enjoy the views / the atmosphere
viajar en el AVE	travel on the AVE high-speed train
pasear por los lagos artificiales	go boating on the artificial lakes
apreciar la arquitectura variada	appreciate the variety of architecture
aprovechar el buen tiempo	make the most of the good weather
Se pueden…	You / One can…
probar platos típicos	try local dishes
practicar deportes acuáticos	do water sports
ver edificios de estilos muy diferentes	see buildings with very different styles
alquilar bolas de agua	hire water balls
practicar senderismo y ciclismo	go hiking / trekking and cycling

En la oficina de turismo | At the tourist office

¿Me puede dar…?	Can you give me…?
un plano de la ciudad	a map of the town / city
más información sobre…	more information about…
¿Cuánto cuesta una entrada?	How much is a ticket?
para adultos / niños	for adults / children
¿Dónde se pueden sacar las entradas?	Where can you get tickets?
¿A qué hora…?	What time…?
sale el autobús?	does the bus leave?
abre…?	does…open?
¿Hay visitas guiadas?	Are there guided tours?
¿Me puede recomendar…?	Can you recommend…?
un restaurante típico	a typical restaurant
un hotel / una excursión	a hotel / a trip

¿Qué haremos mañana? | What will we do tomorrow?

Sacaré muchas fotos.	I will take lots of photos.
Subiremos al teleférico.	We will go up on the cable car.
Bajaremos a pie.	We will go down on foot.
Pasaremos entre las nubes.	We will go through the clouds.
Iremos a la playa / a la montaña / de excursión en barco.	We will go to the beach / to the mountains / on a boat trip.
Haremos piragüismo.	We will go canoeing.
Podremos hacer paddlesurf.	We will be able to go paddlesurfing.
Podrás comprar regalos.	You will be able to buy presents.
será genial / mejor	it will be great / better
nos llevará	he/she will take us
Estoy (muy) a gusto.	I am feeling (very much) at home.
¡Buena idea!	Good idea!
de acuerdo	OK
¡Qué pena! / ¡Qué mal (rollo)!	What a shame! / What a nightmare!
¡Qué triste!	How sad!

¿Qué tiempo hará? | What will the weather be like?

Hará sol / viento.	It will be sunny / windy.
Habrá…	There will be…
nubes / claros / chubascos	clouds / clear spells / showers
una ola de calor	a heat wave
truenos y relámpagos	thunder and lightning
temperaturas más altas / bajas	higher / lower temperatures
granizos / brisas fuertes	hail / strong winds
periodos soleados	sunny periods
lloverá (bastante)	it will rain (quite a bit)
Las temperaturas subirán / bajarán.	The temperatures will rise / fall.
El tiempo…	The weather….
será variable	will be variable
se despejará	will clear up
cambiará	will change
no nos importará	will not matter to us

Las tiendas — Shops

el banco	bank
el estanco	tobacconist's
la cafetería	café
la carnicería	butcher's
la estación de trenes	train station
la farmacia	pharmacy / chemist
la frutería	greengrocer's
la joyería	jeweller's
la librería	book shop
la panadería	bakery
la papelería	stationery shop
la pastelería	cake shop
la peluquería	hairdresser's
la pescadería	fish shop
la tienda de ropa	clothes shop
la zapatería	shoe shop
un regalo	a present
sellos	stamps
una carta / unas cartas	a letter / a few letters
recoger	to pick up
mandar	to send
horario comercial / horas de apertura	business hours / opening hours
de lunes a viernes	from Monday to Friday
abre a la(s)… / cierra a la(s)…	it opens at… / it closes at…
no cierra a mediodía	it doesn't close at midday
cerrado domingo y festivos	closed on Sundays and public holidays
abierto todos los días	open every day

Recuerdos y regalos — Souvenirs and presents

el abanico	fan
el chorizo	chorizo (sausage)
el llavero	key ring
el oso de peluche	teddy bear
los pendientes	earrings
la gorra	cap
la taza	mug
las golosinas	sweets
las pegatinas	stickers
¿Me puede ayudar?	Can you help me?
Quiero comprar…	I want to buy…
¿Tiene uno/a/os/as más barato/a/os/as?	Do you have a cheaper one / cheaper ones?
un billete de (cincuenta) euros	a (fifty) euro note
tengo cambio	I have change

Quejas — Complaints

Quiero devolver…	I want to return…
está roto/a	it is broken
es demasiado estrecho/a / largo/a	it is too tight / long
tiene un agujero / una mancha	it has a hole / a stain
falta un botón	it's missing a button
¿Puede reembolsarme (el dinero)?	Can you reimburse me (the money)?
Podemos hacer un cambio.	We can exchange (it).
¿Qué me recomienda?	What do you recommend?
¿Qué tal…? / ¿Qué te parece(n)…?	What about…? / What do you think of…?
Te queda bien.	It suits you.
Te quedan demasiado grandes.	They are too big on you.
una talla más grande / pequeña	a bigger / smaller size
en rebajas	on sale
Me lo/la/los/las llevo.	I'll take it / them.

De compras — Shopping

Normalmente voy… / Suelo ir…	Usually I go… / I tend to go…
a los centros comerciales	to shopping centres
de tiendas con mis amigos	shopping with my friends
Nunca me ha gustado / Prefiero / Odio…	I've never liked / I prefer / I hate…
comprar en…	shopping in…
cadenas / grandes almacenes	chain stores / department stores
tiendas de diseño / segunda mano	designer shops / second-hand shops
comprar por Internet / en la red	shopping on the internet / online
hacer cola	queueing
porque…	because…
es más económico / práctico / cómodo	it's cheaper / more practical / more convenient
es un buen sitio para pasar la tarde	it's a good place for spending the afternoon
hay más variedad / demasiada gente	there is more variety / there are too many people
los precios son más bajos	the prices are lower
hay más ofertas	there are more offers
ropa alternativa / de moda	alternative clothing / fashionable clothing
gangas	bargains
artículos de marca	branded items

Los pros y los contras de la ciudad — The for and against of living in a city

Lo mejor de vivir en la ciudad es que…	The best thing about living in a city is that…
es tan fácil desplazarse	it's so easy to get around
hay una red de transporte público	there is a public transport system
hay tantas diversiones	there are so many things to do
hay muchas posibilidades de trabajo	there are lots of job opportunities
Lo peor es que…	The worst thing is that…
el centro es tan ruidoso	the centre is so noisy
hay tanto tráfico / tantos coches	there is so much traffic / so many cars
se lleva una vida tan frenética	life is so frenetic
la gente no se conoce	people don't know each other
En el campo…	In the countryside…
el transporte público no es fiable	public transport is not reliable
hay bastante desempleo	there is quite a lot of unemployment
no hay tantos atascos como antes	there are not as many traffic jams as before
Yo conozco a todos mis vecinos	I know all my neighbours

¿Qué harías? — What would you do?

Introduciría más zonas peatonales.	I would introduce more pedestrian areas.
Renovaría…	I would renovate…
algunos edificios antiguos	some old buildings
las zonas deterioradas en las afueras	the dilapidated areas on the outskirts
Mejoraría el sistema de transporte.	I would improve the transport system.
Pondría / Crearía más áreas de ocio.	I would put in / create more leisure areas.
Construiría un nuevo centro comercial.	I would build a new shopping centre.
Invertiría en el turismo rural.	I would invest in rural tourism.
Controlaría el ruido.	I would limit the noise.

Destino Arequipa — Destination Arequipa

Vi / Vimos lugares interesantes.	I saw / We saw interesting places.
Tuvimos un guía.	We had a guide.
Nos hizo un recorrido.	He/She did a tour for us.
Nos ayudó a entender toda la historia	He/She helped us to understand all of the history.
Recorrí a pie el centro histórico.	I walked around the historic centre.
Compré tantas cosas.	I bought so many things.
Alquilé una bici de montaña.	I hired a mountain bike.
Cogí un autobús turístico.	I took a tourist bus.
subimos / bajamos	we went up / we went down
Aprendí mucho sobre la cultura.	I learned a lot about the culture.
Me quedé impresionado con la ciudad.	I was really impressed by the city.
Había vistas maravillosas.	There were amazing views.
La comida estaba muy buena.	The food was very good.
La gente era abierta.	The people were open.
Lo que más me gustó fue / fueron…	What I liked most was / were…
¡Fue una experiencia única!	It was a one-off experience!
¡Qué miedo!	What a scare!
Volveré algún día.	I will go back one day.
Aprenderé a hacer surf.	I will learn to surf.
Trabajaré como voluntario/a.	I will work as a volunteer.

6 De costumbre
Punto de partida 1

- *Describing mealtimes*
- *Talking about daily routine*

1 escuchar

Escucha y apunta los detalles para Zoe y Ángel. (1–4)

1. el desayuno · *Ejemplo: Zoe – 7.15, f, …*
2. la comida / el almuerzo
3. la merienda
4. la cena

2 hablar

Con tu compañero/a, haz diálogos.

- ● ¿A qué hora <u>desayunas</u>?
- ■ *Normalmente <u>desayuno</u> a las…*
- ● ¿Qué <u>desayunas</u>?
- ■ *Depende. A veces <u>desayuno</u>…, pero…*

3 leer

Empareja las mitades de las frases.
¿Qué significan las palabras en negrita?

1. Normalmente desayuno **algo muy rápido**, ya que…
2. Sin embargo, los fines de semana…
3. **Entre semana** almuerzo en casa…
4. **De postre** siempre como **algo dulce**…
5. Por lo general, después del insti…
6. Por la noche no ceno mucho…

a. meriendo **algo ligero, como** fruta o un yogur, por ejemplo.
b. (por ejemplo, un pastel o un helado) porque **soy muy goloso**.
c. dado que no **tengo mucha hambre**.
d. tomo un desayuno **más fuerte** porque tengo más tiempo.
e. **tengo mucha prisa** por la mañana.
f. con mi familia a las dos y media.

¿A qué hora ¿Qué	desayunas? comes / almuerzas? meriendas? cenas?
Desayuno Como / Almuerzo Meriendo Ceno	a las ocho al mediodía
	cereales, churros, tostadas, fruta, galletas, un huevo, un yogur, un pastel, un bocadillo, una hamburguesa, carne, pollo, pescado, marisco, paella, sopa, tortilla, ensalada, verduras, patatas fritas Cola Cao, leche, café, té, zumo de naranja

In Spanish there are different verbs for each meal:

Desayunar	to have breakfast / to have… for breakfast
Comer / Almorzar	to have lunch / to have… for lunch
Merendar	to have tea / to have… for tea
Cenar	to have dinner / to have… for dinner

You can also use the word *tomar*, which means 'to have' (food / drink).

4 escribir

Escribe un texto sobre las comidas en tu casa. Usa expresiones del ejercicio 3.

Entre semana, normalmente desayuno a las…
Suelo desayunar algo…

To add variety to your language:
- use *soler* + infinitive.
  Suelo almorzar a la una.   I **tend to** have lunch at 1.00.
- use verbs in the 'we' form.
  En mi casa **cenamos** *a las diez.*   In my house **we have dinner** at 10.00.

Take care with stem-changing verbs, e.g. *al<u>o</u>rzar* (*alm<u>ue</u>rzo*) and
mer<u>e</u>ndar (*mer<u>ie</u>ndo*).

5 leer **Lee el texto. Copia y completa la tabla.**

activity	time	details
e	6.20	*Hates getting up early in winter*

Me despierto a las seis y veinte y me levanto enseguida. Odio levantarme temprano en invierno. Primero, a las seis y media, voy a la cocina donde desayuno mientras que mi hermana se ducha. A las siete menos cuarto (¡o cuando mi hermana termina!) me ducho y luego me peino. Solo me afeito una vez a la semana. A las siete me visto en mi dormitorio, y después salgo de casa a las siete y cuarto para coger el autobús escolar.

Por la tarde vuelvo a casa a las cuatro y media, o más tarde si tengo actividades deportivas. Finalmente, después de la cena, me lavo los dientes a las diez y media u once menos cuarto y me acuesto enseguida.

Gabriel

6 escuchar **Escucha. Contesta a las preguntas en inglés.**

1 What is Héctor's job and where does he work?
2 What time does he get up?
3 What does he find difficult about this?
4 What does he do to save time? (give <u>two</u> details)
5 What is the worst thing about his routine?
6 What does he like most about it?

Héctor

G *Reflexive verbs* > *Page 211*

Remember, many daily routine verbs are reflexive in Spanish.

me *levanto*	I get up
te *levantas*	you get up
se *levanta*	he/she gets up
nos *levantamos*	we get up
os *levantáis*	you (plural) get up
se *levantan*	they get up

When the verb is used in the infinitive, the correct reflexive pronoun is added to the end.

*No me gusta levantar**me** temprano.*   I don't like getting up early.

Remember that lots of daily routine verbs are also stem-changing.

*Me ac**ue**sto a las once.*   I go to bed at 11.00.
*Prefiero ac**o**star**me** temprano.*   I prefer going to bed early.

⭐ To vary and extend your language:
- use sequencers (**Primero**… **y luego**…)
- use connectives such as **donde**, **cuando** and **para**
- add opinions (*Odio ducharme cuando hace frío*)
- use other persons of the verb (*Mi madre se acuesta más tarde*)

7 hablar **Con tu compañero/a, habla de tu rutina diaria durante <u>un minuto</u>.**

● *Me despierto a las… Prefiero despertarme temprano porque…*

Punto de partida 2

- *Talking about illnesses and injuries*
- *Asking for help at the pharmacy*

1 Lee los textos y escribe la letra correcta.

1 Tengo catarro y tengo tos. También tengo dolor de garganta y estoy muy cansado. Me siento fatal.

2 No me encuentro bien. Tengo diarrea y tengo náuseas. Además, tengo dolor de cabeza.

3 Tengo quemaduras de sol y creo que tengo una insolación. Tengo mucho sueño. También tengo una picadura.

4 Estoy enfermo. Tengo fiebre – primero tengo calor y luego tengo frío. Creo que tengo gripe.

 **a**  **b**  **c**  **d**

2 Estás en la farmacia. Escucha y apunta los detalles en español. (1–5)

Ejemplo: **1** *fiebre, dos días*

¿Desde hace cuánto tiempo?	Desde hace un día / mes una hora / semana más de…
¿Desde cuándo?	Desde ayer / anteayer esta mañana / tarde el (martes) pasado

Remember to use **estar** for temporary states and feelings.

Estoy *enfermo.*   **I am** ill.

Use **tener** to say that that you <u>have</u> something, but also for certain expressions where English uses the verb 'to be'.

Tengo *gripe.*   **I have** flu.
Mi madre **tiene** *sueño.*   My mum **is** sleepy.

3 Escribe consejos para las personas del ejercicio 1.

Tiene(s) que Hay que	beber mucha agua descansar tomar este jarabe / estas pastillas tomar aspirinas ir al hospital / médico / dentista usar esta crema

4 Estás en la farmacia. Con tu compañero/a, haz diálogos.

- ● *Estoy enfermo/a.*
- ■ *¿Qué le pasa?*
- ● *Estoy / Tengo… Además…*
- ■ *¿Desde hace cuánto tiempo? / ¿Desde cuándo?*
- ● *Desde hace… / Desde…*
- ■ *No se preocupe. Hay que… También tiene que…*
- ● *Muchas gracias.*

When saying new words, apply the pronunciation rules you know.

How do you pronounce … ?

aspirinas   jarabe   pastillas   hospital   crema

5 escuchar Escucha y escribe las letras en el orden correcto. (1–3)

b los oídos / las orejas
c los dientes / las muelas
g los ojos
h la cabeza
f la nariz
e el brazo
i la boca
d la mano
j la garganta
k el estómago
l la pierna
m la rodilla
o el pie
a la espalda
n el tobillo

Zona Cultura

La Tomatina es una fiesta que tiene lugar en Buñol (Valencia) el último miércoles de agosto. Cada año, los 20.000 participantes lanzan más de 150.000 tomates en una hora. Después de la batalla los bomberos limpian las calles, que están cubiertas de jugo de tomate.

6 escuchar Escucha. Apunta los detalles en inglés. (1–5)

- What hurts?
- Why?

Me	duele	la pierna
Te	duelen	el tobillo
Le		los ojos
Me he	roto	las muelas
Te has	torcido	etc.
Se ha	cortado	
	quemado	
	hecho daño en	

Doler (to hurt) is a stem-changing verb. It works like *gustar*.

Me *duele la espalda.*   My back hurts.
A *mi abuela* **le** *duelen los oídos.*   My gran has earache.

To say you have hurt/broken/twisted/cut/burned something, use the **perfect tense**. Put the correct **reflexive pronoun** before the verb, and use the **definite article**.

Me *he roto* **la** *pierna.*   I have broken my leg.

7 hablar Tu familia está enferma. El médico no habla inglés. Haz diálogos.

● *Mi padre se ha <u>torcido la rodilla</u> y ahora le duele mucho <u>la pierna</u>.*

■ *¡Qué mala suerte! / ¡Qué desastre! Tiene que <u>descansar</u> y <u>tomar…</u>*

8 escribir Traduce las frases al español.

1 I've had a cold for a week and my stomach aches.
2 I feel awful. I think I have flu because I have a temperature. I also have a sore throat.
3 My sister has hurt her foot. Also, she has a headache.
4 I've broken my leg and I have to rest. What a disaster!

When learning a new verb phrase (e.g. *Me siento mal*), try to learn the infinitive too.

What do you think these infinitives mean?

romperse (el brazo)   *torcerse (el tobillo)*
sentirse (mal)   *hacerse daño (en el pie)*

- Talking about typical foods
- Using the passive
- Spotting words which indicate an increase/decrease

1 leer — Empareja los dibujos con la lista de la compra correcta. Sobra una lista.

Dietas del mundo

¿Qué consume una familia típica cada semana?

Guatemala

Cuba

a
- siete latas de cerveza
- dos botellas de refrescos
- novecientos gramos de queso
- dos barras de pan grandes
- una docena de huevos
- una piña

b
- doce paquetes de patatas fritas
- una caja de cereales
- un paquete de mantequilla
- cien gramos de azúcar
- quinientos gramos de harina
- un bote de mermelada

c
- tres kilos y medio de zanahorias
- veintitrés litros de agua
- una botella grande de aceite
- veintidós kilos de maíz
- dos kilos de judías verdes
- tres coliflores

2 escuchar — Escucha y comprueba tus respuestas. Apunta en inglés otros <u>dos</u> o <u>tres</u> productos mencionados para cada pais.

⭐ Words for quantities or containers are followed by **de**. Find <u>ten</u> examples in exercise 1.

3 escuchar — ¿Qué comen los españoles? Escucha y escribe las letras correctas.

1 Hoy en día la dieta mediterránea en España es…
a más popular que antes.
b menos popular que antes.
c tan popular como antes.

2 Cada vez más españoles comen…
a una dieta variada, equilibrada y sana.
b comida sabrosa.
c comida rápida y sencilla de preparar.

3 Ahora los españoles consumen cada vez menos…
a carne, dulces y aceite de oliva.
b legumbres (judías, guisantes, lentejas).
c lácteos (leche, yogur, queso).

4 Las frutas más populares son…
a los plátanos, las manzanas y las naranjas.
b los melones, las uvas y los pomelos.
c las fresas, las peras y los albaricoques.

🔍 Try to spot phrases which indicate whether something has **increased**, **decreased** or stayed **the same**. For example:

↑	cada vez más	more and more
	un incremento	an increase
↑↓	mismo	same
	seguir	to carry on
↓	cada vez menos	less and less
	perder	to lose
	ya no	no longer

4 hablar — Con tu compañero/a, habla de lo que consume tu familia.

- ¿Qué come tu familia cada semana?
  - *Creo que comemos <u>tres kilos de naranjas</u> porque son <u>sanas</u>. Además,…*
- ¿Y qué bebe tu familia?
  - *Bebemos <u>cinco litros de leche</u> porque es…*

5 leer Lee el texto. Identifica las <u>cuatro</u> frases correctas.

El sabor latino por Víctor Mediavilla

el chairo

el borí borí

¿Has probado la gastronomía latina? Con un sinfín de sabores, la cocina latinoamericana disfruta de gran prestigio mundial. Uno de los platos es *el cebiche*, un plato de pescado que fue inventado en Perú por la población indígena hace dos mil años. Otra joya de la cocina latinoamericana es *el chairo* boliviano, un tipo de guiso que contiene zanahorias, cebolla, carne de ternera y patatas, que fue introducido por el pueblo aimara.

La gastronomía de Venezuela es una mezcla de sabores tropicales y andinos. También incluye *las arepas* (similares a las tortillas mexicanas), preparadas con harina de maíz, que fueron exportadas a las islas Canarias. Si prefieres la cocina caribeña, la República Dominicana lo tiene todo. Por ejemplo, *la bandera dominicana* es un plato suculento que combina el arroz, las judías y la carne.

Sin embargo, mi recomendación personal es *el borí borí* de Paraguay, una sopa muy típica compuesta de harina de maíz, queso fresco y pollo. ¡Está riquísima!

el sinfín	endless number
el sabor	flavour / taste
el guiso	stew

1 La comida latina es muy variada.
2 No es muy conocida internacionalmente.
3 *El cebiche* es un plato bastante nuevo.
4 Su ingrediente principal es el pescado.

5 *El chairo* es el plato nacional de Bolivia.
6 *Las arepas* no fueron inventadas en las islas Canarias.
7 *La bandera* contiene muchas verduras distintas.
8 *El borí borí* no es un plato vegetariano.

6 escuchar **Escucha las entrevistas. Apunta en inglés: (1–4)**

- Name of dish:
- Origin:
- Ingredients:
- Opinion:

7 hablar **Con tu compañero/a, habla de los platos de los ejercicios 5 y 6.**

- ● *¿Has probado el/la/los/las…?*
- ■ *✓ Sí, lo/la/los/las he probado y (no) me gustó/gustaron (mucho/nada).*
- ■ *✗ No, no lo/la/los/las he probado. ¿En qué consiste(n)?*
- ● *Es/Son…*

8 escribir **Escribe un artículo sobre la comida típica de tu país.**

¿Has probado la comida (inglesa)?
Tiene una mezcla de…
Uno de los platos más… es…
Es un plato… que fue…
Si prefieres…

G **The passive** > Page 232

The **passive** is used to say what <u>is / was / will be done</u> to something or someone. To form it, use the correct person and tense of **ser** followed by the **past participle**, which must agree.

Fue inventado hace mil años. **It was invented** a thousand years ago.
Es conocida en todo el mundo. **It's known** throughout the world.

Can you spot the other examples of the passive used in exercise 5?

¿Has probado…?		el gazpacho, la fabada, la ensaladilla rusa, la paella
Es	un tipo de	bebida, guiso, sopa, postre, pescado
	un plato	caliente / frío típico de…
Contiene(n) Consiste(n) en		carne de cerdo / cordero / ternera, pollo marisco, huevos, chorizo, atún, arroz, ajo, cebolla, pepino, pimientos, judías, zanahorias
Fue	inventado introducido	en (Colombia) por (la población indígena)

2 **¡De fiesta!**

- *Comparing different festivals*
- *Avoiding the passive*
- *Paying attention to question words*

1 escuchar

Escucha y lee. Busca los verbos en español.

Fiestas curiosas
¡Las fiestas más raras de España!

La fiesta de **Els Enfarinats se celebra** el 28 de diciembre en el pueblo pequeño de Ibi. Esta extraña tradición, con más de 200 años de historia, **se caracteriza por** una gran batalla en la que **se lanzan** huevos y harina.

Entre el 7 y el 14 de julio **se celebran los Sanfermines**, una tradición antigua en la que más de un millón de españoles y extranjeros visitan la ciudad de Pamplona. Los más valientes se visten de blanco con un pañuelo rojo y corren delante de los toros en 'el encierro', un evento que **se repite** cada día a las ocho de la mañana.

En junio, Alicante **se llena de** música y desfiles para celebrar la llegada del verano con **las Hogueras de San Juan**. Las 'hogueras', que **se construyen** por toda la ciudad, consisten en espectaculares y gigantescas figuras de madera y cartón que **se queman** el 24 de junio, la noche de San Juan. También **se disparan** fuegos artificiales.

el pañuelo	*scarf*
el desfile	*procession*
la hoguera	*bonfire*

1	is filled with	**4**	is characterised by	**7**	are celebrated
2	is celebrated	**5**	are set off	**8**	are built
3	is repeated	**6**	are burned	**9**	are thrown

2 leer

Lee los textos del ejercicio 1 otra vez. Contesta a las preguntas en español.

1 **¿Quiénes** son los visitantes de los Sanfermines?
2 **¿Por qué** son valientes los participantes de los encierros?
3 **¿A qué hora** empieza el encierro?
4 **¿Cómo** se celebra la fiesta de Els Enfarinats?
5 **¿Cuándo** se celebra la llegada del verano en Alicante?
6 **¿Dónde** se construyen figuras enormes?
7 **¿Qué** fiesta <u>no</u> se celebra en verano?

> ⭐ Pay special attention to **question words** to make sure you give the correct information. What do the question words in exercise 2 mean?

> **G** **Avoiding the passive** > *Page 232*
>
> In Spanish the passive is often avoided by using the reflexive pronoun **se**.
>
> *La fiesta **se celebra** en marzo.* — The festival **is celebrated** (literally 'celebrates itself') in March.
>
> Sometimes the subject of the verb comes after the verb.
>
> ***Se lanzan** huevos.* — Eggs **are thrown** (literally 'throw themselves').

3 escuchar

Escucha. Copia y completa la tabla en inglés. (1–3)

	festival	where	when	details
1	Las Fallas	Valencia		

4 hablar

Con tu compañero/a, habla de las fiestas de los ejercicios 1 y 3.

- *¿Qué fiesta te interesa más / menos?*
- *¿Cuándo / Dónde / Cómo se celebra?*
- *¿Por qué (no) te interesa?*

5 escribir **Rellena los espacios en blanco. Escribe la forma correcta del verbo.**

calaveritas de azúcar

El Día de Muertos

Esta costumbre mexicana, que coincide con la fiesta católica de Todos los Santos, es popular hoy en muchos países del mundo. Se celebra el 1 y 2 de noviembre cuando, según la leyenda, los muertos **1** <u>vuelven</u> a ver a sus familiares. En México muchas personas **2** ━━━━━ los cementerios donde **3** ━━━━━ las tumbas y las **4** ━━━━━ con velas y flores. En casa, los mexicanos **5** ━━━━━ altares en honor de los muertos con calaveritas de azúcar, objetos personales y la comida favorita de sus seres queridos. También **6** ━━━━━ 'pan de muerto', un tipo de pan dulce. En muchas ciudades los niños **7** ━━━━━ y **8** ━━━━━ a la calle con sus padres para ver los desfiles de calaveras.

la tumba	*grave*
la vela	*candle*
la calavera	*skull*
la seres queridos	*loved ones*

comer	visitar	disfrazarse	salir
~~volver~~	limpiar	decorar	preparar

⭐ Use the 'they' form of the verb in each of the blanks. Take extra care with reflexive, stem-changing and irregular verbs.

6 hablar **Con tu compañero/a, haz una comparación de las dos fiestas.**

● *En mi opinión, son muy similares porque en las dos fiestas los niños…*

■ *Sí, pero también son diferentes porque en Halloween…, pero en el Día de…*

El Día de Muertos   Halloween

- 1–2 November
- Mexico
- 'bread of the dead'
- altars at home
- decorate graves
- processions

- coincides with All Saints' Day
- celebrated in many countries
- fancy dress
- special food

- 31 October
- US, UK, Canada, Ireland
- toffee apples
- pumpkin lanterns
- 'trick or treat'
- horror films

7 escribir **Escribe un texto en español sobre la Noche de Guy Fawkes.**

an old English tradition

more than four hundred years old

celebrated 5th November every year

children eat toffee apples

dummies (*muñecos*) of Guy Fawkes are burned

bonfires are built

fireworks are set off

Halloween El Día de Muertos	se celebra	en (otoño) el… de…
Muchas personas Los jóvenes Los niños Los ingleses Los mexicanos Los familiares Las familias	comen	manzanas de caramelo pan de muerto
	decoran	las tumbas con… las casas con…
	se disfrazan	de brujas / fantasmas de calaveras
	ven	desfiles películas de terror
	preparan	linternas de calabaza altares
	juegan a 'truco o trato'	

- Describing a special day
- Using reflexive verbs in the preterite
- Inferring meaning in literary texts

1 leer Lee y escribe el número y la letra correctos para cada texto.
Lee los textos otra vez y busca los verbos reflexivos en el presente.

A medianoche comemos doce uvas, una por cada campanada, para tener buena suerte en el nuevo año. Los adultos beben 'cava' (que es parecido al champán) y todos nos acostamos muy tarde. Otra tradición es que ¡llevamos ropa interior roja! **Alba**

Celebramos el final del mes de Ramadán con una rutina especial. Nos levantamos muy temprano, rezamos, nos bañamos, nos lavamos los dientes y nos vestimos con nuestra mejor ropa. Desayunamos algo dulce y luego vamos a la mezquita. Después, mi madre prepara una comida deliciosa y visitamos a los amigos. **Mariam**

Hacemos una cena especial con toda la familia. Cenamos bacalao y pavo, y luego comemos dulces navideños como turrón o mazapanes. Mucha gente va a la iglesia para celebrar la 'Misa del Gallo' y canta villancicos tradicionales. El día siguiente es el Día de Navidad y me despierto temprano para abrir los regalos. **Fer**

1 Nochebuena (24 de diciembre)   **2** Eid al-Fitr   **3** Domingo de Pascua   **4** Nochevieja (31 de diciembre)

a 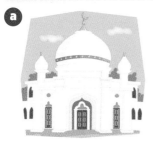   **b**    **c**    **d**

2 escuchar Escucha. ¿Qué día especial celebraron ayer? (1–7)
Ejemplo: **1** Nochebuena

la campanada	stroke (of a bell)
rezar	to pray
el bacalao	cod

3 escuchar Daniel habla de su día especial. Escucha y apunta los detalles en inglés.

- the occasion: *13th birthday and…*
- getting ready / clothes:
- the ceremony:
- the celebration / gifts:

G Preterite tense of reflexive verbs

In the **preterite tense**, reflexive verbs behave in the same way as other verbs but need a reflexive pronoun in front of the verb.

me acosté	**nos** acostamos
te acostaste	**os** acostasteis
se acostó	**se** acostaron

Stem-changing verbs only have a stem change in the present tense, <u>not</u> in the preterite.

infinitive	present	preterite
acostarse	me ac**ue**sto	me ac**o**sté
despertarse	me desp**i**erto	me desp**e**rté

4 hablar Eres Alba, Mariam o Fer. Describe tu día especial de ayer.

- ¿Qué hiciste ayer?
- *Ayer fue… Por la noche cené… Luego comí…*

5 escribir **Traduce el texto al español.**

Proms don't really exist in Spain, so there isn't a word for this. You could use the phrase *el baile de fin de curso* to explain what you mean.

Which verb do you need to use here?

Last Saturday was a very special day because it was the School Prom. In the afternoon I went to the hairdresser's and then had a shower and did my make up. I wore my new dress, which I received for Christmas. Then I went to the hotel with my friends, where we had dinner, danced and took lots of photos. It was an unforgettable night!

Which word do you need for 'in' here?

Don't translate this word for word. Use the reflexive verb *maquillarse*.

6 leer **Lee los dos extractos de una novela. Escribe las letras correctas.**

Alejandro Palomas

Una madre de Alejandro Palomas

Sentados a la mesa del comedor, mamá cuenta uvas y yo doblo las servilletas rojas mientras en el horno se enfría la crema de espárragos y un asado de pavo.

Barcelona. Hoy es 31 de diciembre.

–Seremos cinco –dice mamá. Eso sin contar a Olga, claro. – Olga es la novia de Emma.

–Aunque tío Eduardo llegará un poco más tarde, porque su vuelo lleva retraso –aclara.

* * * * *

Olga y Silvia van metiendo platos y copas en el lavavajillas y organizan el cava, las uvas y el turrón.

Instantes después suena un pequeño tintineo en mi móvil. Lo saco del bolsillo y veo un WhatsApp. Es de ella. "Si es niña, se llamará Sara".

contar	to count
el horno	oven
el bolsillo	pocket

1 For dinner they are going to have…
  a a home-cooked meal.
  b a vegetarian meal.
  c a selection of meats.

2 Including Olga there will be…
  a four people.
  b five people.
  c six people.

3 Emma and Olga are…
  a mother and daughter.
  b sisters.
  c a couple.

4 Uncle Eduardo is travelling…
  a on foot.
  b by plane.
  c by train.

5 The second extract takes place…
  a before dinner.
  b after dinner.
  c after midnight.

6 We suspect that the person who has sent the message…
  a is pregnant.
  b has had a baby girl.
  c knows she is going to have a baby girl.

When reading extracts from novels or plays you often have to 'read between the lines' to infer what is being said.

For example, what can you deduce from these details?

*porque su **vuelo** lleva retraso* (question 4)
***Si** es niña, se llamará Sara* (question 6)

4 **¡A comer!**

- Ordering in a restaurant
- Using absolute superlatives
- Spotting irregular verb patterns in the preterite

1 escuchar **Escucha y lee los anuncios. ¿Qué restaurante recomiendas? (1–8)**

a ## Restaurante El Faro

En el restaurante El Faro te espera un ambiente acogedor. Con más de cincuenta platos innovadores, variados e imaginativos, es el destino ideal para los amantes del marisco y del pescado. Espectacular terraza al aire libre.

Apto para alérgicos, celiacos e intolerancias alimentarias. Acceso para minusválidos.

b ## Parrilla Río Plata

En pleno centro de Madrid, la parrilla Río Plata ofrece la posibilidad de probar los filetes de ternera y de buey más suculentos de la ciudad. Con su iluminación suave también es el lugar perfecto para una cena romántica.

Salón privado disponible para eventos familiares, bodas, comuniones, etc.

c ## Bufé Libre Estrella

Ubicado muy cerca de la estación de Atocha, no hay mejor sitio para comer bien y barato. Disfruta de una amplia selección de pastas, pizzas, ensaladas, carnes y platos vegetarianos en nuestro bufé libre. Algo para todos los gustos.
Menú infantil a mitad de precio.

2 hablar **¿Y tú? ¿Qué restaurante prefieres? ¿Por qué?**

- ● Prefiero… porque me gusta / soy…
- ■ Yo prefiero… porque es / tiene / ofrece…

3 escuchar **Lee el menú. Luego escucha el diálogo y rellena los espacios en blanco.**

- ● Buenos días. ¿Qué va a tomar?
- ■ De primer plato voy a tomar **1** _____.
- ● Muy bien. ¿Y de segundo plato?
- ■ ¿Qué me recomienda?
- ● Le recomiendo la especialidad de la casa, **2** _____. Está riquísimo.
- ■ Bueno, voy a tomar **3** _____, entonces.
- ● ¿Y para beber?
- ■ **4** _____, por favor.
- ● Muy bien. ¡Que aproveche!
  ****
- ● ¿Qué tal la comida?
- ■ Estaba **5** _____.
- ● ¿Quiere postre?
- ■ Sí, voy a tomar **6** _____.
- ● ¿Algo más?
- ■ Nada más, gracias.
  ¿Me trae la cuenta, por favor?

MENÚ DEL DÍA

14 € (servicio incluido)
* * *
Primer plato
Calamares
Sopa de fideos
Albóndigas
Croquetas caseras (atún)
Jamón serrano
* * *
Segundo plato
Filete de cerdo
Chuletas de cordero asadas
Merluza en salsa verde
Trucha a la plancha
Tortilla de espinacas
* * *
Postre
Flan, natillas, melocotón o piña
* * *
pan, agua y vino o cerveza

G *Absolute superlatives*

To say **really** (nice), **extremely** (expensive), etc. use the absolute superlative.
Add **–ísimo** to the end of the adjective, and make it agree.

Este ejercicio es facilísimo.   This exercise is **really** easy.

If the adjective ends in a vowel, remove it before adding the ending.

Estas gambas están buenísimas.   These prawns are **extremely** good.

4 hablar **Con tu compañero/a, haz diálogos. Cambia los detalles del ejercicio 3.**

5 Escucha. Copia y completa la tabla en inglés. (1–3)

	starter	main course	dessert	drink	problem
1	noodle soup				

Me hace falta	un cuchillo un tenedor una cuchara
No hay	aceite vinagre sal
El plato El vaso El mantel La cuchara	está sucio/a está roto/a
El vino La carne	está malo/a está frío/a

6 Lee el texto. Escribe P (positivo), N (negativo) o P+N (positivo y negativo).

1 La comida
2 El servicio
3 El precio
4 El ambiente
5 La limpieza

Platosenlinea.com

Almudena Sánchez (Santander)

Restaurante Mil Maravillas

Vinimos aquí el sábado pasado para celebrar las bodas de plata de mis padres. Cuando llegamos, había mucha gente y por eso tuvimos que esperar media hora. Sin embargo, el ambiente era animado y acogedor, y todo estaba muy limpio.

El camarero era encantador y nos recomendó la especialidad de la casa, las gambas.

A mi padre le encanta el marisco, así que pidió las gambas, mientras que yo pedí pollo al ajillo. Lo malo fue que el camarero se equivocó y me trajo merluza. ¡Soy alérgica al pescado!

Mi madre se quedó un poco decepcionada con el bistec (estaba frío), pero mi padre dijo que las gambas estaban riquísimas. Desafortunadamente, la cuenta tardó mucho tiempo en llegar, y cuando finalmente la recibimos, era carísima: 185 €. ¡No dejamos propina!

7 Lee el texto del ejercicio 6 otra vez. Busca las expresiones en español.

1 silver wedding anniversary
2 we had to wait
3 (he) made a mistake
4 (she) was a bit disappointed
5 (it) took a long time to arrive
6 we didn't leave a tip

8 Escribe una crítica para el foro. Usa el ejercicio 6 como modelo.

El (lunes) pasado fuimos al restaurante… para celebrar…
El ambiente era… y el camarero era… Pedí…, pero…

Use the **preterite tense** for <u>completed actions</u> in the past.

Pedí *cerdo, pero el camarero* **trajo** *pollo.*	**I ordered** pork but the waiter **brought** chicken.

Use the **imperfect tense** for <u>descriptions</u> in the past.

El plato **estaba** *sucio.*	The plate **was** dirty.
¡Había *una mosca en la sopa!*	**There was** a fly in the soup!

G *Irregular verbs in the preterite tense* ⟩ *Page 212*

If you know the 'I' form of the preterite you can usually work out the other forms.

E.g. **tener** (to have):

tuve	I had
tuviste	you had
tuvo	he/she had
tuvimos	we had
tuvisteis	you (plural) had
tuvieron	they had

Now work out the other forms of these verbs.

poner (to put)	→	puse (I put)
poder (to be able to)	→	pude (I was able to)
venir (to come)	→	vine (I came)
traer (to bring)	→	traje (I brought)*
decir (to say)	→	dije (I said)*

*'they' form ends in –jeron

- Talking about a music festival
- Using expressions followed by the infinitive
- Adding interest when narrating a story

1 **escuchar** Escucha y apunta los detalles en inglés. (1–5)

Ejemplo: **1** Likes: *Coldplay – music is original*
Dislikes: …

> ¿Cuál es tu cantante favorito / tu banda favorita?

Zona Cultura

El Festival Internacional de Benicàssim (FIB) se celebra cada año a mediados de julio. Durante cuatro días este festival de música pop, rock, indie y electrónica, entre otros estilos, atrae a más de 150.000 personas de todo el mundo a la costa valenciana.

(No) me gusta Me fascina Admiro No aguanto No soporto	su actitud su comportamiento su determinación su estilo su forma de vestir su talento	
Su música Su voz	(no) es	atrevida(s) imaginativa(s) preciosa(s) repetitiva(s) original(es) triste(s)
Sus coreografías Sus canciones Sus ideas Sus letras	(no) son	

2 **leer** Lee el programa y la página web. Apunta la información en español.

1 La fecha del primer día del festival
2 El precio de las entradas más baratas
3 El nombre del sitio donde se puede acampar
4 Los documentos requeridos para obtener la pulsera
5 La edad mínima para ir al festival solo/a
6 Tres artículos que te hacen falta si hace buen tiempo
7 Una manera de protegerse del ruido
8 Un artículo recomendado en caso de accidente / enfermedad

Julio
16 | 17 | 18 | 19

fib Benicàssim Costa Azahar

JUEVES 16	VIERNES 17	SÁBADO 18	DOMINGO 19

LAS PALMAS

FLORENCE + THE MACHINE	**THE PRODIGY**	**BLUR**	**PORTISHEAD**
CRYSTAL FIGHTERS	**NOEL GALLAGHER'S HIGH FLYING BIRDS**	**LOS PLANETAS**	**BASTILLE**
CLEAN BANDIT	**JAMIE T**	**KAISER CHIEFS**	**VETUSTA MORLA**
L.A.	BRODINSKI	TIMO MAAS	MADEON
SWIM DEEP	MOODOÏD	REVEREND & THE MAKERS	AUGUSTINES
TRAJANO!	NUNATAK	BEACH BEACH	DEBIGOTE
ELYELLA DJ'S			

FIBERFIB.COM - radio 3

GODSPEED YOU! BLACK EMPEROR	**MARK RONSON**	**FFS (FRANZ FERDINAND & SPARKS)**
PALMA VIOLETS	TIGA (DJ)	**PUBLIC ENEMY**
LA BIEN QUERIDA	FRANK TURNER & THE SLEEPING SOULS	THE CRIBS
EVAN BAGGS	HINDS	MØ
MONKI	EDU IMBERNON	A-TRAK
HAMSANDWICH	THE ZOMBIE KIDS (ARTISTA DESPERADOS)	BELAKO
HOLÓGRAMA	LA M.O.D.A.	HUDSON TAYLOR
	PAPAYA	

RED BULL TOUR BUS FIBCLUB

DMA'S	NUDOZURDO	DARWIN DEEZ	JOE CREPÚSCULO
OCELLOT	VESSELS	CURTIS HARDING	CROCODILES
THE LAST DANDIES	POLOCK	LOYLE CARNER	NOVEDADES CARMINHA
MOX NOX	PUBLIC ACCESS T.V.	SIESTA!	THE RIPTIDE MOVEMENT
LUIS LE NUIT	ELSA DE ALFONSO Y LOS PRESTIGIO	THE DEATH OF POP	JONATHAN TOUBIN
MIQUI BRIGHTSIDE	LEY DJ	OPATOV	ALDO LINARES
	DIEGO RJ (RADIO 3)	SUNTA TEMPLETON (XFM)	LITTLE JESUS
		ORLANDO	CELICA XX

ENTRADAS DESDE: 40 €

VIVIENDO EL FESTIVAL

Campfest. Es la zona de acampada gratuita para todos los poseedores de abono de 2, 3 o 4 días.
Cómo moverse. Alquila una bici por 40 € (4 días).
Tu pulsera. Al llegar al festival cambia tu entrada por la pulsera (se necesita pasaporte / DNI).
Menores de 15 años. Siempre deben estar acompañados de un adulto.
Te hace falta… Crema solar, gafas de sol, sombrero/gorra, tapones para los oídos, un minibotiquín (tiritas, aspirinas…).

me/te hace(n) falta	I/you need
DNI	Documento Nacional de Identidad

3 **hablar** Con tu compañero/a, haz diálogos.

- ¿Cuál es tu cantante favorito / tu banda favorita? ¿Por qué?
- ¿Qué bandas / cantantes no aguantas?
- ¿Te gustaría ir al Festival de Benicàssim?
- ¿Qué día del festival te interesa más? ¿Por qué?

4 escuchar

**Escucha a estas personas que hablan del FIB. (1–6)
Apunta:**

- Si es **pasado**, **presente** o **futuro**
- <u>Dos</u> detalles más

> Remember the 'we' forms of –*ar* and –*ir* verbs are identical in the present and preterite:
>
> *Cant**amos** y bail**amos***.   We **sing** and **dance** / We **sang** and **danced**.
>
> Time phrases do not always give you a clue. E.g. Do *en julio* and *este año* help you identify the tense?

5 leer

Lee el texto e identifica las <u>cuatro</u> frases correctas.

Siempre he querido ir al Festival de Benicàssim y por fin tuve la oportunidad de asistir la semana pasada. Acabo de cumplir 17 años, así que pude ir con mis amigos (¡y sin padres!). Decidimos acampar porque era la opción más barata – ¡aunque también la menos cómoda!

Al llegar al festival, montamos la tienda. ¡Nunca habíamos visto tantas tiendas! Por desgracia, mi amigo Roberto se hizo daño con el martillo – se rompió la mano. ¡Es muy torpe! Después de ir al hospital, volvimos al festival para ver las primeras actuaciones.

Durante los cuatro días del festival vi muchas de mis bandas favoritas, incluso el grupo indie *Los Planetas*, que salieron al escenario con una canción nueva, antes de tocar una selección de sus mejores canciones. El sonido era increíble y no me quedé nada decepcionado.

Lo que menos me gustó fue el calor. Por eso, cuando me acosté, decidí dormir con los pies fuera de la tienda (aunque, en realidad, el camping era tan ruidoso que pasé cuatro noches sin dormir). Sin embargo, al día siguiente me desperté con las piernas llenas de picaduras. La proxima vez usaré repelente de mosquitos. O mejor todavía, nos alojaremos en un hotel. ¡Seguro que Roberto preferiría esa opción también!

Álvaro

montar una tienda	to put up a tent
torpe	clumsy

1 Álvaro is nearly 17.
2 He didn't find camping very comfortable.
3 He was surprised by how big the tents were.
4 Roberto cut his hand.

5 *Los Planetas* started their set with a new song.
6 Álvaro was impressed by their performance.
7 It was very hot at night.
8 Álvaro didn't sleep much because of the insects.

 6 leer

Traduce el primer párrafo del texto del ejercicio 5 al inglés.

 7 escribir

**Has ido a un festival de música.
Describe tus experiencias.**

Use ideas from exercise 5 and include:

- different tenses
- time phrases
- expressions followed by the infinitive

> Narrating a story in Spanish is an important exam skill. To add interest, include anecdotes about things that went wrong (e.g. lost something, got ill, arrived late, bad meal, etc).

G *Expressions followed by the infinitive*

To enhance your writing, use a range of expressions which are followed by the infinitive:

para + infinitive	in order to (do)
al + infinitive	on (doing)
sin + infinitive	without (doing)
antes de + infinitive	before (doing)
después de + infinitive	after (doing)

***Al llegar** al festival…*   **On arriving** at the festival…

*Pasé cuatro noches **sin dormir**.*   I spent four nights **without sleeping**.

1 leer — Lee el artículo sobre cómo se celebra 'la quinceañera'.

Tradiciones y rituales de la quinceañera

La celebración de los 15 años varía mucho según los distintos países. En Latinoamérica, donde marca la transición de niña a mujer, la fiesta de 15 años empieza con la llegada de la chica, la 'quinceañera'. Una tradición importante es 'lanzar la muñeca' a las otras niñas invitadas. La muñeca (normalmente una Barbie o alguna muñeca similar) simboliza la última muñeca de la niñez de la joven.

En Uruguay, 'la ceremonia de las 15 velas y 15 rosas' es una de las más frecuentes. La quinceañera baja una escalera mientras se escucha una canción que ella ha escogido. Al pie de la escalera 15 chicos la esperan con rosas, mientras que 15 chicas la esperan con velas. La quinceañera coge las rosas y apaga las velas, y luego va hacia la zona de baile.

Elige la opción correcta para cada frase.

(a) La manera de celebrar los 15 años depende…
- **A** de la persona.
- **B** del clima.
- **C** de los padres.
- **D** del lugar.

(b) En la fiesta la chica lanza…
- **A** un zapato.
- **B** una rosa.
- **C** un juguete.
- **D** una fruta.

(c) La ceremonia de las 15 velas y 15 rosas es una tradición…
- **A** popular.
- **B** cara.
- **C** antigua.
- **D** misteriosa.

(d) Se escucha música…
- **A** tradicional.
- **B** moderna.
- **C** seleccionada por la chica.
- **D** escrita por el padre.

2 leer — Read the article about household accidents. Answer the questions at the top of page 131.

Accidentes navideños

El 30% de los hogares españoles sufre accidentes domésticos durante la Navidad, según un estudio realizado por la División de Hogar de Línea Directa. Los accidentes más comunes son las intoxicaciones alimentarias, pero también son frecuentes las quemaduras por culpa de los fuegos artificiales. Uno de cada cuatro españoles confiesa que ha regalado juguetes 'ilegales' a los niños, es decir, juguetes no homologados* por la Comunidad Europea. Además, la decoración navideña puede provocar problemas (como la electrocución por luces navideñas), y por eso es esencial prestar atención a la calidad del producto.

Según Francisco Valencia de Línea Directa, «Queremos concienciar de los peligros de actividades habituales como cocinar, limpiar o decorar la casa por Navidad». La cocina es el espacio más peligroso para los españoles (80%), y las manos son la parte del cuerpo más afectada en los accidentes domésticos, seguidas de piernas y brazos. Uno de cada cinco españoles no tiene botiquín de primeros auxilios en casa.

homologados = approved

(a) What does the article tell us about accidents in Spanish homes at Christmas? Choose the <u>three</u> correct statements.

A Food poisoning is the greatest problem.
B Burns are often caused by cooking accidents.
C 25% of the toys made in Europe are illegal.
D Faulty toys often lead to electrocution.
E You should check the quality of Christmas decorations.
F Most accidents take place in the kitchen.
G Most accidents cause injuries to the arms or the legs.

3 leer **Translate the following passage into English.**

En muchos países los niños abren sus regalos el 25 de diciembre. Aunque Papá Noel también es popular en España hoy en día, la mayoría de las familias todavía prefieren esperar hasta el 6 de enero. Antes de acostarse el día 5, los niños dejan galletas y leche para los camellos. Al día siguiente se levantan temprano para descubrir si los Reyes Magos los han visitado.

Answer the following questions in English. You do not need to write full sentences.

(b) Which <u>three</u> activities can be dangerous, according to Francisco Valencia?
(c) What item do 20% of Spanish people not have at home?

> Use context to work out the meaning of unfamiliar words. What do you think the following words mean?
>
> un hogar   los peligros
> luces navideñas   peligroso

> Can you work out the meaning of *Papá Noel*, *los camellos* and *los Reyes Magos* by using your common sense and your own knowledge of Christmas?

1 escuchar **Escuchas un reportaje sobre el restaurante Luz Verde. ¿Qué dice? Escoge entre: famoso, barato, estupendo, diferente. Puedes usar las palabras más de una vez.**

(a) El servicio es ⚊⚊⚊ .
(b) El menú es ⚊⚊⚊ .
(c) El pescado es ⚊⚊⚊ .
(d) El vino es ⚊⚊⚊ .
(e) El cocinero es ⚊⚊⚊ .

> In this task you have to draw conclusions from what you hear and decide which adjective best fits each sentence. <u>Before</u> listening to the extract, make sure you are clear about what information you have to listen out for.

2 escuchar **You are listening to an interview about going to a music festival. What advice is given?**

Listen and choose the <u>three</u> correct statements.

A Take care not to lose your mobile phone.
B Drink plenty of water.
C Stay out of the sun.
D Use a high factor sun cream.
E Wear ear plugs.
F Take headache tablets with you.
G Don't wear the same T-shirt as your friends.

A – Role play

1 leer　Look at the role play card and prepare what you are going to say.

Topic: Daily life

Instructions to candidates:

You are talking to your Spanish exchange partner about food. The teacher will play the role of your Spanish friend and will speak first.

You must address your Spanish friend as *tú*.

You will talk to the teacher using the five prompts below.

* where you see – **?** – you must ask a question.
* where you see – **!** – you must respond to something you have not prepared.

Task
Estás hablando con tu amigo/a español/a sobre la comida.

1 Cena – qué hora (normalmente)

2 Comida preferida – razón

3 !

4 ? Comida inglesa – opinión

5 ? Plato español – recomendación

Remember that you don't get extra marks in the role play for giving a complex answer, so keep it simple!

Make sure you give a reason, and don't forget to make adjectives agree with the noun.

The third bullet point is always in the past tense. Remember to use the **preterite** to say what you did, but the **imperfect** to describe something in the past.

You could ask an open question like 'What do you think of …?' or a closed question such as 'Do you like …?'

How could you turn this into a question? (¿Qué …?)

In the picture-based task and general conversation you have to develop your answers fully. However, for the role-play you only need to give the information you are asked to give. Focus on the **accuracy** of what you are saying.

2 escuchar　Practise what you have prepared. Then, using your notes, listen and respond to the teacher.

3 escuchar　Now listen to Freja doing the role play task. **In English**, note down what she says for the first three bullets.

B – Picture-based task

Topic: Cultural life

Mira la foto y prepara las respuestas a los siguientes puntos:

* la descripción de la foto
* tu opinión sobre la Navidad
* lo que hiciste en un día especial reciente
* cómo vas a celebrar tu próximo cumpleaños
* (!)

1 escuchar **Look at the photo and read the task. Then listen to Natalie's response to the first bullet point.**

1 What two things does she say about the boy in the photo?
2 What do you think the following phrases mean: *en el fondo, árbol de Navidad, día de los Reyes Magos*?
3 Why does she think this may **not** be the 25th December?
4 What is her opinion of the children? Why?

2 escuchar **Listen to and read Natalie's response to the second bullet point.**

1 Write down the missing word for each gap.
2 Look at the Answer Booster on page 134. Note down six examples of language which Natalie uses to give a strong answer.

Me chifla la Navidad porque es una fiesta muy especial y **1** ———— para toda la familia. Siempre decoramos la casa con luces y en el salón ponemos un árbol de Navidad con una **2** ———— enorme. También solemos poner un belén para recordar la importancia **3** ———— de esta fiesta. En mi opinión, es una buena oportunidad para pasar tiempo con la familia y descansar. Además, es importante porque se **4** ———— tarjetas a los amigos y a los familiares, y se dan **5** ———— a los seres queridos. Sin embargo, lo malo de las fiestas navideñas es que comemos demasiados **6** ————.

3 escuchar **Listen to Natalie's response to the third bullet point.**
1 **In English**, note down six details that she gives.
2 Can you work out the meaning of *el cuarto domingo de Cuaresma* from the context?

4 escuchar **Listen to Natalie's response to the fourth bullet point. In Spanish**, note down examples of sequencers and other time phrases that she uses.

5 escuchar **Prepare your own answers to the first four bullet points. Try to predict which unexpected question you might be asked. Then listen and take part in the full picture-based task with the teacher.**

⭐ To answer the unexpected question here, you could give a specific example of a festival in each country, and say which one you prefer and why.

C – General conversation

1 escuchar **Listen to Lucas introducing his chosen topic. Complete the sentences in English.**

a Lucas eats lots of…
b He has a quick breakfast because…
c He drinks hot chocolate…
d He never eats…
e After school he has…
f The meal that his brother cooked wasn't…

2 escuchar **The teacher asks Lucas, *'¿Has probado la comida española?'* Which of these adjectives does he use? What do they mean?**

asqueroso/a	*riquísimo/a*	*sabroso/a*	*buenísimo/a*	*frío/a*
salado/a	*dulce*	*picante*	*refrescante*	*típico/a*

⭐ To add variety to your language try to use a wide range of adjectives, including examples of the absolute superlative (e.g. *Estaba buenísimo* – It was extremely nice).

3 escuchar **Listen to Lucas' response to the second question, *'¿Prefieres cenar en casa o en un restaurante?'* Look at the Answer Booster on page 134. Note down six examples of language which Lucas uses to give a strong answer.**

4 hablar **Prepare your own answers to Module 6 questions 1–6 on page 199. Then practise with your partner.**

Answer booster	Aiming for a solid answer	Aiming higher	Aiming for the top
Verbs	**Different time frames**: past, present, near future **Different types of verbs**: regular, irregular, reflexive, stem-changing	**Different persons** of the verb **Verbs with an infinitive**: *tener que, soler, acabar de* **Phrases followed by the infinitive**: *para, sin, antes de, después de, al*	**A wide range of tenses**: present, preterite, imperfect, perfect, future **Conditional**: *iría, sería* **Passive**: *fue fundado* **Avoiding the passive**: *se celebra, se construyen*
Opinions and reasons	**Verbs of opinion**: *me chifla(n), me encanta(n), no aguanto…* **Reasons**: *porque…*	**Exclamations**: *¡Qué miedo!* **Absolute superlatives**: *carísimo, buenísimo*	**Opinions**: *desde mi punto de vista, a mi modo de ver, para mí* **Reasons**: *ya que, por eso, así que, por lo tanto*
Connectives	*y, pero, también*	*además, sin embargo, por desgracia, sobre todo*	*Primero…, segundo…* **Balancing an argument**: *aunque, por un lado… por otro lado…*
Other features	**Qualifiers**: *muy, un poco, bastante, demasiado* **Adjectives**: *sabroso/a, rico/a, emocionante* **Adverbs of frequency**: *siempre, a veces*	**Sentences with *cuando, donde, si***: *si es un día especial…* **Phrases with *tener***: *tener suerte / sueño / hambre / sed / prisa*	**Positive/Negative phrases**: *lo bueno / malo / mejor / peor* **Specialist vocabulary**: *navideño/a, un belén, los seres queridos, los desfiles, la cosecha*

A – Extended writing task

1 leer   Look at the task and answer the questions.

- What **type** of text are you asked to write?
- What is the **purpose** of the text?
- What is each bullet point asking you to do?

2 leer   The third bullet point asks you why festivals are important. Match these sentence halves to give you some ideas. What do the sentences mean in English?

1 Las fiestas son una parte…
2 Te dan la oportunidad de divertirte…
3 Enseñan a los niños a…
4 Te hacen sentir más…
5 Muchas fiestas tienen…
6 Son populares entre los turistas y…

a con tus amigos y tu familia.
b orgulloso de tu cultura.
c importante de nuestra cultura.
d una importancia religiosa o histórica.
e por eso ayudan a la economía.
f valorar las tradiciones del país.

3 leer   Read Matthew's answer on page 135. What do the phrases in **bold** mean?

4 leer   Look at the Answer Booster. Note down <u>eight</u> examples of language which Matthew uses to write a strong answer.

5 escribir   Prepare your own answer to the task.

- Look at the Answer Booster and Matthew's text for ideas.
- Write a detailed plan. Organise your answer in paragraphs.
- Write your answer and carefully check what you have written.

Una fiesta tradicional

Usted ha asistido a una fiesta durante su visita a otro país. Escriba un artículo para informar a los lectores sobre la importancia de las fiestas tradicionales.

Debe incluir los puntos siguientes:

- cómo se celebra la fiesta
- lo que más le gustó y por qué
- por qué las fiestas tradicionales son importantes
- una fiesta a la que le gustaría asistir en el futuro.

Justifique sus ideas y sus opiniones.

Escriba aproximadamente 130–150 palabras **en español**.

El verano pasado fui a Vilafranca del Penedès en España para ver la Fiesta Mayor, que se celebra **a finales de agosto**. Durante tres días las calles se llenan de desfiles, bailes y música. Es **una festividad religiosa en honor de** Sant Fèlix, pero también hay conciertos, procesiones y fuegos artificiales.

Para mí lo mejor de la fiesta fue cuando vimos a los Castellers de Vilafranca, un grupo **que fue fundado en 1948**. En esta tradición antigua **se construyen torres humanas muy altas**. ¡Qué miedo! Fue muy impresionante y saqué muchas fotos, aunque en mi opinión, **debe ser dificilísimo** – ¡y muy peligroso! Creo que son muy valientes.

Desde mi punto de vista, las fiestas tradicionales son importantísimas **por muchas razones**. Primero, te hacen sentir más orgulloso de tu cultura. Segundo, ayudan a la economía, ya que muchos turistas extranjeros asisten a las fiestas y **suelen gastar mucho dinero** (¡como yo!). Sobre todo, las fiestas son divertidas y lo pasas fenomenal.

En el futuro me gustaría ir a la Fiesta de la Vendimia en Argentina, donde se celebra **el fin de la cosecha de la uva**. Después de ver los desfiles en las calles, iría al espectáculo de bailes folclóricos con **más de mil bailarines en el escenario**, y vería la coronación de la Reina Nacional de la Vendimia. ¡Sería guay!

> ⭐ For the final bullet point you have to say which festival you **would** like to attend in the future. Can you remember how to form the **conditional**?

Los Castellers de Vilafranca

B – Translation

1 | escribir

Read the English text and Jamie's translation of it. Correct the <u>eight</u> mistakes in the Spanish translation.

Usually I get up early, have a shower and then have toast with apple juice for breakfast. However, this morning I had to leave the house without having breakfast because I woke up late. Now I'm very hungry and so I'm going to have fish and chips for lunch. I love seafood and my favourite dish is paella.

Normalmente me despierto temprano, me baño y luego desayuno tostadas con zumo de piña. Sin embargo, esta noche tuve que salir de casa sin desayunar porque me acosté tarde. Ahora tengo mucha prisa, así que voy a almorzar carne con patatas fritas. Me encantan las verduras y mi plato favorito es la paella.

2 | escribir

Translate the following passage into Spanish.

Usually we have dinner at eight o'clock and then I go to bed at ten. However, I have just been to a music festival where I spent two nights without sleeping. It was incredible and I saw many of my favourite bands, though today I am very sleepy. Next time I'm not going to camp.

> ⭐ Remember that some phrases do not translate word for word. Take extra care with 'I have just been' and 'I am very sleepy'.

Las comidas / Meals

el desayuno	breakfast
la comida / el almuerzo	lunch
la merienda	tea (meal)
la cena	dinner / evening meal
desayunar	to have breakfast / to have … for breakfast
comer / almorzar	to have lunch / to have … for lunch
merendar	to have tea / to have … for tea
cenar	to have dinner / to have … for dinner
tomar	to have (food / drink)
beber	to drink
entre semana…	during the week…
los fines de semana…	at weekends…
Desayuno a las ocho.	I have breakfast at eight o'clock.
Desayuno / Como / Meriendo / Ceno…	For breakfast / lunch / tea / dinner I have…
un huevo	an egg
un yogur	a yogurt
un pastel	a cake
un bocadillo	a sandwich
una hamburguesa	a hamburger
(el) café / (el) té	coffee / tea

(el) Cola Cao	Cola Cao (Spanish chocolate drink)
(el) marisco	seafood
(el) pescado	fish
(el) pollo	chicken
(el) zumo de naranja	orange juice
(la) carne	meat
(la) ensalada	salad
(la) fruta	fruit
(la) leche	milk
(la) sopa	soup
(la) tortilla	omelette
(los) cereales	cereals
(los) churros	fried doughnut sticks
(las) galletas	biscuits
(las) patatas fritas	chips
(las) tostadas	toast
(las) verduras	vegetables
algo dulce / ligero / rápido	something sweet / light / quick
ser goloso/a	to have a sweet tooth
tener hambre	to be hungry
tener prisa	to be in a hurry
tomar un desayuno fuerte	to have a big (lit. strong) breakfast

Las expresiones de cantidad / Expressions of quantity

cien / quinientos gramos de…	100 / 500 grammes of…
un bote de…	a jar of…
un kilo de…	a kilo of…
un litro de…	a litre of…
un paquete de…	a packet of…

una barra de…	a loaf of…
una botella de…	a bottle of…
una caja de…	a box of…
una docena de…	a dozen…
una lata de…	a tin / can of…

Los alimentos / Food products

el aceite de oliva	olive oil
el agua	water
el ajo	garlic
el arroz	rice
el atún	tuna
el azúcar	sugar
el chorizo	spicy sausage
el maíz	corn
el pan	bread
el queso	cheese
la cerveza	beer
la carne de cerdo / cordero / ternera	pork / lamb / beef
la coliflor	cauliflower
la harina	flour
la mantequilla	butter
la mermelada	jam
los albaricoques	apricots
los guisantes	peas
los lácteos	dairy products
los melocotones	peaches
los melones	melons
los pepinos	cucumbers

los pimientos	peppers
los plátanos	bananas
los pomelos	grapefruits
los refrescos	fizzy drinks
las cebollas	onions
las fresas	strawberries
las judías (verdes)	(green) beans
las legumbres	pulses
las lentejas	lentils
las manzanas	apples
las naranjas	oranges
las peras	pears
las piñas	pineapples
las uvas	grapes
las zanahorias	carrots
¿Has probado…?	Have you tried…?
el gazpacho	gazpacho (chilled soup)
la ensaladilla rusa	Russian salad
la fabada	stew of beans and pork
Es un tipo de bebida / postre.	It's a type of drink / dessert.
Es un plato caliente / frío.	It's a hot / cold dish.
Contiene(n)…	It contains / They contain…
Fue inventado/a / introducido/a…	It was invented / introduced…

Mi rutina diaria / My daily routine

me despierto	I wake up
me levanto	I get up
me ducho	I have a shower
me peino	I brush my hair
me afeito	I have a shave
me visto	I get dressed
me lavo los dientes	I clean my teeth

me acuesto	I go to bed
salgo de casa	I leave home
vuelvo a casa	I return home
temprano / tarde	early / late
enseguida	straight away
odio levantarme	I hate getting up

¿Qué le pasa? / What's the matter?

No me encuentro bien.	I don't feel well.
Me siento fatal.	I feel awful.
Estoy enfermo/a / cansado/a.	I am ill / tired.
Tengo calor / frío.	I am hot / cold.
Tengo catarro.	I have a cold.
Tengo diarrea.	I have diarrhoea.

Tengo dolor de cabeza.	I have a headache.
Tengo fiebre.	I have a fever / temperature.
Tengo gripe.	I have flu.
Tengo mucho sueño.	I am very sleepy.
Tengo náuseas.	I feel sick.
Tengo quemaduras de sol.	I have sunburn.

Tengo tos.	I have a cough.	los ojos	eyes
Tengo una insolación.	I have sunstroke.	¿Desde hace cuánto tiempo?	How long for?
Tengo una picadura.	I've been stung.	desde hace…	for…
Me duele(n)…	My … hurt(s)	un día / un mes	a day / a month
Me he cortado el/la…	I've cut my…	una hora / una semana	an hour / a week
Me he hecho daño en…	I've hurt my…	¿Desde cuándo?	Since when?
Me he quemado…	I've burnt my…	desde ayer	since yesterday
Me he roto…	I've broken my…	desde anteayer	since the day before yesterday
Me he torcido…	I've twisted my…	no se preocupe	don't worry
el brazo / el estómago	arm / stomach	¡Qué mala suerte!	What bad luck!
el pie / el tobillo	foot / ankle	Tiene(s) que / Hay que…	You have to…
la boca / la cabeza	mouth / head	beber mucha agua	drink lots of water
la espalda / la garganta	back / throat	descansar	rest
la mano / la nariz	hand / nose	ir al hospital / médico / dentista	go to the hospital / doctor / dentist
la pierna / la rodilla	leg / knee	tomar aspirinas	take aspirins
los dientes / las muelas	teeth	tomar este jarabe / estas pastillas	take this syrup / these tablets
los oídos / las orejas	ears	usar esta crema	use this cream

Las fiestas — Festivals

la fiesta de…	the festival of…	las calles se llenan de…	the streets are filled with…
esta tradición antigua…	this old tradition…	los niños / los jóvenes…	children / young people…
se caracteriza por…	is characterised by…	los familiares / las familias…	relations / families…
se celebra en…	is celebrated in…	comen manzanas de caramelo	eat toffee apples
se repite…	is repeated…	decoran las casas / las tumbas	decorate houses / graves
se queman figuras de madera	wooden figures are burnt	con flores / velas	with flowers / candles
se construyen hogueras	bonfires are built	preparan linternas / altares	prepare lanterns / altars
se disparan fuegos artificiales	fireworks are set off	se disfrazan de brujas / fantasmas	dress up as witches / ghosts
se lanzan huevos	eggs are thrown	ven desfiles	(they) watch processions

Un día especial — A special day

Abrimos los regalos.	We open presents.	Vamos a la mezquita / iglesia.	We go to the mosque / church.
Buscamos huevos de chocolate.	We look for chocolate eggs.	Ayer fue…	Yesterday was…
Cantamos villancicos.	We sing Christmas carols.	el baile de fin de curso	the school prom
Cenamos bacalao.	We have cod for dinner.	el Día de Navidad	Christmas Day
Comemos dulces navideños /	We eat Christmas sweets /	(el) Domingo de Pascua	Easter Sunday
doce uvas / pavo.	twelve grapes / turkey.	(la) Nochebuena	Christmas Eve
Nos acostamos muy tarde.	We go to bed very late.	(la) Nochevieja	New Year's Eve
Nos levantamos muy temprano.	We get up very early.	Me bañé y luego me maquillé.	I had a bath and then did my make up.
Rezamos.	We pray.		

¿Qué va a tomar? — What are you going to have?

de primer / segundo plato…	for starter / main course…	el menú del día	the set menu
de postre…	for dessert…	la especialidad de la casa	the house speciality
Voy a tomar…	I'm going to have…	está buenísimo/a / riquísimo/a	it's extremely good / tasty
(el) bistec	steak	¡Que aproveche!	Enjoy your meal!
(el) filete de cerdo	pork fillet	¿Algo más?	Anything else?
(el) flan	crème caramel	Nada más, gracias.	Nothing else, thank you.
(el) jamón serrano	Serrano ham	¿Me trae la cuenta, por favor?	Can you bring me the bill, please?
(la) merluza en salsa verde	hake in parsley and wine sauce	No tengo cuchillo / tenedor / cuchara.	I haven't got a knife / fork / spoon.
(la) sopa de fideos	noodle soup	No hay aceite / sal / vinagre.	There's no oil / salt / vinegar.
(la) tortilla de espinacas	spinach omelette	El plato / vaso / mantel está sucio.	The plate / glass / table cloth is dirty.
(la) trucha a la plancha	grilled trout	El vino está malo.	The wine is bad / off.
(los) calamares	squid	La carne está fría.	The meat is cold.
(las) albóndigas	meatballs	dejar una propina	to leave a tip
(las) chuletas de cordero asadas	roast lamb chops	equivocarse	to make a mistake
(las) croquetas caseras	homemade croquettes	pedir	to order / ask for
(las) gambas	prawns	ser alérgico/a…	to be allergic to…
(las) natillas	custard	ser vegetariano/a	to be a vegetarian
¿Qué me recomienda?	What do you recommend?		

Un festival de música — A music festival

Me fascina(n)…	…fascinate(s) me.	atrevido/a(s)	daring
Admiro…	I admire…	imaginativo/a(s)	imaginative
No aguanto / soporto…	I can't stand…	precioso/a(s)	beautiful
su actitud / talento	his/her attitude / talent	repetitivo/a(s)	repetitive
su comportamiento	his/her behaviour	original(es)	original
su determinación / estilo	his/her determination / style	triste(s)	sad
su forma de vestir	his/her way of dressing	Me/Te hace(n) falta…	I/You need…
su música / voz	his/her music / voice	crema solar	sun cream
sus canciones / coreografías	his/her songs / choreography	el pasaporte / DNI	your passport / national ID card
sus ideas / letras	his/her ideas / lyrics	un sombrero / una gorra	a hat / cap

7 ¡A currar!
Punto de partida

- Talking about different jobs
- Discussing job preferences

1 escuchar **Escucha. Copia y completa la tabla. (1–5)**

	trabajo	¿le gusta? (✓ / ✗)	¿por qué (no)?
1	camarera	✗	repetitivo, …

peluquero/a   camarero/a   veterinario/a   jardinero/a   profesor(a)   dependiente/a

ayudar	entrevistas con famosos
contestar	coches
cuidar	llamadas telefónicas
enseñar	platos distintos
hacer	ropa de marca
preparar	comida y bebida
reparar	las plantas y las flores
servir	a los clientes / pacientes / pasajeros / niños
trabajar	en un taller / un hospital / un hotel / una tienda
vender	a bordo de un avión
viajar	por todo el mundo

When saying what job someone does, you don't use the indefinite article.

Soy periodista.   I am **a** journalist.

However, you do use it if giving more specific details.

Es **una** cantante   She's **a** very well
muy conocida.   known singer.

 Masculine and feminine nouns   **> Page 222**

Some nouns have different masculine and feminine forms.

camarero   → camarer**a**
diseñad**or** → diseñad**ora**

Those ending in **–e** or **–ista** are usually invariable.

cantant**e**   → cantant**e**
recepcion**ista** → recepcion**ista**

2 escribir **Escribe <u>tres</u> frases para cada persona.**
Inventa los otros detalles.

Ejemplo: **1** Soy cocinera y trabajo en un restaurante italiano.
Todos los días preparo…
Me gusta mi trabajo porque…

¿En qué trabajas?

Soy cocinera.

Soy enfermero.

Soy azafata.

Soy periodista.

Soy recepcionista.

Soy mecánico.

3 leer **Lee los textos. ¿En qué trabajan? Utiliza un diccionario si es necesario.**

1
Trabajo para una revista de moda, pero no escribo artículos. Tampoco soy modelo ni diseñador gráfico. Nunca salgo sin llevar mi cámara.

2
No soy ni recepcionista ni camarera, pero trabajo en un hotel de lujo. Nunca cocino ni cuido los jardines. Todos los días corto el pelo a los clientes.

3
En mi trabajo viajo por todo el mundo en un crucero enorme. No sirvo comida ni hago manicuras. Tampoco limpio las cabinas. Cada noche canto en un espectáculo.

4
Trabajo en una clínica, pero no soy ni médica ni enfermera. Tampoco trabajo con animales. Ayudo a mis pacientes a cuidar los dientes.

4 Con tu compañero/a, juega a '¿Cuál es mi profesión?'

Ejemplo:

● ¿Trabajas en un hotel?   ■ *Sí, trabajo en un hotel.*
● ¿Sirves comida y bebida?   ■ *No, no sirvo…*

 5 Mira las cuatro listas. Escribe el título correcto. (A–D)

1
bombero/a
médico/a
policía
soldado

2
abogado/a
contable
funcionario/a
guía turístico/a

3
albañil
electricista
fontanero/a
ingeniero/a

4
bailarín/bailarina
diseñador(a)
escritor(a)
músico/a

A Seguridad / Sanidad   **B** Actividades artísticas   **C** Construcción / Ingeniería   **D** Sector servicios

 6 Escucha. ¿Qué trabajos les gustaría hacer? ¿Por qué? (1–5)

Ejemplo: **1** c – *quite serious, …*

a  **b**   **c**  **d**   **e**   **f**

(No) Soy	ambicioso/a	paciente
	comprensivo/a	práctico/a
	creativo/a	responsable
	extrovertido/a	serio/a
	fuerte	trabajador(a)
	inteligente	valiente
	organizado/a	

Es un trabajo	artístico	exigente
	manual	variado
	para personas sociables	
	con responsabilidad	
	con buenas perspectivas	
	con un buen sueldo	

 7 Con tu compañero/a, haz <u>cuatro</u> diálogos. Inventa los detalles.

● ¿Qué tipo de persona eres?
■ *Creo que soy… y…, pero no…*
● *Pues, creo que serías un buen… / una buena… porque es un trabajo…*

☆ Remember that you use the conditional to say what you **would** do.

| *Me gustaría ser fontanero.* | I **would** like to be a plumber. |
| *Serías un buen… / una buena…* | You **would** be a good… |

 8 Traduce las frases al español.

1 I love my job because it's quite varied.
2 My dad is a receptionist. He works in a clinic.
3 I serve food and drink to passengers on board a plane.
4 I would like to be a civil servant because it's a job with good prospects.
5 You are patient and understanding, and so I think you would make a good nurse.

- Talking about how you earn money
- Using *soler* in the imperfect tense
- Using verbs in different forms

1 **Escucha. Apunta los detalles en inglés. (1–5)**

Ejemplo: **1** b – when they need me – 4 € per hour

¿Tienes un trabajo a tiempo parcial?

Sí, tengo un trabajo.

No, no tengo trabajo, pero ayudo en casa

a

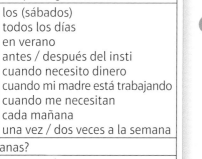

Reparto periódicos.

¿Cuándo trabajas? / ¿Cuándo lo haces?	
Trabajo Lo hago	los (sábados) todos los días en verano antes / después del insti cuando necesito dinero cuando mi madre está trabajando cuando me necesitan cada mañana una vez / dos veces a la semana
¿Cuánto ganas?	
Gano	… euros / libras (a la hora / al día / a la semana)
¡No gano nada!	

b

Hago de canguro.

c

Trabajo de cajero.

d

Cocino y lavo
los platos.

e

Paso la aspiradora
y plancho la ropa.

f

Pongo y quito
la mesa.

g

Paseo al perro y
corto el césped.

2 **Lee el texto. Busca las expresiones en español.**

Soy estudiante, pero también trabajo como socorrista en un parque acuático en Benidorm. Lo hago desde hace seis meses y me encanta. Suelo trabajar dos veces a la semana. Tengo que vigilar a los niños que nadan en la piscina de olas. Me llevo bien con mis compañeros y mi jefe es muy amable. Aunque no gano mucho, es un trabajo divertido y el horario es flexible.

En casa siempre ayudo a mis padres con las tareas domésticas. Arreglo mi habitación y de vez en cuando preparo la cena. Cuando era más joven, solía hacer de canguro para mi hermano, pero ya es mayor. Antes mi hermana y yo solíamos lavar los platos, pero ahora es más fácil – ¡ponemos los platos en el lavavajillas!

1 I've been doing it for six months
2 I have to supervise the children
3 I get on well with my colleagues
4 My boss is very nice
5 I help my parents with the housework
6 I tidy my room
7 but now he's older
8 we used to wash the dishes

G **Soler** *in the imperfect tense*

In the present tense you use **soler** + infinitive to talk about what you <u>usually / tend to</u> do.

> **Suelo** lavar el coche.   **I tend to** wash the car.

You can also use it in the imperfect tense to talk about things you <u>used to</u> do regularly. Alternatively, simply use the imperfect tense of the verb.

> **Solía cortar** el césped.   **I used to** cut the lawn.
> **Cortaba** el césped.   **I used to cut** the lawn.

3 hablar

Imagina que tienes un trabajo a tiempo parcial. Con tu compañero/a, haz diálogos.

- *¿Tienes un trabajo a tiempo parcial?*
- *¿Qué haces?*
- *¿Cuándo lo haces?*
- *¿Cuánto ganas?*
- *¿Te gusta tu trabajo?*
- *¿Ayudas con las tareas en casa?*

4 escuchar

Escucha a Guillermo. Elige la opción correcta.

Guillermo

a **Cocina / Lava los platos / Sirve** en un restaurante.
b Trabaja cada **mañana / tarde / fin de semana**.
c Opina que el salario es **bajo / justo / alto**.
d Se lleva bien con **su jefe / sus compañeros / los clientes**.
e Antes **cocinaba / ponía la mesa / quitaba la mesa**.
f Ya no **pasea al perro / plancha la ropa / pasa la aspiradora**.

5 escribir

Escribe un texto sobre lo que haces en tu trabajo y en casa.

Give details of:

- your part-time job (or invent one!)
  - what you do / when you work
  - how much you earn
  - your opinion of it
- how you help out at home
  - what you do / how often
  - what you used to do
  - what other people in your family do

> You often learn new verbs in the 'I' form of the present tense (e.g. *plancho, reparto*). Make sure you also know the **infinitive** so that you can use them:
>
> - with expressions followed by the **infinitive**
>
>   *Tengo que **pasar** la aspiradora.*   I have **to do** the vacuuming.
>   *Solía **preparar** la cena.*   I used **to prepare** dinner.
>
> - in different tenses / persons of the verb.
>
>   *Ayer planché mi uniforme.*   Yesterday I ironed my uniform.
>   *Mi padre pone la mesa.*   My dad sets the table.
>   *Preparaba la cena.*   I used to prepare dinner.

6 leer

Lee el texto y contesta a las preguntas en inglés.

Buscar empleo para jóvenes de 16 años

Como adolescente, es probable que tengas una buena cantidad de tiempo libre y el deseo de ganar dinero. Los trabajos típicos para los adolescentes incluyen:

- Trabajo en un restaurante de comida rápida
- Dependiente en una tienda
- Repartidor de periódicos

Si tienes 16 años, también existen otras posibilidades de ganar tu propio dinero sin descuidar el colegio:

- Cuidado de niños: Es ideal si haces el curso de la Cruz Roja de primeros auxilios.
- Arreglo de jardines: Los jardines dan trabajo todo el año: en primavera y verano cortar el césped, en otoño barrer las hojas y en invierno quitar la nieve.
- Lavado de coches de los vecinos.
- Enseñar a las personas mayores a usar los ordenadores o Internet.

Si tienes 14 o 15 años, solo puedes trabajar tres horas al día y un máximo de 18 horas a la semana.

descuidar   to neglect
las hojas   leaves

1 Which two things are you likely to have as a teenager?
2 What are you advised to do if you want to look after children?
3 How do gardening tasks vary according to the time of year? (Give <u>three</u> details.)
4 Which job could you do for your neighbours?
5 What is the last idea suggested for earning money?
6 What restrictions apply to younger teenagers?

- *Talking about work experience*
- *Using the preterite and imperfect together*
- *Using alternatives to 'and'*

1 Lee y escribe C (Carolina), E (Eduardo), o C+E (Carolina y Eduardo).

Las prácticas laborales, ¿merecen la pena?

Carolina

Hice mis prácticas en una emisora de radio local. Por desgracia, estaba lejos de mi casa, así que tenía que ir en metro y en tren cada mañana. La primera semana trabajé en el departamento de ventas y marketing. Todos los días sacaba fotocopias y archivaba documentos. Luego, la segunda semana trabajé con el equipo de producción. ¡Qué ilusión! Ayudaba al ingeniero de sonido y me llevaba muy bien con mi jefe. Fue una experiencia tanto divertida como educativa, y aprendí muchísimas cosas.

Eduardo

En mayo pasé quince días trabajando en una granja. Cada día me levantaba a las seis de la mañana para coger el autobús. Empezaba a las siete y terminaba a las cinco, sin tener ni un momento para comer. ¡Me trataban como un esclavo! Tenía que hacer todos los trabajos sucios. No solo tenía que ordeñar las vacas, sino también dar de comer a los cerdos. Fue una pérdida de tiempo y solo aprendí una cosa útil en toda la semana – ¡no quiero ser granjero!

| **merecer / valer la pena** | to be worthwhile |
| **ordeñar** | to milk |

1 No vale la pena hacer prácticas laborales.	**5** Iba en transporte público.
2 Aprendí muchas habilidades nuevas.	**6** No tenía descanso.
3 Pasé dos semanas haciendo prácticas.	**7** Hacía varias tareas administrativas.
4 Trabajé al aire libre.	**8** El horario era muy duro.

2 Lee los textos otra vez. Busca <u>cuatro</u> verbos en el pretérito y <u>ocho</u> verbos en el imperfecto.

> Try using phrases such as these to provide interesting alternatives to **y** (and):
>
> *no solo…, sino también…* not only…, but also…
> *tanto… como…* both… and…

3 Escucha a Antonio. ¿A qué pregunta está contestando? (1–7)

Ejemplo: **1** *c*

a ¿Dónde hiciste tus prácticas?
b ¿Qué tal fue tu primer día?
c ¿Cómo era tu rutina?
d ¿Qué ropa llevabas?
e ¿Qué tareas hacías cada día?
f ¿Cómo era tu jefe?
g ¿Qué cosas aprendiste?

| **la reunión** | meeting |
| **los estantes** | shelves |

> **G** *Using the preterite and the imperfect tense* > Pages **212, 214**
>
> The **preterite** tense is used for completed actions in the past.
>
> *El primer día **llegué** temprano.* On the first day **I arrived** early.
>
> It is also often used for opinions in the past.
>
> ***Me gustó** trabajar allí.* **I liked** working there.
>
> The **imperfect** tense is used for repeated actions in the past, and for descriptions.
>
> *Cada mañana **cogía** el autobús.* Each morning **I caught** the bus.
> *Mis colegas **eran** muy agradables.* My colleagues **were** very pleasant.

4 Escucha otra vez. Apunta <u>dos</u> detalles en inglés para cada pregunta. (1–7)

Ejemplo: **1** *left home at 7.00, …*

5 hablar

Con tu compañero/a, haz diálogos. Usa las preguntas del ejercicio 3.

Hice mis prácticas laborales en… Pasé (quince días) trabajando en…	Mi jefe/a era Mis compañeros eran Los clientes eran	alegre(s) (des)agradable(s) (mal)educado/a(s)
El primer / último día	llegué… conocí a… fui…	(No) aprendí	a trabajar en equipo a usar… nada nuevo
Cada día Todos los dias	empezaba / terminaba a las… llevaba… trabajaba… ayudaba… escribía… cogía… iba…		

 6 escuchar

Escucha. Copia y completa la tabla. Sobra una opción. (1–5)

	cuándo	dónde	opinión
1	hace tres meses	c	experiencia muy positiva

a una agencia de viajes	**b** un polideportivo	**c** una escuela	**d** la empresa de mi madre	**e** una tienda benéfica / solidaria	**f** una fábrica de juguetes

 7 leer

Lee el texto y elige los verbos correctos. Luego traduce el <u>primer</u> párrafo al inglés.

Cada año mi insti organiza prácticas laborales para los alumnos. **1 Decidí / Decidía** ir a trabajar a una empresa cerca de donde vivo. Cada día **2 salí / salía** de casa a las ocho y cuarto y luego **3 fui / iba** a la oficina a pie. **4 Llevé / Llevaba** un traje azul oscuro que **5 recibí / recibía** por Navidad. Todos los días **6 hice / hacía** muchas tareas diferentes.

Mis compañeros de trabajo **7 fueron / eran** amables y siempre **8 pasé / pasaba** la hora de comer con ellos. Lo mejor fue el último día, cuando mi jefe **9 organizó / organizaba** una pequeña fiesta de despedida para mí. Mis prácticas fueron una experiencia muy positiva y **10 aprendí / aprendía** muchas habilidades nuevas.

 8 escribir

Escribe un texto sobre tus prácticas laborales.

Use the **preterite** to give details about:
- When / where you did your placement
- Your first / last day
- What you learned + your opinion

Use the **imperfect** to give details about:
- How you travelled each day
- What time you started / finished
- What you wore
- Your daily tasks
- The people you worked with

> Try to include some other tenses, such as the **present**, the **perfect**, the **future** or the **conditional**. For example:
>
> *Creo que las prácticas laborales (no)* ***merecen*** *la pena.*
>
> ***He decidido*** *que (no)* ***voy a ser…*** *en el futuro.*
>
> *(No)* ***recomendaría*** *estas prácticas a otro alumno.*

- Talking about the importance of learning languages
- Using the present and the present continuous
- Using **saber** and **conocer**

1 escuchar Escucha. ¿Cuál es la ventaja <u>más importante</u> para cada persona? (1–4)

el cerebro brain

a Te abre la mente.

b Aumenta tu confianza.

c Te hace parecer más atractivo.

d Mejora tus perspectivas laborales.

e Te ayuda a conocer nuevos sitios.

f Te permite hacer nuevos amigos.

g Te permite trabajar o estudiar en el extranjero.

h Estimula el cerebro.

i Te permite descubrir nuevas culturas.

j Te ayuda a mejorar tu lengua materna.

Diez ventajas de aprender un idioma

2 leer Lee y apunta las opiniones del ejercicio 1 que mencionan.
Ejemplo: **Paulina:** *d, …*

In exercise 1 you have to identify the **most important** reason for each person. Beware of distractors and listen out for clue words such as *más*, *sobre todo*, *principal*, *más que nada*.

No domino el inglés, pero lo hablo bastante bien. También hablo un poco de ruso. Creo que es más fácil encontrar trabajo si sabes hablar otro idioma, y a veces aun ganas un salario más alto. Además, te permite viajar a lugares más exóticos, conocer a mucha gente distinta y establecer nuevas amistades. Finalmente, mejora la memoria y te ayuda a solucionar problemas.

Paulina

Saber hablar otro idioma te da la oportunidad de buscar un empleo o ir a la universidad en otro país. Por ejemplo, yo pasé un año estudiando en Estados Unidos. También te ayuda a apreciar la vida cultural de otros países – el cine, la literatura, la música e incluso el humor. Reduce los prejuicios y el racismo porque te hace una persona más abierta a las diferencias. Además, te permite aprender cosas sobre tu propio idioma que no sabías.

Íñigo

| dominar | to master / be fluent in |
| aun / incluso | even |

3 leer Lee los textos del ejercicio 2 otra vez. Traduce al inglés las <u>cuatro</u> frases donde se usa 'saber' o 'conocer'.

The verbs **saber** and **conocer** both mean 'to know'.

saber – to know (facts / information), to know how to (do something)

| **No sé** la respuesta. | I **don't know** the answer. |
| ¿**Sabes** conducir? | Do **you know how** to drive? |

conocer – to know / be acquainted with (person / place / thing), to get to know / meet

| ¿**Conoces** a Eva? | Do **you know** Eva? |
| **Conocí** a mucha gente. | I **got to know / met** lots of people. |

4 escribir **Traduce el texto al español. Utiliza frases de los ejercicios 1 y 2 como modelo.**

I'm not fluent in Spanish, but I speak it quite well. I also speak a bit of French. In my opinion, if you know how to speak another language it allows you to meet lots of different people. Furthermore, it improves your job prospects. Above all, it increases your confidence and opens your mind.

5 escuchar **Escucha y lee el texto. Luego apunta la información en inglés.**

Susana

Trabajo como corresponsal de guerra para un canal de televisión. Es el trabajo de mis sueños porque me permite hacer todas las cosas que me interesan: viajar, conocer a gente nueva y, sobre todo, compartir historias importantes con el resto del mundo. Aunque es un trabajo emocionante, también puede ser peligroso, y siempre hay que recordar que esto no es ninguna película de Hollywood. La realidad de la guerra es muy triste y afecta a la vida de tanta gente inocente.

Para hacer bien mi trabajo me hace falta hablar idiomas extranjeros. Pasé diez años aprendiendo inglés cuando era más joven, y antes de venir aquí hice un curso de árabe. Esto me permite hacer entrevistas, leer documentos y escuchar las noticias locales para preparar mis reportajes. Más que nada, me ayuda a establecer buenas relaciones con la gente – algo esencial para un buen periodista.

recordar	to remember
compartir	to share

Ejemplo: **1** *Her job: war correspondent for a…*

1 Her job:
2 Why it's her dream job:
3 How she describes the job:

4 Why it's not like a film:
5 Her language studies:
6 How languages help her:

6 hablar **Mira las fotos. Con tu compañero/a, haz diálogos.**

● ¿Qué está haciendo <u>este hombre / esta mujer</u>?
■ *Está <u>trabajando como…</u> y está…*
● *En tu opinión, ¿cómo usa los idiomas en su trabajo?*
■ *Creo que <u>organiza…</u> También…*
● *¿Y tú? ¿Qué idiomas hablas?*
■ *Domino… y hablo…*
● *¿Por qué es importante aprender idiomas?*
■ *En mi opinión, es importante porque… Además,…*

guía turístico

is working in a hotel
is helping people

organises excursions
answers phone calls
solves problems

G *Present and present continuous* > *Page 218*

Use the **present continuous** to talk about what he/she <u>is doing</u> in the photo.

Use the **present tense** to talk about what he/she <u>does</u> more generally.

> ***Está escogiendo** ropa.* **She is choosing** clothes.
> *Todos los días **soluciona** problemas.* Every day **he solves** problems.

Remember, the present continuous uses the present tense of ***estar*** + present participle (*–ando / –iendo*).

compradora de moda

is visiting a company
is buying clothes

travels a lot
meets lots of people
writes emails

- Applying for a summer job
- Using indirect object pronouns
- Writing a formal letter

1 leer Lee los anuncios y contesta a las preguntas.

A

Animadores

¿Has terminado los exámenes? ¿Te apetece pasar el verano trabajando en Menorca? ¿Eres un(a) fanático/a del deporte? Se buscan animadores con buen nivel de inglés y español para campamento de verano. Precioso entorno rural. No hace falta experiencia.

B

Au pair

Estamos buscando a un(a) joven británico/a agradable y cariñoso/a para compartir nuestro hogar en Ibiza y cuidar de nuestros dos hijos encantadores. No se requiere experiencia. Flexibilidad horaria necesaria. Salario a convenir.

C

Varios puestos

¿Quieres trabajar en un parque de atracciones en Mallorca? Se requieren operarios de atracciones, camareros, ayudantes de cocina y dependientes. Experiencia deseable. Buenas capacidades de comunicación esenciales.

Zona Cultura

Destino:	ISLAS BALEARES
Ubicación:	Mar Mediterráneo, a 100 km de la costa valenciana.
Población:	1,1 millones (¡y más de 13 millones de turistas cada año!)
Famosas por:	Sus playas, su paisaje hermoso y su vida nocturna.

¿Te apetece…?	Do you fancy…? / Does… appeal to you?
cariñoso/a	affectionate
el hogar	home

¿Qué anuncio/trabajo…

1 te permite negociar el sueldo?
2 requiere buenas habilidades lingüísticas?
3 te ofrece alojamiento?
4 prefiere una persona con experiencia?
5 te permite disfrutar del campo?
6 te da la oportunidad de trabajar en una tienda?
7 no tiene horario fijo?

2 escuchar Escucha a Rafa. Copia y completa la tabla.

anuncio	ventaja	inconveniente
A	*trabajar al aire libre*	

3 hablar Con tu compañero/a, haz diálogos.

- ¿Te apetece ser <u>animador(a)</u>?
- ■ Sí / No, (no) me apetece ser… porque…
- ¿Te apetece trabajar en…?

(No) soy una persona…
(No) he trabajado en…
(No) me interesa (+ infinitive)
(No) tengo experiencia trabajando en/como…
Me da la oportunidad de (+ infinitive)

G Indirect object pronouns › Page 228

me	(to) me	**nos**	(to) us
te	(to) you	**os**	(to) you
le	(to) him/her/you (formal, singular)	**les**	(to) them/you (formal, plural)

The indirect object pronoun usually comes before the verb.

> **Me** apetece trabajar en España. Working in Spain appeals **to me**.

With verbs followed by the infinitive it can come before or after.

> **Le** voy a escribir / Voy a escribir**le**. I am going to write **to you**.

In English we often miss out the word 'to'.

> **Nos** da la oportunidad de… It gives **us** the opportunity to…

4 leer — Lee y completa la carta de presentación con las palabras del recuadro.

Muy Señor mío:

En referencia a su **1** _____ publicado en la página web www.empleosdeverano.es, le escribo para solicitar el **2** _____ de animador.

Aunque no tengo **3** _____ previa en un campamento de verano, he **4** _____ con niños pequeños en el polideportivo local y también he hecho de canguro para mis **5** _____. Soy responsable y **6** _____, practico muchos deportes en mi tiempo libre y me gusta trabajar en **7** _____.

Le adjunto mi currículum vitae. Como podrá ver, además del inglés (mi lengua materna) hablo bien el español y tengo **8** _____ de alemán.

Le agradezco su amable atención y quedo a la espera de su respuesta.

Atentamente,

Tom Hughes

vecinos	anuncio
equipo	puesto
experiencia	trabajado
trabajador	conocimientos

> Just like in English, you have to follow special conventions when writing a formal letter. Can you spot these phrases in Spanish?
>
> Dear Sir
> I'm enclosing my CV
> Thank you for your kind attention
> Yours sincerely
>
> Remember to use the **usted** (formal singular) form of the verb.

5 escribir — Escribe una carta de presentación para uno de los puestos del ejercicio 1.

Mention:

- the job you are applying for and where you saw it advertised
- your previous experience
- your personal qualities and interests
- your language skills / other skills

6 leer — Lee la entrevista. Empareja las preguntas con las respuestas.

1 ¿Por qué quiere ser (ayudante de cocina)?
2 ¿Qué asignaturas ha estudiado?
3 ¿Qué experiencia laboral tiene?
4 ¿Ha trabajado (en equipo) antes?
5 ¿Qué cualidades tiene usted?
6 ¿Qué otras habilidades tiene?

a He estudiado todas las asignaturas típicas, tales como las matemáticas, las ciencias y la informática, pero también he hecho un curso optativo de pastelería.

b Soy una persona honrada, amable y sincera. También tengo buen sentido del humor y me llevo bien con la gente.

c Sí, estoy haciendo un programa especial que se llama el 'Duke of Edinburgh Award'. Tenemos que trabajar en grupos para hacer una expedición.

d Me interesa este trabajo porque me encanta cocinar y quiero aprender más. En el futuro me gustaría ser cocinero.

e Domino el español y entiendo el francés escrito. También tengo buenas capacidades de comunicación y de resolución de problemas.

f El año pasado hice mis prácticas laborales en una carnicería, donde aprendí mucho. También tengo un trabajo a tiempo parcial en una cafetería.

7 escuchar — Escucha y comprueba tus respuestas.

tales como *such as*

8 hablar — Con tu compañero/a, haz una entrevista para un trabajo. Utiliza las preguntas del ejercicio 6.

- Discussing gap years
- Revising the conditional
- Using the 24-hour clock

1 **escuchar** Escucha y elige la respuesta correcta. (1–4)

¿Cómo pasarías un año sabático?

1 Marc iría a España, donde…

- **a** enseñaría inglés.
- **b** mejoraría su nivel de español.
- **c** ganaría mucho dinero.

2 Fernanda pasaría un año en Honduras, donde…

- **a** apoyaría un proyecto medioambiental.
- **b** trabajaría en un orfanato.
- **c** ayudaría a construir un colegio.

3 Ramón buscaría un trabajo para tres meses y luego…

- **a** viajaría como mochilero por el mundo.
- **b** visitaría Latinoamérica.
- **c** haría un viaje en Interrail por Europa.

4 Pilar dice que trabajaría en una estación de esquí, donde…

- **a** aprendería a esquiar.
- **b** el alojamiento sería muy caro.
- **c** nunca olvidaría la experiencia.

el orfanato	orphanage
viajar como mochilero/a	to go backpacking

G **The conditional** > Page **220**

Remember to use the **conditional** to say what you would do.

Enseñaría inglés.	**I would teach** English.
Trabajaríamos en un orfanato.	**We would work** in an orphanage.

To form the conditional, add the imperfect endings of –er/–ir verbs to the infinitive.

Some verbs have an irregular stem. They include:

hacer → haría (I would do)
poder → podría (I would be able to)
tener → tendría (I would have)

2 **hablar** Con tu compañero/a, haz diálogos.

- ¿Cómo pasarías un año sabático?
- Primero…, donde… Luego…

1 job (4 months) + earn money
2 Interrail (Europe)
3 Colombia + help build orphanage
= never forget

1 Argentina + improve Spanish
2 backpack (Latin America)
3 job (hotel) + earn money
= learn a lot

3 **leer** Lee el texto y tradúcelo al inglés.

Si pudiera tomarme un año sabático, lo aprovecharía para trabajar como voluntaria porque, en mi opinión, es importantísimo ayudar a los demás. Sin embargo, no me gustaría trabajar como profesora – ¡estoy harta de los colegios! Iría a Costa Rica, donde trabajaría en un proyecto medioambiental para salvar las tortugas marinas. Creo que el voluntariado aumenta tu confianza y te permite mejorar tus habilidades sociales. Después, viajaría como mochilera por los países de Centroamérica (¡si tuviera bastante dinero!).

These phrases use a form of the verb called the **imperfect subjunctive**.

Si **pudiera** tomarme un año sabático…	If **I could** take a gap year…
Si **tuviera** bastante dinero…	If **I had** enough money…
Si **fuera** más ambicioso/a…	If **I were** more ambitious…

aprovechar	to make the most of
estar harto/a	to be fed up
el voluntariado	volunteering

4 leer Lee la página web. ¿Quién habla? Escribe el nombre correcto.

Tu año sabático.com

¿Cómo viajarías?

Cogería el tren, ya que es más cómodo y puedes ver vídeos en tu tableta mientras viajas. También puedes dejar la maleta en la consigna mientras visitas una ciudad. No viajaría en autobús porque no me gusta nada esperar en la parada de autobús. **Óscar (Bilbao)**

Para viajar entre diferentes ciudades cogería el autocar dado que es rápido – normalmente hay pocos atascos en las autopistas. No iría en tren porque los conductores siempre están en huelga. Y lo peor es que los billetes son carísimos. **Conchita (Vigo)**

No viajaría en autobús, pues las carreteras están en muy mal estado en muchos sitios. También tengo miedo a volar, y suele haber muchos retrasos en los aeropuertos. Creo que iría en tren. Por lo menos los trenes tienen aire acondicionado y no contaminan el medio ambiente. **Lourdes (Jaén)**

1 I'm scared of flying.
2 Train drivers are always on strike.
3 I can't stand waiting at bus stops.
4 Motorways are congestion-free.

5 You can store your luggage.
6 I can do other things while travelling.
7 The roads are poor.
8 Tickets are really expensive.

5 escribir ¿Cómo pasarías un año sabático? ¿Cómo viajarías? Escribe un texto.

Give details of:

- Where you would go
- What you would do
- How you would travel, and why

6 escuchar Escucha y mira la información. Corrige los errores. (1–5)

Ejemplo: **1** *Retraso – 10 min*

Destino	Salida	Llegada	Vía	Observaciones
Gijón	09:39	15:32	5	Retraso – 12 min
Málaga	09:41	12:47	8	
Zaragoza	09:46	11:25	11	Cancelado
Coruña	09:53	15:20	4	Tren AVE
Toledo	09:58	10:29	7	

Train stations and airports often use the 24-hour clock. When listening to announcements be prepared to hear the hour (0–23) followed by the minutes (up to 59).

las catorce	14:00
las quince cero dos	15:02
las dieciséis cuarenta y siete	16:47

7 escuchar Escucha y rellena los espacios en blanco. (1–3)

En la taquilla

● *Buenos días. ¿Qué desea?*
■ *Quisiera* **a** ⸺ *billete(s) de* **b** ⸺ *a*
  c ⸺, *por favor.*
● *¿A qué hora?*
■ *A las* **d** ⸺ *¿De qué andén sale?*
● *Sale del andén* **e** ⸺.
■ *¿Y a qué hora llega?*
● *Llega a las* **f** ⸺.
■ *¿Es directo o hay que cambiar?*
● **g** ⸺.

el tren con destino a	*the train to*
efectuará su salida	*will leave / depart*
de la vía / del andén (dos)	*from platform (two)*
un billete de ida	*a single ticket*
un billete de ida y vuelta	*a return ticket*

8 hablar Con tu compañero/a, haz diálogos. Utiliza la información del ejercicio 6 e inventa los otros detalles.

- *Discussing plans for the future*
- *Using the subjunctive with cuando*
- *Using different ways to express future plans*

1 Escucha y escribe las <u>dos</u> letras correctas. (1–5)

> ¿Qué planes tienes para el futuro?

a Quiero montar mi propio negocio.

b Espero aprobar mis exámenes.

c Tengo la intención de casarme.

d Pienso trabajar como voluntario/a en…

e Voy a aprender a conducir.

f Me gustaría tener hijos.

g Espero ser feliz.

h ¡Seré famoso/a!

2 Escucha otra vez. Apunta las <u>dos</u> razones que mencionan. (1–5)

Ejemplo: **1** *success is important to him, …*

(No)	el desempleo / paro
Me gusta(n)	el dinero
Me interesa(n)	el éxito
Me importa(n)	el matrimonio
Me preocupa(n)	la responsabilidad
	la independencia
	la pobreza
	los niños
	las notas

Zona Cultura

En España casi la mitad de los adultos menores de 30 años (el 49%) todavía vive con sus padres, comparado con el 26% en el Reino Unido. Es menos común irse de casa para compartir piso con amigos o una pareja. Por un lado, es una consecuencia del problema del paro juvenil, pero por otro lado, muestra la importancia tradicional de la familia.

3 Con tu compañero/a, haz diálogos.

- ¿Vas a <u>aprender a conducir</u>?
- Sí, voy a <u>aprender a conducir</u> porque me importa el/la…
- ¿Tienes la intención de…?
- No, no tengo la intención de… ya que…

> When asking questions don't forget to use the **tú** form of the verb. For reflexive verbs the pronoun also has to change.
>
> Quier**o** casar**me** → ¿Quier**es** casar**te**?

G *Talking about future plans* > *Page 216*

You can express future plans with a variety of phrases followed by the infinitive:

quiero	I want to
tengo la intención de	I intend to
espero	I hope to
pienso	I plan to / intend to
voy a	I am going to
me gustaría	I would like to
Espero ir a la universidad.	I hope to go to university.
Tengo la intención de casarme.	I intend to get married.

You can also use the simple future tense.

Buscaré un trabajo.	**I will look for** a job.

4 leer Lee los textos. Busca el equivalente de las expresiones en español.

Tomás

Me interesan las asignaturas prácticas, así que el próximo año pienso ir a otro instituto para hacer un ciclo de formación profesional. Espero obtener el título de Técnico en Cocina y Gastronomía. La formación profesional es una buena opción si quieres un oficio en sectores como la gestión administrativa o la hostelería. Cuando termine el curso buscaré un trabajo como cocinero. Más tarde cuando me enamore me casaré, ya que me importa el matrimonio.

Lina

Estoy en cuarto de ESO y espero sacar buenas notas en los exámenes porque me preocupa el paro y hay que tener éxito en los estudios para conseguir un buen empleo. Cuando termine los exámenes seguiré estudiando en mi insti, donde haré el bachillerato. Luego tengo la intención de ir a Londres para hacer una carrera universitaria. Cuando gane bastante dinero voy a aprender a conducir.

el oficio   trade / profession

1 to do a vocational training course
2 I hope to qualify as
3 such as business management
4 when I fall in love
5 I'm in Year 11
6 to get a good job
7 where I will do A Levels
8 a university degree

5 leer Lee los textos del ejercicio 4 otra vez. Escribe <u>cinco</u> detalles en inglés para cada persona.

6 escuchar Escucha. Copia y completa la tabla. (1–6)

	when…	I will…
1	I go to university	buy…

⭐ If your plans aren't certain, use words like **quizás** or **tal vez** (maybe/perhaps).

7 escribir Escribe un texto sobre tus planes para el futuro.

Include:

- Details of your plans for study and work
- Personal ambitions (learning to drive, relationships, etc.)
- A range of verbs for talking about future plans
- Phrases such as *me interesa(n)*
- *Cuando* + subjunctive

G Cuando + *present subjunctive*   ❯ *Page 234*

When using the word **cuando** to talk about future plans you have to use a form of the verb called the **subjunctive**.

To form the present subjunctive, start with the 'I' form of the present tense, remove the *–o* and add these endings:

	gan**ar** (to earn / win)	vend**er** (to sell)	viv**ir** (to live)
(yo)	gan**e**	vend**a**	viv**a**
(tú)	gan**es**	vend**as**	viv**as**
(él/ella/usted)	gan**e**	vend**a**	viv**a**
(nosotros/as)	gan**emos**	vend**amos**	viv**amos**
(vosotros/as)	gan**éis**	vend**áis**	viv**áis**
(ellos/ellas/ustedes)	gan**en**	vend**an**	viv**an**

Verbs which are irregular in the present subjunctive include:

ser (to be) → **sea**   **ir** (to go) → **vaya**

el amo/a de casa househusband / housewife

Cuando…	buscaré un trabajo
sea mayor	compartiré piso con…
me enamore	me compraré un coche / una casa
gane bastante dinero	seguiré estudiando en mi insti
vaya a la universidad	iré a otro insti / a la universidad
tenga… años	me casaré
Cuando termine…	me iré de casa
este curso	me tomaré un año sabático
el bachillerato	trabajaré como…
la formación profesional	
la licenciatura	

1 leer **Read what the people say about where they work.**

Hay buenos beneficios para los empleados, como un restaurante subvencionado y días adicionales de vacaciones por antigüedad – cuando cumpla diez años en la empresa, tendré una semana extra de vacaciones. Valoran mucho la formación y ofrecen buenos programas de desarrollo profesional. **Teresa**

No estaba contento en el departamento de ventas porque tenía un jefe muy exigente. He cambiado de puesto y ahora me siento más feliz. Aunque me gustaría tener un sueldo más alto, el horario es flexible y esto te ayuda a mantener el equilibrio entre el trabajo y la vida personal. **Diego**

Hay buenas perspectivas para los que quieren progresar en la empresa, como yo. Cada año los jefes dan premios a la persona que falta menos días al trabajo, la que vende más productos, etc. Es una buena manera de incentivar a la gente. **Gorka**

Si pudiera cambiarme de trabajo lo haría, ya que no soporto a mi jefa. No es nada comprensiva. El problema es que con la crisis actual no sería nada fácil encontrar otro trabajo con un sueldo tan alto – ite tratan mal, pero te pagan bien! **Lidia**

Who says what? Write either Teresa, Diego, Gorka or Lidia.

(a) ——— does not like their current boss.
(b) ——— appreciates the quality of the training offered.
(c) ——— says that the salary is good.
(d) ——— is ambitious for promotion in the future.

Answer the following questions in English. You do not need to write full sentences.

(e) How exactly are employees rewarded for length of service?
(f) What do flexible working hours enable you to do?

2 leer **Read the article about unemployment in Spain.**

Los profesionales formados en matemáticas y estadística y los dedicados a servicios de seguridad tienen las tasas de paro más bajas de España, según los últimos datos de la Encuesta de Población Activa (EPA). En concreto, el paro afecta al 5,7% de los profesionales dedicados a las matemáticas y estadística, y al 7,45% de los que trabajan en servicios de seguridad.

Otros sectores con tasas de paro bajas son el derecho (10,63%), la veterinaria (10,65%) y la salud (12,18%). De los 38,5 millones de españoles mayores de 16 años, las tasas de paro más elevadas corresponden a las personas que han estudiado como máximo la Enseñanza Secundaria Obligatoria o el bachillerato y no han seguido estudios universitarios (62,12%).

Answer the following questions in English. You do not need to write full sentences.

(a) Which sector has the second lowest unemployment rate?
(b) As well as veterinary medicine, which <u>two</u> other sectors have low unemployment?
(c) Who experiences the highest rate of unemployment?
(d) Which age group does this study cover?

When reading texts with lots of statistics, pay attention to words like 'high' and 'low', and those which suggest an increase or decrease. What do the following words mean?

bajo   aumentar   reducir   menor
disminuir   elevado   mayor   alto

3 leer Read the extract from a play in which two candidates are waiting for a job interview.

El método Grönholm by Jordi Galcerán (abridged and adapted)

Enrique:	¿Has venido en coche?
Fernando:	Sí.
Enrique:	Yo también. Mucho tráfico, ¿no?
Fernando:	Como cada día.
Enrique:	Yo ya he hecho tres entrevistas. No sé qué más quieren saber de mí. Y tú, ¿cuántas llevas?
Fernando:	Tres.
Enrique:	Vengo de una empresa pequeña, y no he trabajado nunca en una multinacional. ¿Y tú?
Fernando:	Yo he trabajado en muchos sitios.
Enrique:	Y las condiciones son increíbles. El sueldo es… Bueno, no sé qué ganas tú, pero yo ganaría casi el doble… Tenía miedo de llegar tarde. Estaba en la avenida Diagonal, atascado, y pensaba, 'ahora llegarás tarde'. Estas cosas son importantes. A veces los pequeños detalles son los que hacen tomar una decisión. La manera de vestir, el coche…

Choose the correct word(s) for each phrase.

(a) Today there was…
  A more traffic than normal.
  B less traffic than normal.
  C as much traffic as normal.
  D hardly any traffic.

(b) Enrique has worked…
  A in a multinational company.
  B in lots of places.
  C in a small company.
  D abroad.

(c) If he gets the job, Enrique will…
  A earn more than he does now.
  B earn less than he does now.
  C be able to arrive later.
  D have to work later.

(d) On the avenida Diagonal there were lots of…
  A people.
  B traffic jams.
  C accidents.
  D traffic lights.

1 escuchar **You are listening to an English girl being interviewed for a job in Spain.**

Listen and choose the <u>three</u> correct statements.

  A Spanish is compulsory at her school.
  B She is hardworking.
  C She speaks Spanish fluently.
  D Her first language is Urdu.
  E She has a part-time job.
  F She has experience of looking after children.
  G She did six weeks' work experience in an office.

Shakila

2 escuchar **You are listening to Begoña, a careers adviser, talking about gap years.**

Listen and answer the following questions in English.

  (a) (i)   Where do many people decide to travel to?
      (ii) Why is this more difficult later in life?
      (iii) Which skill will you develop in particular?

  (b) (i)   What does Begoña think is a waste of time?
      (ii) What advice does she give? Give <u>two</u> details.

⭐ In tasks like this, try to avoid writing down the answer as soon as you hear it. Otherwise, you may miss the answer to the next question. Trust your short-term memory and write down the answers when you hear the 'beep'.

A – Role play

 1 leer   Look at the role play card and prepare what you are going to say.

Topic: Work

Instructions to candidates:

You are phoning a Spanish hotel to ask for information about a summer job. The teacher will play the role of the receptionist and will speak first.

You must address the receptionist as *usted*.

You will talk to the teacher using the five prompts below.

• where you see – **?** – you must ask a question.
• where you see – **!** – you must respond to something you have not prepared.

Task

Usted está llamando a un hotel en España. Quiere pedir información sobre un trabajo de verano y habla con el/la recepcionista.

1 Información - trabajo
2 Trabajo - tipo
3 !
4 ? Sueldo - semana
5 ? Mensaje - dejar

Use either the **perfect tense** to say what you **have done**, or the **preterite tense** to say what you **did** (e.g. last year).

Which question word means 'How much …?'?

Read the second sentence of the instructions (above the bullet points). Can you adapt it?

Remember that you are phoning a hotel. What kind of jobs will be available there?

To turn this into a question you could start with 'Can I …?'

⭐ In Spain people often answer the phone by saying *¡Dígame!* (literally 'Tell me!').

If you ask to speak to someone, you might also hear:

¿De parte de quién?   Who's calling?
Lo siento, no está.   I'm sorry, he/she isn't here.

If you need to leave a message, you can ask:

¿Puedo dejar un mensaje, por favor?

 2 escuchar   Practise what you have prepared. Using your notes, listen and respond to the teacher.

3 escuchar   Now listen to Bethany doing the role play task.
In English, note down what she says for bullets 2 and 3.

⭐ To say what you **want** to / **would like** to do, or to ask if you **can** do something, remember to use:

Quiero…
Me gustaría… ⎬ + infinitive
¿Puedo…?

B – Picture-based task

Topic: Ambitions

Mira la foto y prepara las respuestas a los siguientes puntos:

• la descripción de la foto
• tu opinión sobre tomarse un año sabático
• un ejemplo de cuándo has ayudado a otras personas
• tus planes para continuar estudiando en el futuro
• (!)

1 escuchar **Look at the photo and read the task. Then listen to Oliver's response to the first bullet point.**

1 How does he describe the adult in the middle?

2 Write down the <u>three</u> verbs he uses in the present continuous.

2 escuchar **Listen to and read Oliver's response to the second bullet point.**

1 Write down the missing word for each gap.

2 Look at the Answer Booster on page 156. Note down <u>six</u> examples of language which Oliver uses to give a strong answer.

Desde un punto de vista **1** —————, un año sabático te da la oportunidad de viajar, descubrir culturas distintas y **2** ————— a gente nueva. Además, no solo te permite aumentar tu **3** —————, sino también mejorar tus habilidades sociales, ya que haces muchísimos amigos nuevos. Sin embargo, a mi modo de ver, no **4** ————— la pena tomarse un año sabático si no **5** ————— el tiempo para ayudar a los demás también. Para mí, esto es importantísimo, y si tuviera bastante dinero iría a Latinoamérica, donde **6** ————— a los niños que viven en la calle.

3 escuchar **Listen to Oliver's response to the third bullet point. Note down <u>six</u> details that he gives, in English.**

4 escuchar **Listen to Oliver's response to the fourth bullet point. In Spanish, note down <u>five</u> different expressions which he uses to refer to his future plans.**

Ejemplo: Espero sacar…

 Remember that phrases for referring to future plans usually include the **infinitive**, unless the verb is in the simple future tense:
*Quiero **ir** a la universidad.*
Iré a otro insti.

5 escuchar **Prepare your own answers to the first <u>four</u> bullet points. Try to predict which unexpected question you might be asked. Then listen and take part in the full picture-based task with the teacher.**

C – General conversation

1 escuchar **Listen to Mark introducing his chosen topic. Make notes in English about his <u>current</u> job under these headings:**

Job   Opinion   When   Tasks   Pay

2 escuchar **The teacher asks Mark, '¿Qué planes tienes para el futuro?' Listen to his response and look at the Answer Booster on page 156. Note down <u>six</u> examples of language which Mark uses to give a strong answer.**

3 escuchar **The teacher then asks Mark, '¿Qué opinas de ir a la universidad?' Look at the following statements and decide if they are for or against. Then listen to Mark's answer and note down which ones he mentions.**

a Las personas con títulos universitarios ganan más.

b Abre muchas puertas en el mundo laboral.

c Es muy caro – terminas la licenciatura con deudas.

d Pasar tres años estudiando es una pérdida de tiempo.

e Aprendes a ser más independiente.

f Para muchos trabajos no es necesario.

g Haces amigos para toda la vida.

4 hablar **Prepare your own answers to Module 7 questions 1–6 on page 199. Then practise with your partner.**

Answer booster	Aiming for a solid answer	Aiming higher	Aiming for the top
Verbs	**Different time frames**: past, present, near future **Different types of verbs**: regular, irregular, reflexive, stem-changing	**Verbs with an infinitive**: *tener que, soler, acabar de* **Phrases with an infinitive**: *para, sin, antes de, después de, al…* **Phrases to refer to future plans**: *espero, pienso, quiero, tengo la intención de* + infinitive	**A wide range of tenses**: present, present continuous, preterite, imperfect, perfect, future, conditional **Avoiding the passive**: *se pueden traducir* ***Cuando* + subjunctive**: *cuando sea mayor, cuando termine…*
Opinions and reasons	**Verbs of opinion**: *me chifla(n), me encanta(n), me interesa(n), no aguanto* **Reasons**: *porque…*	**Opinions**: *me importa(n), me preocupa(n)* **Absolute superlatives**: *muchísimo, importantísimo*	**Opinions**: *desde mi punto de vista, a mi modo de ver, a mi juicio…* **Reasons**: *ya que, dado que, por lo tanto, por eso, así que*
Connectives	*y, pero, también*	*además, sin embargo, sobre todo*	*aunque, a pesar de, ya, todavía* **Alternatives to 'and'**: *no solo… sino también, tanto… como…*
Other features	**Qualifiers**: *muy, un poco, bastante, demasiado* **Negatives**: *no, nunca* **Sequencers**: *luego, después, más tarde*	**Different uses of *saber / conocer*** **Desde hace**: *estudio… desde hace…* **Indirect object pronouns**: *te da la oportunidad de…, te permite…*	**Complex sentences with *si***: *si tuviera bastante…* **More complex vocabulary**: *valer / merecer la pena, defenderse, aprovechar* **Other complex structures**: *por si eso fuera poco, ¡Ojalá pudiera…!*

A – Extended writing task

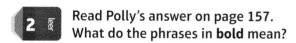

1 leer **Look at the task and answer the questions.**

- What **type** of text are you asked to write?
- What is each bullet point asking you to do?
- Which tense(s) will you need to use to answer each one?

2 leer **Read Polly's answer on page 157. What do the phrases in bold mean?**

3 leer **Look at the Answer Booster. Note down <u>eight</u> examples of language which Polly uses to write a strong answer.**

4 leer **Complete the essay plan based on Polly's answer.**

5 escribir **Prepare your own answer to the task.**

- Look at the Answer Booster and Polly's plan for ideas.
- Think about how you can develop your answer for each bullet point.
- Write a detailed plan. Organise your answer in paragraphs.
- Write your answer and carefully check what you have written.

La importancia de los idiomas

Usted ha pasado un mes haciendo prácticas laborales en España.

Escriba un artículo para convencer a los alumnos de la importancia de aprender otros idiomas.

Debe incluir los puntos siguientes:

- sus habilidades lingüísticas
- las ventajas de aprender idiomas
- detalles sobre sus prácticas laborales en España
- sus planes para tomarse un año sábatico en el futuro.

Justifique sus ideas y sus opiniones.

Escriba aproximadamente 130–150 palabras **en español**.

Paragraph 1
- My first language
- How long…

Paragraph 2
-

En mi opinión, las lenguas son importantísimas. Mi lengua materna es el inglés, pero también estudio español desde hace cinco años. Aunque todavía no lo domino, **me defiendo** bastante bien. Mi madre nació en Galés y es bilingüe. ¡**Ojalá yo pudiera hablar** galés también!

Como todo el mundo sabe, aprender otros idiomas no solo te ayuda a mejorar tus perspectivas laborales (ya que **muchas empresas valoran** las habilidades lingüísticas), sino también a viajar a sitios distintos y establecer nuevas amistades. **Por si eso fuera poco**, te permite comprender otras culturas, incluso la literatura, la música y el humor (¡muchos chistes no se pueden traducir de una lengua a otra!).

Acabo de volver de Gran Canaria, donde hice prácticas laborales en una escuela de equitación. Cada día ayudaba a los niños, daba de comer a los caballos y limpiaba los establos. **A pesar del olor**, aprendí mucho y **por eso valió la pena**. Sobre todo, pasé tres semanas **sin hablar ni una palabra de inglés**.

Cuando termine los exámenes de 'A Level' (equivalentes al bachillerato), espero tomarme un año sabático **antes de empezar la carrera universitaria**. Me gustaría trabajar en un proyecto medioambiental en Latinoamérica. Después, si tuviera bastante dinero, viajaría como mochilera por Perú (¡y **cumpliría mi sueño de** subir a Machu Picchu!).

Polly

B – Translation

1 escribir **Translate the passage into Spanish.**

Which words do you **not** need to translate here?

Which person of the verb do you need?

Do you need *ser* or *estar* here? In which tense?

My mum used to be a hairdresser but now she is a chef. Usually she does all the household chores, but yesterday my brother and I cooked because she was tired. In the future I hope to be a nurse because I am very understanding. When I earn enough money I will leave home because independence is important to me.

Remember to use *cuando* + present subjunctive.

Do not translate this word for word. Start with *Me importa…*

2 escribir **Now translate the following passage into Spanish. Use your answer to exercise 1 to help you.**

I don't like my part-time job because I don't earn much money. Usually I deliver newspapers, but yesterday I also helped in the shop because my boss was ill. When I am older I would like to be a journalist because it's a varied job with a good salary. Unemployment worries me, so I hope to pass my exams.

⭐ Take care with words which are similar but mean different things.

un(a) enfermero/a (a nurse)	*enfermo/a* (ill)
un(a) cocinero/a (a cook/chef)	*cocinar* (to cook)
un(a) periodista (a journalist)	*un periódico* (a newspaper)

¿En qué trabajas? — What is your job?

Soy… / Es… — I am… / He/She is…
Me gustaría ser… — I would like to be…

abogado/a	lawyer
albañil	bricklayer / builder
amo/a de casa	housewife / househusband
azafato/a	flight attendant
bailarín(a)	dancer
bombero/a	firefighter
camarero/a	waiter / waitress
cantante	singer
cocinero/a	cook
contable	accountant
dependiente/a	shop assistant
diseñador(a)	designer
electricista	electrician
enfermero/a	nurse
escritor(a)	writer
fontanero/a	plumber
fotógrafo/a	photographer
funcionario/a	civil servant
guía turístico/a	tour guide
ingeniero/a	engineer
jardinero/a	gardener
mecánico/a	mechanic
médico/a	doctor
músico/a	musician
peluquero/a	hairdresser
periodista	journalist
policía	police officer
profesor(a)	teacher
recepcionista	receptionist
socorrista	lifeguard
soldado	soldier
veterinario/a	vet

Es un trabajo… — It's a … job

artístico / emocionante	artistic / exciting
exigente / importante	demanding / important
fácil / difícil	easy / difficult
manual / monótono	manual / monotonous
variado / repetitivo	varied / repetitive
con responsabilidad	with responsibility
con buenas perspectivas	with good prospects
con un buen sueldo	with a good salary

Tengo que… / Suelo… — I have to… / I tend to…

cuidar a los clientes / pacientes / pasajeros	look after the customers / patients / passengers
contestar llamadas telefónicas	answer telephone calls
cuidar las plantas y las flores	look after the plants and flowers
enseñar / vigilar a los niños	teach / supervise the children
hacer entrevistas	do interviews
preparar platos distintos	prepare different dishes
reparar coches	repair cars
servir comida y bebida	serve food and drink
trabajar en un taller / en un hospital / en una tienda / a bordo de un avión	work in a workshop / in a hospital / in a shop / aboard a plane
vender ropa de marca	sell designer clothing
viajar por todo el mundo	travel the world

¿Qué tipo de persona eres? — What type of person are you?

Creo que soy… — I think I'm…

ambicioso/a	ambitious
comprensivo/a	understanding
creativo/a	creative
extrovertido/a	extroverted / outgoing
fuerte	strong
inteligente	intelligent
organizado/a	organised
paciente	patient
práctico/a	practical
serio/a	serious
trabajador(a)	hardworking
valiente	brave

¿Qué haces para ganar dinero? — What do you do to earn money?

¿Tienes un trabajo a tiempo parcial?	Do you have a part-time job?
Reparto periódicos.	I deliver newspapers.
Hago de canguro.	I babysit.
Trabajo de cajero/a.	I work as a cashier.
Ayudo con las tareas domésticas.	I help with the housework.
Cocino.	I cook.
Lavo los platos.	I wash the dishes.
Paso la aspiradora.	I do the vacuuming.
Plancho la ropa.	I iron the clothes.
Pongo y quito la mesa.	I lay and clear the table.
Paseo al perro.	I walk the dog.
Corto el césped.	I cut the lawn.
Lo hago…	I do it…
los sábados	on Saturdays
antes / después del insti	before / after school
cuando necesito dinero	when I need money
cuando mi madre está trabajando	when my mum is working
cuando me necesitan	when they need me
cada mañana	each / every morning
una vez / dos veces a la semana	once / twice a week
Gano … euros / libras a la hora / al día / a la semana	I earn … euros / pounds per hour / day / week
Me llevo bien con mis compañeros.	I get on well with my colleagues.
Mi jefe/a es amable.	My boss is nice.
El horario es flexible.	The hours are flexible.

Mis prácticas laborales — Work experience

Hice mis prácticas laborales en…	I did my work experience in…
Pasé quince días trabajando en…	I spent a fortnight working in…
un polideportivo	a sports centre
una agencia de viajes / una granja	a travel agency / a farm
una escuela / una oficina	a school / an office
una fábrica de juguetes	a toy factory
una tienda benéfica / solidaria	a charity shop
la empresa de mi madre	my mum's company
El primer / último día conocí a / llegué…	On the first / last day I met / I arrived…
Cada día / Todos los días…	Each / Every day…
archivaba documentos	I filed documents
ayudaba…	I helped…
cogía el autobús / el metro	I caught the bus / underground
empezaba / terminaba a las …	I started / finished at…
hacía una variedad de tareas	I did a variety of tasks
iba en transporte público	I went by public transport
llevaba ropa elegante	I wore smart clothes
ponía folletos en los estantes	I put brochures on the shelves
sacaba fotocopias	I did photocopying
Mi jefe/a era…	My boss was…
Mis compañeros eran…	My colleagues were…
Los clientes eran…	The customers were …
alegre(s)	cheerful
(des)agradable(s)	(un)pleasant
(mal)educado/a(s)	polite (rude)
El trabajo era duro.	The job was hard.
Aprendí…	I learned
muchas nuevas habilidades	lots of new skills
a trabajar en equipo	to work in a team
a usar…	to use…
No aprendí nada nuevo.	I didn't learn anything new.

¿Por qué aprender idiomas? — Why learn languages?

Aumenta tu confianza.	It increases your confidence.
Estimula el cerebro.	It stimulates the brain.
Mejora tus perspectivas laborales.	It improves your job prospects.
Te abre la mente.	It opens your mind.
Te hace parecer más atractivo.	It makes you appear more attractive.
Te ayuda a…	It helps you to…
Te permite…	It allows you to…
apreciar la vida cultural de otros países	appreciate the cultural life of other countries
conocer a mucha gente distinta	meet lots of different people
conocer nuevos sitios	get to know new places
encontrar un trabajo	find a job
descubrir nuevas culturas	discover new cultures
establecer buenas relaciones	establish good relationships
hacer nuevos amigos	make new friends
mejorar tu lengua materna	improve your first language
solucionar problemas	solve problems
trabajar o estudiar en el extranjero	work or study abroad
Me hace falta saber hablar idiomas extranjeros.	I need to know how to speak foreign languages.
(No) Domino el inglés.	I (don't) speak English fluently.
Hablo un poco de ruso.	I speak a bit of Russian.

Solicitando un trabajo — Applying for a job

Se busca / Se requiere…	… required.
(No) hace falta experiencia.	Experience (not) needed.
Muy señor mío	Dear Sir
Le escribo para solicitar el puesto de…	I'm writing to apply for the post of…
Le adjunto mi currículum vitae.	I'm enclosing my CV.
Le agradezco su amable atención.	Thank you for your kind attention.
Atentamente	Yours sincerely/faithfully
Me apetece trabajar en…	Working in… appeals to me.
(No) Tengo experiencia previa.	I (don't) have previous experience.
He estudiado / trabajado…	I've studied / worked…
He hecho un curso de…	I've done a course in…
Tengo…	I have…
buen sentido del humor	a good sense of humour
buenas capacidades de comunicación / resolución de problemas	good communication / problem-solving skills
buenas habilidades lingüísticas	good language skills

Un año sabático — A gap year

Si pudiera tomarme un año sabático…	If I could take a gap year…
Si tuviera bastante dinero…	If I had enough money…
apoyaría un proyecto medioambiental	I would support an environmental project
aprendería a esquiar	I would learn to ski
ayudaría a construir un colegio	I would help to build a school
buscaría un trabajo	I would look for a job
enseñaría inglés	I would teach English
ganaría mucho dinero	I would earn a lot of money
haría un viaje en Interrail	I would go Interrailing
iría a España, donde…	I would go to Spain, where…
mejoraría mi nivel de español	I would improve my level of Spanish
nunca olvidaría la experiencia	I would never forget the experience
pasaría un año en…	I would spend a year in…
trabajaría en un orfanato	I would work in an orphanage
viajaría con mochila por el mundo	I would go backpacking around the world

¿Cómo viajarías? — How would you travel?

Cogería el / Viajaría en autobús / autocar / avión / tren.	I would catch the / travel by bus / coach / plane / train.
Es más barato / cómodo / rápido.	It's cheaper / more comfortable / quicker.
Puedes…	You can…
ver vídeos mientras viajas	watch videos whilst you travel
dejar tu maleta en la consigna	leave your suitcase in the left-luggage office
Hay muchos / pocos atascos / retrasos…	There are lots of / few traffic jams / delays…
en las autopistas / las carreteras	on the motorways / roads
Los billetes son carísimos.	The tickets are extremely expensive.
Los conductores están en huelga.	The drivers are on strike.
Odio esperar en la parada de autobús.	I hate waiting at the bus stop.
Tengo miedo a volar.	I'm scared of flying.

Viajando en tren — Travelling by train

El tren con destino a…	The train to…
efectuará su salida…	will leave / depart…
de la vía / del andén dos	from platform two
el (tren) AVE	high-speed train
la taquilla	the ticket office
Quisiera un billete de ida a…	I would like a single ticket to…
Quisiera un billete de ida y vuelta a…	I would like a return ticket to…
¿De qué andén sale?	From which platform does it leave?
¿A qué hora sale / llega?	What time does it leave / arrive?
¿Es directo o hay que cambiar?	Is it direct or do I have to change?

El futuro — The future

Me interesa(n)…	…interest(s) me.
Me importa(n)…	…matter(s) to me.
Me preocupa(n)…	…worry/worries me.
el desempleo / el paro	unemployment
el dinero / el éxito	money / success
el fracaso / el matrimonio	failure / marriage
la responsabilidad	responsibility
la independencia / la pobreza	independence / poverty
los niños / las notas	children / marks
Espero…	I hope to…
Me gustaría …	I would like to…
Pienso…	I plan to/intend to…
Quiero…	I want to…
Tengo la intención de…	I intend to…
Voy a…	I am going to…
aprender a conducir	learn to drive
aprobar mis exámenes	pass my exams
casarme	get married
conseguir un buen empleo/trabajo	get a good job
estudiar una carrera universitaria	study a university course
montar mi propio negocio	set up my own business
sacar buenas notas	get good marks
ser feliz	be happy
tener hijos	have children
trabajar como voluntario/a	work as a volunteer
Cuando…	When…
gane bastante dinero…	I earn enough money…
me enamore…	I fall in love…
sea mayor…	I'm older…
tenga … años…	I'm … years old…
vaya a la universidad…	I go to university…
termine este curso / el bachillerato / la formación profesional / la licenciatura…	I finish this course / my A Levels / my vocational course / my degree
buscaré un trabajo	I will look for a job
compartiré piso con…	I will share a flat with…
compraré un coche / una casa	I will buy a car / house
iré a otro insti / a la universidad	I will go to another school / to university
me casaré	I will get married
me iré de casa	I will leave home
seguiré estudiando en mi insti	I will carry on studying at my school
seré famoso/a	I will be famous
me tomaré un año sabático	I will take a gap year
trabajaré como…	I will work as…

8 Hacia un mundo mejor
Punto de partida 1

● Describing types of houses
● Talking about the environment

1 escuchar

Escucha y escribe la letra correcta. (1–4)

¿Dónde vives?

Hogar, dulce hogar

Vivo en…
un bloque de pisos
una casa individual
una casa adosada
una residencia de ancianos
una finca / granja

Está en…
un barrio de la ciudad
las afueras
el campo
la costa
la montaña / sierra

2 escuchar

Escucha otra vez. Escribe <u>dos</u> detalles en inglés.

el entorno   surrounding area

3 leer

Lee los textos. Apunta los detalles en inglés para cada texto.

Rooms mentioned: Would change:
Positive(s):   Ideal house would be/have:
Negative(s):

Zona Cultura

casa cueva en Granada

Las casas cueva eran típicas de la región de Andalucía. Hay gente que vive todavía en estas viviendas subterráneas y son una opción popular entre los turistas.

Vivimos en el cuarto piso de un edificio antiguo. El apartamento tiene tres dormitorios, dos cuartos de baño y una cocina amplia y bien equipada, que me encanta. Pintaría el salón de otro color porque es demasiado oscuro. Mi casa ideal sería una finca en el campo, que tendría una piscina climatizada y mi propio cine en casa.
Verena

Alquilamos esta casa amueblada. La habitación que más me gusta es el comedor porque está recién renovado y tiene una mesa y unas sillas nuevas. Además, el estudio es útil para estudiar. Sin embargo, el aseo necesita una reforma, y cambiaría los demás muebles porque son muy anticuados. Mi casa ideal tendría una gran sala de fiestas en el sótano.
Eduardo

amueblado/a   furnished

quinto	5°
cuarto	4°
tercero	3°
segundo	2°
primero	1°
planta baja	
sótano	

4 hablar

Con tu compañero/a, haz un diálogo.

● ¿Dónde vives?
● ¿Cómo es tu casa?
● ¿Te gusta dónde vives? ¿Qué cambiarías?
● ¿Cómo sería tu casa ideal? ¿Qué tendría?

'First' and 'third' drop the -o in front of masculine singular nouns:

Está en el primer / tercer piso.
It is on the 1st/3rd floor.

Piso can mean 'flat' or 'floor'.

5 leer **Empareja las frases con los dibujos.**

¿Cómo se debería cuidar el medio ambiente en casa?

Para cuidar el medio ambiente,
se debería…
1 apagar la luz.
2 ducharse en vez de bañarse.
3 separar la basura.
4 reciclar el plástico y el vidrio.
5 cerrar el grifo.
6 desenchufar los aparatos
   eléctricos.

No se debería…
7 malgastar el agua.
8 usar bolsas de plástico.

6 escuchar **Escucha. Apunta las <u>dos</u> letras
correctas del ejercicio 5. (1–4)**

G Se debería ⟩ Page 220

Se debería + infinitive means 'you/we should'. It is the conditional
form of **se debe**.

Se debería ahorrar energía.   **You/We should** save energy.
No se debería tirar basura al suelo.   **You/We shouldn't** throw
   rubbish on the ground.

7 escuchar **Escucha y lee la entrevista.
Busca las expresiones en español.**

– ¿Qué se debería hacer para cuidar el medio ambiente, Marta?

– ¡Mucho! Se debería ahorrar energía y no malgastar el agua.

– Y, ¿qué hacéis en casa?

– Ya hacemos bastantes cosas. Todos desenchufamos los aparatos eléctricos,
y nos duchamos en vez de bañarnos. Mi hermana menor tiene la mala
costumbre de no cerrar el grifo cuando se lava los dientes, pero me ayuda
a separar la basura. Cuando vamos al colegio, siempre vamos en bici o a
pie. Así hacemos todo lo posible para ser verdes.

Marta

1 save energy
2 we already do quite a few things
3 we all unplug the electrical appliances
4 bad habit
5 she helps me to
6 to be green

8 escribir **Traduce el texto al español.**

Use *para* + infinitive here.

This is we/one
in general.

There is a lot that we should do in order to save
energy. At home we all help. I turn the lights off
and my dad separates the rubbish. When we go
shopping we never use plastic bags. They are
small things, but we should do everything possible
to look after the environment.

Ayudar means 'to help'.
Don't forget to change
the ending for 'we help'.

What two things do you
have to remember about
adjectives in Spanish?

Change the verb
ending to match the
subjects 'I' and 'my dad'.

Use *para* + infinitive here.

Punto de partida 2

1 escuchar
Escucha y mira el diagrama.
Completa la tabla. (1–4)

Los nutrientes

a proteínas

b minerales

c grasa

d sal

e vitaminas

f azúcar

g gluten

Los alimentos

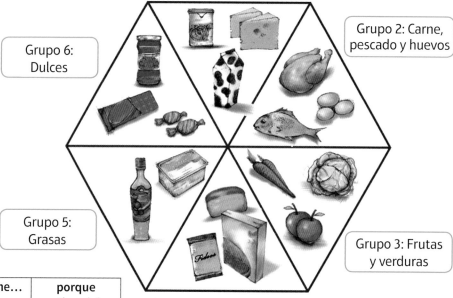

Grupo 1: Lácteos

Grupo 2: Carne, pescado y huevos

Grupo 6: Dulces

Grupo 5: Grasas

Grupo 3: Frutas y verduras

Grupo 4: Cereales

	come... (grupo)	porque / aunque contiene(n)...	no come...	porque contiene(n)...
1	3	e		

2 leer
Lee los textos. Completa las frases con las palabras de abajo. Sobran <u>dos</u> palabras.

Como zanahorias y ensalada a menudo porque es importante comer verduras, ya que contienen muchas vitaminas, aunque no me gusta mucho el sabor. La fibra de la fruta y la verdura también es importante porque protege contra el cáncer y combate la obesidad. **Timo**

Soy vegana, así que no como carne de ningún tipo. Tampoco consumo huevos, lácteos ni miel. A mi madre le preocupa porque piensa que mi dieta tiene pocas proteínas, pero suelo comer una variedad de frutos secos, legumbres y cereales. **Soraya**

Suelo saltarme el desayuno porque nunca tengo hambre por la mañana. En el recreo me compro un trozo de pizza. Sé que no es saludable porque tiene demasiada grasa y sal, pero está rica. **Isabel**

las legumbres *pulses*

1 A Timo no le gustan mucho las _____.

2 La fibra _____ el riesgo de ciertas enfermedades.

3 Soraya no _____ alimentos de origen animal.

4 Su madre cree que Soraya necesita comer más _____.

5 Soraya opina que lleva una dieta _____.

6 Isabel no _____ nada por la mañana.

7 La pizza no es sana, pero está _____.

8 Isabel lleva una _____ bastante malsana.

come   deliciosa   energía   malsana   equilibrada

verduras   come   dieta   reduce   proteínas

3 hablar

Con tu compañero/a, haz un diálogo.

● *¿Qué comes / no comes? ¿Por qué?*
● *¿Qué se debe comer todos los días para estar en forma?*
● *¿Crees que llevas una dieta sana? ¿Por qué (no)?*

Suelo Intento	comer beber evitar	mucho/a/os/as… demasiado/a/os/as… tanto/a/os/as…	
(No) Se debe Es importante Es necesario Es esencial Hay que			
porque / aunque contiene(n)	mucho/a poco/a demasiado/a	azúcar fibra grasa sal	
	muchos/as pocos/as demasiados/as	minerales proteínas vitaminas	

4 escuchar

Escucha. Apunta los detalles en inglés para cada persona. (1–3)

* the problems
* how they want to change their lifestyle

Ahora
suelo comer / beber…
como / bebo…
   galletas
   refrescos
   agua
   comida rápida
(no) desayuno
(no) tengo tiempo para cocinar
(no) tengo energía
(no) tengo hambre / sed
me causa sueño

En el futuro
(No) Voy a…
   evitar comer / beber…
   comer / beber más…
   cambiar mi dieta
   preparar comida con
      ingredientes frescos
(No) Quiero…
   engordar
   saltarme el desayuno
   praticar más deporte

5 escribir

Escribe un párrafo sobre tu dieta.

Include:
* whether you have / don't have a healthy diet
* one problem with your diet
* what people must do to keep in shape generally
* what you are going to do to lead a healthier life (diet, exercise, etc.)

6 leer

Lee el artículo. Contesta a las preguntas en inglés.

Solo un 7,5% de los niños en España toma un desayuno adecuado compuesto por hidratos de carbono, lácteos y fruta. El 8% de los niños se salta completamente el desayuno, mientras que el 59,5% de los niños dedica menos de 10 minutos a su desayuno. Uno de los efectos de saltar el desayuno es la disminución de la atención en las primeras horas de clase. También se ha demostrado que el fenómeno de la obesidad es más alto en las personas que no toman un desayuno equilibrado.

1 According to the article, what should a balanced breakfast consist of?
2 What percentage of children skip breakfast altogether?
3 What do 59.5% of Spanish children do?
4 What can happen in school as a result of not eating a good breakfast?
5 What is the connection between obesity and breakfast?

1 ¡Piensa globalmente…!

- Considering global issues
- Using the present subjunctive
- Listening for high numbers

1 escuchar

Escucha y lee. Escribe la letra correcta.

Ejemplo: **1** c

Parlamento de la Juventud

¿Cuáles son los problemas globales más serios hoy en día?

1 Lo que más me preocupa es la diferencia entre ricos y pobres en el mundo. No es justo que haya tanta desigualdad social y que muchos no tengan para comer. Es esencial que apoyemos proyectos de ayuda y que compremos productos de comercio justo.
Silvio, Guatemala

3 A mi parecer, el mayor problema es la crisis económica. Es terrible que haya tanta gente sin trabajo y sin techo. Es importante que creemos oportunidades de trabajo y que recaudemos dinero para organizaciones de caridad.
Maya, España

2 Me preocupan sobre todo los problemas del medio ambiente. Por ejemplo, en mi país destruyen la selva, y por consecuencia amenazan la supervivencia de muchas especies de fauna. Es muy importante que cuidemos el planeta. Es necesario que hagamos proyectos de conservación y que usemos productos verdes.
Óscar, Bolivia

4 En mi país lo más preocupante son los problemas de la salud. Hay tanta gente obesa y tantos drogadictos. Es esencial que hagamos campañas publicitarias sobre los riesgos de estas enfermedades y que ayudemos a evitar el consumo de sustancias perjudiciales.
Eduardo, Estados Unidos

a el paro / desempleo

b
los animales en peligro de extinción

c
el hambre

d
la drogadicción

| amenazar | to threaten |
| sin techo | homeless |

2 leer

Lee los textos del ejercicio 1 otra vez. Empareja cada problema con uno de los textos.

a la obesidad
b los sin hogar
c la pobreza
d la deforestación

3 leer

Busca las frases en español en los textos del ejercicio 1.

1 it's necessary that we do conservation projects
2 it's essential that we support aid projects
3 it's not fair that there is so much social inequality
4 it's important that we create job opportunities
5 it's essential that we do publicity campaigns

G The present subjunctive ❯ *Page* **234**

You have already learned to use the subjunctive with *cuando*.

The subjunctive is also used to express points of view, using the structure **Es** + adjective + **que**:

Es *importante* **que**…   *No* **es** *justo* **que**…
Es *esencial* **que**…   **Es** *terrible* **que**…
Es *necesario* **que**…

ahorrar →
*Es esencial que ahorr**emos** energía.*
It is essential that we save energy.

aprender →
*Es importante que aprend**amos** más sobre el medio ambiente.*
It is important that we learn more about the environment.

permitir →
*No es justo que permit**amos** la deforestación.*
It is not right that we allow deforestation.

Verbs which are irregular in the present subjunctive include:
ser (to be) → **sea**   **ir** (to go) → **vaya**
dar (to give) → **dé**   **haber** (there is/are) → **haya**

4 escuchar
Escucha. Apunta el problema en inglés. (1–5)

la ley   the law
la sociedad de usar y tirar   throwaway society

> As you listen, you will hear these verbs in the subjunctive. See if you can pick them out in order to write the phrases in Spanish.
>
> ***ahorrar*** (to save), ***construir*** (to build), ***recaudar*** (to collect), ***cambiar*** (to change), ***consumir*** (to consume)

5 escuchar
Escucha otra vez y apunta las soluciones en español.

> Es importante / esencial que…

> we build more houses

> we consume less

> we save water

> we collect money for aid projects

> we change the law

6 hablar
Con tu compañero/a, haz diálogos.

- ¿Cuál es el problema global más serio hoy en día?
  - ■ *Para mí, el mayor problema es la crisis económica.*
  - ■ *Lo que más me preocupa son los problemas del medio ambiente.*

- ¿Cuál es la solución?
  - ■ *Es esencial que actuemos rápidamente.*
  - ■ *Es terrible que haya…*

7 escuchar
Escucha y escribe la cifra correcta. (1–5)

La crisis del agua

1 Al menos ——— millones de personas en todo el mundo beben agua que está contaminada.
2 Unos ——— millones de personas no tienen servicios sanitarios.
3 Cada ——— horas mueren ——— niños por falta de agua y saneamiento.
4 Para producir un kilo de arroz hacen falta unos ——— litros de agua, mientras que para un kilo de carne son necesarios unos ——— litros.
5 La demanda mundial de agua para la fabricación se incrementará en un ——— entre los años ——— y ———.

> 95% = el noventa y cinco por ciento
> 1.000 = mil
> 3.574 = tres mil quinientos setenta y cuatro
> 1.000.000 = un millón
> Use a **full stop** to separate thousands and a **comma** for decimals.

8 leer
Lee el artículo y completa las frases en inglés.

¿Es posible una guerra mundial del agua?

En 2000 hubo una 'guerra del agua' en Cochabamba, Bolivia. La empresa multinacional Aguas del Tunari triplicó los precios del servicio del agua, lo que provocó una revuelta masiva. Hubo manifestaciones, luchas y al menos una muerte, pero finalmente los ciudadanos ganaron. La acción colectiva consiguió defender el agua como un bien común y frenar la privatización.

Actualmente existen conflictos por la escasez de agua entre varios países, incluso hay una disputa entre México y Estados Unidos sobre el río Bravo.

La Asociación Mundial del Agua (GWP) ya ha advertido sobre una crisis en el planeta hacia el 2025, afirmando que la falta de agua podría llevar a una guerra mundial. Es importante que cuidemos este elemento esencial.

la escasez   shortage / scarcity
consiguió   managed to
frenar   to stop

1 In 2000 there was…
2 The multinational company Aguas del Tunari…
3 This provoked…
4 The people's action managed to…
5 Currently there are…
6 The Global Water Partnership has already warned of…
7 The lack of water could…
8 It is important…

● *Talking about local actions*
● *Using the subjunctive in commands*
● *Presenting a written argument*

1 leer **Lee los comentarios. Empareja el problema 1–6 con el consejo apropiado a–f.**

1 La destrucción de los bosques es un problema muy serio.
2 El aire está contaminado.
3 Hay demasiada basura en las calles.
4 La polución de los mares y ríos me preocupa mucho.
5 Hay demasiada gente sin espacio para vivir.
6 Los combustibles fósiles se acaban.

a No corte tantos árboles.

b No tire basura al suelo.

c No construya tantas casas grandes.

d No vaya en coche si es posible ir a pie.

e No malgaste energía.

f No eche tantos desechos químicos en los mares.

2 escuchar **Escucha y comprueba tus respuestas. (1–6)**

3 escuchar **Escucha otra vez. Apunta otro consejo en español e inglés. (1–6)**

Ejemplo: **1** *Plante más bosques y selvas.*
Plant more woods and forests.

4 escribir **Escribe un slogan para cada póster. Usa la forma *usted*.**

desenchufar	el plástico y el papel
no utilizar	el agua
reciclar	las luces
apagar	bolsas de plástico
no malgastar	los aparatos eléctricos

G *The subjunctive in commands* > *Page 233*

The present subjunctive is also used:

For **all negative** commands.

*us**ar** (to use)*
*¡No us**es** tanta agua! (tú)*
*¡No us**e** tanta agua! (usted)*

For **formal positive** commands.
*¡Us**e** menos agua!*

There are a few spelling changes to keep the same pronunciation:

*apag**ar** (to switch off)* → *apag**ue***
*prote**ger** (to protect)* → *prote**ja***
*utiliz**ar** (to use)* → *utili**ce***

1

2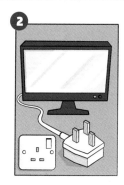

3

4

5

5 · leer · Lee el blog. ¿Es la casa A, la casa B, las casas A + B?

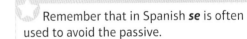

Creo que es posible llevar una vida más verde y salvar el planeta. ¿Soy demasiado optimista? Aquí tenéis unos pequeños ejemplos de cómo la gente intenta reducir la huella de carbono con sus casas.

A **Casas de plástico**

Desde hace más de ocho años un chileno, Santi Morales, lleva un proyecto de construcción de casas de botellas de plástico recicladas. Las botellas se llenan de arena o tierra y así forman 'eco-ladrillos'. Santi Morales comentó: 'Es esencial que busquemos soluciones nuevas. Con este proyecto reciclamos la basura de cada día en una casa económica para muchos años.'

B **Casas prefabricadas**

Sencilla, cálida, ecológica y más barata. Así definen a Cas4, una casa prefabricada de Argentina que utiliza recursos naturales. Es ecológica porque utiliza paneles solares para generar energía. El techo de la casa recoge el agua de lluvia que sirve incluso para el consumo. Las casas se hacen en una fábrica, lo que acelera el proceso de construcción (90 días) y de montaje (una semana). Otro aspecto positivo es que son móviles. Si la persona se muda, puede llevarse su casa al nuevo domicilio.

1 Se usan materiales reciclados.
2 Las casas se construyen en Chile.
3 El proceso de construcción es rápido.
4 Las casas cuestan menos que las casas tradicionales.
5 Las casas son transportables.
6 Las casas usan energía renovable.

> Remember that in Spanish **se** is often used to avoid the passive.
> *Las botellas **se llenan** de arena.*
> The bottles **are filled** with sand.

6 · leer · Lee el blog otra vez. Contesta a las preguntas en inglés.

1 What are people trying to reduce with their houses?
2 In text A, how are the eco-bricks made?
3 According to Santi Morales, what are the <u>two</u> advantages of his houses?

4 Apart from the cost, list <u>three</u> further characteristics of the Cas4 houses.
5 What does the roof of the Cas4 do?
6 Where exactly are these Argentinian houses made?

7 · escribir · Escribe una redacción *en contra* del argumento 'No se puede salvar el planeta'.

- Say it is true there are a lot of problems
- Say which problems most concern you

- Say you believe it is possible to solve the problems
- Say what it is important to do globally
- Say what you should do locally

Es verdad que…
Para mí, el mayor problema es (la contaminación del aire). Otro problema que me preocupa es (la pobreza).
Es posible solucionar…
Es importante que (cambiemos la ley) para…
Localmente se debería (reciclar)…

8 · hablar · Presenta tu redacción en clase.

> When saying what we need to do, e.g. to protect the environment, we usually use structures such as **Se debería**, **Hay que**, etc. + infinitive, whereas in a poster we use commands for giving instructions.

- *Discussing healthy lifestyles*
- *Understanding different tenses*
- *Giving extended reasons*

1 Escucha y lee. Empareja los textos con los dibujos a–d.

1 Por un lado, **no me parece un problema serio** porque todos mis amigos lo hacen. Por otro lado, **daña los pulmones** y el corazón, **provoca mal aliento** y **mancha los dientes de amarillo**. ¡Qué asco!

3 En mi opinión, **es muy perjudicial para la salud**. También **afecta tu capacidad para tomar decisiones**. Sin embargo, tomar una copa con tus amigos también **te hace sentir bien**.

2 Aunque no es tan peligroso como tomar heroína o cocaína, tiene muchos riesgos y **es un vicio muy caro**. Algunos dicen que fumar porros **te hace sentir más adulto**, pero en realidad **causa el fracaso escolar**.

4 **Produce una fuerte dependencia física**, y por eso **es ilegal y peligroso**. Además, **es fácil engancharse** y la rehabilitación es larga y dura.

beber alcohol

tomar drogas blandas

fumar cigarrillos

tomar drogas duras

2 Lee los textos otra vez. Completa la tabla con las frases en **negrita**.

	en contra	a favor
fumar	*daña los pulmones*	*no me parece un problema serio*

3 Escucha. Apunta los detalles en inglés. (1–4)

Ejemplo: **1** *boyfriend smokes spliffs, …*

- bad habit
- opinion
- reason (<u>two</u> details)

| **me emborracho (emborracharse)** | I get drunk |
| **parar** | to stop |

4 Con tu compañero/a, haz un diálogo.

- ● *¿Tienes algún vicio?*
- ■ *Sí / No. A veces <u>bebo / fumo</u>.*
- ● *¿Qué opinas de beber alcohol / fumar / tomar drogas duras / blandas?*
- ■ *Creo que <u>beber alcohol</u> es una tontería porque…*

> Use the language from exercise 2 to give extended reasons.
>
> E.g. … *porque el alcohol afecta a tu capacidad para tomar decisiones. Por otro lado, …*

Creo que…	Por un lado, … por otro lado, …
En mi opinión…	Desde mi punto de vista…
Sin embargo…	

beber alcohol / emborracharse	no es tan malo
fumar (cigarrillos / porros)	es una tontería
tomar drogas blandas / duras	es (muy) perjudicial

porque	te relaja
ya que	te quita el estrés / sueño / control
dado que	causa la depresión
	es un malgasto de dinero
	te engancha

5 leer Lee el blog de Lorenzo. Elige las respuestas correctas.

Antes llevaba una vida sana en todos los aspectos: comía y bebía bien, hacía ejercicio todos los días y cuidaba mi cuerpo. Pero hace un año cedí ante la presión de grupo y probé un cigarrillo en una fiesta, y luego caí en el hábito de fumar cuando salía con mis amigos.

Después de unos meses me di cuenta de que era adicto a la nicotina. Ya no tenía ganas de entrenar y lo pasaba muy mal. Un día, cuando veía la tele en casa, vi un maratón y decidí cambiar mi estilo de vida. Todavía me queda mucho por hacer, porque no estoy en forma y todavía no he dejado de fumar, pero creo que en seis meses tendré el mismo nivel de estado físico que antes. Luego espero participar en una carrera patrocinada de 20 km.

Lorenzo

1 Lorenzo **has / had** a healthy lifestyle.

2 He **looks / used to look** after his body.

3 Smoking **is / was** a regular habit when he **goes / went** out with friends.

4 He **still smokes / has quit smoking**.

5 He **has / will have** the same level of fitness as before.

6 He **hoped / hopes** to do a 20k sponsored run.

6 leer Lee el texto del ejercicio 5 otra vez. Busca las frases en español.

1 I fell into the habit of
2 I realised that
3 I was having a really bad time
4 I decided to change
5 There is still a lot for me to do
6 I still haven't stopped

☆ Look carefully at the verb endings to help you work out the tense.

The **imperfect** (*–aba, –ía* endings) describes a scene, what you used to do, or repeated actions in the past.

The **preterite** (*–é, –í* endings) refers to finished actions in the past.

The **future** (infinitive + *–é*) expresses what you 'will / shall' do.

Remember that there are several ways to express future meaning: future tense, near future tense, *esperar* + infinitive, *querer* + infinitive.

7 escuchar Escucha. Completa la tabla con los detalles en inglés. (1–2)

	in the past (2)	now (2)	in the future (3)
1			

8 escribir Escribe un post para el blog *Estilo de vida*. Usa tu imaginación.

Incluye:

• un vicio que tenías
• por qué era un problema
• cómo es la situación ahora
• tus planes para el futuro
• tus recomendaciones para una vida sana

Antes	Ahora	A partir de ahora
tenía (mucho estrés / la mala costumbre de…)	no puedo parar	voy a
fumaba, comía, bebía, hacía, llevaba, lo pasaba…	estoy un poco obsesionado/a	mejorar…
cedí ante la presión de grupo	ya no bebo / fumo…	dejar de…
empecé a (saltarme el desayuno)	ya he empezado a…	entrenar…
probé…	todavía no he dejado de…	cambiar…
caí en el hábito de…		hacer…
decidí…		llevar…
perdí peso		También debo…
		Intentaré…
		Luego espero…

4 **¡El deporte nos une!**
● *Talking about international sporting events*
● *Using the pluperfect tense*
● *Explaining your point of view*

1 **Escucha. Apunta la letra y los <u>dos</u> beneficios correctos. (1–3)**
Ejemplo: **1** *b 3, …*

> ¿Para qué sirven los eventos deportivos internacionales?

a

la Copa Mundial de Fútbol

b

los Juegos Olímpicos

c

la Vuelta a España

Sirven para…
1 promover la participación en el deporte.
2 regenerar los centros urbanos.
3 elevar el orgullo nacional.
4 transmitir los valores de respeto y disciplina.
5 unir a la gente.
6 animar el turismo.

2 **Escucha otra vez. Apunta otros detalles en inglés.**
Ejemplo: **1** *raise national pride, …*

> 🔊 We often rephrase what we say in order to explain our ideas or give more detail. Listen out for clue words such as *en otras palabras* (in other words), *o sea* (I mean) and *es decir* (that is to say).

3 **Lee los posts. Apunta <u>dos</u> opiniones del ejercicio 1 y las desventajas que se mencionan.**

💬 **Natalia**
Soy una fan de los grandes acontecimientos deportivos, sobre todo de los Juegos Paralímpicos. Me inspiran a ser una buena persona, es decir, a respetar a los demás. Siempre estoy muy orgullosa de ser española cuando gana uno de mis compatriotas. No obstante, no se puede hablar de los eventos deportivos sin mencionar la batalla contra el dopaje. Otro inconveniente es el tráfico que producen estos eventos.

💬 **Lorena**
Por una parte, los eventos deportivos dan un impulso económico, sobre todo a los sectores de la construcción y la hostelería. Además, fomentan el espíritu de solidaridad. Por otra parte, los costes de organización son muy altos, y a menudo resultan en deudas para la ciudad anfitriona. Otra desventaja es el riesgo de ataques terroristas durante la temporada del evento.

la ciudad anfitriona host city

Una / Otra desventaja es…	
el riesgo de ataques terroristas	el dopaje
el coste de la organización / de la seguridad	la deuda
	el tráfico

> 🔊 The opinions are not given in the same words as in exercise 1, so pay attention to the overall meaning and look for expressions that mean the same thing.

4 **Con tu compañero/a, haz un diálogo.**
● *¿Qué evento deportivo internacional es el más interesante para ti?*
● *¿Qué piensas de los eventos deportivos internacionales?*
● *¿Hay otros beneficios?*
● *¿Hay desventajas?*

■ *El evento que me interesa más es… porque…*
■ *Desde mi punto de vista, sirven para…*
■ *Sí, también unen a la gente.*
■ *Sí, una desventaja es el dopaje.*

5 escuchar Escucha y lee el comentario. ¿Las frases se refieren a Maribel (M), a Pedro (P), o a los dos (M+P)?

Voluntarios olímpicos comparten sus experiencias

Mi abuela Maribel y yo conseguimos puestos de voluntariado en los JJ. OO. Decidí solicitarlo porque **nunca había trabajado como voluntario**. Mi abuela estaba disponible porque **había dejado de trabajar dos meses antes**. Además, **ya había hecho un voluntariado** en los JJ. OO. de 1992 en Barcelona. Ella **siempre había dicho** que fue una experiencia inolvidable.

La primera semana, fui embajador de los valores olímpicos: la amistad, la armonía y la solidaridad. Tuve que saludar a los visitantes y guiarlos a los eventos, lo que fue muy gratificante. Hice muchos amigos durante esta semana y me gustó mucho trabajar en equipo. La segunda semana trabajé en la piscina olímpica. Yo soy estudiante y un fanático de la natación, pero **nunca había visto de cerca a mis modelos**. Asistí a los nadadores y trabajé de socorrista en la piscina. ¡Qué ilusión!

Mi abuela era asistente del equipo colombiano y lo pasó fenomenal. Los ayudó a organizar sus visitas turísticas. Aprovechó su experiencia porque **antes había sido guía turística en la ciudad**. A mi parecer, el voluntariado es una experiencia muy buena porque te permite desarrollar tus habilidades comunicativas. Se la recomendaría a todos, ¡jóvenes y jubilados! **Pedro**

JJ. OO.	*Juegos Olímpicos*
desarrollar	*to develop*

1 Hizo el trabajo voluntario con otro miembro de su familia.
2 Trabajó en la piscina olímpica.
3 Le gustó trabajar con otras personas.
4 Aprovechó su experiencia previa de voluntario.
5 Vio a sus ídolos.

6 leer Lee los textos otra vez. Traduce las expresiones en **negrita** al inglés.

7 escuchar Escucha *Voluntarios: ¡Inspiración en acción!* Apunta los detalles en inglés. (1–2)

Opinion of volunteering:
Event:
Reason for applying:
Tasks (<u>two</u> details):
Opinion:
Future plans:

me ocupé de	*I was in charge of*

 **G** **The pluperfect tense** **›** *Page 231*

The **pluperfect** is used to talk about what someone <u>had</u> done, referring to a past action which happened earlier than another action.

	haber	past participle
(yo)	había	
(tú)	habías	
(él/ella/usted)	había	trabaj**ado**
(nosotros/nosotras)	habíamos	quer**ido**
(vosotros/vosotras)	habíais	viv**ido**
(ellos/ellas/ustedes)	habían	

Remember that some past participles are irregular:
hacer ➞ **hecho** (done)   **ver** ➞ **visto** (seen)
poner ➞ **puesto** (put)   **decir** ➞ **dicho** (said)

8 escribir Escribe un artículo sobre tus experiencias como voluntario/a en un evento deportivo. Usa tu imaginación. Incluye:

- lo que opinas del voluntariado — *A mi parecer, el voluntariado es una buena experiencia porque…*
- por qué solicitaste un trabajo voluntario — *Solicité un trabajo voluntario porque…*
  (Nunca) había sido…
  Antes ya había trabajado como…
- qué hiciste — *Tuve que… Ayudé a… Trabajé con…*
  La gente / El trabajo era…
- tus planes para el voluntariado — *En el futuro, pienso trabajar como voluntario/a en…*

5 ¡Apúntate!

- *Talking about natural disasters*
- *Using the imperfect continuous*
- *Using grammar knowledge in translation*

1 escuchar

Escucha y lee. Empareja los tuits con las fotos. Sobra <u>una</u> foto. (1–5)

> ¿Qué **estabas haciendo**?

1 **Estaba durmiendo** y de repente me desperté. ¡El edificio **se estaba moviendo**!

2 **Estábamos ensayando** para un concierto en el colegio, pero **estaba nevando** tanto que nos tuvimos que ir a casa.

3 Me asomé por la ventana y ¡la calle **se estaba convirtiendo en** un río! El agua **estaba entrando** en la casa.

4 Los niños **estaban leyendo** en la biblioteca cuando se sintió el seísmo. Tenían miedo porque los libros se **estaban cayendo**.

5 **Estaba conduciendo** por la ciudad. ¡A mi alrededor había coches que **estaban volando** por el aire!

a

un temblor, Colombia

b

unas inundaciones, Bolivia

c

una tormenta de nieve, Estados Unidos

d

un incendio forestal, Mallorca, España

e

un huracán, Estados Unidos

f

un tornado, México

2 leer

Lee los tuits otra vez. Busca el equivalente de estas frases.

1 it was snowing
2 the children were reading
3 we were rehearsing
4 I was sleeping
5 the building was moving
6 the books were falling
7 the street was turning into a river
8 What were you doing?

me asomé por la ventana	I looked out of the window
se sintió el seísmo	the earthquake was felt

G *Imperfect continuous* > *Page 230*

The **imperfect continuous** translates as 'was / were …ing'.
***Estaba cenando** cuando la tormenta azotó al pueblo.*
I was having dinner when the storm hit the town.

	estar (to be)	**gerund**
(yo)	estaba	
(tú)	estabas	
(él/ella/usted)	estaba	trabaj**ando**
(nosotros/as)	estábamos	beb**iendo**
(vosotros/as)	estabais	escrib**iendo**
(ellos/ellas/ustedes)	estaban	

To form the gerund, take the infinitive, remove the –ar, –er or –ir and add the endings –ando, –iendo, –iendo.

3 escuchar

Escucha y completa la tabla. (1–6)

	desastre natural	¿qué estabas haciendo?	¿cómo te enteraste?
Santi			

4 Con tu compañero/a, pregunta y contesta. Cierra el libro.
Utiliza tus respuestas al ejercicio 3.

● *¿Cómo te enteraste <u>del temblor / de las inundaciones</u>?*

■ *Estaba <u>viendo las noticias</u> cuando <u>encontré un reportaje</u>.*

 5 Escucha y lee. Traduce las frases en **negrita** al inglés.

una Shelterbox

Alba

¿Cómo te enteraste de la acción humanitaria para Nepal, Alba?

Estaba buscando información en Internet para mis deberes de geografía y encontré un artículo sobre *Interact*.

¿Y eso qué es?

Es una organización internacional de servicio voluntario para los jóvenes. El artículo contaba la historia de una chica en Nepal que no tenía ni siquiera cepillo de dientes. **Su casa fue destruida por el terremoto que dejó a miles de personas sin hogar**.

¿*Interact* hacía una campaña para las víctimas?

Sí. Mi club local estaba preparando una caja de supervivencia, una *Shelterbox*, para mandar a Nepal. Tiene todo lo esencial para vivir seis meses.

¿Qué hiciste tú?

Decidí apuntarme. Tuvimos que recaudar fondos, así que organizamos algunos eventos en el instituto y en la ciudad.

¿Qué tipo de eventos?

Hicimos un concierto y un espectáculo de baile. **Otros miembros del grupo participaron en una carrera de bici apadrinada**. Yo organicé una venta de pasteles cada viernes en el insti. También **escribimos cartas a tiendas de la ciudad para solicitar donativos**. Ya tenemos la caja completa y **la mandaremos a Nepal** la semana que viene.

Otros jóvenes se podrían apuntar, ¿cómo les convencerías?

Diría que es importante ser solidario porque te hace sentir más conectado con los demás. ¡Apúntate!

This is the passive. What does *por* mean here?

que refers back to the earthquake.

Which tense is this?

Remember the group is raising money. What sort of activity is this?

Use the context again here. Why might you write letters to local shops?

Is there a time phrase to help you decide which tense this is?

ni siquiera not even

We can't translate word for word here. What captures the idea of solidarity?

 6 Escucha y contesta a las preguntas en inglés.

1 How did Manolo find out about the campaign being run by Ciudades Refugio?
2 Who are they trying to help?
3 What is being done to raise awareness of the issues?
4 What sort of aid is being offered by the organisation?
5 Why did Manolo decide to sign up to work with them?
6 What are the benefits of being involved with aid work, according to Manolo?

los refugiados refugees

 7 Escribe un post sobre tus actividades benéficas.

Me enteré de… cuando estaba… Es un grupo / una organización que… La organización hacía una campaña para (las víctimas de…) Decidí apuntarme porque… Tuvimos que recaudar fondos, así que organicé… Diría que es importante ser solidario porque… El mes que viene vamos a…

1 leer **Read the extract. Armand Sauvelle has recently passed away.**

Las luces de septiembre by Carlos Ruiz Zafón

Tras seis meses de sufrimiento, una enfermedad había quitado la vida a Armand Sauvelle. Armand Sauvelle se llevó a la tumba su magia y su risa* contagiosa, pero sus numerosas deudas no lo acompañaron en el último viaje.

Colegios de prestigio y ropa impecable fueron sustituidos por empleos a tiempo parcial y ropa más modesta para Irene y Dorian. Lo peor, sin embargo, cayó sobre Simone, su madre. Retomar su empleo como profesora no era suficiente para hacer frente al torrente de deudas de Armand.

Semanas más tarde, apareció la promesa de un buen empleo para su madre en un pequeño pueblo de la costa. Lazarus Jann, inventor y fabricante de juguetes, necesitaba un ama de llaves para cuidar su residencia en el bosque de Cravenmoore.

La paga era generosa y, además, Lazarus Jann les ofrecía la posibilidad de instalarse en la Casa del Cabo, una modesta residencia construida al otro lado del bosque de Cravenmoore.

* risa = laughter

Choose the correct answer for each question.

Ejemplo: Armand Sauvelle died… *D*

   A six months ago.
   B from an unknown illness.
   C after seeing a ghost.
   D after several months of suffering.

(a) He was a… man.
   A funny
   B sad
   C lonely
   D hard working

(b) After their father's death, Irene and Dorian…
   A wore smarter clothes.
   B tried harder in school.
   C got part-time jobs.
   D went on to college.

(c) When their mother, Simone, went back to teaching…
   A the financial situation was resolved.
   B she was relieved.
   C there were still debts.
   D she was exhausted.

(d) Luckily, then there was…
   A a trip to the coast.
   B a new job offer.
   C a holiday in the country.
   D the arrival of a rich uncle.

(e) A further advantage was the…
   A modest income.
   B peaceful countryside.
   C offer of accommodation.
   D generous bonus.

2 leer **Lee el artículo sobre un evento deportivo en Madrid.**

La Fiesta de la Bici

Vuelve la Fiesta de la Bici. Un evento sano, deportivo, colorido, festivo… Un evento familiar. El recorrido será igual al de años anteriores.

Durante el recorrido encontrarás zonas de animación con música, actividades y disfraces, así que la Fiesta de la Bici es una gran experiencia para los más pequeños. Si vas con los niños, tu objetivo principal debe ser su vigilancia e integridad. Hay que darles instrucciones en caso de pérdida.

la Puerta de Alcalá, Madrid

Antes de la fiesta es aconsejable hacer una revisión básica de la bicicleta. Asegúrate de que las ruedas llevan la presión necesaria, y sobre todo, debes revisar la tensión de los frenos*.

La Fiesta de la Bici es una marcha no competitiva de carácter popular. Si vas de carreras puedes provocar accidentes y molestias a otros participantes.

* los frenos = brakes

Contesta a las preguntas en español. No tienes que escribir frases completas.

(a) ¿Cómo sabemos que no es el primer año que se celebra este evento?

(b) ¿Por qué esta fiesta es una gran experiencia para los niños?

(c) ¿Qué deben hacer los padres si van con sus niños?

(d) Antes de la fiesta, ¿qué es lo más importante que tienen que hacer los participantes?

(e) ¿Qué puede pasar si los ciclistas son competitivos?

> Work out what the question means and identify the relevant detail(s). To answer you can usually lift the words directly from the text. However, when asked *¿Cómo sabemos…?* (How do we know…?), it is useful to start your answer with *Dice que…* (It says that…).

3 leer **Translate the following passage into English.**

Marco está en ruta hacia Bolivia. Solicitó un trabajo como voluntario en un orfanato, donde va a pasar seis meses. ¡Tiene muchas ganas de empezar a trabajar con los niños! Piensa que el voluntariado ofrece muchos beneficios, sobre todo la oportunidad de ayudar a los demás. Ganará mucha experiencia, y después todavía tendrá tiempo suficiente para explorar Sudamérica.

1 escuchar **You are listening to a news report about Mexico.**

Listen and answer the following questions in English.

(a) Mexico is the world's greatest consumer of which product?

(b) According to the report, what are the consequences of this? Give <u>two</u> details.

(c) What has been the response by the *Alianza por la Salud Alimentaria*?

(d) Why has the organisation done this? Give <u>two</u> reasons.

> Use the questions to give you clues about the information you are looking for. For example, what could the *Alianza por la Salud Alimentaria* be? How does this help you predict which sort of product you are listening out for in question (a)?

2 escuchar **Oyes a un experto meteorólogo hablando del tiempo.**

Rellena el espacio de cada frase con una palabra del recuadro. Hay más palabras que espacios.

Gran Bretaña	solo	~~caluroso~~	extremo
pasado	en casa	muertes	España
nuevos países	olas de calor	frecuente	pobreza

Ejemplo: Se habla de un tiempo <u>caluroso</u>

(a) El fenómeno es ———.

(b) 28° significa una ola de calor en ———.

(c) La situación es grave en Asia, donde hay más ———.

(d) Las olas de calor ocurrirán en ——— en el futuro.

(e) Lo más importante es no estar ———.

A – Role play

1 *leer* Look at the role play card and prepare what you are going to say.

Topic: Ambitions

Instructions to candidates:

You are in Spain and want to do some voluntary work in an organisation. The teacher will play the role of the organisation employee and will speak first.

You must address the employee as *usted*.

You will talk to the teacher using the five prompts below.

- where you see – **?** – you must ask a question
- where you see – **!** – you must respond to something you have not prepared

Task

Usted está en una organización benéfica en España. Habla con el/la empleado/a sobre un trabajo voluntario.

1 Trabajo voluntario – motivo

2 Carácter- descripción

3 !

4 ? Trabajo - horario

5 ? Uniforme

Imagine how the examiner may ask this question (e.g. 'Why…') to help you start your answer.

Stick to language you can pronounce confidently. Start with 'I am…'

What information might you be asked to give? Think about typical interview scenarios.

What can you add to turn this into a question?

Use either 'Do I have to…' or 'Is there..?' to ask the question here.

---

2 *escuchar* Practise what you have prepared. Then, using your notes, listen and respond to the teacher.

3 *escuchar* Now listen to Arthur doing the role play task. Note down the unexpected question and how he answers it.

> Role play tasks often require you to say or ask if you **have to** do something. Remember to use the infinitive after the following:
>
> Tengo que…
> Es obligatorio…   } + infinitive
> Hay que…

B – Picture-based task

Topic: Environmental issues

Mira la foto y prepara las respuestas a los siguientes puntos:

- la descripción de la foto
- tu opinión sobre el reciclaje
- qué hiciste recientemente para ser más verde
- lo que el gobierno debería hacer para proteger el medio ambiente
- (!)

1 escuchar

Look at the photo and read the task. Then listen to Ed's response to the first bullet point.

1 How does he describe the boy?
2 Where does he suggest the boy lives, and why does he think this?
3 What do you think *los cubos de basura* are? How can you work this out?
4 What do you think *Quizás le importa el medio ambiente* means?

2 escuchar

Listen to and read Ed's response to the second bullet point.

1 Write down the missing word for each gap.
2 Look at the Answer Booster on page 178. Note down <u>six</u> examples of language which Ed uses to give a strong answer.

Los problemas globales relacionados con el medio ambiente me preocupan mucho. En mi opinión, reciclar es una cosa **1** ———— que podemos hacer para cuidar el medio ambiente, ya que **2** ———— muy poco tiempo. Sin embargo, no solo se debería reciclar, sino también **3** ———— ahorrar energía. Por ejemplo, creo que siempre se debería **4** ———— los aparatos, como el ordenador o la tele, cuando no los estamos utilizando. Además, es **5** ———— que no usemos tanta agua. Si todos hacemos estos pequeños **6** ————, podremos reducir nuestra huella de carbono.

3 escuchar

Listen to Ed's response to the third bullet point. Note down <u>six</u> details that he gives, in English.

4 escuchar

Listen to Ed's response to the fourth bullet point. In Spanish, note down <u>five</u> examples of the subjunctive, and match them to the correct infinitives below. Not all of these verbs are used in the subjunctive.

transmitir	consumir	apoyar	haber	hacer
mejorar	insistir	regenerar	cambiar	tomar

5 escuchar

Prepare your own answers to the first <u>four</u> bullet points. Try to predict which unexpected question you might be asked. Then listen and take part in the full picture-based task with the teacher.

C – General conversation

1 escuchar

Listen to Alison introducing her chosen topic. Complete the sentences in English.

a In her view, Spain's greatest problem is…
b It's important that the government…
c One solution would be to…
d In South America, what most worries her is…
e It is not fair that…
f She thinks that…
g Last term…
h In the future she hopes to…

2 escuchar

The teacher asks Alison, *'¿Para qué sirven los eventos deportivos internacionales?'* **Listen to her response and look at the Answer Booster on page 178. Note down <u>six</u> examples of language which Alison uses to give a strong answer.**

3 escuchar

Listen to Alison's response to the second question, *'¿Qué opinas de los grandes eventos musicales?'*

1 What does the following phrase mean?
Sirven para crear conciencia sobre las injusticias mundiales.
2 Note down <u>two</u> examples of present, preterite and future tense verbs.

⭐ Improve the complexity of your answers by including more than one tense, even when the question itself does not require it. Which <u>two</u> of these strategies does Alison use?

• refers to future plans
• contrasts then and now
• narrates a past event
• states what should or would happen

4 hablar

Prepare your own answers to Module 8 questions 1–6 on page 199. Then practise with your partner.

Answer booster	Aiming for a solid answer	Aiming higher	Aiming for the top
Verbs	**Different time frames**: past, present, near future **Different types of verbs**: regular, irregular, reflexive, stem-changing	**Verbs/Expressions with an infinitive**: *poder, intentar, se debería, servir para* **Phrases with an infinitive**: *para, antes de, después de* **Phrases to refer to future plans**: *espero, pienso, tengo la intención de* + infinitive	**A wide range of tenses**: present, present continuous, conditional, preterite, perfect, pluperfect, future ***Si* + present + future** ***Es... que* + subjunctive**: *es esencial que usemos...*
Opinions and reasons	**Verbs of opinion**: *me chifla(n), me encanta(n), me interesa(n)* **Reasons**: *porque...*	**Opinions**: *me apasiona(n), me preocupa(n), me importa(n)* **Absolute superlatives**: *muchísimo, importantísimo*	**Opinions**: *desde mi punto de vista, a mi juicio, en mi opinión, creo que* **Reasons**: *ya que, por lo tanto, por eso, así que* **Opinions in the preterite**: *me encantó*
Connectives	*y, pero, también*	*además, sin embargo, sobre todo, no obstante, por ejemplo*	*gracias a* **Alternatives to 'and'**: *no solo..., sino también...* **Balancing an argument**: *un / otro beneficio, un inconveniente, a pesar de, aunque*
Other features	**Qualifiers**: *muy, bastante, un poco, poco, demasiado* **Sequencers**: *luego, después, más tarde*	**Sentences with *cuando, donde, si* *para* + infinitive**: *para ayudar* ***Tan, Tanto/a/os/as***: *tan grande* **Indirect object pronouns**: *te da la oportunidad de..., te permite...*	**Complex sentences with *si***: *si tuviera bastante...* **Specialist vocabulary**: *una sociedad de usar y tirar, la huella de carbono*

A – Extended writing task

1 **leer** Look at the task and answer the questions.

- What **type** of text are you asked to write?
- What is each bullet point asking you to do?
- Which tense(s) will you need to use to answer each one?

2 **leer** Read Alexandra's answer on page 179. What do the phrases in **bold** mean?

3 **leer** Look at the Answer Booster. Note down <u>six</u> examples of language which Alexandra uses to write a strong answer.

4 **leer** Complete the essay plan, based on Alexandra's answer.

5 **escribir** Prepare your own answer to the task.

- Look at the Answer Booster and Alexandra's plan for ideas.
- Think about how you can develop your answer for each bullet point.
- Write a detailed plan. Organise your answer in paragraphs.
- Write your answer and carefully check what you have written.

La importancia de ser solidario

Usted ha participado en un evento para una campaña de UNICEF.

Escriba un artículo para convencer a otras personas de la importancia de ser solidario.

Debe incluir los puntos siguientes:

- el problema más serio en el mundo, en su opinión
- lo que todos podemos hacer
- su participación en un evento de UNICEF
- sus planes para ser solidario/a en el futuro.

Justifique sus ideas y sus opiniones.

Escriba aproximadamente 130–150 palabras **en español**.

Paragraph 1
- Social inequality
-

Paragraph 2
-
-

Me preocupa sobre todo la desigualdad social. **No es justo que haya** gente que muera por falta de comida y de agua potable. Además, la pobreza **no solo afecta a los países en desarrollo**, sino también a muchos niños en mi país. Sin embargo, si todos ayudamos **podremos crear** un mundo mejor para todos.

Hay muchas cosas que podemos hacer para mejorar la situación, y es esencial que actuemos pronto. Por ejemplo, cuando compramos productos de comercio justo, **estamos apoyando** a familias en el tercer mundo. Además, podemos colaborar en eventos patrocinados* para recaudar fondos para organizaciones caritativas **o globales o locales**.

El año pasado decidí participar en **una caminata patrocinada de 20 km**. Fue organizada por UNICEF **para crear conciencia sobre** la crisis de los refugiados en zonas de conflicto. Luego hicimos un día de silencio organizado en mi instituto **para la misma campaña**. Fue la primera vez que **colaboré** en un evento solidario tan grande, pero me encantó.

Desde mi punto de vista, es muy importante ser solidario porque te da la oportunidad de hacer algo concreto para ayudar a los demás. **Ya me he afiliado al** club de Amnistía Internacional en mi insti y escribimos cartas cada semana. **Si tuviera más tiempo**, **participaría** en todavía más eventos. Después de hacer el bachillerato, solicitaré un trabajo voluntario en una escuela primaria en África porque pienso ser profesora un día.

> Use your imagination to help you produce a longer, more interesting answer. Remember that in an exam you don't have to tell the truth, as long as what you write is plausible!

* *patrocinado = sponsored (for events, e.g. a sponsored walk)*
apadrinado = sponsored (for people, e.g. a sponsored child in Africa)

B – Translation

> Think carefully about which person and tense you need. Take extra care with verbs that do not translate word for word, for example 'it's cold', or where you need to choose between verbs, for example *ser* or *estar* for 'would be in the country'.

1 Read the English text and Gillian's translation of it. Write down the missing word(s) for each gap.

I used to live in a flat in the city, but my family and I now have an old house on the outskirts. Two months ago I decorated my bedroom and therefore it's my favourite room. I tend to eat in the kitchen because it's cold in the dining room. My ideal house would be in the country.

1 _____ en un apartamento en la ciudad, pero ahora mi familia y yo **2** _____ una casa antigua en las afueras. Hace dos meses **3** _____ mi dormitorio y por eso **4** _____ mi habitación favorita.
5 _____ en la cocina porque **6** _____ frío en el comedor. Mi casa ideal **7** _____ en el campo.

2 Translate the following passage into Spanish.

My house in the country was old, but very comfortable. However, for six months we've been living in a large, modern flat. The only bad thing is the small garden because I would like to have a bigger space to plant flowers. Last week my dad bought a farm in Wales and in two months we will go to live there.

¿Cómo es tu casa?

Vivo en…	I live in…
un bloque de pisos	a block of flats
una casa individual	a detached house
una casa adosada	a semi-detached / terraced house
una residencia de ancianos	an old people's home
una finca / granja	a farmhouse
Alquilamos una casa amueblada.	We rent a furnished house.
Está en…	It is in / on…
un barrio de la ciudad	a district / suburb of the city / town
las afueras	the outskirts
el campo	the country
la costa	the coast
la montaña / sierra	the mountains
el cuarto piso de un edificio antiguo	the fourth floor of an old building
Mi apartamento / piso tiene…	My apartment / flat has…
tres dormitorios	three bedrooms
dos cuartos de baño	two bathrooms
una cocina amplia y bien equipada	a spacious, well-equipped kitchen
un comedor recién renovado	a recently refurbished dining room
un estudio	a study
un aseo	a toilet
un sótano	a basement / cellar
un salón	a living room
una mesa	a table
unas sillas	some chairs
Mi casa ideal sería…	My ideal house would be…
Tendría…	It would have…
una piscina climatizada	a heated swimming pool
mi propio cine en casa	my own home cinema
una sala de fiestas	a party room
Cambiaría los muebles.	I would change the furniture.
Pintaría … de otro color.	I would paint … another colour.

¿Cómo se debería cuidar el medio ambiente en casa?

How should you look after the environment at home?	
Para cuidar el medio ambiente se debería…	To care for the environment you / one should…
apagar la luz	turn off the light
ducharse en vez de bañarse	have a shower instead of taking a bath
separar la basura	separate the rubbish
reciclar el plástico y el vidrio	recycle plastic and glass
desenchufar los aparatos eléctricos	unplug electric appliances
ahorrar energía	save energy
cerrar el grifo	turn off the tap
hacer todo lo posible	do everything possible
no se debería…	you / one should not…
malgastar el agua	waste water
usar bolsas de plástico	use plastic bags

¿Cuáles son los problemas globales más serios hoy en día?

What are the most serious global issues today?	
Me preocupa(n)…	I am worried about…
el paro / desempleo	unemployment
el hambre / la pobreza	hunger / poverty
la deforestación	deforestation
la diferencia entre ricos y pobres	the difference between rich and poor
la drogadicción / la salud / la obesidad	drug addiction / health / obesity
la crisis económica	the economic crisis
los problemas del medio ambiente	environmental problems
los sin hogar / techo	the homeless
los animales en peligro de extinción	animals in danger of extinction
Es necesario / esencial que…	It's necessary / essential that (we)…
cuidemos el planeta	look after the planet
hagamos proyectos de conservación	do conservation projects
compremos / usemos productos verdes / de comercio justo	buy / use green / fairtrade products
apoyemos proyectos de ayuda	support aid projects
creemos oportunidades de trabajo	create job opportunities
ayudemos a evitar el consumo de sustancias perjudiciales	help to avoid the consumption of harmful substances
ahorremos agua	save water
construyamos más casas	build more houses
cambiemos la ley	change the law
consumamos menos	consume less
hagamos campañas publicitarias	carry out publicity campaigns
recaudemos dinero	raise money
para organizaciones de caridad en el tercer mundo	for charities in the third world
No es justo / Es terrible que haya…	It's not fair / terrible that there is…
tanta desigualdad social / contaminación	so much social inequality / pollution
tanta gente sin trabajo y sin techo	so many people out of work and homeless
tanta gente obesa y tantos drogadictos	so many obese people and so many drug addicts

¡Actúa localmente!

Act locally!	
Hay demasiada…	There is / are too much / many…
basura en las calles	rubbish on the streets
gente sin espacio para vivir	people with nowhere to live
destrucción de los bosques	destruction of woodland / forest
polución de los mares y ríos	pollution of seas and rivers
El aire está contaminado.	The air is polluted.
Los combustibles fósiles se acaban.	Fossil fuels are running out.
No corte tantos árboles.	Don't cut down so many trees.
No vaya en coche si es posible ir a pie.	Don't go by car if it's possible to walk.
No tire basura al suelo.	Don't throw rubbish onto the ground.
No malgaste energía.	Don't waste energy.
No construya tantas casas grandes.	Don't build so many large houses.
No eche tantos desechos químicos.	Don't release so much chemical waste.
Plante más bosques y selvas.	Plant more woods and forests.
Reduzca las emisiones de los vehículos.	Reduce vehicle emissions.
Recicle el papel, el vidrio y el plástico.	Recycle papel, glass and plastic.
Use energías renovables.	Use renewable energy.
Diseñe casas más pequeñas.	Design smaller houses.
Introduzca leyes más estrictas.	Introduce stricter laws.
llevar una vida más verde	(to) live a greener life
salvar el planeta	(to) save the planet
reducir la huella de carbono	(to) reduce your carbon footprint
ecológico/a	environmentally-friendly
el techo	roof
el agua de lluvia	rain water
el domicilio	home
los recursos naturales	natural resources
los paneles solares	solar panels
la arena	sand
los (eco-)ladrillos	(eco-)bricks
una fábrica	a factory
mudarse (de casa)	(to) move house

Una dieta sana

A healthy diet	
los alimentos	foods
lácteos	milk products
carne, pescados y huevos	meat, fish and eggs
frutas y verduras	fruit and vegetables
cereales	cereals
fideos	noodles
grasas	fats
dulces	sugars / sweet things
legumbres	pulses
frutos secos	nuts and dried fruit
los nutrientes	nutrients
proteínas	proteins

minerales — *minerals*
grasa — *fat*
sal — *salt*
vitaminas — *vitamins*
azúcar — *sugar*
gluten — *gluten*
el sabor — *taste*
vegetariano / vegano — *vegetarian / vegan*
saludable / sano / malsano — *healthy / healthy / unhealthy*
(No) Tengo hambre / sed / sueño. — *I am (not) hungry / thirsty / tired.*
tiempo para cocinar — *time to cook*
contiene / contienen — *it contains / they contain*

¡Vivir a tope! — *Live life to the full*
Beber alcohol… — *To drink / Drinking alcohol…*
Fumar cigarrillos / porros… — *To smoke / Smoking cigarettes / joints…*
Tomar drogas blandas / duras… — *To take / Taking soft / hard drugs…*
Es / No es… — *It is / isn't…*
ilegal / peligroso — *illegal / dangerous*
un malgasto de dinero — *a waste of money*
una tontería / un problema serio — *stupid / a serious problem*
un vicio muy caro — *an expensive habit*
muy perjudicial para la salud — *very damaging to your health*
tan malo — *as bad*
provoca mal aliento — *causes bad breath*
daña los pulmones — *damages the lungs*
mancha los dientes de amarillo — *stains your teeth yellow*
causa el fracaso escolar / depresión — *causes failure at school / depression*
produce una fuerte dependencia física — *produces a strong, physical dependence*

¡El deporte nos une! — *Sport unites us!*
¿Para qué sirven…? — *What are…for?*
los eventos deportivos internacionales — *international sporting events*
los grandes acontecimientos deportivos — *big sporting events*
los Juegos Paralímpicos / Olímpicos — *the Paralympics / Olympics*
la Copa Mundial del Fútbol — *the Football World Cup*
Sirven para… — *They serve to…*
promover… — *promote / foster / encourage…*
la participación en el deporte — *participation in sport*
el espíritu de solidaridad — *team spirit*
regenerar los centros urbanos — *regenerate city centres*
elevar el orgullo nacional — *increase national pride*
transmitir los valores de respeto y disciplina — *convey / instil the values of respect and discipline*
unir a la gente — *unite people*

¡Apúntate! — *Sign up!*
¿Qué estabas haciendo? — *What were you doing?*
Estaba / Estábamos / Estaban… — *I/He/She/It was / We were / They were…*
ensayando — *rehearsing*
nevando — *snowing*
entrando en casa — *coming into the house*
durmiendo — *sleeping*
conduciendo por la ciudad — *driving through the city*
leyendo — *reading*
volando por el aire — *flying through the air*
Se estaba convirtiendo en un río. — *It was turning into a river.*
Se estaba moviendo. — *It was moving.*
a mi alrededor — *around me*
Se estaban cayendo. — *They were falling.*
¿Cómo te enteraste del/de la/ de las…? — *How did you find out about the…?*
temblor — *tremor*
incendio forestal — *forest fire*
huracán — *hurricane*
tornado — *tornado*
terremoto — *earthquake*
tormenta de nieve — *snow storm*
acción humanitaria — *humanitaria campaign*
inundaciones — *floods*

La fibra… — *Fibre…*
protege contra el cáncer — *protects against cancer*
combate la obesidad — *combats obesity*
reduce el riesgo de enfermedades — *reduces the risk of diseases*
evitar comer / beber… — *avoid eating / drinking…*
cambiar mi dieta — *change my diet*
llevar una dieta equilibrada — *have a balanced diet*
preparar con ingredientes frescos — *prepare with fresh ingredients*
engordar — *to put on weight*
saltarse el desayuno — *to skip breakfast*
practicar más deporte — *to do more sport*

tiene muchos riesgos — *has many risks*
afecta a tu capacidad para tomar decisiones — *affects your capacity to make decisions*
te relaja / te quita el estrés — *relaxes you / relieves stress*
te quita el sueño / control — *robs you of sleep / self-control*
te hace sentir bien / más adulto — *makes you feel good / more adult*
Es fácil engancharse. — *It is easy to get hooked.*
¡Qué asco! — *How disgusting!.*
Cedí ante la presión de grupo. — *I gave in to peer pressure.*
Caí en el hábito de… — *I fell into the habit of…*
Empecé a… — *I started to…*
Perdí peso. — *I lost weight.*
No puedo parar. — *I can't stop.*
Ya he empezado a… — *I've already started to…*
Todavía no he dejado de… — *I still haven't given up…*
A partir de ahora intentaré… — *From now on I will try to…*

dar un impulso económico — *give a boost to the economy*
inspirar a la gente — *inspire people*
Una / Otra desventaja es… — *A / Another disadvantage is…*
el riesgo de ataques terroristas — *the risk of terrorist attacks*
el tráfico — *the traffic*
el dopaje — *doping*
la deuda — *the debt*
el coste de organización de la seguridad — *the cost of organising the security*
la ciudad anfitriona — *the host city*
el voluntariado — *volunteering*
Solicité un trabajo voluntario porque… — *I applied for a volunteering job because…*
(Nunca) Había sido… — *I had (never) been…*
Antes ya había trabajado como… — *Previously I had already worked as…*

Estaba… — *I / He/She was…*
mirando/viendo las noticias / la tele — *watching the news / the TV*
buscando informaciones en línea — *looking for information online*
charlando con un amigo / una amiga — *chatting with a friend*
leyendo un post en Facebook — *reading a Facebook post*
cuando… — *when…*
encontré un reportaje / un artículo — *I found a report / an article*
recibí un SMS — *I received a text message*
(lo) vi en las noticias — *I saw (it) on the news*
mi novio me llamó / me contó la historia — *my boyfriend called me / told me the story*
una organización de servicio voluntario — *a voluntary organisation*
una campaña para las víctimas — *a campaign for the victims*
una caja de supervivencia — *a survival box*
Decidí apuntarme. — *I decided to sign up.*
recaudar fondos / solicitar donativos — *to raise funds / ask for donations*
organizamos algunos eventos — *we organised some events*
un concierto / un espectáculo de baile — *a concert / a dance show*
una carrera de bici apadrinada — *a sponsored bike race*
una venta de pasteles — *a cake sale*
ser solidario — *showing solidarity / supporting…*
Te hace sentir más conectado con los demás. — *Makes you feed more connected to others.*

1 *leer* — *Refresh your memory!* **Translate these adjectives into Spanish. Write a sentence about a past holiday using each one.**

Ejemplo: **1** *picturesque – pintoresco/a*

*El verano pasado fuimos a Barcelona y vi unos monumentos **pintorescos**.*

1 picturesque	**5** unforgettable
2 amazing	**6** lively
3 luxurious	**7** noisy
4 cosy	

> Remember to make adjectives agree. Is the noun masculine or feminine and is it singular or plural?

2 *escribir* — *Refresh your memory!* **Rewrite these sentences in the past tense. Do you need the preterite or the imperfect for each verb?**

Ejemplo: **1** ***Saqué*** *fotos cuando **estaba** en la montaña.*

1 Saco fotos cuando estoy en la montaña.

2 La pensión está cerca de la costa, pero no tiene piscina.

3 Vamos a la playa y hacemos una barbacoa cuando hace calor.

4 Voy solo y me quedo en un parador pequeño que tiene mucho ambiente.

5 El hotel tiene vistas al mar y además, es muy cómodo.

6 Lo paso muy bien porque hago el vago y leo mis libros.

3 *escuchar* — *Refresh your memory!* **Listen to these people talking about their holidays. (1–4)**

Note down **in English**:

- where they stayed
- what was good about the holiday
- what was bad about it

4 *escuchar* — **You are listening to a radio advert for a hotel in Costa Rica. What does the hotel offer? Write down the letters of the <u>three</u> correct statements.**

A tropical fishing expeditions

B sustainable tourism

C somewhere to appreciate nature

D children's tennis lessons

E wifi available at extra cost

F lively entertainment in the restaurant

G rooms with fantastic views

> Don't jump to conclusions! Listen to the whole section before choosing your answer. E.g. you may hear the word *tenis*, but is option D correct?

Costa Rica

5 leer Read what these tourists write about a campsite in Spain. Answer questions A–D by writing **Eva**, **Andrés**, **Miguel** or **Sara**. Then answer questions E and F **in English**.

Eva: Nos encanta viajar en nuestra caravana, y visitamos este camping maravilloso desde hace cuatro años. Siempre está muy limpio y tiene un montón de actividades de las que se puede disfrutar. Aparte de la tienda, cuenta con un gimnasio y una piscina climatizada.

Miguel: El camping tiene grandes parcelas con sombra o sol. Te dan un documento con las normas del camping. Me parecen necesarias y no son nada estrictas. La tienda no tenía mucha variedad de productos, pero los precios no son caros.

Andrés: El lugar no era grande, pero estaba lleno de gente. Por eso los baños estaban muy sucios. Hay demasiadas normas y muchos perros ruidosos. Lo bueno es que se podía alquilar equipos deportivos, como cañas de pescar.

Sara: La atención del personal fue muy buena. Sin embargo, en las caravanas muchas cosas estaban estropeadas, como la ducha, y no te dan toallas ni papel higiénico. Creo que sería mejor si llevaras tu propia tienda de campaña.

*Example: **Miguel** mentions that there are sunny and shady plots available.*

(a) ▬▬▬▬ says that some of the equipment is broken.
(b) ▬▬▬▬ approves of the rules in the campsite.
(c) ▬▬▬▬ explains why they keep returning to the campsite.
(d) ▬▬▬▬ thinks the campsite was overcrowded.
(e) What are the employees like at the campsite?
(f) What is the good thing about the shop?

6 leer Translate into English Eva's text from exercise 5.

7 escribir Look at the task card and do this extended writing task.

Los intercambios escolares

Usted ha hecho un intercambio con un colegio español en Madrid. Escriba un artículo para una revista española para interesar a otros estudiantes en hacer un intercambio.

Debe incluir los puntos siguientes:

- lo que hizo en el intercambio
- lo más interesante de su visita y por qué
- por qué los intercambios son importantes
- un viaje que le gustaría hacer en el futuro

Justifique sus ideas y sus opiniones.

Escriba aproximadamente 130–150 palabras **en español**.

> ⭐ To answer the third bullet point, look back at page 144 about why languages are important. Could you adapt any ideas from there to use here?

8 escribir Translate the text into Spanish.

Often people go on holiday to the mountains and, if the weather is good, it is fun to be outside. According to a survey, last winter many families stayed in apartments instead of luxury hotels. However, I am going to stay at home because last year I had a skiing accident.

1 escribir

Refresh your memory! **Look back at Module 2 and find examples of the following. Then close the book and write them down from memory.**

- <u>five</u> items of school uniform, e.g. *una chaqueta*
- <u>five</u> opinion verbs/phrases to say what you think of your school, e.g. *me interesa…*
- <u>five</u> reasons for liking or disliking teachers, e.g. *explica bien*
- <u>five</u> phrases about your primary school (in the imperfect), e.g. *no había laboratorios*

2 escuchar

Refresh your memory! **Listen to a girl talking about school rules. Note down in English the <u>four</u> things you are <u>not</u> allowed to do in her school.**

3 escuchar

Escucha a un alumno que habla de sus experiencias en el instituto. Rellena el espacio de cada frase con una palabra del recuadro. Hay más palabras que espacios.

divertidos	fácil	buscar empleo	idioma
aburrido	instrumento	excelente	serio
~~éxito~~	problema	antipáticos	seguir estudiando

Ejemplo: Según el alumno, para la mayoría, el sistema educativo español es un <u>éxito</u>.

(a) Para este alumno, el problema es que ciertos alumnos son _____.

(b) Su profesor de ciencias es _____.

(c) Cree que el dibujo es _____.

(d) Después del colegio va a _____.

(e) También quiere aprender un _____.

> Before listening, read each statement through and look for possible answer options in the box. This will help you focus on finding the correct information more easily while listening.

4 leer Read the text about what the narrator's life was like as a girl. Answer the following questions **in English**. You do not need to write in full sentences.

Mi país inventado by Isabel Allende (abridged)

Algunas familias [...] mandaban a sus hijas a la universidad, pero no era el caso de la mía [...] Se esperaba que mis hermanos fueran profesionales – en lo posible abogados, médicos o ingenieros. [...] En esos años las mujeres profesionales provenían en su mayoría de la clase media [...] Eso ha cambiado y hoy el nivel de educación de las mujeres es incluso superior al de los hombres. Yo no era mala estudiante, pero como ya tenía novio, a nadie se le ocurrió que podía obtener una profesión [...] Terminé la secundaria a los dieciséis años confundida e inmadura, [...] pero siempre tuve claro que debía trabajar.

Isabel Allende

(a) Who did some families send to university?
(b) What jobs did her family want her brothers to do? (Give <u>two</u> examples.)
(c) Why did her family think she would not need a job?
(d) How old was she when she left school?

> When faced with a complex text, read the questions first to give you an idea of what the text is about and what information you will need to find. Try not to worry if the first few sentences contain unfamiliar words or difficult grammar. Keep going and focus on the answers you have to find!

5 hablar Prepare and perform this role play.

Topic: School Exchange

Instructions to candidates:

You are at a Spanish school during an exchange visit. The teacher will play the role of your Spanish friend and will speak first.

You must address your Spanish friend as *tú*.

You will talk to the teacher using the five prompts below.

- where you see – **?** – you must ask a question.
- where you see – **!** – you must respond to something you have not prepared.

Task

Estás hablando con tu amigo/a español/a en un colegio en España.

  1 Profesor(a) preferida – razón
  2 Actividades extraescolares – en tu país
  3 !
  4 ? Clases – horario mañana
  5 ? Planes – después del colegio

6 escribir Translate the text into Spanish.

My friend is addicted to her mobile. At school she takes photos of everyone and downloads music at break time. She never wants to talk with us and she does not have time to read or do anything else. Last week she lost it on the bus and we had to go to the police station.

1 escribir

Refresh your memory! **Complete the sentences with an appropriate word or phrase. Look back through Module 3 for ideas.**

1 Siempre uso aplicaciones para ———.
2 Mi móvil es útil para ———.
3 En este momento estoy ——— en casa.
4 No puedo ir al concierto porque tengo que ———.
5 Quiero ——— porque está lloviendo.
6 Creo que leer en formato digital ———.

> ✛ Think carefully about which of the phrases in exercise 1 require a verb in the infinitive and which require a different verb form.

2 escuchar

Refresh your memory! **Listen to Ángel and Cristina talking about reading.**

1 What does Ángel like and dislike reading?
2 Why does Cristina like reading?
3 What do they each think about e-books and why?

Ángel   Cristina

3 escribir

Refresh your memory! **Choose __four__ family members or friends. Note down __two__ physical characteristics and __two__ character traits for each of them. Then write out a full description of __one__ of them.**

Example: Mi hermano – pelo corto, bajo, tonto, travieso
Mi hermano es bastante bajo y tiene el pelo corto. Creo que es muy tonto y es travieso.

4 escuchar

Your Spanish friend invites you to an event. Listen to the message he has recorded for you. Write down the letters of the __two__ correct answers for each question.

(a) He knows you will want to come because…

    A you are interested in science fiction films.
    B you are looking for a job in IT.
    C you love everything to do with technology.
    D it is free for students.
    E you will both learn a lot.

(b) Before you buy the ticket you should…

    A read more about it online.
    B prepare a competition entry.
    C buy an outfit to wear.
    D download a programme of events.
    E read the rules of the competition.

> ✛ Prepare by reading each statement and deciding which words you need to listen for. E.g. In question (a), if option C is correct, you might expect to hear '*trabajo / trabajar*' or '*empleo*' and '*informática*'.

5 leer Read this magazine article about social media. What does the article tell us? Write down the letters of the <u>three</u> correct statements. Then answer questions (b) and (c) **in English.**

Hoy en día los adolescentes dedican gran parte de su tiempo libre a las redes sociales. Millones de usuarios chatean y mandan mensajes a través de Facebook, Twitter, Snapchat y muchas otras redes. Sin embargo, muchos adolescentes no conocen los peligros existentes en las redes sociales.

Un gran problema de las redes sociales es la privacidad. Por ejemplo, se pueden recibir y aceptar solicitudes de amistad de extraños. También las fotos que sube un adolescente pueden ser vistas por personas desconocidas. Esto puede representar un peligro para la seguridad de los adolescentes.

Un experimento reciente alertó de los peligros que pueden suponer las redes sociales. En el experimento, un hombre contactó con tres niñas adolescentes de 12, 13 y 14 años. Las tres menores de edad conocían los peligros de contactar con extraños en las redes sociales, y sin embargo, las tres accedieron a tener una cita con el desconocido.

Los padres y educadores deberían dar más consejos a los jóvenes sobre cómo utilizarlas y apoyarlos en cualquier problema con el que se pueden encontrar.

(a)

  A Privacy is one of the big issues with social media.
  B Most teenagers know that many sites are dangerous.
  C Snapchat was used in an experiment to show the dangers of communicating online.
  D Some teenage boys were contacted by a man they did not know.
  E The teenagers involved were aware of the dangers of meeting strangers.
  F You cannot receive friend requests from strangers on most sites.
  G In the experiment, the young people agreed to go on a date with a stranger.

(b) What does the article say about photos?
(c) According to the article, how should parents and teachers support young people? (Give <u>one</u> detail.)

6 hablar Prepare and perform this picture-based task.

Topic: Cultural life

Mira la foto y prepara las respuestas a los siguientes puntos.

  • la descripción de la foto
  • la importancia de leer libros
  • la última vez que pasaste tiempo con tus amigos
  • otras actividades que te gustaría hacer con tus amigos
  • (!)

⭐ Use the preparation time to think about what the unexpected question (!) might be. What else could you be asked about? Brainstorm some ideas in Spanish on a separate sheet.

7 escribir Translate this text into Spanish.

I am quite tall and I have long curly hair. My friends tell me that I am a little lazy, but it's not true. I met my best friend three years ago at school. We get on very well. For me, a good friend is someone who never judges you. I hope to be his friend forever.

1 *escuchar*

Refresh your memory! Listen to Mónica talking about her leisure activities and note down the following: (1–5)

1 what hobbies she does regularly
2 what she likes to do most and why
3 how her taste in films has changed

4 what she does to relax
5 something she has done recently

2 *escribir*

Refresh your memory! Complete the following sentences with an appropriate phrase. Look back through Module 4 for ideas.

1 Gasto mi paga en ━━━━.
2 Acabo de ━━━━.

3 Suelo ver ━━━━.
4 ¿Has leído ━━━━?

3 *escribir*

Refresh your memory! Make a list of <u>ten</u> adjectives that you could use to describe a book, film or leisure activity. Avoid the obvious ones like *interesante*, *aburrido/a* and *divertido/a*!

> ✪ Having a bank of interesting and less common adjectives at your fingertips will raise the level of your Spanish. Create your own top ten!

4 *escuchar*

You are on holiday in Málaga and you hear two Spanish people talking about their plans and experiences. What do they say? Write the letter of the correct phrase to complete each sentence.

Example: They discuss where they will go for… C

    A the Easter holidays.
    B their summer vacation.
    C Christmas Eve.
    D New Year's Eve.

(a) They both plan to spend the time…
    A with lots of friends.
    B with family members.
    C with their best friend.
    D on their own.

(b) It will be…
    A noisy.
    B busy.
    C boring.
    D quiet.

(c) Last year they could not…
    A listen to the radio.
    B watch a film.
    C go to England.
    D eat at the table.

(d) This year they will…
    A play board games.
    B watch TV.
    C buy some videogames.
    D eat in a restaurant.

(e) They are now planning…
    A a trip to England.
    B a night out.
    C a holiday next month.
    D a shopping trip.

(f) They will…
    A go home early.
    B eat out.
    C spend their pocket money.
    D not need much money.

5 leer Lee el artículo. Escribe la letra de la respuesta correcta para cada pregunta.

El festival nacional de lectura

En mayo va a tener lugar la Feria del Libro de Madrid, que se celebra una vez al año. Autores y fanáticos de la lectura van a asistir y habrá un ambiente perfecto para encontrar los últimos libros. Hay más de trescientas casetas dedicadas a libros, revistas y tebeos. Es uno de los eventos de ocio más importantes de la capital.

El año pasado, aunque hizo mal tiempo, la feria reunió a miles de visitantes. Éstos aprovecharon para hablar de sus libros favoritos y participaron en muchos de los eventos. En el pabellón infantil, los niños suelen hacer actividades y escuchar cuentos emocionantes.

las casetas   *stalls / stands*

Ejemplo: La feria tiene lugar en… A

- **A** España.
- **B** Francia.
- **C** las islas Baleares.
- **D** Latinoamérica.

(a) Esta feria…
- **A** es muy pequeña.
- **B** es algo nuevo.
- **C** tiene lugar cada año.
- **D** empezó el año pasado.

(b) La feria se dirige a…
- **A** niños pequeños.
- **B** personas a las que les encanta leer.
- **C** solo autores y a sus editores.
- **D** empleados de librerías.

(c) Los libros de la feria…
- **A** son muy antiguos.
- **B** fueron escritos en los años treinta.
- **C** muestran una gran variedad de literatura.
- **D** nunca contienen dibujos.

(d) Durante la feria del año pasado…
- **A** hizo buen tiempo.
- **B** no vino mucha gente.
- **C** hubo muchos problemas técnicos.
- **D** la gente tomó parte en varias actividades.

(e) Normalmente los visitantes más pequeños…
- **A** escuchan historias.
- **B** cantan.
- **C** ganan premios.
- **D** no pagan entrada.

6 leer Translate into English the first paragraph of the text from exercise 5.

> ⭐ Don't try to understand every word as you read. It will take too long and you may get stuck on certain phrases. Read through quickly to get the gist, then look at the questions to see what information you need to find.

7 escribir Look at the task card and do this shorter writing task.

Una visita al cine

Acabas de ver una película. Escribe un artículo para una revista española para adolescentes sobre la película.

Debes incluir los siguientes puntos:
- cuándo fuiste y con quién
- el tema de la película
- tu opinión de la película
- tus planes para el sábado que viene

Escribe aproximadamente 80–90 palabras **en español**.

8 escribir Translate the text into Spanish.

In my free time, I love to use the computer at home. I have just played a new videogame, which has amazing graphics, and I am already a fan! Sometimes my friends and I go to the cinema. Last month we went to the circus and I would love to see another similar show.

1 escribir

Refresh your memory! **Look back at Module 5 and write down:**

- <u>four</u> phrases which use *estar* to describe the location of a town or village, e.g. *Está al lado de las montañas.*
- <u>five</u> adjectives to describe a city, e.g. *famosa*
- <u>five</u> phrases which use verbs in the future tense, e.g. *Iremos a la playa.*
- exclamations to enhance your speaking or writing, e.g. *¡Qué bien!*

2 escuchar

Refresh your memory! **Listen to these conversations in different shops. Note down in English the problem and the outcome in each case. (1–3)**

3 hablar

Refresh your memory! **In pairs, take five minutes to look at the pros and cons of living in a city on page 104, then close the book. Who can remember the most statements?**

- *Lo mejor es…*
- *Lo peor es…*

4 escuchar

Escuchas una entrevista con la directora de una cadena de tiendas de moda. ¿Qué dice la directora? Escoge entre: barata, informal, cara, nueva. Puedes usar las palabras más de una vez.

Ejemplo: Mucha ropa en sus tiendas es <u>barata</u>

(a) Toda la ropa en las tiendas es ━━━

(b) La falda que más se vende es ━━━

(c) En el futuro, quiere tener más ropa ━━━

(d) Su ropa nunca va a ser más ━━━

(e) Piensa que la moda tiene que ser ━━━

> ⭐ In this type of activity, you need to listen carefully to the meaning of the <u>whole sentence</u>. If you hear a negative sentence using one of the adjectives, you will need to answer with the opposite adjective. For example, if you heard *'la ropa no es barata'* then you would need to write *cara* as your answer.

5 leer

Read the extract. Mateo is describing Barcelona.
Write the letter of the correct words to finish each sentence.

El día de mañana by
Ignacio Martínez de Pisón

> Lo que más me gustaba era subir la torre de la iglesia, que era el punto más alto de la ciudad, y observarlo todo desde allí arriba: los campos, las carreteras cercanas, las calles, el mar. Para mí, el día más feliz de todos fue el de la gran Navidad del 1962. Durante toda la Nochebuena no paró de nevar y, cuando nos despertamos por la mañana, había casi un metro de nieve por todas partes.
>
> Salimos al jardín e hicimos una guerra de bolas de nieve y cuando subí las escaleras de la iglesia me sentí feliz al ver Barcelona. Las calles, los coches y hasta los barcos del Puerto estaban cubiertos de nieve. Eso fue para mí un momento de felicidad absoluta, mirando en silencio aquella Barcelona tan blanca y tan hermosa…

Example: The thing Mateo liked most was… B
- **A** playing on the pitch.
- **B** climbing the church tower.
- **C** climbing the hill near home.
- **D** being very tall.

(a) He liked this because he…
- **A** could have some time alone.
- **B** was with his friends.
- **C** could see everything from there.
- **D** couldn't hear the traffic.

(b) From the tower, Mateo states he could see…
- **A** roads and fields.
- **B** the sea and horses.
- **C** streets and rubbish.
- **D** fields and trees.

(c) He remembers Christmas 1962 because…
- **A** he received many gifts.
- **B** it was a boring day.
- **C** he spent it relaxing at home.
- **D** it was the happiest of days.

(d) Mateo went out into the garden and…
- **A** looked at the church.
- **B** threw snowballs.
- **C** saw a small amount of snow.
- **D** played on his own.

(e) Mateo describes Barcelona as…
- **A** a quiet city.
- **B** a beautiful city.
- **C** an old city.
- **D** a happy city.

6 hablar

Prepare and perform this role play.

Topic: Travel and tourist transactions

Instructions to candidates:

You are in a shop in Argentina. The teacher will play the role of the shop assistant and will speak first.

You must address the shop assistant as *usted*.

You will talk to the teacher using the five prompts below.
- where you see – **?** – you will must ask a question
- where you see – **!** – you must respond to something you have not prepared

Task

Usted está en una tienda de recuerdos en Argentina. Quiere cambiar un regalo.

1 Regalo – problema
2 Artículo comprado - cuándo
3 **!**
4 **?** Cambiar
5 **?** Reembolso

7 escribir

Translate this text into Spanish.

My area is located in a valley which has beautiful landscapes. The best thing is that there are incredible views and lots of great shops to visit in the city centre. Last summer, my Spanish friend and I took a tourist bus to see all the old buildings. If the weather is good tomorrow, we will go to the beach.

1 leer **Refresh your memory!** Put the food and drink from the box into <u>four</u> lists using the headings below. Then translate each item into English.

- Lácteos
- Carnes y pescados
- Frutas y verduras
- Bebidas

una lata de cerveza	unas chuletas de cerdo	queso de cabra
un kilo de zanahorias	un filete	un yogur de frambuesa
medio kilo de albaricoques	dos cebollas	un zumo de pomelo
un litro de leche semidesnatada		

2 escuchar **Refresh your memory!** Listen to people describing music festivals. (1–3)

Note down **in English**:

- the type of music mentioned
- whether the festival is in the past or the future
- any positive and negative aspects mentioned

Time expressions do not always tell you whether something is in the past or the future, so listen for the tense of the verb used. E.g.

*El jueves **fuimos** a un concierto.*
On Thursday we went to a concert.

*El jueves **vamos a ir** a un concierto.*
On Thursday we are going to go to a concert.

3 escuchar You are listening to a radio programme about eating out in San Sebastián.

Write down the letter of the correct phrase to finish each sentence.

(a) The cuisine of San Sebastián is…
  A a closely kept secret.
  B well known in parts of Spain.
  C famous in Spain and abroad.
  D the best in Spain.

(b) In San Sebastián you can…
  A eat lots of different seafood dishes.
  B find something for everyone.
  C visit many vegetarian restaurants.
  D mainly find locals eating the tapas.

(c) If you do not want to spend much money you should…
  A avoid all the restaurants and bars.
  B visit the area outside the city centre.
  C eat in your hotel.
  D eat small dishes called 'pinchos'.

San Sebastián

(d) The dishes he refers to are normally…
  A eaten standing up.
  B brought to your table to share.
  C made of meat.
  D served with wine.

(e) The dishes he prefers are…
  A vegetarian.
  B meat-based.
  C fish-based.
  D the most expensive ones.

4 leer Read the newspaper article below.

A pesar del alto nivel de desempleo, este verano tres nuevos restaurantes de la Costa Brava están buscando gente con energía, buen humor y lenguas extranjeras para trabajar en sus establecimientos. Son buenas noticias para nuestra juventud. Pronto se abrirá un restaurante tradicional y se ofrecerán ocho puestos de trabajo para servir comida típica española como marisco, arroces y paellas. También habrá muchos puestos en dos restaurantes internacionales que venderán comida típica inglesa y comida japonesa.

El trabajo será muy variado, desde fregar platos y doblar servilletas, hasta conversar con los clientes. Es una gran oportunidad para los jóvenes que viven aquí, que están encontrando problemas para conseguir trabajo o para ganar un buen sueldo.

Costa Brava

Answer the following questions **in English**. You do not have to write full sentences.

(a) What good news is there for young people in the Costa Brava?
(b) Apart from energy and good humour, what skills are required?
(c) Which <u>three</u> new restaurants are mentioned?
(d) Summarise the types of work which will be required.

5 leer Translate into English the section of the text in exercise 4 from *'Pronto se abrirá…'* to *'…comida japonesa'*.

6 escribir Look at the task card and do this extended writing task.

Los eventos benéficos

Usted ha asistido a un festival musical benéfico. Escriba un artículo para una revista española para interesar a los lectores en los eventos musicales benéficos.

Debe incluir los puntos siguientes:

- lo que hizo
- lo que más le gustó y por qué
- por qué son importantes los eventos benéficos de este tipo
- lo que va a hacer en el futuro por una organización benéfica.

Justifique sus ideas y sus opiniones.

Escriba aproximadamente 130–150 palabras **en español**.

⭐ Look back through the book to find verbs you could use to answer the third bullet point. E.g. *recaudar* (to collect) and *mostrar* (to show). Also think about which form of the verb you will need to use. E.g. *Los eventos benéficos* **recaudan**…, **muestran**…

7 escribir Translate the text into Spanish.

I am very interested in Spanish culture and therefore last year I went to a very exciting festival in Spain with my parents. They let off lots of fireworks and we loved the processions and the music. Next year I hope to go back again, as I would like to take more photos.

1 *hablar*

Refresh your memory! In pairs, look at pages 158–159 and memorise as many jobs and adjectives as you can in <u>two</u> minutes. Then take it in turns to say a sentence about a job.

● *Me gustaría ser jardinero/a porque es un trabajo variado.*
■ *Quiero ser profesor(a) porque es un trabajo importante.*

2 *escribir*

Refresh your memory! Copy and complete the grid with the first person singular and plural forms of the verbs.

infinitive	present	preterite	imperfect	conditional
ganar (to earn)	gano ganamos	gané ganamos	ganaba ganábamos	ganaría ganaríamos
ayudar (to help)		ayudamos		
tener (to have)		tuvimos		tendría
hacer (to do)	hago			haríamos
ir (to go)	voy		iba	

> ⭐ Try to use the *nosotros* (we) form in your spoken and written work. It will add variety to your work.

3 *escuchar*

Refresh your memory! Listen and answer the questions.

1 What job does Lucía do?
2 What are the good and bad points?

3 What has helped her career?
4 What does she want to do next?

4 *escuchar*

Two young people discuss their jobs as part of a radio podcast. What do María and Javier say?
Write the letter of the correct phrase to complete each sentence.

Example: María works in marketing… A

  A for an international cosmetics company.
  B for a international clothing company.
  C for an international bank.
  D for a charitable organisation.

(a) She loves her job because…
  A her clients are based nearby.
  B she often travels abroad.
  C she is given lots of free products.
  D she writes about her experiences on internet sites.

(b) Javier believes that… broadens your horizons.
  A working in a bank
  B having lots of friends
  C changing jobs
  D speaking another language

(c) Javier's job requires him to use foreign languages…
  A from time to time.
  B when he is abroad.
  C for interviews and reading documents.
  D if translators are unavailable.

5 leer

Read what these two people have written about their first jobs. Answer the questions **in English**. You do not need to write in full sentences.

Rafael: Mi primer trabajo fue en una empresa de marketing y lo recuerdo perfectamente. Era un trabajo administrativo, así que sacaba muchas fotocopias, archivaba documentos y me encargaba de repartir el correo. No era un trabajo muy interesante, pero mis colegas eran muy amables y aprendí mucho sobre el mundo laboral.

Elena: Mi primera experiencia de trabajo tuvo lugar en la biblioteca de la universidad. El sueldo no era muy bueno, sin embargo, el horario era fantástico porque me permitía asistir a clase y aún tenía tiempo para estudiar. Mis tareas eran muy variadas: colocaba y organizaba los libros, estaba en la recepción dando la bienvenida a estudiantes y muchas veces ayudaba en la sala de ordenadores.

(a) Apart from photocopying, what did Rafael do? (Name <u>one</u> thing.)

(b) Name <u>one</u> positive aspect he mentions about this job.

(c) What does Elena say about her pay?

(d) Why were the hours Elena worked good for her?

(e) Apart from helping to organise the books, what did her role entail? (Name <u>one</u> thing.)

> ⭐ When reading or listening for opinions, watch out for connectives, which can change a negative statement into a positive one or vice-versa. E.g.
>
> *Mi trabajo no era muy interesante, **sin embargo**, el sueldo era excelente.*

6 leer

Translate Rafael's text into English.

7 hablar

Prepare and perform this picture-based task.

Topic: Work

Mira la foto y prepara las respuestas a los siguientes puntos:

- la descripción de la foto
- tu opinión sobre la importancia de las prácticas laborales
- lo que has hecho en casa o en el mundo laboral para ganar dinero
- lo que te gustaría hacer cuando termines el colegio
- (!)

> ⭐ Use every possible opportunity to show you can use different tenses. E.g.
>
> *Para ganar dinero, normalmente **ayudo** a mis padres con algunas tareas en casa, pero antes **lavaba** el coche de mi madre.*

8 escribir

Translate this text into Spanish.

I love my job now because I work outside. I used to work in a hospital, but the salary was very bad. I used to start at 10am and finish at 4pm. I had to answer telephone calls. I used to get on well with my boss because he was very understanding and I learned lots of new things.

1 leer

Refresh your memory! **Read and unjumble these sentences about the importance of international sporting events. Then translate them into English.**

1 para a eventos la Los sirven internacionales gente deportivos unir

2 de el Fomentan solidaridad espíritu

3 valores y Sirven los transmitir respeto para de disciplina

4 costes desventaja altos son una Los

2 escribir

Refresh your memory! **In pairs, choose <u>three</u> of the following headings and create a mind map for each. Write at least <u>three</u> phrases for each one.**

Example:

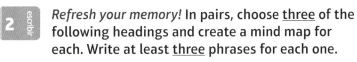
el alcohol

Afecta a tu capacidad para tomar decisiones.

- el desempleo
- las drogas
- la contaminación ambiental
- la pobreza mundial
- la violencia

Make sure you have a good supply of opinion phrases to discuss complex issues. E.g.

Me parece muy importante el tema de…
Para mí, el problema más… es…

Look back through Module 8 and write down at least <u>six</u> other opinion phrases.

3 escuchar

Refresh your memory! **Listen to the conversation about environmental issues and note down which of the following are not mentioned.**

Floods

Pollution of rivers and seas

Too much rubbish

Air pollution

Fossil fuels running out

Deforestation

4 escuchar

You are listening to a radio programme. A head teacher from a school in Mexico is talking about the problems his students face. Answer the following questions in English.

(a) What does he say is the biggest problem for young people?

(b) Which <u>two</u> things contribute to this problem?

(c) Who was in trouble with the police yesterday?

(d) What should schools do to help those most at risk?

It's a good idea to make notes in Spanish as you listen the first time, then write your answers during or just after the second time the recording is played.

5 leer

Lee el texto sobre los problemas que afectan a las islas Galápagos.
Contesta en español. No tienes que escribir frases completas.

Las islas Galápagos forman el archipiélago medioambiental más diverso del mundo. Son uno de los grupos volcánicos más activos del mundo y se consideran Patrimonio Natural de la Humanidad desde 1978. Desafortunadamente, algunas de las especies de plantas y varios animales están en peligro de extinción debido a la actividad humana en tiempos anteriores.

En enero de 2001, un barco petrolero derramó trescientas toneladas de petróleo en la costa de las Galápagos, y el agua estuvo contaminada durante años. Este accidente se considera uno de los mayores desastres naturales. Ahora las islas se enfrentan a otros problemas como la sobrepoblación, la contaminación y el exceso de turismo. Muchos turistas quieren explorar las aguas de las islas, que ofrecen la oportunidad de ver arrecifes de coral, tortugas gigantes, iguanas y cientos de variedades de peces.

El gobierno de Ecuador ha tomado medidas para la conservación del espacio ecológico de las islas: ha regulado el turismo y la navegación. Por ejemplo, existen cuarenta y cinco sitios aprobados para el turismo con la finalidad de proteger la vegetación y los animales salvajes de las islas. Siempre hay que visitar estos sitios con un guía naturalista profesional. Actualmente, el énfasis de las soluciones propuestas por el gobierno está en la educación de la población para cuidar el medio ambiente.

las islas Galápagos

los arrecifes de coral   coral reefs

(a) ¿Qué problema existe para los animales y las plantas de las islas?
(b) ¿Qué consecuencia tuvo el accidente de 2001?
(c) Aparte del turismo, ¿cuáles son los problemas que existen en las islas?
(d) ¿Cómo han regulado el turismo?
(e) ¿Cómo sabemos que el gobierno todavía protege la naturaleza de las islas?

6 escribir

Look at the task card and do this longer writing task.

Los eventos deportivos internacionales

Usted ha ido a un evento deportivo internacional.

Escriba un artículo para una revista deportiva para interesar a los lectores en los eventos deportivos internacionales.

Debe incluir los puntos siguientes:

- lo que vio e hizo durante el evento
- lo que piensa del evento y por qué
- por qué valen la pena los eventos deportivos internacionales
- los planes que tiene para asistir a otros eventos deportivos

Justifique sus ideas y sus opiniones.

Escriba aproximadamente 130–150 palabras **en español**.

To impress in your writing, try to present both sides of the argument. E.g.
*Los eventos deportivos sirven para promover el turismo, **pero** un inconveniente es el tráfico que producen estos eventos.*

7 escribir

Translate this text into Spanish.

In my opinion, there are many global problems, which we have to change very soon. Last year I worked as a volunteer in a big hospital and I saw a lot of poverty and obesity. I am also worried about the environment and unemployment. After finishing exams, some of my friends will be looking for jobs, but there are few job opportunities.

The Edexcel Spanish course is made up of several topics (e.g. *holidays*, *cultural life*), which are grouped into five **themes**:

- Theme 1 – Identity and Culture
- Theme 2 – Local area, holiday and travel
- Theme 3 – School
- Theme 4 – Future aspirations, study and work
- Theme 5 – International and global dimension

Module 1
Theme: Local area, holiday and travel (holidays; travel and tourist transactions)

1 ¿Qué haces en verano?
2 ¿Dónde prefieres pasar las vacaciones? ¿Por qué?
3 ¿Adónde fuiste de vacaciones el año pasado?
4 ¿Dónde te alojaste?
5 ¿Cómo era el pueblo/la ciudad?
6 ¿Qué fue lo mejor de tus vacaciones?
7 ¿Qué planes tienes para el próximo verano?
8 ¿Por qué son importantes las vacaciones?
9 ¿Por qué veranea tanta gente en el extranjero?
10 ¿Adónde irías si tuvieras mucho dinero? ¿Por qué?

Module 2
Theme: School (what school is like; school activities)

1 ¿Cómo es tu insti? ¿Qué instalaciones tiene / no tiene?
2 ¿Qué asignaturas te gustan y no te gustan? ¿Por qué?
3 ¿Qué opinas del uniforme escolar?
4 ¿Qué piensas de las otras normas de tu insti?
5 ¿Qué actividades extraescolares haces?
6 ¿Qué planes tienes para este trimestre?
7 ¿Qué es lo bueno / malo de tu insti?
8 Compara tu escuela primaria con tu instituto.
9 ¿Hay diferencias entre los institutos españoles y tu instituto?
10 ¿Puedes describir un intercambio o un viaje escolar que hiciste en el pasado?

Module 3
Theme: Identity and culture (who am I?; cultural life)

1 Describe a un buen amigo tuyo / una buena amiga tuya.
2 ¿Qué aplicaciones usas para estar en contacto con tus amigos y con tu familia?
3 ¿Estás enganchado/a a tu móvil?
4 ¿Qué piensas de las redes sociales?
5 ¿Qué te gusta leer? ¿Por qué?
6 ¿Te llevas bien con tu familia? ¿Por qué (no)?
7 Describe a una persona de tu familia.
8 ¿Quiénes son más importantes, tus amigos o tus padres? ¿Por qué?
9 ¿Cómo es un buen amigo / una buena amiga?
10 ¿Qué planes tienes con tus amigos este fin de semana?

Module 4
Theme: Identity and culture (who am I?; cultural life)

1 ¿Qué sueles hacer en tus ratos libres?
2 ¿Eres teleadicto/a? ¿Por qué (no)?
3 ¿Prefieres ver películas en casa o en el cine? ¿Por qué?
4 ¿Te gusta la música? ¿Por qué (no)?
5 ¿Tus padres te dan dinero? ¿Qué haces con la paga?
6 ¿Qué planes tienes para este fin de semana?
7 ¿Eres muy deportista? ¿Por qué (no)?
8 Háblame de la última vez que participaste en un deporte.
9 ¿En qué consiste un buen modelo a seguir?
10 ¿Quién es tu modelo a seguir?

For the General Conversation, you can choose a **topic** (e.g. *school activities*) from **one** of the themes for your discussion. You will be allowed to speak about this for up to one minute at the start. After that you will be required to continue with the discussion on your chosen topic (or the wider theme). Your teacher will then ask you questions on a second theme. You can use the questions below in order to help prepare.

Module 5
Themes: Local area, holiday and travel (town, region and country); Identity and culture (daily life)

1 ¿Cuál es tu ciudad favorita? ¿Por qué te gusta?
2 ¿Cómo es la ciudad o el pueblo donde vives?
3 ¿Qué es mejor, vivir en la ciudad o en el campo? ¿Por qué?
4 ¿Qué hay para turistas en tu zona? ¿Qué se puede hacer?
5 ¿Qué hiciste recientemente en tu zona?
6 ¿Cómo cambiarías tu zona?
7 ¿Qué harás en tu ciudad este fin de semana, si hace buen tiempo? Y ¿si hace mal tiempo?
8 ¿Dónde te gusta comprar? ¿Por qué?
9 ¿Adónde fuiste de compras la última vez y qué compraste? ¿Qué hiciste?
10 Describe una visita que hiciste a una ciudad (en Gran Bretaña o en otro país).

Module 6
Theme: Identity and culture (daily life; cultural life)

1 ¿Qué te gusta comer? ¿Por qué?
2 ¿Has probado la comida española? ¿Te gusta? ¿Por qué (no)?
3 ¿Prefieres cenar en casa o en un restaurante? ¿Por qué?
4 Háblame de lo que hiciste en un día especial reciente con tus amigos o tu familia.
5 ¿Cómo vas a celebrar tu próximo cumpleaños?
6 ¿Has asistido a un festival de música? ¿Puedes describirlo?
7 Háblame de lo que hiciste por Navidad el año pasado.
8 ¿Cuál es la fiesta más importante, en tu opinión?
9 ¿Crees que las fiestas tradicionales son importantes? ¿Por qué (no)?
10 Háblame de una fiesta a la que te gustaría asistir.

Module 7
Theme: Future aspirations, study and work (using languages beyond the classroom; ambitions; work)

1 ¿Tienes un trabajo a tiempo parcial? ¿Qué haces?
2 ¿Qué planes tienes para el futuro?
3 ¿Qué opinas de ir a la universidad? ¿Por qué?
4 ¿Cómo ayudas con las tareas domésticas?
5 ¿Dónde hiciste tus prácticas laborales?
6 ¿En qué te gustaría trabajar? ¿Por qué?
7 ¿Crees que es importante aprender otras lenguas? ¿Por qué (no)?
8 ¿Cómo pasarías un año sabático? ¿Por qué?
9 ¿Qué otras ambiciones tienes?
10 ¿Qué cosas te importan más en la vida? ¿Por qué?

Module 8
Theme: International and global dimension (bringing the world together; environmental issues)

1 ¿Cuáles son los problemas globales más serios hoy en día?
2 ¿Cómo se pueden solucionar los problemas?
3 ¿Para qué sirven los eventos deportivos internacionales?
4 ¿Qué opinas de los grandes eventos musicales?
5 ¿Cómo se debería cuidar el medio ambiente?
6 ¿Te gusta tu casa? ¿Por qué (no)?
7 Si fueras millonario, ¿cómo sería tu casa ideal? ¿Qué tendría?
8 ¿Qué haces en casa para proteger el medio ambiente?
9 ¿Es importante ser solidario? ¿Por qué (no)?
10 ¿Si tuvieras mucho dinero, cómo ayudarías a los demás?

Te toca a ti: Módulo 1

1 *leer* **Match the sentence halves and copy them out in a logical order. Then translate them.**

1 El último día fuimos a Terra Mítica, un parque de…

2 Mis vacaciones fueron inolvidables, pero lo…

3 Hace dos años fui de vacaciones a Benidorm…

4 Luego, por la tarde fui al centro de la…

5 Al día siguiente por la mañana hice…

6 El primer día hizo mucho calor. Cuando…

a ciudad y compré recuerdos para mis amigos.

b llegamos al hotel, decidimos ir a la playa.

c mejor fue cuando aprendí a bucear en el mar. ¡Qué guay!

d turismo. Subí a la Torre Morales y saqué muchas fotos.

e con mi familia. Viajamos en avión y en autocar.

f atracciones, donde vomité en una montaña rusa. ¡Qué horror!

2 *escribir* **Write a paragraph about your holidays, using exercise 1 as an example.**

3 *leer* **Read the texts and questions. Write I (Isabel), T (Tomás) or I+T (Isabel and Tomás).**

Isabel-98
La Palma

¡Hotel horroroso!
Pasé un finde en este hotel y no era nada barato – 150 € por noche. ¡Qué timo! Las habitaciones estaban muy sucias, la ducha estaba estropeada y no había toallas. También había basura en la piscina. Cuando fuimos a cenar, la comida estaba fría y había un insecto en mi sopa. Pero lo peor fue que el recepcionista tenía muy mala actitud.

TomásFG
Bilbao

Experiencia malísima
No recomiendo este hotel. No tenía ni wifi ni aire acondicionado en las habitaciones. Tampoco tenía aparcamiento. El gimnasio no estaba abierto y el ascensor estaba estropeado. Había una discoteca que tenía la música muy alta, y por eso era imposible dormir. Además, el camarero en el restaurante era muy maleducado. Pero lo peor fue que había una serpiente en el balcón. ¡Qué miedo!

Who mentions…

1 the rooms?

2 the staff?

3 the food?

4 the noise?

5 the sports facilities?

6 the price?

7 the bathroom?

8 a scary reptile?

el finde el fin de semana (slang)
¡Qué timo! What a con!

4 *escribir* **Write about a holiday from hell, using the pictures. Add extra details.**

Te toca a ti: Módulo 2

1 leer · **Read Lina's text and join the English sentence halves correctly.**

Mi instituto es grande, mixto y tiene muy buena fama, dado que los alumnos siempre sacan buenas notas. Además, no hay ni mucho acoso escolar ni falta de disciplina. El año pasado mi insti ocupó el primer lugar en el ranking oficial de colegios en Madrid.

A mi parecer, mi instituto ofrece muy buenas oportunidades extraescolares, sobre todo si eres músico. En junio mis amigos y yo participamos en un concurso de bandas jóvenes, y los profesores de música nos ayudaron con la grabación y el vídeo. ¡Fue genial!

Otra cosa buena es que no tenemos que llevar uniforme porque es mucho más cómodo llevar ropa de calle. Sin embargo, el nuevo director introduce muchas normas más estrictas. ¡Qué pesado! Por ejemplo, por desgracia ahora está prohibido llevar maquillaje.

No todo es malo porque el nuevo director tiene planes para mejorar las instalaciones deportivas. Vamos a tener un polideportivo, un taller de baile y un gimnasio amplio con un muro de escalada. Va a ser el insti mejor equipado de todo el país. A todos los alumnos nos encanta la posibilidad de tener más clubs y actividades.

Lina

1	My school is large, mixed and has…	**a**	more clubs and activities.
2	Last year my school…	**b**	very good extracurricular opportunities.
3	In my view, my school offers…	**c**	helped with the competition recording and video.
4	The music teachers…	**d**	a very good reputation.
5	The new headteacher is…	**e**	going to be the best equipped school in the country.
6	The new headteacher has…	**f**	plans to improve the sports facilities.
7	It is…	**g**	took first place in the official ranking of schools in Madrid.
8	All the pupils love the prospect of…	**h**	introducing lots of stricter rules.

2 leer · **Re-read the text from exercise 1 and find the <u>three</u> correct statements. Correct the false statements.**

1 La disciplina en el insti no es buena.
2 El instituto de Lina es el mejor colegio de Madrid.
3 A Lina le gusta mucho la música.
4 El nuevo director va a introducir un uniforme escolar.
5 Lina está de acuerdo con las nuevas normas.
6 El director también tiene propósitos positivos para el insti.
7 El instituto no tiene ningún club.

3 escribir · **Write a text about your school. Use exercise 1 as a model.**

Include:

- a description of your school
- extracurricular opportunities
- past achievements
- uniform and rules
- future plans for your school

⭐ Try to link sentences and paragraphs together. Look at how Lina uses the following:

a mi parecer   dado que   otra cosa buena es que

sin embargo   por desgracia

1 leer Match the web profiles to the statements below. There is one extra statement.

 www.amorcitos.es

mi media naranja *my other half*
mi alma gemela *my soulmate*

♥ ♥ ♥ ♥ ♥ Tu gran historia de amor te espera ♥ ♥ ♥ ♥ ♥ ♥

1 Busco a mi media naranja. Mi pareja ideal es alguien trabajador, responsable, romántico, pero también deportista.

2 Quiero casarme porque me importa la estabilidad, pero no quiero tener niños porque mi carrera es más importante.

3 Mi alma gemela es una persona inteligente, con un buen sentido del humor. Me interesa la política, así como la cultura popular.

4 Soy bastante solitaria, pero busco alguien con quien compartir mi amor a la literatura y a las ideas.

a Busco una relación amorosa, aunque me comprometo con mi trabajo.
b Soy extrovertida, y me interesa viajar y hablar de muchos temas diferentes.
c Soy un verdadero ratón de biblioteca.
d Mi profesión me ocupa bastante tiempo, pero me gusta mantenerme en forma.
e Soy graduado en historia, pero también me encanta la música pop.

2 leer Read the article and complete the sentences in English.

la boda wedding

Casarse ya no está de moda

En España se casan menos personas, y mucho más tarde. La edad media para casarse es de 34, 5 años. El motivo es, sobre todo, económico. Debido a la crisis económica todavía hay mucho desempleo y el coste medio de una boda se sitúa entre 11.000 y 21.000 euros. Otro factor son las tasas elevadas de divorcio. El año pasado, siete de cada diez matrimonios en España acabaron en separación o divorcio. Además, antes la mayoría de gente se casaba por la iglesia, mientras que ahora prefieren una ceremonia civil.

1 In Spain fewer people ━━━━.
2 The average age for ━━━━ is ━━━━.
3 The economic crisis means that ━━━━.
4 Another factor is the ━━━━.
5 Last year ━━━━.
6 When people marry now, the majority ━━━━.

3 leer Match the sentence halves. Then translate the views about marriage into English.

1 El matrimonio es una promesa de vivir…
2 Para mí, casarse…
3 Después del matrimonio…
4 Se dice que los casados son…
5 No me gusta la idea de una boda tradicional,…
6 Si quieres formar una familia,…

a es un rito anticuado y mi amor a mi pareja no depende de un papel.
b más felices que los solteros.
c así que prefiero la opción de entrar en una unión civil.
d juntos para siempre. Te da mucha seguridad.
e creo que el matrimonio es la opción más estable para los niños.
f viene el divorcio, así que en mi opinión, no vale la pena.

4 escribir Use the exercises above to help you answer the following questions.

• ¿Cómo es tu pareja ideal?
• Creo que el matrimonio todavía es relevante. Y tú, ¿qué opinas?
• ¿Quieres casarte algún día? ¿Por qué (no)?
• ¿Quieres formar una familia? ¿Por qué (no)?

1 leer   Write out these jumbled sentences correctly. Then match each one to the correct question.

a fanático Soy las policíacas de series un.

b ambiente al porque mejor ir Prefiero cine el es.

c hinchas y mi Chelsea hermana del yo somos Sí.

d me porque relajarme ayuda chifla a Me.

e monto y monopatín Juego en al futbolín.

f iba e balonmano Jugaba pesca de al.

1 ¿Qué sueles hacer en tu tiempo libre?

2 ¿Eres aficionado/a de un equipo?

3 ¿Qué deportes hacías cuando eras más joven?

4 ¿Dónde prefieres ver las películas?

5 ¿Qué tipo de programas te gusta ver?

6 ¿Por qué te gusta escuchar música?

2 escribir   Write your own answers to the questions above. Try to give extra details.

3 leer   Read the news article and answer the questions in English.

Los gustos deportivos del español medio

Según una encuesta reciente, el Real Madrid no es solo el club más premiado de España y de Europa, también es el club con más aficionados en nuestro país (37,9% de los encuestados). Una de cada cuatro personas (25,4%) tiene como su equipo favorito al Barça.

Deportes más seguidos

– Fútbol. Casi la mitad de los encuestados (48%) lo consideran como el deporte que les interesa más.

– Tenis. Los éxitos de Rafa Nadal lo hacen el segundo deporte en interés (21,4%).

– Baloncesto. En el pasado, el deporte de Pau Gasol, Ricky Rubio, etc., ha sido considerado el segundo de España, pero de momento solo ocupa el tercer lugar (17,1%).

Deportes más practicados

– El ciclismo. Montar en bici es el deporte más practicado, con un 18,6%.

– Carrera a pie. El 17,1% de los españoles salen a correr habitualmente.

– Natación. Un 16,1% de los españoles están enganchados a esta práctica sana.

– Fútbol. Aunque verlo es muy popular, solo un 14,7% lo practica.

– Montañismo / Senderismo. Las rutas a pie por el campo son la quinta preferencia para hacer deporte.

1 How do we know that Real Madrid is a successful club?

2 Which is the second most popular football team?

3 What has happened to the popularity of basketball?

4 Which sport is described as healthy?

5 How does the popularity of playing football compare with watching it?

6 Which is the fifth most popular sport?

> To work out the meaning of a new word ask yourself whether it is similar to one you already know. E.g.
>
> *un premio* = a prize   *el club más premiado* = ?
> *una encuesta* = a survey   *los encuestados* = ?

1 leer — Translate the clues into English. Which city is it?
Do some research, if necessary.

1 Se habla español allí.
2 Está al oeste del país.
3 No está en la costa.
4 Está cerca de un lago enorme.
5 Está rodeada de montañas.
6 Perú está a su izquierda.
7 No es la capital oficial del país.
8 Es una de las ciudades más altas del mundo.
9 Su nombre significa lo contrario de 'guerra'.

2 escribir — Write in Spanish about a city of your choice. Ask your partner to guess the city.

3 leer — In the following extract, the writer describes arriving in a new place. Read the text and answer the questions in English.

Donde aprenden a volar las gaviotas by Ana Alcolea (abridged and amended)

Un tren y tres aviones tuve que coger desde Zaragoza hasta Trondheim, que está en el centro de Noruega y es la tercera ciudad del país. Llegué después de pasear todo el día entre nubes y aeropuertos. Me esperaba toda la familia: el padre, que se llamaba Ivar; Inger, la madre, de larga melena rubia, que parecía sacada de un cómic; y Erik, el hijo, que me llevó las maletas hasta el coche. La primera impresión que tuve de Noruega fue que a finales de junio hacía frío, y la segunda que había mucha luz: a pesar de haber llegado a las once y media de la noche, los rayos del sol aún se veían sobre el fiordo.

1 What <u>two</u> details does the writer give about Trondheim?
2 How long did the writer spend travelling?
3 What <u>two</u> pieces of information are we given about Erik?
4 What was the writer's first impression of Norway?
5 Why does the writer comment on the fact that the sun was shining?

⭐ Focus on the details you need to answer the questions and don't get distracted by unfamiliar words in the text.

4 escribir — Write a text about arriving in a new city. Use your imagination, and use exercise 3 as an example.

- Say how you got there
- Say where the city is
- Say how long you spent travelling
- Say who met you on arrival
- Give one detail about each person
- Give your first impression of the city

Tuve que coger… desde… hasta…
que está en…
Llegué después de…
Me esperaba(n)…
El padre, que se llamaba…
La primera impresión que tuve de… fue…

el AVE

🔵 Zona Cultura

AVE (Alta Velocidad Española) es el nombre para los trenes superrápidos españoles que circulan a una velocidad máxima de 310 km/h. El AVE conecta muchas ciudades en España, por ejemplo: Madrid, Barcelona, Sevilla, Málaga, Valencia y Zaragoza.

1 leer Read the texts and choose the correct title for each one.
There is one title too many.

el Día de la Madre   Nochebuena   Diwali

el Día de San Valentín   el Día de Reyes

un roscón de Reyes

1 Ayer decoramos la casa con lámparas de colores y cocinamos platos riquísimos. Fue un día importante porque celebramos el nuevo año hindú.

2 Anoche salí con mi novia y fuimos a un restaurante, donde le regalé un ramo de rosas rojas. Fue muy romántico, pero me costaron 40 euros. ¡Qué timo!

3 Me desperté temprano para abrir mis regalos. Más tarde comimos el roscón de Reyes, un bollo dulce especial que se come el 6 de enero.

4 Me levanté temprano porque quería preparar el desayuno para mi mamá. También le di una tarjeta y un regalo.

2 escribir Write two or three sentences for the title you did not use in exercise 1.
Use your imagination to describe what you did on that day.

3 leer Read the text. Complete each sentence with details from the text.

El 8 de mayo voy a cumplir dieciséis años y no puedo esperar. Cuando era más pequeña, mis padres siempre organizaban una fiesta de disfraces para mi cumpleaños y a veces poníamos un castillo hinchable en el jardín. Generalmente me compraban juguetes o videojuegos. Sin embargo, el año pasado fuimos a la bolera y luego fuimos a un restaurante chino. Mis abuelos me regalaron un reloj, y recibí un montón de tarjetas. Lo pasé fenomenal.

He decidido que este año me gustaría ir de compras por la mañana para gastar el dinero que me regalan. Luego, por la tarde haremos una barbacoa (¡si no llueve, claro!). Pero lo mejor es que mis tíos me van a comprar una entrada para un festival de música. ¡Qué suerte!

Margarita

regalar   to give (a present)

1 When she was younger…
2 Last year she…
3 This year she…

4 escribir Write a text about your birthday. Use exercise 3 as a model.

Describe:
- how you **used to celebrate** it when you were younger (imperfect)
- how you **celebrated** last year (preterite)
- how you **are going to celebrate** this year (future)

1 leer Read the adverts and match each one with the requirements below.

BuscamosEmpleo.com

a
LIMPIO Y PLANCHO
Se ofrece chica para limpieza de casas. Soy trabajadora y responsable. También sé cocinar. He trabajado en varios lugares y tengo carné de conducir y coche propio. Horarios flexibles.

c
CLASES PARTICULARES
Doy clases individuales de francés e inglés (ESO / Bachillerato) adaptadas a las necesidades de cada alumno. He terminado la carrera universitaria y soy profesional y paciente.

b
BUEN NIVEL DE INGLÉS
Busco trabajo como recepcionista o secretaria. Tengo diez años de experiencia y he pasado un año trabajando en Inglaterra. Soy seria, puntual y educada, con muchas ganas de trabajar.

d
DOS CHICOS BUSCAN TRABAJO
Tenemos experiencia en albañilería, pintura, carpintería y fontanería. Hemos hecho un ciclo formativo de grado medio en Construcción y somos trabajadores, dinámicos y honestos.

1 Queremos ampliar la cocina y construir una nueva terraza.
2 Los idiomas son dificilísimos. Siempre saco malas notas.
3 Buscamos chico/a para ayudar con las tareas domésticas.
4 Empresa británica busca administrativo/a con buenas habilidades lingüísticas.

> ⭐ Don't jump to conclusions. Read each text carefully and beware of distractors!

2 escribir Write adverts for these people who are looking for work.

- Almudena: waitress – 3 years' experience – has spent year working in Italy – sociable, honest, organised – has driving licence

- Iván: lifeguard – lots of experience – has spent 6 months working in sports centre – punctual, practical, hardworking – has own car

3 leer Read the text and answer the questions in English.

¿Qué es Sabática?
Sabática es un consultor educativo que promueve programas de trabajo, voluntariado y formación en todo el mundo.

¿Quién puede inscribirse en un proyecto de Sabática?
Para inscribirte en Sabática debes:
- tener entre 18 y 70 años (algunos proyectos requieren una edad mínima de 21–23 años)
- estar en forma y gozar de buena salud
- tener la capacidad de adaptarte e integrarte
- tener nivel intermedio del idioma del destino

¿Qué tipo de gente participa en los programas de voluntariado?
Hay gente de diversas edades con objetivos comunes: ganas de aventura, de hacer un cambio en su vida, de descansar, de aprender, de ayudar a los demás o de conocer nuevas culturas.

¿Es esencial tener experiencia?
Puedes inscribirte en muchos proyectos sin experiencia previa, pero si quieres hacer un voluntariado en sectores específicos como salud, veterinaria, etc., sí es necesario tener títulos o experiencia en el sector.

estar en forma to be in shape

1 What <u>three</u> types of programme does Sabática offer?
2 Where do they take place?
3 What are the age requirements?

4 Which <u>two</u> things must you be able to do?
5 Give <u>four</u> reasons why people join these projects.
6 What is required for health or vet's services?

1 leer · Read the text and note down <u>five</u> details in English. Then complete each recommendation with the correct verb.

El Día de la Tierra

La celebración del Día de la Tierra es el 22 de abril y comenzó en 1970. Hoy es un evento a nivel mundial reconocido en más de 192 países. Nos invita a considerar la situación actual de nuestro hogar, las pequeñas acciones que dañan el medio ambiente y nuestros hábitos de consumo. Todos tenemos en nuestras manos la llave del cambio. Aquí tienes algunas propuestas para celebrar la Tierra y cuidarla.

1 ――――― el coche y usa otras formas de movilidad.
2 ――――― algún deporte al aire libre.
3 ――――― algo en tu casa que ibas a tirar.
4 ――――― una recogida de basura en tu pueblo.
5 ――――― tu ropa usada a una organización caritativa.
6 ――――― vegetariano/a por un día.
7 ――――― una comida con alimentos de cultivo local.
8 ――――― todos los aparatos eléctricos antes de salir de tu casa.

reutiliza · sé · evita · dona

practica · organiza · desenchufa · prepara

2 leer · Read the text and find the Spanish for the words below.

Cómo ser un ciudadano del mundo

El ciudadano del mundo…

- **valora** la diversidad y **defiende** la multiculturalidad.
- **habla** otros idiomas y **aprecia** el acto de viajar para conocer otras culturas.
- **contribuye** a la comunidad, desde lo local a lo global.
- **cuida** los recursos a nivel local y **protege** el medio ambiente.
- **combate** los estereotipos y **reacciona** contra la xenofobia y la intolerancia.
- **aprende** sobre otros países y **se interesa** por las noticias internacionales.
- **apoya** la justicia social.
- **es** una persona con iniciativa propia que **actúa** con independencia de las modas.

1 world citizen
2 at a local level
3 other countries
4 the news
5 own initiative
6 whatever the fashion

3 leer · Read the text again. Translate the verbs in **bold** into English.

4 escribir · Write a declaration about being a world citizen, using verbs in the subjunctive. Rank the statements in order of importance to you.

> Es importante que valoremos la diversidad y defendamos la multiculturalidad.
> Es esencial que…
> Es necesario que…

> ⭐ Look back at p.151 to remind yourself how to form the subjunctive of regular verbs.
> Remember that *ser* is irregular in the subjunctive → *sea*.

Gramática Hay que saber bien

The present tense – regular verbs

What is it and when do I use it?

The present tense is used to talk about the present. You use it to talk about:

- What usually happens — *Normalmente **como** fruta.* — **I** normally **eat** fruit.
- What things are like — *La ciudad **es** grande.* — The city **is** big.
- What is happening now — ***Vivimos** en Liverpool.* — **We live** in Liverpool.

Why is it important?

Verbs are the building blocks of a language. Using the correct tense helps Spanish people to understand what you want to say. For GCSE, you need to be able to use all the different persons of the verb correctly.

Things to watch out for

The verb ending! This tells you who is speaking. You do not need to include *yo* (I) or *tú* (you), etc. before the verb unless you need to add extra emphasis.

How does it work?

To form the present tense you replace the infinitive ending (*–ar*, *–er* or *–ir*) with the present tense endings like this:

	escuchar (to listen)	**comer** (to eat)	**vivir** (to live)
(yo)	escuch**o**	com**o**	viv**o**
(tú)	escuch**as**	com**es**	viv**es**
(él/ella/usted)	escuch**a**	com**e**	viv**e**
(nosotros/as)	escuch**amos**	com**emos**	viv**imos**
(vosotros/as)	escuch**áis**	com**éis**	viv**ís**
(ellos/ellas/ustedes)	escuch**an**	com**en**	viv**en**

Stem-changing verbs

Stem-changing verbs are formed in the same way as regular present tense verbs. However, a vowel change occurs in the stem in some of their forms (I, you (singular), he/she/it/you polite (singular), they/you polite (plural)). They are usually regular in their endings.

There are three common groups.

	o → ue po**d**er (to be able to)	e → ie qu**e**rer (to want)	e → i pe**d**ir (to ask for)
(yo)	**pue**do	**quie**ro	**pi**do
(tú)	**pue**des	**quie**res	**pi**des
(él/ella/usted)	**pue**de	**quie**re	**pi**de
(nosotros/as)	podemos	queremos	pedimos
(vosotros/as)	podéis	queréis	pedís
(ellos/ellas/ustedes)	**pue**den	**quie**ren	**pi**den

Other examples of stem-changing verbs:

u/o → ue
jugar → *j**ue**go*	I play
costar → *c**ue**sta*	it costs
acostarse → *me ac**ue**sto*	I go to bed
dormir → *d**ue**rmen*	they sleep
encontrar → *enc**ue**ntras*	you find
llover → *ll**ue**ve*	it rains
volver → *v**ue**lvo*	I return

e → ie
despertarse → *se desp**ie**rta*	she wakes up
empezar → *emp**ie**zan*	they begin
entender → *ent**ie**ndo*	I understand
nevar → *n**ie**va*	it snows
pensar → *usted p**ie**nsa*	you think
perder → *p**ie**rde*	he loses
preferir → *pref**ie**ro*	I prefer
recomendar → *recom**ie**ndas*	you recommend

e → i
repetir → *rep**i**to*	I repeat
servir → *s**i**rven*	they serve
vestir(se) → *me v**i**sto*	I get dressed

1 Choose the correct form of the verb to complete each sentence.

1 Cuando estoy de vacaciones **come / como / comemos** muchos helados.
2 En verano mis amigos y yo **nadamos / nadan / nadas** en el mar.
3 A veces mi hermano **leo / lees / lee** novelas o manda correos.
4 ¿Vosotros nunca **descargas / descargan / descargáis** música?
5 Todos los días, me relajo y **tocamos / tocáis / toco** la guitarra.
6 Mi familia **vivís / vive / viven** en el noroeste de Inglaterra.
7 Mi amigo **prefiere / prefieren / preferimos** ir a la playa.
8 ¿Y tú? ¿Qué deportes **practica / practicas / practicamos** en el colegio?
9 ¿Cuánto **cuestan / cuesto / cuesta** una habitación individual con desayuno incluido?

2 Complete the sentence with the correct form of the verb. Then translate each sentence into English.

1 En el instituto   estudiar varias asignaturas y no tienes que llevar uniforme. (*poder*)
2 Muchas personas   unos vaqueros y una camiseta. (*llevar*)
3 Las clases   a las nueve y   a las tres y media. (*empezar / terminar*)
4 Me gustan las ciencias, pero   las matemáticas. (*preferir*)
5 Mi amigo estudia historia porque   aprender más del pasado. (*querer*)
6 La profesora de inglés   muy bien y   un buen ambiente de trabajo. (*enseñar / crear*)
7 Los alumnos de mi colegio   mucho durante las vacaciones. (*estudiar*)
8 Mis amigos y yo   en varias actividades extraescolares. (*participar*)
9 Desafortunadamente, hay alumnos que   intimidación en mi insti. (*sufrir*)

3 Translate these sentences into Spanish.

1 Every year we spend the summer holidays in Spain.
2 I read a lot and I sometimes download videos.
3 We do sport every day and sometimes we listen to music.
4 How much does a double room cost?
5 I would like to change rooms because the shower does not work.
6 We need three towels and a hairdryer.
7 Juan plays an instrument at school but his brother prefers to play football.
8 Classes last forty minutes and break lasts fifteen minutes.
9 My friends wear grey trousers, a white shirt and a black jacket at school.

The present tense – irregular verbs

What are they and when do I use them?
Irregular verbs do not follow the normal patterns of regular –ar, –er and –ir verbs. Many of the most common and most useful verbs in Spanish are irregular.

Why are they important?
You can't speak a language without knowing a wide range of verbs, and some of the most important verbs like 'to be', 'to have', 'to do' and 'to go' are irregular. For your GCSE, you need to use all parts of these verbs accurately.

Things to watch out for
You must learn irregular verbs by heart. Sometimes, just the **yo** form is irregular.

How does it work?
These verbs are only irregular in the 'I' form (the first person)

conducir → conduzco	I drive	hacer → hago	I make/do	salir → salgo	I go out
conocer → conozco	I know	poner → pongo	I put	traer → traigo	I bring
dar → doy	I give	saber → sé	I know		

Other verbs are more irregular.

	ser (to be)	estar (to be)	tener (to have)	ir (to go)
(yo)	soy	estoy	tengo	voy
(tú)	eres	estás	tienes	vas
(él/ella/usted)	es	está	tiene	va
(nosotros/as)	somos	estamos	tenemos	vamos
(vosotros/as)	sois	estáis	tenéis	vais
(ellos/ellas/ustedes)	son	están	tienen	van

Look at the verb tables on page 237 for more irregular present tense verbs.

Look at the verb tables on page 237 for more irregular present tense verbs.

Preparados

1 Complete these sentences with the yo (I) form of the verb.

1 Normalmente   a las ocho. (salir)
2   a toda la clase. (conocer)
3 Siempre   que llevar uniforme. (tener)
4   mucho de los edificios de mi colegio. (saber)
5 A veces   deportes acuáticos con mi familia. (hacer)
6 De vez en cuando   un paseo. (dar)

Listos

2 Complete these sentences with the correct form of ser, estar, tener or ir. Then translate each sentence into English.

1 Mi amiga   adicta a la tele y por lo tanto no practica mucho deporte.
2 El clima   muy soleado en verano pero a veces   nublado.
3 Durante las vacaciones mis amigos y yo   al cine.
4   que llevar uniforme pero no nos gusta.
5 El colegio   un biblioteca grande y tres pistas de tenis.
6 Salgo de casa a las ocho y   al colegio andando.

¡Ya!

3 Translate the text into Spanish.

In my school we all have to wear uniform. The worse thing it that I have to wear a brown skirt. I think it is really ugly. Every day my brother and I go to school on the bus. The journey is easy and we normally leave the house at eight o'clock. We have six classes a day and, for me, the best subject is Spanish as my teacher is fun. The rules in my school are too strict and some pupils are a bad influence.

The present tense – reflexive verbs

What are they and when do I use them?
Reflexive verbs are verbs that include a reflexive pronoun. They describe actions that we do to ourselves.

Why are they important?
They are useful verbs when describing your relationships with others and your daily routine.

Things to watch out for
Check you are using the correct reflexive pronoun as well as the correct ending.

How does it work?
Reflexive verbs are formed in the same way as regular present tense verbs but they include a reflexive pronoun. In the infinitive the pronoun is shown at the end of the verb, *levantarse*. In the present tense the pronoun precedes the verb and changes according to the person (*me levanto*).

	levantarse (to get up)	divertirse (to enjoy oneself)	llevarse con (to get on with)
(yo)	**me** levanto	**me** div**ie**rto	**me** llevo
(tú)	**te** levantas	**te** div**ie**rtes	**te** llevas
(él/ella/usted)	**se** levanta	**se** div**ie**rte	**se** lleva
(nosotros/as)	**nos** levantamos	**nos** divertimos	**nos** llevamos
(vosotros/as)	**os** levantáis	**os** divertís	**os** lleváis
(ellos/ellas/ustedes)	**se** levantan	**se** div**ie**rten	**se** llevan

Preparados

1 Complete these sentences with the correct form of the verb.

  1 _____ a las siete y media. (*ducharse, yo*)
  2 Normalmente _____ bien con mi padre. (*llevarse, yo*)
  3 Mi hermano y yo _____ mucho en casa. (*divertirse, nosotros*)
  4 ¿_____ con tus hermanos o con tus padres? (*pelearse, tú*)
  5 Mis padres _____ bien y se apoyan en todo. (*llevarse, ellos*)

Listos

2 Complete the second and third rows of the table with the 'you' form and the 'he/she' form of the underlined verbs.

yo	<u>Me levanto</u> todos los días y me digo que mi vida va a cambiar. <u>Pienso</u> que <u>soy</u> una persona simpática. <u>Me llevo</u> muy bien con mucha gente y <u>me divierto</u> cuando <u>puedo</u>.
tú	_____ todos los días y te dices que tu vida va a cambiar. _____ que _____ una persona simpática. _____ muy bien con mucha gente y _____ cuando _____.
él/ella	_____ todos los días y se dice que su vida va a cambiar. _____ que _____ una persona simpática. _____ muy bien con mucha gente y _____ cuando _____.

¡Ya!

3 Complete these sentences with the correct form of the verb.

  1 Mi amigo y yo _____ fenomenal porque _____ mucho en común. (*llevarse / tener*)
  2 Siempre _____ con mi padre porque nos interesan los deportes. (*divertirse*)
  3 Mis hermanos _____ en casa todos los días, pero siempre _____ en el instituto. (*pelearse / apoyarse*)
  4 _____ mal con mi profesor de religión porque él no _____ buen sentido de humor. (*llevarse / tener*)
  5 Siempre _____ muy tarde los fines de semana porque no tengo sueño. (*acostarse*)
  6 Normalmente mi hermana _____ primero y _____ en la cocina mientras yo _____. (*ducharse / desayunar / vestirse*)

Gramática Hay que saber bien

The preterite tense

What is it and when do I use it?
The preterite tense is sometimes known as the 'simple past'. It is used to talk about completed actions in the past.

Fui a la playa.   **I went** to the beach.
Viajó en coche.   **He travelled** by car.

Why is it important?
You often want to say what you or someone else did. Without the preterite tense you could not tell a story in Spanish. It is a key tense to learn and understand for GCSE.

Things to watch out for
● Some forms of regular verbs in the preterite take an accent. Be careful that you use accents correctly as using them incorrectly can change the meaning of a word.

    escuch**o** (I listen), but escuch**ó** (he listened)

● Irregular verbs don't take accents in the preterite.

● The verbs *ir* and *ser* are the same in the preterite.

How does it work?
Regular preterite verbs
The preterite tense is formed by taking the infinitive of a verb, removing the infinitive endings (*–ar*, *–er* or *–ir*), and then adding the following preterite endings. Note that *–er* and *–ir* verbs take the same endings in the preterite.

	visitar (to visit)	**comer** (to eat)	**salir** (to go out)
(yo)	visit**é**	com**í**	sal**í**
(tú)	visit**aste**	com**iste**	sal**iste**
(él/ella/usted)	visit**ó**	com**ió**	sal**ió**
(nosotros/as)	visit**amos**	com**imos**	sal**imos**
(vosotros/as)	visit**asteis**	com**isteis**	sal**isteis**
(ellos/ellas/ustedes)	visit**aron**	com**ieron**	sal**ieron**

● When you are using stem-changing verbs make sure you have the correct infinitive:

    encuentro (I find) ➔ encontrar (to find) ➔ encontré (I found)

Irregular preterite verbs
● The most common irregular verbs are:

	ser/ir (to be/to go)	**ver** (to see)	**hacer** (to do/make)	**tener** (to have)
(yo)	fui	vi	hice	tuve
(tú)	fuiste	viste	hiciste	tuviste
(él/ella/usted)	fue	vio	hizo	tuvo
(nosotros/as)	fuimos	vimos	hicimos	tuvimos
(vosotros/as)	fuisteis	visteis	hicisteis	tuvisteis
(ellos/ellas/ustedes)	fueron	vieron	hicieron	tuvieron

● Other irregular preterite verbs include:

andar	to walk	*poner*	to put
dar	to give	*querer*	to want
decir	to say	*saber*	to know
estar	to be	*traer*	to bring
poder	to be able to	*venir*	to come

Look at the verb tables on page 237 for more irregular preterite tense verbs.

- Some preterite verbs have **irregular spellings** just in the first person singular (*yo*). For example:

sacar	→ sa**qu**é	I got/took	empezar	→ empe**c**é	I started
tocar	→ to**qu**é	I played	jugar	→ ju**gu**é	I played
cruzar	→ cru**c**é	I crossed	llegar	→ lle**gu**é	I arrived

- Some preterite verbs have irregular spellings in the third person singular (él/ella/usted) and third person plural (ellos/ellas/ustedes):

caer → ca**y**ó, ca**y**eron   he/she fell, they fell   leer → le**y**ó, le**y**eron   he/she read, they read

Preparados

1 **Look at the list of phrases and decide if the verbs are in the present or the preterite tense. Then translate each sentence into English.**

1 Desayuno a las diez.
2 Fuimos al museo antes de comer.
3 Hace mucho sol aquí.
4 Mi amigo decidió comprar unos recuerdos.
5 Practiqué natación en el mar cerca de mi casa.

6 Nunca hacéis vuestros deberes.
7 Observé a la gente en el restaurante.
8 En el colegio comemos a las doce y media.
9 Anoche mis amigos fueron al cine.
10 Silvia jugó al fútbol el sábado.

Listos

2 **Write the correct form of the verb in brackets in the preterite. Then translate each sentence into English.**

1 La semana pasada yo   un libro muy bueno. *(leer)*
2 Ayer yo   un reloj y luego fui al cine. *(comprar)*
3 La semana pasada mi amiga   paella. *(comer)*
4 Mis amigos   una fiesta para celebrar sus cumpleaños. *(hacer)*
5 ¿Cuándo   a la piscina? Ayer no te vi. *(ir)*
6 Mis vacaciones   increíbles. *(ser)*
7 Ayer mis amigos y yo no   nada que hacer. *(tener)*
8 Anteayer fui en metro al centro y   una obra de teatro. *(ver)*
9 Mi hermano   ocho asignaturas en el colegio. *(estudiar)*
10 Mi madre   a Inglaterra en avión. *(volver)*

¡Ya!

3 **Write the following story in the past. Change all the present tense verbs into the preterite tense. Then translate the text into English.**

¡Un buen día!

Por la mañana **1** *voy* a la bolera y **2** *juego* a los bolos con mi familia. **3** *Bebemos* refrescos pero no **4** *comemos* nada. Mis padres me **5** *dan* cuatro euros para gastar el fin de semana y **6** *es* suficiente para salir por la tarde. **7** *Llamo* a mi amiga y **8** *vamos* al centro comercial para ir de compras. En la tienda de ropa no **9** *veo* nada bonito pero mi amiga **10** *compra* una gorra. **11** *Volvemos* a casa para escuchar música y **12** *descansamos* un poco. Por la noche, **13** *salgo* y **14** *voy* al cine con mi novio pero no **15** *nos gusta* la película. Después yo **16** *vuelvo* a casa para cenar. Mis hermanos **17** *juegan* con el ordenador, pero yo **18** *hago* mis deberes. Finalmente, **19** *leo* un poco y **20** *mando* mensajes a mi novio.

Gramática Hay que saber bien

The imperfect tense

What is it and when do I use it?

The imperfect tense is another way of talking about the past. It is used in Spanish for:

- Descriptions in the past (what someone or something was like or was doing):
  *En mi escuela primaria, las instalaciones **eran** mejores.*
  In my primary school, the facilities **were** better.

- Repeated actions in the past:
  ***Tenía** clases de gimnasia cada semana.*   **I had** gymnastics classes every week.

- What people used to do and what things used to be like:
  *Antes **jugábamos** al fútbol, pero ahora preferimos hacer kárate.*
  Before **we used to** play football, but now we prefer to do karate.

Why is it important?

To tell a story in the past successfully you need to be able to use the imperfect for descriptions and repeated actions. The imperfect tense is important for GCSE because you need to describe different types of past events to be successful. If you can combine the imperfect with the preterite tense correctly, you will create more complex and detailed phrases.

Things to watch out for

You use the **preterite tense** for single events in the past and the **imperfect tense** for repeated actions and things you used to do in the past.

How does it work?

- The imperfect tense is formed by taking the infinitive of a verb, removing the infinitive endings (*–ar*, *–er*, *–ir*) and then adding the following endings. Note that *–er* and *–ir* verbs take the same endings in the imperfect.

	jugar (to play)	**hacer** (to do/make)	**vivir** (to live)
(yo)	jug**aba**	hac**ía**	viv**ía**
(tú)	jug**abas**	hac**ías**	viv**ías**
(él/ella/usted)	jug**aba**	hac**ía**	viv**ía**
(nosotros/as)	jug**ábamos**	hac**íamos**	viv**íamos**
(vosotros/as)	jug**abais**	hac**íais**	viv**íais**
(ellos/ellas/ustedes)	jug**aban**	hac**ían**	viv**ían**

- There are three verbs that are irregular in the imperfect tense.

	ir (to go)	**ser** (to be)	**ver** (to see)
(yo)	**iba**	**era**	**veía**
(tú)	**ibas**	**eras**	**veías**
(él/ella/usted)	**iba**	**era**	**veía**
(nosotros/as)	**íbamos**	**éramos**	**veíamos**
(vosotros/as)	**ibais**	**erais**	**veíais**
(ellos/ellas/ustedes)	**iban**	**eran**	**veían**

- The imperfect tense of ***hay*** (there is) is ***había*** (there was/were) and the preterite is ***hubo*** (there was/were). *Había* is very useful for describing things and saying what things used to be like and *hubo* is used for completed actions and specific past events.

  *En el hotel **había** una piscina cubierta.*   In the hotel **there was** an indoor pool.
  *El fin de semana pasado **hubo** un accidente*   Last weekend **there was** an accident
  y llegué tarde al aeropuerto.   and I arrived at the airport late.

1 Translate the sentences into English. Write the correct letters next to each sentence to explain why the imperfect is required – D (descriptions in the past), RA (repeated action in the past) or UT ('used to' phrase).

1 La pensión estaba en las afueras de la ciudad.
2 Cada sábado montaba a caballo con mis amigos.
3 Mi escuela primaria era muy pequeña y no había aulas de informática.
4 Cuando tenía doce años, era aficionado de Real Madrid.
5 Antes mi hermano no era muy deportista y nunca jugaba al baloncesto.
6 Cuando era más pequeña hacía deportes acuáticos con mi familia.
7 El albergue juvenil estaba cerca del centro de la ciudad pero no tenía piscina.
8 En el verano íbamos a la playa todos los días.
9 Lo bueno del pueblo era que tenía muchos espacios verdes y era muy tranquilo.
10 La gente era muy simpática y la comida estaba muy buena.

2 Complete the sentences with the correct form of the imperfect tense. Translate each sentence into English.

1 Antes mi colegio no **teníamos / tenía / tener** un patio grande y no **había / hay / hubo** un teatro pero ahora las instalaciones son muy buenas.
2 Cuando mi padre **tenías / tenía / tenían** quince años **iba / íbamos / ir** al colegio en moto y **jugaba / juega / jugaban** al fútbol todos los días.
3 El hotel **es / era / había** muy grande y **tiene / teníais / tenía** una piscina bonita, pero no **hay / había / era** ni restaurante ni cafetería.
4 El año pasado mis amigos y yo **usábamos / usamos / usaban** nuestros móviles demasiado y siempre **chateábamos / chateo / chateamos** durante muchas horas.
5 ¿Qué **hacías / hacía / hacían** usted cuando **tuviste / tenía / tiene** nueve años?
6 En mi escuela primaria lo malo **eran / éramos / era** que **hay / había / habíamos** poco espacio pero las clases **eran / era / erais** más cortas.
7 Antes yo **era / soy / fui** aficionado del Atlético de Bilbao y mis amigos y yo **iba / íbamos / vamos** a casi todos los partidos pero ahora no me gusta nada el fútbol.
8 Antes mi madre **fuma / fumaba / fumaban** mucho para quitar el estrés, pero ya no fuma nunca.
9 Durante mis prácticas laborales yo **cogía / cogías / cogían** el tren cada día y **llevábamos / llevabais / llevaba** ropa elegante.
10 Los clientes **éramos / era / eran** bastante maleducados pero mi jefe **éramos / era / eran** muy simpático.

3 Complete the sentences with either the preterite or imperfect tense.

1 Fui de vacaciones a España y el hotel donde nos quedamos   bastante lujoso. *(ser)*
2 Ayer mi madre   recuerdos pero yo   en el hotel. *(comprar, descansar)*
3 Antes Juan   en una cafetería todos los sábados, pero ahora quiere ser peluquero. *(trabajar)*
4 Mis padres y yo   al parque para jugar al tenis, pero   mucho y por lo tanto   un desastre. *(ir, llover, ser)*
5 Mi amiga   a Francia de vacaciones. El camping   cerca de la playa y   muy barato y bastante acogedor. *(ir, estar, ser)*
6 Siempre   mucha gente en la playa porque era agosto. *(haber)*
7 Me dijeron que mi abuelo era muy alto y   el pelo negro como yo. *(tener)*
8 Hicimos nuestros deberes el domingo y después   juntas. *(salir)*
9 Mi hermano   al rugby cada semana pero ahora tiene que estudiar mucho. *(jugar)*
10 Ya no hago mucho deporte, pero antes   baile, gimnasia y equitación cada semana. *(hacer)*

Gramática Hay que saber bien

The future tense

The near future tense

What is it and when do I use it?

The near future is used to describe what **is going to happen** (for example, tonight, tomorrow, next week, etc.).
It is the most common tense in Spanish for describing future plans.

Voy a practicar el español.	**I am going to practise** Spanish.
Vamos a ir de excursión.	**We are going to go** on a trip.

Why is it important?

You often want to say what you or someone else is going to do. You also need to be able to understand and refer to future events for your GCSE.

Things to watch out for

Don't forget to use the preposition **a** when using the near future.

How does it work?

To form the near future, you need:

ir (in the present tense) + **a** + **infinitive**

(yo)	voy		comer
(tú)	vas		jugar
(él/ella/usted)	va	a	tener
(nosotros/as)	vamos		salir
(vosotros/as)	vais		comprar
(ellos/ellas/ustedes)	van		hacer

The future tense

What is it and when do I use it?

The future tense is used to describe what **will happen** in the future.

Mañana **iremos** al centro comercial.	Tomorrow **we will go** to the shopping centre.

Why is it important?

You often want to say what you or someone else will do. Using two types of future tense will add variety and complexity to your texts.

Things to watch out for

Don't forget to include the accents on future tense verb endings.

How does it work?

To form the future tense of most verbs, you take the infinitive of the verb and add the following endings (these are the same for –ar, –er and –ir verbs):

(yo)	ser**é**
(tú)	ser**ás**
(él/ella/usted)	ser**á**
(nosotros/as)	ser**emos**
(vosotros/as)	ser**éis**
(ellos/ellas/ustedes)	ser**án**

- The following verbs have irregular stems in the future tense. You need to use these stems instead of the infinitive, but the endings stay the same as for regular verbs.

decir	to say	→ **dir**é, **dir**ás, …
hacer	to do/make	→ **har**é, **har**ás, …
poder	to be able to	→ **podr**é, **podr**ás, …
poner	to put	→ **pondr**é, **pondr**ás, …
querer	to want	→ **querr**é, **querr**ás, …
saber	to know	→ **sabr**é, **sabr**ás, …
salir	to leave/go out	→ **saldr**é, **saldr**ás, …
tener	to have	→ **tendr**é, **tendr**ás, …
venir	to come	→ **vendr**é, **vendr**ás, …

- The future tense of *haber* is **habrá** (there will be).

1 Rewrite the Spanish sentence to include the missing part of the near future tense.

1 I am going to attend lessons. – Voy asistir a clases.
2 We are going to wear casual clothes. – Vamos a ropa de calle.
3 What are you going to do? – ¿Qué a hacer?
4 She is going to arrive on Thursday. – Va llegar el jueves.
5 My family is going to travel by car. – Mi familia va a en coche.
6 In the morning they are going to do a guided tour. – Por la mañana a hacer una visita guiada.
7 My brother is going to participate in a tournament. – Mi hermano a participar en un torneo.
8 Tomorrow they are going to do ice skating. – Mañana van a patinaje sobre hielo.
9 I'm going to go to France. – Voy ir a Francia.
10 Are you going to work as a volunteer? – ¿Vas a como voluntario?
11 My friends are going to visit other cities. – Mis amigos a visitar otras ciudades.
12 Today you are all going to play football. – Hoy vosotros a jugar al fútbol.

2 Find all of the near future verbs in this blog and change them into the future tense. Watch out for the irregular ones! Then translate the text into English.

¿Qué vas a hacer mañana? Yo voy a hacer muchas cosas porque mis primos van a venir a visitarnos. Por la mañana mis primos y yo vamos a ir al centro de la ciudad. Mis primos van a comprar unas camisetas y yo voy a comprar unos zapatos. Luego mis padres nos van a llevar a la playa en coche. Mi prima María no va a nadar porque odia el mar, pero mi primo José va a hacer windsurf conmigo. Mis padres van a tomar el sol y van a descansar. Después vamos a pasear por el casco viejo de la ciudad y vamos a ir a un restaurante barato donde se puede comer una gran variedad de marisco.

3 Complete the conversation with the correct future tense of one of the verbs in the box:

A: ¿Qué haremos mañana?
B: Pues, primero tú y yo **1**   al teleférico porque desde allí las vistas son increíbles.
A: ¡Qué guay? ¿Y nosotros qué **2**   después?
B: Depende del tiempo. Si hace sol y no llueve, tú **3**   fotos de Barcelona y luego nosotros **4**   un café en la terraza.
A: ¿A qué hora nosotros **5**   otra vez en teleférico?
B: A las once, más o menos. Después yo **6**   que ir a mi clase de tenis pero tú **7**   visitar unos monumentos.
A: De acuerdo, ¿Y nosotros dónde **8**   ? ¿En un restaurante o en tu casa?
B: Pues si no estamos demasiado cansados, nosotros **9**   a mi restaurante favorito para comer tapas, pero está un poco lejos del centro, y por eso **10**   en metro. Finalmente, a las cinco mis amigos **11**   a mi casa para jugar a los videojuegos.
A: ¡Buena idea! ¡El día **12**   fantástico!

sacar
ir
poder
almorzar
bajar
hacer
tener
venir
ser
tomar
viajar
subir

Gramática Hay que saber bien
The present continuous tense

What is it and when do I use it?
The present continuous is used to say what you are doing at the moment. It is made up of two parts: the present tense of **estar** and the present participle.

¿Qué estás haciendo?	What **are you doing**?
Estoy pensando en salir.	**I am thinking** about going out.

Why is it important?
For GCSE, it is important to be able to use this form of the present tense to help give your writing or speaking more grammatical variety. You also need to recognise and understand this tense in listening or reading texts.

Things to watch out for
Sometimes in English, we use the present participle when in Spanish you need to use an infinitive.

Cantar es divertido.	**Singing** is fun.
Le gusta nadar.	She likes **swimming**.

How does it work?
Take the present tense of **estar** and add the present participle (the '–ing' form). To form the present participle, take the infinitive of the verb, remove the –ar, –er or –ir and add the endings: **–ando, –iendo, –iendo**.

Estamos viendo la tele.   **We are watching** TV.

(yo)	estoy		
(tú)	estás		hablando
(él/ella/usted)	está	+	comiendo
(nosotros/as)	estamos		saliendo
(vosotros/as)	estáis		
(ellos/ellas/ustedes)	están		

- Stem changing –ir verbs (but not –ar or –er verbs) change their spellings for the present participle:

  o → u *dormir*   to sleep → *durmiendo* sleeping
  e → i *pedir*   to ask   → *pidiendo* asking

- Some **irregular present participles** include:

leer	to read	→ *leyendo*	reading	*poder*	to be able to	→ *pudiendo*	being able to
oír	to hear	→ *oyendo*	hearing	*reír*	to laugh	→ *riendo*	laughing

Preparados

1 Write the present continuous for each of these verbs.

1 (yo) jugar
2 (vosotros) repasar
3 (ustedes) beber
4 (tú) hacer
5 (nosotras) escribir
6 (él) dormir

Listos

2 Use your imagination and a verb from the box to create an answer in the present continuous for each of the questions.

comer	dormir	jugar	andar	navegar	leer

1 ¿Qué está haciendo la chica?
2 ¿Qué está haciendo Lucía?
3 ¿Qué están haciendo Pepe y Paco?
4 ¿Qué estás haciendo?
5 ¿Qué estamos haciendo?
6 ¿Qué está haciendo Juan?

¡Ya!

3 Translate the sentences into Spanish.

1 What are you doing right now?
2 I am listening to music and my friend is watching a film.
3 We are not doing anything special.
4 They are reading some comics on the bus.
5 He is writing an email and having a coffee in a café.
6 Are you all revising for the exams?

The perfect tense

What is it and when do I use it?
The perfect tense is used to talk about what you **have done**.

He descargado unas canciones nuevas.   **I have downloaded** some new songs.

Things to watch out for
When you want to say that someone has **just** done something you do not use the perfect tense. You use the present tense of the verb **acabar** (a regular –ar verb) followed by the preposition **de**.

Acabamos de comer pizza.   **We have just** eaten pizza.

How does it work?
The perfect tense is formed by using the verb **haber** in the present tense and the past participle of the verb. The past participle is formed by taking the infinitive, removing the –ar, –er or –ir and adding the endings: **–ado**, **–ido**, **–ido**.

(yo)	he		
(tú)	has		
(él/ella/usted)	ha	+	hablado
(nosotros/as)	hemos		comido
(vosotros/as)	habéis		salido
(ellos/ellas/ustedes)	han		

Some common **irregular past participles** are:

abrir	to open	→	abierto	opened		poner	to put	→	puesto	put
decir	to say	→	dicho	said		romper	to break	→	roto	broken
escribir	to write	→	escrito	written		ver	to see	→	visto	seen
hacer	to do/make	→	hecho	done/made		volver	to return	→	vuelto	returned
morir	to die	→	muerto	died						

1 Put the words in the correct order for each sentence.

1 Delia / el / descargado / ha / videojuego
2 el / he / iPad / roto
3 ha / Pablo / comedia / estupenda / visto / una
4 hemos / palomitas / comido / muchas
5 en / mi / cine / perdido / he / móvil / el
6 emocionantes / leído / han / libros / muchos

2 Write about what you have done and what you have never done.

descargar música	montar a caballo	hacer remo	romperse el brazo	leer periódicos
ver un buen culebrón	gastar mi paga en unas zapatillas de marca		asistir a un espectáculo de baile	

1 …frecuentemente.
2 …recientemente.
3 …muchas veces.
4 …pocas veces.
5 …una vez.
6 No…nunca.

3 Write about what Pedro and Maite have done today. Change the verbs in brackets into the perfect tense.

Me llamo Pedro y hoy mi amiga Maite y yo **1** (hacer) muchas cosas. Primero, Maite **2** (compartir) muchas fotos en Instagram y yo **3** (descargar) varias canciones nuevas. Luego Maite y yo **4** (comprar) por Internet dos entradas para ver la última peli de Robert Pattinson esta noche. También yo **5** (ver) un reality mientras Maite **6** (escribir) su blog. Mis hermanos **7** (jugar) al ping-pong y **8** (hacer) ciclismo.

Gramática Hay que saber bien

The conditional

What is it and when do I use it?

The conditional tense is used to describe what you **would** do in the future.

En mi ciudad **mejoraría** el sistema de transporte.   In my city **I would improve** the transport system.

Why is it important?

You need the conditional to talk successfully about your future plans and ideas.

Things to watch out for

Don't confuse conditional verbs with imperfect verbs. The conditional is formed by using the future stem and adding the imperfect endings for –er/–ir verbs.

How does it work?

The conditional tense is formed in the same way as the future tense. You take the infinitive of the verb and add the following endings (these are the same for –ar, –er and –ir verbs):

	ser (to be)
(yo)	ser**ía**
(tú)	ser**ías**
(él/ella/usted)	ser**ía**
(nosotros/as)	ser**íamos**
(vosotros/as)	ser**íais**
(ellos/ellas/ustedes)	ser**ían**

- The verbs which have irregular stems in the future also have irregular stems in the conditional tense. For example:

  hacer   (to do/make) → **har**ía, **har**ías, …   (would do/make)
  poder   (to be able to) → **podr**ía, **podr**ías, …   (would be able to)
  tener   (to have)   → **tendr**ía, **tendr**ías, … (would have)

  Other verbs which have irregular stems in the future are listed on page 237.

- The conditional tense of haber is **habría** (there would be).

- The conditional tense can be used to express future ideas by using the verb **gustar** followed by an infinitive:

  En el futuro, **me gustaría** hablar más idiomas.   In the future, **I would like** to speak more languages.

- The conditional tense of **poder** is used to express the notion of something that you could do.

  Podríamos ir al cine.   **We could** go to the cinema.

- The conditional tense of **deber** is used to express the notion of something that you should do.

  Deberíamos reciclar el plástico y el vidrio.   **We should** recycle plastic and glass.

Preparados

1 Read these sentences about making an ideal city. Complete with the correct conditional tense.

1 ¿Qué es lo que _____ de tu ciudad? *(cambiar)*

2 Lo único que yo _____ las afueras.
(cambiar, ser)

3 Mis padres _____ algunos edificios porque creen que son muy feos. *(renovar)*

4 En un mundo ideal, mi ciudad no _____ tanta contaminación. *(tener)*

5 Mis amigos y yo _____ más áreas de ocio en nuestra zona. *(poner)*

6 Yo sé que mi abuelo _____ más el ruido y le reducir el tráfico. *(controlar, gustar)*

7 ¿Qué _____ tú para mejorar la ciudad? *(hacer)*

8 Yo _____ más árboles en el centro e _____ más zonas peatonales. *(plantar, introducir)*

9 ¡Mis hermanos _____ una pista de monopatín cerca de nuestra casa! *(construir)*

10 Mi profesor de geografía _____ en el turismo rural y _____ las zonas deterioradas. *(invertir, renovar)*

Listos

2 What would you do if you had the time? Translate these examples into Spanish.

1 My brother would play football a lot more.

2 My friends would swim in the sea every day.

3 I would look for and I would download more music.

4 Manuel would go to the cinema every Sunday.

5 Rosa would watch television every evening.

6 My brother would go to a concert every weekend.

7 Would you do water sports?

8 You would all chat more and send more messages.

9 I would visit a museum every month.

10 My friends would read more books.

¡Ya!

3 Give advice to your friends. What would you do in their position? Use as many of the verbs in the box as you can.

| estudiar   practicar   comprar   descansar   hacer   jugar   salir   dejar |

1 Maite fuma demasiado.

2 Juan no asiste a ningún club.

3 Mohamed juega demasiados videojuegos.

4 Alfonso nunca hace ningún deporte.

5 Alina lleva una vida frenética.

6 Marisol nunca lee.

7 Elena usa las redes sociales demasiado.

8 Iker es teleadicto.

9 Belén no habla con sus padres.

10 Roberto no tiene novia.

Gramática Hay que saber bien

Nouns and articles

Nouns

What are they and when do I use them?
Nouns are words that name things, people and ideas. You use them all the time!

How do they work?
In Spanish each noun has a gender: masculine or feminine.
Generally, nouns ending in **–o** are masculine (**el** libro) and those ending in **–a** are feminine (**la** casa). However, there are exceptions which you need to learn, for example: el día, el problema, la mano, la foto, etc.

- There are some other endings that are generally either masculine or feminine.

  Masculine: nouns ending in: **–or** (actor, pintor), **–ón** (peatón, salchichón) and **–és** (escocés, estrés).

  Feminine: nouns ending in: **–ción** (tradición, educación), **–dad** and **–tad** (ciudad, libertad).

- To form the plural of nouns you normally add:
  –s to words ending in a vowel   **–es** to words ending in a consonant
  bolígrafo pen   →   bolígrafo**s**   pens   actor   actor   →   actor**es**   actors

- Nouns which end in **–z** in the singular, end in **–ces** in the plural.

  vez   time   →   veces   times

Articles

What are they and when do I use them?
Articles are used with nouns. There are definite articles **el / la / los / las** (the) and indefinite articles **un / una** (a, an) and **unos / unas** (some).

How do they work?
In Spanish the **definite article** changes according to whether the noun is masculine or feminine, singular or plural.
   el piso   →   **los** pisos   **la** casa   →   **las** casas

- The definite article is sometimes used in Spanish where we don't use it in English. You need to use it to:

  Talk about languages (except when the language comes straight after a verb):
    El inglés es fácil.   English is easy.   Ella habla francés.   She can speak French.

  Refer to school subjects (except when the subject comes straight after a verb):
    La geografía es genial.   Geography is great.   Estudio religión.   I study religion.

  Express an opinion, for example, me gusta or me encanta:
    Me gusta el pescado.   I like fish.   Las telenovelas son aburridas.   Soap operas are boring.

  Refer to days of the week and mean 'on…'
    Voy al cine el sábado.   I am going to the cinema on Saturday.

The **indefinite article** also changes according to whether the noun is masculine or feminine, singular or plural.
  un piso   a flat   →   un**os** pisos   some flats
  un**a** casa   a house   →   un**as** casas   some houses

- The indefinite article is sometimes not used in Spanish where we do use it in English. You do **not** need to use it when:

  You talk about jobs:
    Soy médico.   I am a doctor.
  It comes after the verb **tener** in negative sentences:
    No tengo coche.   I don't have a car.
  It comes after **sin** or **con**:
    Salí con gorra.   I went out with a cap on.
    Sin duda.   Without a doubt.

1 Write the plural form for each of the nouns and the correct article.

1 película (some)

2 ordenador (the)

3 montaña (the)

4 ciudad (some)

5 móvil (the)

6 recuerdo (some)

7 habitación (the)

8 secador (the)

9 lugar (some)

10 noche (the)

2 Complete these sentences with the correct article.

1 Vivo en   norte de Gales.

2 Veo   tele los sábados.

3 Nos encanta usar   ordenador.

4   piscinas del hotel son estupendas.

5 ¿Cuánto cuesta   habitación doble?

6 El parador tiene   gimnasio pequeño y   cafetería bonita.

7   aire acondicionado no funciona y necesito   secador.

8 Me interesan   dibujo,   matemáticas y   religión.

9 En mi insti hay   salón de actos,   laboratorios y   biblioteca.

10 Nos quedamos en   pensión en   centro de   ciudad.

3 Complete these sentences with the correct article. Be careful, you may not need to use one. Then translate each sentence into English.

1 Prefiero veranear en   extranjero.

2 Mi madre no habla   francés ni   alemán.

3 Viajé en   autocar y en   barco.

4 Creo que   inglés es muy difícil.

5 Quisiera reservar   habitación con   baño.

6 Estudio   matemáticas,   español y   geografía.

7   química es más difícil que   informática.

8 En mi insti no hay   pistas de tenis ni   campos de fútbol.

9 Mi novia va a   concierto   viernes.

10   uniforme limita   individualidad, pero es   regla más importante del insti.

What are they and when do I use them?

Adjectives are describing words. You use them to describe a noun, a person or thing.

Why are they important?

Adjectives are important to describe things you are talking or writing about. They make your work more interesting and personal. Make sure you can use a variety of adjectives accurately.

Things to watch out for

- In Spanish adjectives have to agree with the person or thing they describe. They may have different endings in the masculine, feminine, singular and plural.

- Most Spanish adjectives come after the noun.

How do they work?

These are the common patterns of adjective endings.

adjective ending	masculine singular	feminine singular	masculine plural	feminine plural
–o	bonit**o**	bonit**a**	bonit**os**	bonit**as**
–e	elegant**e**	elegant**e**	elegant**es**	elegant**es**
–ista	pesim**ista**	pesim**ista**	pesim**istas**	pesim**istas**
–or	acoged**or**	acoged**ora**	acoged**ores**	acoged**oras**
other consonants	azul	azul	azul**es**	azul**es**

- Some adjectives of nationality which do not end in **–o** follow the same pattern as **–or** above.

adjective ending	masculine singular	feminine singular	masculine plural	feminine plural
–s	inglés	ingles**a**	ingles**es**	ingles**as**
–l	español	español**a**	español**es**	español**as**
–n	alemán	aleman**a**	aleman**es**	aleman**as**

- Some adjectives don't change and always take the masculine singular form. They are mostly colours made up of two words (*azul claro*, *rojo oscuro*, etc.)

- The majority of adjectives will come after the noun that they are describing.

  una chaqueta anticuada   an old-fashioned jacket
  un vestido gris   a grey dress

  When two adjectives are used to describe a noun, they can come after the noun separated by *y*.
  *Es una persona **generosa y amable.***

- However, there are a few adjectives that often come before the noun.

  mucho, bueno, malo
  primero, segundo, tercero…
  alguno, ninguno

  *No tengo **mucho** tiempo.*   I don't have a lot of time.

- Some adjectives are shortened when they come before a masculine singular noun.

bueno	good	→	*buen*	*Hace buen tiempo.*
malo	bad	→	*mal*	*Hace mal tiempo.*
primero	first	→	*primer*	*Vivo en el primer piso.*
tercero	third	→	*tercer*	*Es el tercer hijo.*
alguno	some, any	→	*algún*	*¿Has leído algún libro interesante últimamente?*
ninguno	none	→	*ningún*	*No, no tengo ningún bolígrafo.*

- ***Grande*** is shortened when it comes before both a masculine and a feminine noun.

  *Es un/a **gran** actor/actriz.*   He/She is a great actor/actress.

Preparados

1 Choose the correct adjective.

1 Era un hotel **pequeñas / pequeña / pequeño**.

2 Nos alojamos en una pensión **caras / cara / caros**.

3 El pueblo era demasiado **turístico / turísticos / turística**.

4 Tenemos que llevar una chaqueta **negro / negra / negras**.

5 Tengo que llevar una corbata a rayas **rojos / roja / rojas**.

6 Mi profesora de empresariales es muy **severas / severos / severa**.

7 Asistimos a un **gran / grande / grandes** instituto en el centro.

8 Mi novio es **española / español / españolas**, pero vive en Inglaterra.

9 Hay unos alumnos que son muy **divertido / divertidas / divertidos**.

10 En mi insti hay una pista de tenis **nuevo / nueva / nuevas**.

Listos

2 Look at the picture and the description of this family. Put an appropriate adjective, and one that agrees with the noun, in each space.

marrones	alto	castaña	liso	alargada	corto
azul	moreno	gordo	colombiana	simpáticos	

Me llamo María, soy **1**   y tengo siete años. En mi familia todos tenemos el pelo **2**   y somos muy enérgicos. En la foto, mi madre lleva una camisa **3**   y mi padre tiene bigote. Mi madre tiene el pelo **4**   y corto, y tiene los ojos **5**   . Mi padre no es ni **6**   ni bajo, y es un poco **7**   . Mis tíos son muy **8**   , y mi tío tiene la cara **9**   y el pelo **10**   como mi hermano. Me gusta mucho mi familia.

¡Ya!

3 Rewrite these sentences using the adjective provided. Make sure that the ending and the position of the adjective is correct.

1 Mi novio se llamaba Juan. *(primero)*

2 Me gusta leer libros. *(español)*

3 Mi prima es una persona. *(hablador)*

4 Las niñas son. *(español)*

5 Me llevo bien con mis hermanas porque son. *(fiel)*

6 Para mí, es un problema impresionante. *(serio)*

7 Me gusta mi trabajo porque tengo un jefe. *(bueno)*

8 La clase no tiene idea. *(ninguno)*

9 Vivimos en una casa. *(grande)*

Gramática Hay que saber bien

Adverbs

What are they and when do I use them?
Adverbs are words that describe how **an action** is done (slowly, quickly, regularly, suddenly, badly, well, very…).

Why are they important?
Adverbs are important because they help you give useful information and are an easy way to extend your sentences. Using several adverbs accurately will add interest and complexity to your texts.

Things to watch out for
- Adverbs often end in **–mente** (like '**–ly**' in English).
- Some of the most useful adverbs are irregular!

How do they work?
To form a regular adverb, you add **–mente** to the feminine form of the adjective.

    lento/a   slow   →   lent**a**mente   slowly

- The adverbs from **bueno** (good) and **malo** (bad) are irregular and you just have to learn them.

    bien   well   mal   badly

- You can learn some adverbs in pairs of opposites.

    mucho   a lot   –   poco   a little
    aquí   here   –   allí   there

- Other irregular adverbs are used to describe **when** you do something (adverbs of frequency).

siempre	always	de vez en cuando	from time to time
a menudo	often	ahora	now
a veces	sometimes	ya	already

- Adverbs usually follow the verbs they describe. However, they can come before a verb 'for emphasis'.

    Hablamos **rápidamente**.   We speak **quickly**.
    Siempre habla en inglés.   He **always** talks English.

Preparados

1 Change these adjectives into adverbs and translate them into English.

1 general
2 rápido
3 tranquilo
4 amable
5 sincero

6 final
7 fácil
8 feliz
9 constante
10 frecuente

Listos

2 Rewrite the sentences with the correct adverb in the correct position.

1 Ana usa el móvil en clase. *(always)*
2 Nadamos en el mar. *(slowly)*
3 Mis amigos estudian para los exámenes. *(constantly)*
4 Toco la guitarra. *(well)*
5 Mi profe siempre habla. *(calmly)*

6 Viajas en avión. *(a little)*
7 Mi padre habla francés. *(badly)*
8 Montas a caballo. *(easily)*
9 Tuvimos un pinchazo. *(unfortunately)*
10 Fueron a la comisaría. *(quickly)*

¡Ya!

3 Translate these sentences into Spanish.

1 We sometimes have a barbecue if it's sunny.
2 I quickly learned to sail.
3 Often you can see lots of boats in the port.
4 My teacher teaches well.
5 They usually leave home at eight o'clock.

6 Do you sing in the choir now?
7 I am editing my photos perfectly.
8 We look for and download music frequently.
9 I use an app to monitor my physical activity easily.
10 My friends suffer from bullying frequently.

Negatives

Which ones do I need to know?

no…	not	*no … ni … ni…*	neither … nor…
no … nada	nothing / not anything	*no … ningún / ninguna*	no / not any
no … nunca	never	*no … nadie*	nobody / not anybody
no … jamás	never (stronger than *nunca*)	*tampoco*	not either

How do they work?

In Spanish the simple negative is **no** and it goes immediately **before** a verb (or before a reflexive pronoun or object pronoun).

No *como.*	I **don't** eat.
No *me levanto temprano.*	I **don't** get up early.
No *me dan mucho dinero.*	They **don't** give me much money.

- Negative expressions go either side of the verb, forming a sandwich around it.

No *compro* **nada**.	I **don't** buy **anything**.
No *hacemos* **nunca** *deporte.*	We **never** do sport.
No *fumo* **jamás**.	I **never** smoke.
No *soy* **ni** *alto* **ni** *bajo.*	I **am neither** tall **nor** short.
Ella **no** *tiene* **ningún** *libro.*	She **doesn't** have **any** books.
No *hablamos con* **nadie**.	We **don't** speak to **anybody**.

- Sometimes, for emphasis, the negative expression can be placed before the verb and in this case *no* is not used.

Nunca *vamos a ir allí.*	We are **never** going to go there.
El hotel **tampoco** *tenía lavandería.*	The hotel **didn't** have a launderette **either**.

- **Sino** means 'but' (with the meaning 'rather' or 'instead'). **Sino** is used to connect a negative first statement with a second statement that is expressing a different opinion.

No *bebo agua,* **sino** *zumo de naranja.*	I don't drink water but orange juice.

Preparados

1 Make each statement negative and then translate it into English.

1 Mis abuelos viven en el norte del país.
2 Quiero cambiar de habitación.
3 Perdimos el equipaje en el aeropuerto.
4 Los profesores nos dan buenas estrategias.
5 Jaime se levanta a las ocho y media.
6 Mi madre me compró saldo para el móvil.

Listos

2 Put the words in the correct order to form a negative phrase.

1 a / Elena / caballo / nunca / monta
2 toco / jamás / la / no / trompeta
3 asistimos / no / a / sábados / clase / nunca / los
4 no / cubierta / el / ninguna / parador / tenía / piscina
5 compartir / no / enganchada / está / a / fotos / todavía
6 come / no / examen / un / Juan / de / nada / antes

¡Ya!

3 Match up the sentence halves and translate each sentence into English.

1 Juan no lleva…
2 La escuela primaria no tenía…
3 Ana no aprende…
4 Miguel tampoco…
5 Gabriela no escribe…
6 Antonia no hace…

a …nunca cartas, sino correos electrónicos.
b …ni laboratorios ni biblioteca ni pista de tenis.
c …ni alemán ni francés.
d …uniforme.
e …nada porque siempre está escuchando música.
f …tiene ganas de ir a un festival.

Gramática Para sacar buena nota

Pronouns

What are they and when do I use them?

Pronouns are used in place of a noun, to avoid repeating it. Make sure the pronoun agrees with the noun it replaces!

How do they work?

- **Subject pronouns** are often only used for emphasis in Spanish, because the verb ending usually indicates who is doing the action: *yo, tú, él, ella, usted, nosotros/as, vosotros/as, ellos, ellas, ustedes*

- **Object pronouns** can be direct or indirect. They replace something or someone that has already been mentioned (e.g. Did you buy **the car**? Yes I bought **it**.)

English	direct	indirect
me	*me*	*me*
you	*te*	*te*
him/her/it	*lo/la*	*le*
us	*nos*	*nos*
you	*os*	*os*
them	*los/las*	*les*

Direct: ***Lo*** *compré.*   I bought **it**.

           Los *veo allí.*   I see **them** over there.

Indirect object pronouns usually have the meaning of 'to' or 'for someone' in Spanish where we wouldn't necessarily say that in English.

Indirect: ***Le*** *compré un regalo.*   I bought **him** a present. = I bought a present **for him**.

            Te *voy a escribir.*   I am going to write **to you**.

- Object pronouns normally go:
  Before the verb:

  Lo *tenemos.*   We have **it**.   ***Lo*** *has hecho.*   You have done **it**.

  After the negative word:

  *No **lo** quiero.*   I don't want **it**.   *Nadie **lo** estudia.*   Nobody studies **it**.

  Attached to the end of the infinitive, gerund or imperative:

  *Van a hacer**lo**.*   They are going to do **it**.   *Estoy haciéndo**lo**.*   I am doing **it**.
  *Haz**lo**.*   Do **it**.

Listos

1 Rewrite these sentences using direct or indirect object pronouns.

1 El profesor da el libro a Pablo.
2 Hacemos los deberes.
3 Voy a preparar la cena esta noche.
4 Mandó un correo electrónico a su jefe.
5 Reparten periódicos antes de ir al instituto.

6 Compré una gorra para mi tía.
7 Va a enseñar inglés a niños pequeños.
8 Todos los días cortamos el pelo a los clientes.
9 Nadie lava el coche en mi familia.
10 Nunca sacaba fotocopias.

¡Ya!

2 Translate these sentences into Spanish.

1 I like newspapers and I read them every day.
2 He writes to her every day.
3 I am going to send messages to you (plural).
4 My grandmother is going to give us money.
5 I told them everything.

6 It gives us the opportunity to work in Spain.
7 You are going to look after them.
8 We met him last year.
9 Do you know how to use it?

Connectives

Which ones do I need to know?

a pesar de	despite / in spite of	ya que	since	que	that/which
así que	so / therefore	por eso / por lo tanto	therefore	sin embargo	however
aún / aún (si)	even / even if	cuando	when	para	in order to
aunque	although	donde	where	si	if
mientras (que)	while / whilst	como	like/as		

Why are they important?

Using connectives to make extended sentences makes your speaking and writing sound more natural and adds complexity. Try to avoid just using **pero, y** and **o.**

How do they work?

● Connectives link different sentences or phrases together.

*A las ocho voy a la cocina **donde** preparo el desayuno **mientras que** mi madre se viste.*
At eight o'clock I go to the kitchen **where** I make breakfast **whilst** my mother gets dressed.

● *Remember that **y** changes to **e** if it comes before words beginning with 'i' or 'hi' and **o** changes to **u** if it comes before words beginning with o– or ho–.*

*Estudio matemáticas **e** inglés.* I study Maths **and** English.
*Puede ser un problema para mujeres **u** hombres.* It can be a problem for women **or** men.

Preparados

1 Complete each sentence with a different connective from the box.

o	ya que	aunque	como	cuando
si	sin embargo	por eso	mientras que	donde

1 Mi hermano puede estudiar inglés, matemáticas   geografía.
2 A mi amigo le encanta jugar con su ordenador   es divertido.
3 Vuelven a casa tarde   tienen actividades deportivas   el tenis.
4 Suelo almorzar a las doce y media   a veces no puedo.
5 Practican varios deportes en el instituto y   prefieren descansar en casa.
6 Fuimos a un restaurante peruano   probamos varios platos típicos.

Listos

2 Match up the sentence halves and translate each sentence into English.

1 Mi amigo nunca va al parque,…
2 Estoy en el supermercado,…
3 José juega al baloncesto…
4 Muchos extranjeros visitan España…
5 Viajábamos en coche,…
6 Iré al campo el sábado…

a …aunque tiene dos perros.
b …a pesar de ser muy bajo.
c …para disfrutar de las fiestas.
d …cuando tuvimos un pinchazo.
e …si hace buen tiempo.
f …donde voy a comprar el pescado.

¡Ya!

3 Complete the sentence with the correct connective.

1 Tengo una prima   habla italiano perfectamente.
2 Había mucha gente en el restaurante   llegamos para celebrar el cumpleaños.
3 A menudo vamos de paseo   hace buen tiempo.
4 Se debería usar el transporte público,   los autobuses o el metro.
5 Estaban en el supermercado,   vieron a Manuel.
6 Mi profesor de inglés es paciente,   se enfada a veces   no escuchamos.

Gramática Para sacar buena nota

The imperfect continuous tense

What is it and when do I use it?

It describes something that **was happening** at a particular moment in the past.

Estaba trabajando en el centro cuando la tormenta de nieve azotó el pueblo.
I was working in the town centre when the snow storm hit.

Why is it important?

You need to be able to understand texts that may use this tense. In addition, using this tense in your own writing or speaking will show that you can use an excellent variety of past tenses.

Things to watch out for

In English, we do not distinguish between the imperfect and the imperfect continuous when we translate it.

Alicia **estaba leyendo / leía** un libro cuando su amigo llegó.
Alicia **was reading** a book when her friend arrived.

How does it work?

Use the imperfect tense form of the verb *estar* together with the present participle (the '–ing' form). To form the present participle, take the infinitive of the verb, remove the –ar, –er or –ir and add the endings: **–ando, –iendo, –iendo**.

(yo)	estaba		
(tú)	estabas		hablando
(él/ella/usted)	estaba	+	comiendo
(nosotros/as)	estábamos		saliendo
(vosotros/as)	estabais		
(ellos/ellas/ustedes)	estaban		

Estaba haciendo mis deberes cuando leí el correo.   **I was doing** my homework when I read the email.

- Remember that there are some irregular present participles to watch out for:

| dormir | → | durmiendo | sleeping | | poder | → | pudiendo | being able to |
| leer | → | leyendo | reading | | reír | → | riendo | laughing |

---

1 Complete the sentences. Use the verbs in the box in the correct form of the imperfect continuous tense.

| descargar | conducir | correr | dormir | enseñar |
| buscar | jugar | leer | trabajar | tomar |

1 Mi padre ___ por la ciudad cuando escuchó la noticia del huracán.
2 Mi madre ___ el periódico cuando recibió un SMS de su amiga.
3 Nosotros ___ una película cuando hubo un problema con el ordenador.
4 Mi primo ___ información por Internet cuando le llamé.
5 José ___ cuando se cayó en la calle y se rompió la pierna.
6 Yo ___ como voluntario cuando decidí apuntarme a la campaña.

2 Translate the sentences into Spanish.

1 I was working as a volunteer in the hospital, my brother was playing football and my sister was travelling on the bus when the storm hit.
2 We were reading and looking for information online in the school library when we heard about the earthquake in the south of the country.
3 Carla was watching the news and José was listening to music when the earthquake was felt but they were not scared.

The pluperfect tense

What is it and when do I use it?

The pluperfect tense describes what someone **had done** or what **had happened** at a particular moment in the past.

*Antes ya **había trabajado** como voluntario/a.*   **I had already worked** as a volunteer before.

Why is it important?

Using the pluperfect tense means that you can talk about events in the past in more detail. Using this tense correctly will add variety and complexity to your speaking and writing.

How does it work?

The pluperfect tense is formed using the imperfect tense of the verb ***haber*** followed by the past participle of a verb.

Remember that the past participle is formed by taking the infinitive, removing the *–ar*, *–er* or *–ir* and adding **–ado** for *–ar* verbs (*hablado, comprado,* etc.) and **–ido** for *–er* and *–ir* verbs (*bebido, vivido,* etc.).

(yo)	había		
(tú)	habías		hablado
(él/ella/usted)	había	+	comido
(nosotros/as)	habíamos		salido
(vosotros/as)	habíais		
(ellos/ellas/ustedes)	habían		

*Marta **había conocido** a mucha gente durante el evento deportivo.*
Marta **had made** many friends during the sporting event.

See page 219 for irregular past participles.

● Remember that nothing comes between the part of the verb ***haber*** and the past participle. All negatives and pronouns (reflexive, object, etc.) come before ***haber***.

*No **me habían dado** el uniforme correcto.*   **They hadn't given me** the correct uniform.

Listos

1 Insert the correct form of the verb to make these sentences pluperfect.

1 Mi abuela ya   en el sector de la hostelería. *(trabajar)*
2 Mi amigo y yo nunca   un proyecto de conservación. *(hacer)*
3 La empresa multinacional   demasiada agua. *(malgastar)*
4 Mi instituto ya   dinero para organizaciones de caridad. *(recaudar)*
5 El gobierno no   suficientes casas en los últimos años. *(construir)*
6 Nunca   tan fácil encontrar oportunidades para cuidar el medio ambiente. *(ser)*

¡Ya!

2 Translate these sentences into Spanish.

1 I had already visited many cities in Spain.
2 They had already worked as volunteers during the Olympics in London.
3 Sara had wanted to be a tourist guide but she did not speak English or French.
4 My grandparents had spoken about the floods that left thousands of people homeless.
5 I had already read the book about the dangerous tornado in Mexico but I had not seen the film.
6 We had already been to the restaurant to eat meatballs when we arrived at the cinema.

Gramática Hay que saber bien

The passive

What is it and when do I use it?

The passive is used to describe something that is/was/will be done to something or someone. The object becomes the subject of the sentence:

my teacher wrote the text   →   the text was written by my teacher.
subject   object

*El texto **fue escrito** por mi profesor(a).*   The text **was written** by my teacher.
*La comida italiana **es conocida** en todo el mundo.*   Italian food **is known** throughout the world.

Why is it important?

You may want to use the passive when describing events and you need to be able to understand it in spoken and written texts.

Things to watch out for

English uses the passive more often than Spanish. In Spanish, when you don't know who or what has done the action, the passive is often avoided. For example, you can use the passive to translate this sentence:

English **is spoken** by lots of people. → *El inglés **es hablado** por mucha gente.*

However, if you do not know who has done the action, then you can avoid the passive. You do this by using the pronoun **se**:

English **is spoken**. → ***Se habla** inglés.*

How does it work?

To form the passive, you use the correct tense of the verb **ser**, followed by the past participle (see page 219). Note that the past participle must agree in number and gender with the object.

*Los tomates **serán lanzados** por muchísimos turistas.*   **The tomatoes will be thrown** by many tourists.

Listos

1 Avoid the passive! Use the reflexive pronoun *se* with the correct form of a suitable verb from the box.

| celebrar | repetir | lanzar | hablar | desenchufar | disparar |

1 The event is celebrated in the Summer. –   el evento en verano.
2 Fireworks are set off. –   fuegos artificiales.
3 Eggs are thrown. –   huevos.
4 The procession is repeated every year. – Cada año   el desfile.
5 Spanish is spoken in Bolivia. – En Bolivia   español.
6 Electrical devices are unplugged. –   los aparatos eléctricos.

¡Ya!

2 Make a list of all the passive phrases or phrases that avoid using the passive, and their meanings. Then translate the whole text into English.

El Carnaval de Cádiz es conocido mundialmente por ser una fiesta 'de la calle'. Son muchos días de baile, música, teatro y, sobre todo, participación popular. La ciudad entera se llena de gente que sale a reír, a cantar y, en definitiva, a pasarlo bien. Se realizan dos cabalgatas y el público se convierte en un desfile multicolor. Las canciones se oyen por toda la ciudad durante las celebraciones. También se disparan muchos fuegos artificiales y hay muchísimas actividades que contribuyen a la diversión de la gente. Toda la ciudad se transforma en una fiesta increíble.

Gramática Para sacar buena nota

The imperative

What is it and when do I use it?
The imperative is a form of the verb that is used to give commands and instructions ('Go to sleep!', 'Don't do that!').

How does it work?
The imperative has a different form depending on whether the command is positive ('Sit down!') or negative ('Don't sit down!') and who is receiving it.

Positive imperatives
- The positive imperative for one person (*tú*) is formed by removing the **–s** from the **tú** form of the verb.

  girar ➔ *(tú) giras* ➔ *¡Gira!*   Turn! (you)   *coger* ➔ *(tú) coges* ➔ *¡Coge!*   Catch! (you)

- These verbs have irregular imperatives in the *tú* form:

decir	➔	*di*	say	*salir*	➔	*sal*	go / get out
hacer	➔	*haz*	do	*tener*	➔	*ten*	have
ir	➔	*ve*	go	*venir*	➔	*ven*	come
poner	➔	*pon*	put				

- The positive imperative for more than one person (*vosotros/as*) is formed by taking the infinitive and changing the **–r** to a **–d**.

  tomar ➔ *¡Tomad!*   Take! (you plural)

- A formal command is given using the present subjunctive. (See page 234)

  tomar ➔ *¡Tome!*   Take! (you polite)   *comer* ➔ *¡Coman!*   Eat! (you polite plural)

Negative imperatives
- You use the present subjunctive form for all negative commands. (See page 234 on the present subjunctive for more information on how to form this tense.)

pasar	➔	*¡No pases!*	Don't pass! (you)	*seguir*	➔	*¡No sigáis!*	Don't follow! (you plural)
coger	➔	*¡No cojas!*	Don't take! (you)	*girar*	➔	*¡No giren!*	Don't turn! (you polite plural)
cruzar	➔	*¡No cruce!*	Don't cross! (you polite)				

Preparados

1 Make these statements into *tú* commands.

1 la segunda calle a la derecha. *(tomar)*
2 el buen tiempo. *(aprovechar)*
3 más despacio. *(comer)*

4 los semáforos. *(pasar)*
5 español, por favor. *(hablar)*
6 algo. *(decir)*

Listos

2 Make these statements into *vosotros/as* commands. Then translate each one into English.

1 la primera calle a la derecha. *(tomar)*
2 a la izquierda. *(girar)*
3 el puente. *(pasar)*

4 a la torre. *(subir)*
5 ¡   cuidado! *(tener)*
6 la calle. *(cruzar)*

¡Ya!

3 Use the present subjunctive to make formal commands and negative commands. Then translate each one into English.

1 los semáforos. *(pasa, usted)*
2 No   el autobús número 39. *(coger, tú)*
3 más bosques y selvas. *(plantar, usted)*

4 No   tantos árboles. *(cortar, vosotros/as)*
5 No   la selva. *(destruir, ustedes)*
6 No   basura al suelo. *(tirar, tú)*

Gramática Para sacar buena nota

The present subjunctive

What is it and when do I use it?

The present subjunctive is a form of the verb which we do not really use anymore in English but which is used a lot in Spanish. The subjunctive has to be used:

- After the word **cuando** when talking about the future.

  *Cuando **sea** mayor, me tomaré un año sabático.*   When **I am** older, I will take a gap year.

- With negative commands and formal commands (*usted/ustedes*). See page 233 for more information.

- After feelings which use the structure *es + adjective + que*:

  Es esencial que… / Es importante que… / Es necesario que… / No es justo que…

  *Es importante que no **malgastemos** la energía.*   It's important that **we** do not **waste** energy.

- After verbs of wishing, command, request and emotion and to express purpose, e.g. *querer, pedir*, etc.

  *Quiero que **escuches**.*   I want **you** to **listen**.
  *Piden que no **hagamos** tanto ruido.*   They ask that **we** don't **make** so much noise.
  *Me alegro que **estés** aquí.*   I'm glad **you're** here.

- After the expression *ojalá*.

  *Ojalá **haga** sol.*   Let's hope **it is** sunny.

Why is it important?

Knowing some of the situations in which you use the subjunctive will allow you to be more accurate in your communication in Spanish. If you can use it correctly in your GCSE, it will impress your examiner and add complexity to your speaking and writing.

Things to watch out for

As English no longer uses the subjunctive, it won't come naturally to you. If you want to use it successfully you must learn by heart the situations when you will need it.

How does it work?

To form the present subjunctive, take the first person singular (*yo*) of the present tense, remove the final **-o** and add these endings.

	hablar (to talk)	**com**er (to eat)	**viv**ir (to live)
(yo)	habl**e**	com**a**	viv**a**
(tú)	habl**es**	com**as**	viv**as**
(él/ella/usted)	habl**e**	com**a**	viv**a**
(nosotros/as)	habl**emos**	com**amos**	viv**amos**
(vosotros/as)	habl**éis**	com**áis**	viv**áis**
(ellos/ellas/ustedes)	habl**en**	com**an**	viv**an**

If the first person singular (*yo*) is irregular, the subjunctive will take the same form, for example, *hago – haga*. There are some irregular present subjunctive verbs:

ir → *vaya, vayas, vaya, …*   **ser →** *sea, seas, sea, …*   **hay →** *haya*

The present subjunctive

1 Complete these sentences with the correct present subjunctive form of a suitable verb from the box.

trabajar	tener	aprobar	ser	terminar	ganar	enamorarse

1 Cuando yo   este curso, iré a otro insti.
2 Cuando mi mejor amigo   mayor, trabajará como médico.
3 Cuando nosotros   bastante dinero, compraremos un piso.
4 Cuando yo   , me casaré.
5 Cuando mi hermano   dieciocho años, hará formación profesional.
6 Cuando los alumnos   los exámenes, podrán apuntarse a los cursos.

Listos

2 Complete each of the sentences with the correct present subjunctive verb. Then translate them into English.

1 Es importante que mis amigos no   . *(fumar)*
2 Cuando   a España, compraré un abanico bonito. *(ir)*
3 No quiero que mis profesores   antipáticos. *(ser)*
4 Ojalá tú   venir conmigo a la disco. *(poder)*
5 Pedimos que nuestro barrio   un polideportivo nuevo. *(tener)*
6 No es justo que Juan no   trabajo como voluntario. *(encontrar)*

¡Ya!

3 Translate this text into Spanish. Watch out for the underlined verbs that need to be in the present subjunctive!

When I finish my exams, I am going to learn to drive and then I will look for a job. I don't think that it is easy to find work at the moment but let's see. Let's hope I am successful! I also want to share a flat with some friends when I earn enough money. It is important that the flat has a big kitchen because I love cooking.

Gramática Para sacar buena nota

The imperfect subjunctive

What is it and when do I use it?

The imperfect subjunctive is a past form of the verb which is not really used anymore in English but which is used a lot in Spanish.

You use the imperfect subjunctive as the past tense equivalent of the present subjunctive (see page 234). You also need to use it when you use an **'if' clause** in the past tense that also requires the conditional tense.

Si **tuviera** dinero, <u>visitaría</u> Latinoamérica.   If **I had** money, I <u>would visit</u> Latin America.
    imperfect subjunctive   conditional tense

Si **pudiera** tomarme un año sabático, trabajaría en un orfanato.

If **I could** take a gap year, I would work in an orphanage.

Si **fuéramos** ricos, compraríamos una casa grande en el centro de la ciudad.

If **we were** rich, we would buy a big house in the city centre.

Why is it important?

Learning and using some phrases in the imperfect subjunctive in your writing or speaking will add complexity and grammatical variety to your work. You may also need to recognise it to fully understand a spoken or written text.

Things to watch out for

You will need to know the preterite tense thoroughly to form this correctly!

How does it work?

To form the imperfect subjunctive, take the third person plural of the preterite tense (ellos/ellas), remove the final **–ron** and add these endings:

	hablar (to talk)	**comer** (to eat)	**vivir** (to live)
(yo)	habla**ra**	comie**ra**	vivie**ra**
(tú)	habla**ras**	comie**ras**	vivie**ras**
(él/ella/usted)	habla**ra**	comie**ra**	vivie**ra**
(nosotros/as)	hablá**ramos**	comié**ramos**	vivié**ramos**
(vosotros/as)	habla**rais**	comie**rais**	vivie**rais**
(ellos/ellas/ustedes)	habla**ran**	comie**ran**	vivie**ran**

- If the third person plural of the preterite tense (ellos/ellas) is irregular, the subjunctive will take the same form, for example:

  hicieron → hiciera   fueron → fuera

Listos

1 Change these verbs from the infinitive to the 'I' (yo) form of the imperfect subjunctive (using the third person plural of the preterite tense).

1 ser   **2** poder   **3** tener   **4** ir   **5** estudiar   **6** hacer

¡Ya!

2 Translate these sentences into English.

1 Si yo pudiera tomarme un año sabático, trabajaría como voluntario.
2 Si tuviéramos bastante dinero, viajaríamos con mochila por el mundo.
3 Si pudieran viajar a Colombia, ayudarían a construir un colegio nuevo.
4 Si tuvieras más tiempo, ¿qué te gustaría hacer?
5 Si Carlota ganara más dinero, viviría más cerca de sus padres.
6 ¡Si yo estudiara cada día, aprobaría todos mis exámenes!

Verb tables

 These verbs are continued overleaf. ➔

infinitive		pronouns (only include for emphasis)	present	future	conditional	preterite
hablar – to speak (regular **-ar** verb)	I you he/she/you (polite) we you (plural) they/you (polite plural)	yo tú él/ella/usted nosotros/as vosotros/as ellos/ellas/ustedes	habl**o** habl**as** habl**a** habl**amos** habl**áis** habl**an**	hablar**é** hablar**ás** hablar**á** hablar**emos** hablar**éis** hablar**án**	hablar**ía** hablar**ías** hablar**ía** hablar**íamos** hablar**íais** hablar**ían**	habl**é** habl**aste** habl**ó** habl**amos** habl**asteis** habl**aron**
comer – to eat (regular **-er** verb)	I you he/she/you (polite) we you (plural) they/you (polite plural)	yo tú él/ella/usted nosotros/as vosotros/as ellos/ellas/ustedes	com**o** com**es** com**e** com**emos** com**éis** com**en**	comer**é** comer**ás** comer**á** comer**emos** comer**éis** comer**án**	comer**ía** comer**ías** comer**ía** comer**íamos** comer**íais** comer**ían**	com**í** com**iste** com**ió** com**imos** com**isteis** com**ieron**
vivir – to live (regular **-ir** verb)	I you he/she/you (polite) we you (plural) they/you (polite plural)	yo tú él/ella/usted nosotros/as vosotros/as ellos/ellas/ustedes	viv**o** viv**es** viv**e** viv**imos** viv**ís** viv**en**	vivir**é** vivir**ás** vivir**á** vivir**emos** vivir**éis** vivir**án**	vivir**ía** vivir**ías** vivir**ía** vivir**íamos** vivir**íais** vivir**ían**	viv**í** viv**iste** viv**ió** viv**imos** viv**isteis** viv**ieron**
dar – to give	I you he/she/you (polite) we you (plural) they/you (polite plural)	yo tú él/ella/usted nosotros/as vosotros/as ellos/ellas/ustedes	**doy** das da damos **dais** dan	daré darás dará daremos daréis darán	daría darías daría daríamos daríais darían	**di** **diste** **dio** **dimos** **disteis** **dieron**
decir – to say	I you he/she/you (polite) we you (plural) they/you (polite plural)	yo tú él/ella/usted nosotros/as vosotros/as ellos/ellas/ustedes	**digo** **dices** **dice** decimos decís **dicen**	**diré** **dirás** **dirá** **diremos** **diréis** **dirán**	**diría** **dirías** **diría** **diríamos** **diríais** **dirían**	**dije** **dijiste** **dijo** **dijimos** **dijisteis** **dijeron**
estar – to be	I you he/she/you (polite) we you (plural) they/you (polite plural)	yo tú él/ella/usted nosotros/as vosotros/as ellos/ellas/ustedes	**estoy** **estás** **está** estamos estáis **están**	estaré estarás estará estaremos estaréis estarán	estaría estarías estaría estaríamos estaríais estarían	**estuve** **estuviste** **estuvo** **estuvimos** **estuvisteis** **estuvieron**
hacer – to do / make	I you he/she/you (polite) we you (plural) they/you (polite plural)	yo tú él/ella/usted nosotros/as vosotros/as ellos/ellas/ustedes	**hago** haces hace hacemos hacéis hacen	**haré** **harás** **hará** **haremos** **haréis** **harán**	**haría** **harías** **haría** **haríamos** **haríais** **harían**	**hice** **hiciste** **hizo** **hicimos** **hicisteis** **hicieron**
ir – to go	I you he/she/you (polite) we you (plural) they/you (polite plural)	yo tú él/ella/usted nosotros/as vosotros/as ellos/ellas/ustedes	**voy** **vas** **va** **vamos** **vais** **van**	iré irás irá iremos iréis irán	iría irías iría iríamos iríais irían	**fui** **fuiste** **fue** **fuimos** **fuisteis** **fueron**

Verb tables

	pronouns (only include for emphasis)	imperfect	gerund (for present and imperfect continuous tenses)	past participle	present subjunctive	imperative
hablar (continued)	yo tú él/ella/usted nosotros/as vosotros/as ellos/ellas /ustedes	habl**aba** habl**abas** habl**aba** habl**ábamos** habl**abais** habl**aban**	habl**ando**	habl**ado**	habl**e** habl**es** habl**e** habl**emos** habl**éis** habl**en**	habl**a** (tú) habl**ad** (vosotros/as)
comer (continued)	yo tú él/ella/usted nosotros/as vosotros/as ellos/ellas/ustedes	com**ía** com**ías** com**ía** com**íamos** com**íais** com**ían**	com**iendo**	com**ido**	com**a** com**as** com**a** com**amos** com**áis** com**an**	com**e** (tú) com**ed** (vosotros/as)
vivir (continued)	yo tú él/ella/usted nosotros/as vosotros/as ellos/ellas/ustedes	viv**ía** viv**ías** viv**ía** viv**íamos** viv**íais** viv**ían**	viv**iendo**	viv**ido**	viv**a** viv**as** viv**a** viv**amos** viv**áis** viv**an**	viv**e** (tú) viv**id** (vosotros/as)
dar (continued)	yo tú él/ella/usted nosotros/as vosotros/as ellos/ellas/ustedes	daba dabas daba dábamos dabais daban	dando	dado	**dé** **des** **dé** **demos** **deis** **den**	da (tú) dad (vosotros/as)
decir (continued)	yo tú él/ella/usted nosotros/as vosotros/as ellos/ellas/ustedes	decía decías decía decíamos decíais decían	**diciendo**	**dicho**	**diga** **digas** **diga** **digamos** **digáis** **digan**	**di** (tú) decid (vosotros/as)
estar (continued)	yo tú él/ella/usted nosotros/as vosotros/as ellos/ellas/ustedes	estaba estabas estaba estábamos estabais estaban	estando	estado	**esté** **estés** **esté** estemos estéis **estén**	**está** (tú) estad (vosotros/as)
hacer (continued)	yo tú él/ella/usted nosotros/as vosotros/as ellos/ellas/ustedes	hacía hacías hacía hacíamos hacíais hacían	haciendo	**hecho**	**haga** **hagas** **haga** **hagamos** **hagáis** **hagan**	**haz** (tú) haced (vosotros/as)
ir (continued)	yo tú él/ella/usted nosotros/as vosotros/as ellos/ellas/ustedes	**iba** **ibas** **iba** **íbamos** **ibais** **iban**	**yendo**	**ido**	**vaya** **vayas** **vaya** **vayamos** **vayáis** **vayan**	**ve** (tú) id (vosotros/as)

Verb tables

 These verbs are continued overleaf. ➝

infinitive		pronouns (only include for emphasis)	present	future	conditional	preterite
poder – to be able to	I you he/she/you (polite) we you (plural) they/you (polite plural)	yo tú él/ella/usted nosotros/as vosotros/as ellos/ellas/ustedes	**puedo** **puedes** **puede** podemos podéis **pueden**	**podré** **podrás** **podrá** **podremos** **podréis** **podrán**	**podría** **podrías** **podría** **podríamos** **podríais** **podrían**	**pude** **pudiste** **pudo** **pudimos** **pudisteis** **pudieron**
poner – to put	I you he/she/you (polite) we you (plural) they/you (polite plural)	yo tú él/ella/usted nosotros/as vosotros/as ellos/ellas/ustedes	**pongo** pones pone ponemos ponéis ponen	**pondré** **pondrás** **pondrá** **pondremos** **pondréis** **pondrán**	**pondría** **pondrías** **pondría** **pondríamos** **pondríais** **pondrían**	**puse** **pusiste** **puso** **pusimos** **pusisteis** **pusieron**
querer – to want / love	I you he/she/you (polite) we you (plural) they/you (polite plural)	yo tú él/ella/usted nosotros/as vosotros/as ellos/ellas/ustedes	**quiero** **quieres** **quiere** queremos queréis **quieren**	**querré** **querrás** **querrá** **querremos** **querréis** **querrán**	**querría** **querrías** **querría** **querríamos** **querríais** **querrían**	**quise** **quisiste** **quiso** **quisimos** **quisisteis** **quisieron**
salir – to go out	I you he/she/you (polite) we you (plural) they/you (polite plural)	yo tú él/ella/usted nosotros/as vosotros/as ellos/ellas/ustedes	**salgo** sales sale salimos salís salen	**saldré** **saldrás** **saldrá** **saldremos** **saldréis** **saldrán**	**saldría** **saldrías** **saldría** **saldríamos** **saldríais** **saldrían**	salí saliste salió salimos salisteis salieron
ser – to be	I you he/she/you (polite) we you (plural) they/you (polite plural)	yo tú él/ella/usted nosotros/as vosotros/as ellos/ellas/ustedes	**soy** **eres** **es** **somos** **sois** **son**	seré serás será seremos seréis serán	sería serías sería seríamos seríais serían	**fui** **fuiste** **fue** **fuimos** **fuisteis** **fueron**
tener – to have	I you he/she/you (polite) we you (plural) they/you (polite plural)	yo tú él/ella/usted nosotros/as vosotros/as ellos/ellas/ustedes	**tengo** **tienes** **tiene** tenemos tenéis **tienen**	**tendré** **tendrás** **tendrá** **tendremos** **tendréis** **tendrán**	**tendría** **tendrías** **tendría** **tendríamos** **tendríais** **tendrían**	**tuve** **tuviste** **tuvo** **tuvimos** **tuvisteis** **tuvieron**
venir – to come	I you he/she/you (polite) we you (plural) they/you (polite plural)	yo tú él/ella/usted nosotros/as vosotros/as ellos/ellas/ustedes	**vengo** **vienes** **viene** venimos venís **vienen**	**vendré** **vendrás** **vendrá** **vendremos** **vendréis** **vendrán**	**vendría** **vendrías** **vendría** **vendríamos** **vendríais** **vendrían**	**vine** **viniste** **vino** **vinimos** **vinisteis** **vinieron**
ver – to see	I you he/she/you (polite) we you (plural) they/you (polite plural)	yo tú él/ella/usted nosotros/as vosotros/as ellos/ellas/ustedes	**veo** ves ve vemos **veis** ven	veré verás verá veremos veréis verán	vería verías vería veríamos veríais verían	**vi** viste **vio** vimos visteis vieron

Verb tables

	pronouns (only include for emphasis)	imperfect	gerund (for present and imperfect continuous tenses)	past participle	present subjunctive	imperative
poder (continued)	yo tú él/ella/usted nosotros/as vosotros/as ellos/ellas/ustedes	podía podías podía podíamos podíais podían	**pudiendo**	podido	**pueda** **puedas** **pueda** podamos podáis **puedan**	**puede** (tú) poded (vosotros/as)
poner (continued)	yo tú él/ella/usted nosotros/as vosotros/as ellos/ellas/ustedes	ponía ponías ponía poníamos poníais ponían	poniendo	**puesto**	**ponga** **pongas** **ponga** **pongamos** **pongáis** **pongan**	**pon** (tú) poned (vosotros/as)
querer (continued)	yo tú él/ella/usted nosotros/as vosotros/as ellos/ellas/ustedes	quería querías quería queríamos queríais querían	queriendo	querido	**quiera** **quieras** **quiera** queramos queráis **quieran**	**quiere** (tú) quered (vosotros)
salir (continued)	yo tú él/ella/usted nosotros/as vosotros/as ellos/ellas/ustedes	salía salías salía salíamos salíais salían	saliendo	salido	**salga** **salgas** **salga** **salgamos** **salgáis** **salgan**	**sal** (tú) salid (vosotros/as)
ser (continued)	yo tú él/ella/usted nosotros/as vosotros/as ellos/ellas/ustedes	**era** **eras** **era** **éramos** **erais** **eran**	siendo	sido	**sea** **seas** **sea** **seamos** **seáis** **sean**	**sé** (tú) sed (vosotros/as)
tener (continued)	yo tú él/ella/usted nosotros/as vosotros/as ellos/ellas/ustedes	tenía tenías tenía teníamos teníais tenían	teniendo	tenido	**tenga** **tengas** **tenga** **tengamos** **tengáis** **tengan**	**ten** (tú) tened (vosotros/as)
venir (continued)	yo tú él/ella/usted nosotros/as vosotros/as ellos/ellas/ustedes	venía venías venía veníamos veníais venían	**viniendo**	venido	**venga** **vengas** **venga** **vengamos** **vengáis** **vengan**	**ven** (tú) venid (vosotros/as)
ver (continued)	yo tú él/ella/usted nosotros/as vosotros/as ellos/ellas/ustedes	**veía** **veías** **veía** **veíamos** **veíais** **veían**	viendo	**visto**	**vea** **veas** **vea** **veamos** **veáis** **vean**	ve (tú) ved (vosotros/as)